American Perspectives

READINGS IN AMERICAN HISTORY

Volume II
Fourth Edition

Custom Edition for the Houston Community College System

Custom Publishing

New York   Boston   San Francisco
London   Toronto   Sydney   Tokyo   Singapore   Madrid
Mexico City   Munich   Paris   Cape Town   Hong Kong   Montreal

Cover Art: Courtesy of Comstock

Printed in the United States of America

10 9 8 7 6 5 4 3

2008300035

KC/LD

**Pearson
Custom Publishing**
is a division of

www.pearsonhighered.com

ISBN 10: 0-555-04439-4
ISBN 13: 978-0-555-04439-1

Copyright Acknowledgments

Contents
American Perspectives:
Readings in American History, Volume II

Introduction to the Fourth Edition

American Perspectives: Readings in American History is a collection of various articles designed to enhance students' knowledge and interest in different facets of American history. The articles are also designed to allow individual faculty members to choose from the selections and tailor their courses to suit their needs. The articles allow for students to delve more deeply into specific topics that often get overlooked in many American history survey courses. Members of the history faculty at Houston Community College chose each of the selections found in both volume one and two, and in addition to the objectives stated above the articles found in *American Perspectives* also represent a canon of American historians as many of the articles were written by some of the most prominent historians in the United States and brought together as part of unique collection for the use of students at Houston Community College.

In volume two, students will find articles by several noted historians including Harvey Wasserman, Page Smith, John Milton Cooper, Gabriel Kolko, Charles L. Mee, Jr., and George Herring. In addition to these prominent writers, students will also find a selection by Eric Alterman, a noted media critic who visited with students at Houston Community College in 2005. In addition to articles by these prominent authors, one selection included in volume two allows for three key participants in the Civil Rights Movement, Martin Luther King, Jr., Malcolm X, and Cesar Chavez to be read in their own words as students are invited to read from some of the important works these activists left behind.

Faculty should utilize the selections found in *American Perspectives* to broaden the understanding of American history by assigning articles in conjunction with survey lecture topics, readings assigned from the textbook, along with other books that students are required to read for their courses. Students should look for specific ways in which the assigned readings provide more detailed information on the problems and conflicts caused by the rapid industrialization of the American economy following the Civil War, the United States' emergence as a global power, racism and its impact on American society, and finally the current controversies that periodically flare up over the role religion plays in American life, who controls the media, and what energy policies should the United States pursue as we enter an age of declining resources and rising prices for fuel

In the end, the incorporation *American Perspectives* into the American History survey courses offered at Houston Community College will prove to be a richly rewarding experience for students and faculty alike.

The Robber Barons

Harvey Wasserman

The Civil War made a few businessmen very rich.

The North and the South both gave army deferments to the rich. The Confederacy exempted owners of more than fifty slaves; the Union let those who had it buy their way out for $300.

Among those who paid their $300 were J. Pierpont Morgan, John D. Rockefeller, Andrew Carnegie, James Mellon, Philip Armour, and Jay Gould. Mellon just listened to his father, who told him in a letter that "a man may be a patriot without risking his own life or sacrificing his health. There are plenty of lives less valuable."

Accordingly, young Mellon bought his way out and joined a few thousand men like J. P. Morgan and Jay Cooke in the business of war profiteering.

To Cooke the war meant about $3 million a year in commissions alone. A wealthy banker and speculator, he wormed his way into the government as official promoter of Union bonds. After four years of war the national debt had skyrocketed from $75 million to almost $3 billion. Cooke became a multimillionaire and the most powerful banker in the country. The national debt, he announced, was "a national blessing."

J. P. Morgan, son of a millionaire banker, took his cut dealing gold and guns. Through a middleman, the 24-year-old Morgan bought obsolete carbines from the War Department at $3.50 apiece. His partner then resold them to Union General Fremont a $22.00 each.

Meanwhile Philip Armour supplied the Union Army with beef. Jay Gould speculated gold and securities while Cornelius Vanderbilt dealt rotten hulks to the Navy and began putting together a railroad empire. Jim Fisk ran contraband southern cotton through the Union blockade, and John D. Rockefeller piled up profits as a Cleveland merchant and invested them in oil refineries.

America's first crop of "war millionaires" was taking shape. Mellon wrote his father that there were men starting in business who "continue growing richer and don't care when the war closes."

Reprinted from *Harvey Wasserman's History of the United States*, (1972), Harper & Row.

The War Profiteers Play Monopoly

For the millions who actually fought or who watched the two war machines wreck their farms, towns, and lives, the Civil War meant unimaginable horror, four years of unmitigated slaughter and devastation. Five hundred thousand people died, and the romantic spirit of the thirties and forties was consumed into a mangled, bloody mess.

The economic root of the war was a collision of the rising factory owners of the North against the slave-owning ruling caste of the South. Both wanted control of the federal government and both wanted the land west of the Mississippi, then being taken from the Indians.

Between them were the growing agrarian masses, who wanted free land for homesteading. After four decades of political strife, in the midst of a collapsed railroad boom and a national depression, the small farmers joined the industrialists to elect Abraham Lincoln on the slogan "Vote Yourself a Farm!" War over slavery, union, and control of the Mississippi River and the West followed almost immediately.

With the slaveowners out of Washington, the farmers and factory owners sped construction of the national industrial machine and prepared to open the West. A homestead act was passed as well as an immigration act, high tariffs, and a reform of the national banking system.

Industrial entrepreneurs poured into the capitol for huge "grants" of money and land. The Pacific Railway Act of 1862 gave the promoters of the Union Pacific and Central Pacific Railways five square miles of land for every mile of track they would lay across the west.

Two years later, after an amazing round of bribery, the members of Congress decided to up the grant to ten square miles in addition to the allotment of as much as $48,000 for every mile of track.

By 1872 a bought Congress had given various industrial con artists more than $700 million and 200 million acres of public land, an area roughly the size of Maine, New Hampshire, Vermont, Massachusetts, Rhode Island, Connecticut, New York, and Pennsylvania. Grants by the individual states swelled the money and land totals even higher, and by the time land grant colleges and independent speculators got through, virtually all the homestead land was in the hands of eastern finance.

Actual construction of the railroads was also quite profitable. The directors of the Union Pacific, which began cross-country construction in Omaha, hired the Credit Mobilier Corporation to do the road work. The directors of the Union Pacific also happened to control the Credit Mobilier, which charged the UP about $23 million more than construction had actually cost, money which came out of the federal subsidy and the public sale of worthless stock. The Central Pacific ring of California did even better, picking up $121 million for $58 million in actual construction.

Thus, with the railroad grants as their key capital base, a few men began to carve giant private empires out of public money and land. Many of them, like Rockefeller, Vanderbilt, Carnegie, and Jim Hill, had begun life in dire poverty. Most were of Scottish or old Yankee descent.

Vanderbilt was one of the few who got his start before the Civil War. He was born to Dutch parents in 1794. As a youth he ran a ferry boat from Staten Island to Manhattan, slowly building capital to buy more boats. By the 1850s he was a full-fledged pioneer in the free-enterprise system, whose methods he perfected. "Whenever his keen eye detected a line that was making a large profit," wrote a biographer, "he swooped down and drove it to the wall by offering better service and lower rates."

Then, with the competition driven out of business, "he would raise his rates without pity, to the lasting misery of his clients."

Vanderbilt slowly collected a fleet of ships, and in the crazed years of the Gold Rush he made a fortune running the prospectors from New York across Nicaragua by boat and stage and then on to California. He was at his best in the jungles, where he drove his men to the breaking point, setting the example by fourteen to sixteen hours a day of sleepless vigilance and labor.

> *The engineers were appalled but on he went. Sometimes he got over the rapids by putting on all steam; sometimes, when this did not avail, he extended a heavy cable to great trees up stream and warped the boat over. . . . The engineers reported that he "tied down the safety-valve and 'jumped' the obstructions, to the great terror of the whole party."*

The tall, gaunt Commodore swelled his fortune by carrying the mail, studiously keeping postage rates high through his power in Congress.

During the Civil War he began piecing together a railway system with capital from his fleet, capital he added to by buying boats like the *Niagara* for the Union Navy. Gustavus Myers wrote in *Great American Fortunes* that

> *Vanderbilt was one of the few men in the secret of the Banks' expedition; he knew that the ships had to make an ocean trip. Yet he bought for $10,000 the Niagara, an old boat that had been built nearly a score of years before for trade on Lake Ontario. "In perfectly calm weather," reported Senator Grimes, of Iowa, "with a calm sea, the planks were ripped out of her and exhibited to the gaze of the indignant soldiers on board, showing that her timbers were rotten. The committee have in their committee room a large sample on one of the beams of this vessel to show that it has not the slightest capacity to hold a nail."*

As early as 1853 the dour, semiliterate Commodore was worth about $11 million, little of which he spent on his wife and nine children, who led a notably sparse existence. His son William, whom he considered stupid, was shipped off to a farm on Staten Island.

One day, however, William cheated his father in a small business deal; Cornelius then considered his son "fit" and brought him into the business, eventually leaving him around $100 million. "Law!" the Commodore once screamed, "What do I care about the Law! Hain't I got the power?"

Vanderbilt's early foe in the railroad game was "Uncle" Dan Drew, a financial manipulator of whom an admirer noted "no hardships or privations could deter him from the pursuit of money."

Like most of his contemporaries, Drew was deeply religious, an avid churchgoer, and a sponsor of cathedrals and seminaries. "He holds the honest people of the world to be a pack of fools," said Henry Clews, a Wall Street contemporary. "When he has been unusually lucky

4

in his trade of fleecing other men, he settles accounts with his conscience by subscribing toward a new chapel or attending a prayer meeting."

Drew got his start as a cattle drover, buying the animals from the midwestern farmers and driving them over the Alleghenies to market. It was as a dover that Drew pioneered the practice of "stock-watering."

During the long drive to market Drew kept the cows from getting water and often, in fact, fed them salt. Then, just before selling them, he let the thirst-crazed animals bloat themselves, multiplying their weight and price but adding nothing of value.

Drew perfected financial "stock-watering" on the Erie Railroad, the first truck line from New York City to the Great Lakes. The road was built at a cost of around $15 million, and its completion in 1851 brought celebrations and "tremendous barbecues" all over the country. The Erie was hailed as a monument at once of engineering skill and commercial enterprise."

Unfortunately, the rails were made of weak iron which had to be replaced, and the engines and cars were rickety and cheap. Furthermore, $26 million in stock—watered stock—was issued on around half that in real assets. The difference went to men on the inside, like Drew.

In the late sixties Vanderbilt squared off against Drew, Jim Fisk, and Jay Gould for control of the Erie. Vanderbilt wanted to add it to his New York Central; the "Erie Ring" wanted it for their stock-watering games and their thriving business into New York City, which they multiplied by dealing through Tammany Hall and by blackmailing farmers and merchants along the road who had no other way to get their goods to market.

When Vanderbilt tried to buy up the Erie stock the Ring began printing fresh shares like confetti. Certificates flew all over Wall Street, followed by court injunctions which each side got from their own judges.

Suddenly, Vanderbilt took the upper hand—

At ten o'clock the astonished police saw a throng of panic-stricken railway directors—looking more like a frightened gang of thieves, disturbed in the division of their plunder, than like the wealthy representatives of a great corporation—rush headlong from the doors of the Erie office and dash off in the direction of the Jersey ferry. In their hands were packages and files of papers, and their pockets were crammed with assets and securities. One individual bore away with him in a hackney-coach bales containing six millions of dollars in greenbacks. Other members of the board followed under cover of the night; some of them, not daring to expose themselves to the publicity of a ferry, attempted to cross in open boats concealed by darkness and a March fog.

The Erie directors holed up in the Taylor Hotel in Jersey City, which they surrounded with armed guards. When a rumor spread that Vanderbilt was offering $50,000 reward for the return of Drew to New York, "a standing army was organized from the employees of the road, and a small navy equipped. The alarm spread through Jersey City; the militia was held in readiness; in the evening the stores were closed and the citizens began to arm; while a garrison of about one hundred and twenty-five men entrenched themselves around the directors, in their hotel."

But it was a false alarm, and a little later a rumor circulated that Gould had left for Ohio. Soon thereafter he surfaced in Albany with a valise containing $500,000 for "legal expenses." There, said Charles Francis Adams, he undertook the task of cultivating a thorough understanding between himself and the members of the legislature—

Fabulous stories were told of the amounts which the contending parties were willing to expend; never before had the market quotations of votes and influence stood as high.

Faced with an apparently endless expense, the Commodore called a truce. He let Drew back into New York and agreed to a temporary settlement. "Vanderbilt allus told me that I acted very foolish in goin' to Jersy City," said Uncle Dan. "I tole him I didn't know but what I was circumstanced in an ockered light."

After the Vanderbilt fight Drew played a smaller and smaller role on Wall Street and eventually died a pauper.

The following year—1869—Fisk and Gould fought Pierpont Morgan for the Albany & Susquehanna, a key link to some rich Pennsylvania coal fields. In a snowstorm of legal paper, Fisk, now known as "the Prince of Erie," sauntered into a stockholder's meeting with a gang of thugs, expecting to take over.

A group of Morgan men (recruited from the Bowery) met him and threw him down a flight of stairs, where he was "arrested" and taken to the local police station. The "policeman" that "arrested" him turned out to be a Morgan man in costume, and Fisk walked out of jail a little later.

Soon Morgan took control of the Albany terminal of the road, while the Erie Ring held the station at Binghamton. With injunctions flying right and left both sides sent out a trainload of thugs. The two locomotives rammed each other at a tunnel fifteen miles east of Binghamton, where "there was a crash and a smash, and the Albany locomotive rolled off the track, leaving the other without cowcatcher, headlight, or smokestack."

A pitched battle ensued, which the better-armed Morgan men won. The Erie Army retreated into the tunnel and regrouped. Morgan's men charged but were afraid to attack in the dark. Night fell, the militia marched in and the battle reverted to the courts, where Morgan eventually won.

That same year Gould cornered the national gold exchange and sent the price skyrocketing. When it peaked he poured his gold onto the open market, taking a gigantic profit and incidentally crashing the entire economy. "Let everyone carry out his own corpse!" yelled the irrepressible Fisk.

The Crash of '73

Four years later eastern speculators noticed their money was drying up again, as it had in 1819, 1837, and 1857. This time the Franco-Prussian War had thrown European money sources into disarray, while the postwar orgy of speculation in the United States put thousands of operators out on a limb, holding paper empires with nothing real under them.

Jay Cooke was sunk deep over his head in the Northern Pacific Railroad. Morgan, whose father had just arranged a $50 million loan to save the French government, wanted to add the NP to his expanding empire. He began publishing stories in his newspaper aimed at undermining the market value of Cooke's stock.

Under the strain Cooke's cash reserves disappeared. He was forced to duel Morgan on the floor of Congress for a $300 million "loan." Morgan won.

On September 17, 1873, President Ulysses S. Grant visited Cooke's palace in Philadelphia and spent the night. In the morning, while Grant slept, oblivious to what was going on, Cooke rode downtown and closed the doors of his bank. The national money supply disappeared. Millions of farmers and workers were thrown into a desperate struggle for existence. Mortgage money dried up, unemployment skyrocketed, families wandered from city to city in search of work.

For Morgan, Vanderbilt, and a few others with big money, crash meant good times. Labor was cheap. Giant factories stood idle, waiting to be picked off for next to nothing. With Cooke out of the way Morgan became the most powerful banker in the country. Vanderbilt and Gould added property after property to their empires while Rockefeller put the final touches on his oil kingdom. Bit by bit they took it all—

> *Just as a number of German barons planted their castles along the banks of the Rhine, in order to tax the commerce between East and West, which was obliged to make use of this highway, so it is with these economic narrows. Wherever they are found, monopolies plant themselves in the shape of "rings," "corners," "pools," "syndicates," or "trusts."*

Rockefeller's position was pretty well set by the 1873 depression. Rising as a merchant during the Civil War, he invested his capital in Cleveland oil refineries, taking care as he grew to commandeer all the railroad support he could get. By the early seventies he was the most powerful oil man in Cleveland.

Like Drew, Rockefeller was deeply religious. He read the Bible every night before retiring to bed, where he would discuss the day's business with himself. "These intimate conversations with myself had a great influence upon my life," he wrote in his autobiography.

The Baron of Oil had "the soul of a bookkeeper," kept all his accounts in his head, and was exceedingly taciturn, almost never displaying any emotion of any kind. On making a large profit, however, Rockefeller was known to clap his hands with delight, or throw his hat in the air and yell "I'm bound to be rich! *Bound to be rich!*"

With ruthless precision Rockefeller trimmed waste from his refineries while forcing rebates from the roads that carried his oil, carefully insuring that they charged his competitors more—

> *Wilkerson and Company received car of oil Monday 13th—70 barrels which we suspect slipped through at the usual fifth class rate—in fact we might say we know it did—paying only $41.50 freight from here. Charges $57.40. Please turn another screw.*

In the depression of the seventies Rockefeller consolidated virtually the entire oil industry in his own hands. Dominating the railroad, underselling and, in at least one instance, blowing up would-be competitors, Standard Oil simply strong-armed the rest of the industry out of existence. "I tried to make friends with these men," explained John D. "I admitted their ability and the value of their enterprise. I worked to convince them that it would be better for both to cooperate."

By 1880 Rockefeller refined 80 percent of the nation's oil. Its gigantic capital fund allowed the Standard machine to pile railroads, ore mines, shipping companies, pipelines, state governments, and U.S. senators one on top of the other into a mushrooming empire that was probably the most powerful single organization in the world.

By the 1880s Standard and the other baronies growing with it—Carnegie Steel, the Morgan and Mellon Banks, James Duke's American Tobacco Company, Swift and Armour Meat Packing, the railroads of Gould, Jim Hill, Tom Scott, and the Central Pacific ring—filled every corner of American life.

The Big Three

The wreckage of the 1893 collapse left three barons in control of the heart of the economy—Morgan, Rockefeller, and Carnegie, the baron of steel.

Morgan was born in Hartford in 1847. Cold and colorless, he studied mathematics in Germany and then settled into his father's banking business. In his old age his face was disfigured by a rare disease that made his nose swollen and red. He had the mind of a computer, the passion of a Swiss watch.

Morgan, in his position as the leading banker on Wall Street, had taken to "reorganizing" as many railroads as he could get his hands on, which by the nineties was about half the track in the country.

After the Erie War of 1869 he worked himself and his father's capital into the role of "peacemaker" among warring corporations. When a major struggle loomed he would invite the directors to his yacht *Corsair* (*Corsair II*, 204 feet long, was sold to the navy for use in conquering Cuba) and preside over a settlement. Any new stocks or bonds that resulted were handled by the House of Morgan and often interlocking directorates were created. A typical settlement occurred when General Electric and Westinghouse threatened to engage in "ruinous competition." Morgan settled the fight, took a directorship in both corporations, and the two companies pooled their patents.

The only man as big as Morgan was Rockefeller. Allied with E. H. Harriman of the Illinois Central, Rockefeller in the 1890s sat atop complete control of the oil industry, a widespread network of controlled or affiliated railroads, huge coal and iron mining interests, and a gigantic yearly income that allowed him to buy properties, ruin competitors, and manipulate national prices and markets at will.

Between Morgan and Rockefeller, Andrew Carnegie held the key. Outgoing, well-read and articulate, the lively Scotsman was known to the world as a philanthropist, to his associates as a pirate, and to the workers in his factories as a killer. An outspoken advocate of peace and human community, Carnegie built an empire on the tools of war and paid other men to use them. He was a pioneer preacher of the gospel of wealth, a leader of men "who in the words of Jack London invoked the name of the Prince of Peace in their diatribes against war, and who put rifles in the hands of Pinkertons with which to shoot down strikers in their own factories."

Carnegie built his empire of steel from the untiring efforts of a few devoted engineers who helped him cash in on the Bessemer process. Later he brought Henry Frick, the coke king, into his operation as plant manager, thus tying most of his raw materials under one roof. By the nineties he held undisputed control over the nation's key growth industry.

In 1899 friction developed between Carnegie and the Pennsylvania Railroad, where he had begun as an office boy. He threatened to "go to war" and build his own railroad to the Great Lakes, a move that upset both Rockefeller and Morgan.

Rockefeller offered to buy him out but the deal fell through. In 1900 Morgan told Carnegie to name his price and then paid over $492 million.

Quickly Morgan added his own steel holdings to the Carnegie properties and on April Fool's Day, 1901, the House of Morgan offered the first billion dollar trust—the United States Steel Corporation—for public consumption. *Cosmopolitan* magazine declared it a turning point in American economic history—

> *The old competitive system, with its ruinous methods, its countless duplications, its wastefulness of human effort, and its relentless business warfare, is hereby abolished.*

King Dollar

As the wealth of the barons mushroomed, so did their power. From the days of Jackson the spoils system carried through the Civil War to the "Great Barbeque" of Grant, when the flood of corporate money into the government became a tidal wave. With amazing speed an efficient, loosely centralized political machine grew out of corporate money. "It was simple," wrote William Allen White—

> *A state boss collected money from the railroads, the packing houses, the insurance companies, and the banks in his state.*
>
> *This money he sent to his henchmen in the counties, who distributed the largesse to their followers, who controlled the county conventions. The object and aim of all county conventions was to control the nomination of those Republicans who would run for the legislature and the state senate. When they were elected, as all good Republicans were, they would follow the boss.*
>
> *On most matters they were free; but where legislation touched the banks, the railroads, the insurance companies, or the packing houses, they were bound in honor to vote with the boss, and on his candidate for United States senator and for the tie-up he made with a candidate for state printer.*
>
> *The two united made a winning majority. So, over the United States, our senators went to Washington obligated to the large corporate interests of their states. . . .*
>
> *The railroad lobbyists and bosses in Washington amalgamated their forces. Thus the plutocracy built its mighty fortress.*

In mass elections "votes" equaled "dollars." No candidate could win without a political party and thus real issues were eliminated because "the same monopolies that run the Republican run the Democratic party." A political party, explained Secretary of State William Seward, was "a joint-stock company in which those who contribute the most direct the action and management of the concern."

The parties were essentially rival corporations competing for the spoils of power. The bigger barons usually contributed to both, often supporting candidates against each other to cover their bets.

Washington was a bad joke. Congress was "transformed into a mart where the price of votes was haggled over, and laws, made to order, were bought and sold." In 1877, after troops crushed a bloody national rail strike, President Rutherford B. Hayes looked in amazement at what had become of American government—

> *Shall the railroads govern the country, or shall the people govern the railroads? . . . This is a government of the people, by the people, and for the people no longer. It is a government of corporations, by corporations, and for corporations. How is this?*
>
> *At the turn of the century the U.S. Senate—ninety men—included no less than 25 of the country's 4000 millionaires.*

The Legal Backstop

Nonetheless, as early as the seventies popular hostility to the money power was too great to be denied by electoral manipulation. At all levels of government the American people demanded that the corporations be brought under some degree of popular control.

This pushed the issue to the last line of legal defense—the Supreme Court.

After the Civil War, Congress passed the Fourteenth Amendment, guaranteeing the right of ex-slaves by forbidding any state to "deprive any person of life, liberty, or property without due process of law . . . ."

In 1886 the Supreme Court voided some 230 state laws meant to regulate corporations on the ground that they deprived the corporations of their property "without due process of law."

This insane ruling meant that a corporation—an organization of property—got the same legal rights as a human being. At the same time the corporations were never held liable on a human basis for criminal offenses—maltreatment of human beings and murder, for example, as literally thousands of workers were killed in factories where safety devices were "unprofitable."

In 1874, in *Schulenburg v. Harriman*, the Court stopped an attempt to take back a public land grant from a railroad which had not completed its contract. In 1895 the Court ruled an income tax law unconstitutional.

In 1887 Congress passed the Interstate Commerce Act to regulate the railroads and other businesses dealing across state lines. Almost immediately the law became the tool of the corporations themselves. Richard Olney, a lawyer for the Boston & Maine and Attorney General under Cleveland, advised a railroad president that

> *The Commission, as its functions have now been limited by the courts, is, or can be made, of great use to the railroads. It satisfies the public clamor for a government supervision of railroads, at the same time that that supervision is almost entirely nominal.*

Further, the older such a commission gets to be, the more inclined it will be found to take the business and railroad view of things. It thus becomes a sort of barrier between the railroad corporations and the people. . . .

The Sherman Anti-Trust Act, passed in 1890, served the same function. Republican Senator Orville Platt of Connecticut explained why Congress bothered to pass it at all—

> *The conduct of the Senate . . . has not been in the line of honest preparation of a bill to prohibit and punish trusts. It has been in the line of getting some bill with that title that we might go to the country with.*
>
> *The questions of whether the bill would be operative, of how it would operate, . . . have been whistled down the wind in this Senate as idle talk, and the whole effort has been to get some bill headed: "A Bill to Punish Trusts" with which to go to the country.*

If there was ever any doubt, the Supreme Court wiped out the Sherman Act's effectiveness against the trusts five years after its passage. In 1895 it ruled that the E. C. Knight Company, which refined 98 percent of the nation's sugar, restrained trade only "indirectly."

But from 1890 to 1897 the Sherman Act was used twelve times to break labor strikes. "What looks like a stone wall to a layman," said the humorist Mr. Dooley, "is a triumphal arch to a corporation lawyer."

The Barrel of the Gun

But if the system seemed to run on money and legalities, there was no mistaking that ultimately it rested on brute force. From the thirties on, federal, state, and local armies, militia, and police were in ceaseless use breaking up demonstrations, strikes, and labor unions. In the name of property, law, and order, jails were constantly filled and official violence brought down on those who advocated worker control of factories, the right to organize, a black-white alliance in the South, and a redistribution of wealth and power.

In a pinch the barons also had their private armies of Pinkerton "detectives," professional guards, strikebreakers, vigilantes, and citizen's leagues to handle the untidy work of doing away with rebels. In a nation with a solid unemployment rate and an average income below the subsistence level, a man like Jay Gould wasn't kidding when he boasted "I can hire one-half the working class to kill the other half!"

Atop this flexible tyranny sat the Four Hundred, a group of four to six hundred families centered in New York and including the biggest of the barons and their entourage—a self-proclaimed "nobility of wealth." Frederick Townshend Martin spoke their creed in *The Passing of the Idle Rich*—

> *The class I represent, care nothing for politics. . . . It matters not one iota what political party is in power or what president holds the reigns of office.*
>
> *We are not politicians or public thinkers; we are the rich; we own America; we got it, God knows how, but we intend to keep it if we can by throwing all the tremendous weight of our support, our influence, our money, our political connections, our purchased senators, our hungry congressmen, our public-speaking demagogues, into the scale against any legislature, any political platform, any presidential campaign that threatens the integrity of our estate.*

The Machine

The American industrial machine was clearly becoming the biggest in the world. Each land-mark of growth, each statistic of wealth, was hailed by the barons with excitement and pride.

Upon completion of the transcontinental railroad in 1869, Jay Gould could hardly control his delight. "WE have made the country rich," he yelled. "WE have developed the country, coal mines and cattle raising, as well as cotton. . . . WE have created this earning power by developing the system!"

With great national fanfare the Union and Central Pacific lines were joined at Promon-tory Point, Utah. A gold and a silver spike were to be driven into the final tie by one of the many dignitaries carried to Utah for the ceremony. But none of them could handle a sledge-hammer. A construction worker had to be called out of the crowd to knock in the spikes.

By 1888 the American industrial system was killing 100 workers every day—around 35,000 were killed each year, with over 500,000 reported injured.

More than 700,000 American workers were killed in industrial "accidents" from 1888 to 1908. Nearly a million industrial injuries were reported in 1913. The railroads alone killed ten workers a day, the coal mines about the same. If you only get maimed you were lucky—

A brakeman with both hands and all his fingers was either remarkably skillful, incredibly lucky or new on the job.

A substantial part of the work force was made up of children, especially in the mines and in the textile mills of New England towns like Lawrence, Massachusetts, where half the work-ers were girls between the ages of fourteen and eighteen—

A considerable number of the boys and girls die within the first two or three years after beginning work. . . . Thirty-six of every 100 of all the men and women who work in the mill die before or by the time they are twenty-five years of age.

The life-span of the average mill worker in Lawrence was twenty-two years shorter than that of an owner.

To help guarantee a large work force for their factories, the barons advertised Ameri-can all over Europe as the land of the rich, where anyone "good enough" could become wealthy in no time. The plains of Montana were hailed as fertile, jungle-like farmland and became known as "Jay Cooke's Banana Belt." Steamship companies and rail lines starving for pas-sengers uplifted entire peasant villages and set them down in the West.

For the immigrants the voyage to America was a journey of hope, an escape from the poverty of Europe's dying peasant culture. America meant a new chance at life. But for Andrew Carnegie, himself an immigrant, people coming to America meant a "cheap and mobile labor force," as he pointed out in 1905—

Taking the cost, the value of a man, a an or a child, in this Republic as low as you put the slave, and that was average of about $1000, you are getting 400,000 a year and that means $4,000,000 cash value.

Utterly powerless and confused, piled into the ghettoes of New York, Chicago, Philadelphia, Baltimore, and Boston, or shuttled to the crippled western farm community, the new arrivals were at the disposal of employers without whom they literally could not get food, clothing, housing. The bitter prewar diatribe of a South Carolina senator began to make a perverted sort of sense—

The difference between us is that our slaves are hired for life. . . . Yours are hired by the day, not cared for, and scantily compensated which may be proved in the most deplorable manner, at any hour in any street of your large towns. . . .

American industry was paid for in the broken backs and dead eyes of men, women, and children who were valued only as fuel. "Men are cheap and machinery is dear," explained Woodrow Wilson. "You can discard your man and replace him; there are others ready to come into his place; but you can't without great cost, discard your machine and put a new one in its place."

Who Do You Trust?

At the turn of the century it was generally accepted that the free enterprise system had finally passed away. It was hoped by many that the "community of interest" arrangements between the banks and the big trusts would help rationalize the economy. Wasteful competition would be eliminated, and professional, "progressive" management would take charge.

But the trusts brought no basic changes. From its very beginning the long-awaited United States Steal Corporation was half water. Morgan floated $1.4 billion in stock over 5,682 million in real assets and took a $62 million "commission" for handling the issue. By 1903 U.S. Steel stock had dropped from 40 to 8. The price of a ton of the company's steel jumped from $24 to $28 soon after the trust was formed.

As for efficiency, the giant corporations were at best unwieldy, impersonal bureaucracies. And they turned out to be powerful, destructive barriers to technological progress.

For while many of them could and did conduct expensive scientific research, they also used their power to buy up new inventions and bury them in the patent office, keeping them out of the hands of the public.

Small innovations were indeed used to cut short-range production costs. But major changes that might require expensive retooling or complicated reorganization were suppressed time and again. "A huge organization," wrote *Engineering News,* "is too clumsy to take up the development of an original idea. With the market closely controlled and profits certain by following standard methods, those who control our trusts do not want the bother of developing anything new."

Woodrow Wilson, before he became President, agreed—

I am not saying that all invention has been stopped by the growth of the trusts, but I think it is perfectly clear that invention in many fields has been discouraged. . . and that mankind has been deprived of many comforts and conveniences, as well as the opportunity of buying at lower prices.

Urban Pollution—
Many Long Years Ago

Joel A. Tarr

To many urban Americans in the 1970s, fighting their way through the traffic's din and gagging on air heavy with exhaust fumes, the automobile is a major villain in the sad tale of atmospheric pollution. Yet they have forgotten, or rather never knew, that the predecessor of the auto was also a major polluter. The faithful, friendly horse was charged with creating the very problems today attributed to the automobile: air contaminants harmful to health, noxious odors, and noise. At the beginning of the twentieth century, in fact, writers in popular and scientific periodicals were decrying the pollution of the public streets and demanding "the banishment of the horse from American cities" in vigorous terms. The presence of 120,000 horses in New York City, wrote one 1908 authority for example, is "an economic burden, an affront to cleanliness, and a terrible tax upon human life." The solution to the problem, agreed the critics, was the adoption of the "horseless carriage."

A concern with clean streets and with the horse as a principal obstacle to them was nothing new. European cities had shown concern for the problem as early as the fourteenth century, as had American cities from their beginnings. But it required a more statistically minded age to measure the actual amount of manure produced by the horse. Sanitary experts in the early part of the twentieth century agreed that the normal city horse produced between fifteen and thirty pounds of manure a day, with the average being something like twenty-two pounds. In a city like Milwaukee in 1907, for instance, with a human population of 350,000 and a horse population of 12,500, this meant 133 tons of manure a day, for a daily average of nearly three-quarters of a pound of manure for each resident. Or, as health officials in Rochester, New York, calculated in 1900, the fifteen thousand horses in that city produced enough manure in a year to make a pile 175 feet high covering an acre of ground and breeding sixteen billion flies, each one a potential spreader of germs.

Milwaukee and Rochester resembled other American cities in 1900 in having thousands of horses at work in their streets even after the automobile and electric streetcar had been introduced. Chicago had 83,330, Detroit 12,000, and Columbus 5,000. Overall, there

Reprinted from *American Heritage*, 1971, by permission of American Heritage Publishing Co.

were probably between three and three and a half million horses in American cities as the century opened, compared with about seventeen million living in more bucolic environments. (Today, at a time when horseback riding for pleasure is on the rise, the total number of horses in the United States is somewhat over seven million.) The ratio of horses to people was much higher in cities where traction lines were not yet completely electrified. In 1890, even after electrification had already begun, twenty-two thousand horses and mules were still required simply for pulling streetcars in New York City and in Brooklyn, with a total of ten thousand performing similarly in Philadelphia and Chicago. Ten years earlier, when New York and Brooklyn had counted no electric railways and 1,764,168 souls, they had a total equine population of 150,000 to 175,000.

To a great extent nineteenth-century urban life moved at the pace of horse-drawn transportation, and the evidence of the horse was everywhere—in the piles of manure that littered the streets attracting swarms of flies and creating stench, in the iron rings and hitching posts sunk into the pavements for fastening horses' reins, and in the numerous livery stables that gave off a mingled smell of horse urine and manure, harness oil and hay. In 1880 New York and Brooklyn were served by 427 blacksmith shops, 249 carriage and wagon enterprises, 262 wheelwright shops, and 290 establishments dealing in saddles and harnesses. They were eminently necessary. On a typical day in 1885 an engineer, Francis V. Greene, making a study of urban traffic conditions, counted 7,811 horse-drawn vehicles, many with teams of two or more horses, passing the busy corner of Broadway and Pine Street.

While some of these conveyances were fine carriages drawn by spirited teams, the most common city horses were commercial or work animals. City streets were crowded with large team-pulled drays guided by husky and colorfully profane drivers and piled high with heavy freight. Among these, single-horse spring wagons twisted their way, making deliveries of ice, milk, and goods of every kind to residential areas. Their sides were often brightly decorated with advertisements, catching the eyes of passers-by and of the riders in the many omnibuses and hacks plying their routes. The horse remained essential in urban civilization, even after the development of the steam engine. As the *Nation* noted in 1872, though great improvements had been made in the development of such "agents of progress" as the railroad, the steamboat, and the telegraph, modern society's dependence on the horse had "grown almost *pari passu* with our dependence on steam." For it was the horse who fed the railroads and steamboats with passengers and freight, and who provided transportation within the cities.

Yet this hard-working animal, so vital to the functioning of urban society, posed problems that were recognized by even the earliest American city dwellers. The question of clean streets was most obvious. In eighteenth-century Boston and New York, money was allocated by the city fathers for street cleaning, and householders were required to sweep the road in front of their doorways. Cities made sporadic attempts during the mid-nineteenth century to mechanize the tasks of sanitation. In 1855 New York introduced street-sweeping machines and self-loading carts, and in 1865 urban entrepreneurs formed the New York Sanitary and Chemical Compost Manufacturing Company for the purpose of "cleansing cities, towns, and villages in the United States" with several varieties of mechanical devices adapted to the task. By 1880 almost all cities over thirty thousand in population employed street-cleaners.

American cities made their most sustained efforts to clean the streets under the stimulus of the fear induced by epidemics of cholera, smallpox, yellow fever, or typhoid. Many eighteenth- and nineteenth-century medical authorities believed that such diseases were caused by "a combination of certain atmospheric conditions and putrefying filth," among which horse manure was a chief offender. In 1752 Boston selectmen allocated extra funds to clean the streets because of the fear that street dirt might contain smallpox infection, and in 1795, during the yellow-fever season, town officials invited neighboring farmers to collect the manure from the streets free of charge. The city fathers of New York, faced by the threat of cholera in 1832, made special efforts to cleanse the cobblestones, thereby divesting the city "of that foul aliment on which the pestilence delights to feed."

But unless jolted by rampant disease, city authorities and citizens tolerated a great deal of "that foul aliment" in their streets. One reason, perhaps, was a reluctance to spend money on such an unsatisfying, if crucial, municipal effort. Some cities tried to cover the cost of street cleaning by selling the manure for fertilizer. In 1803 the New York superintendent of scavengers expended about twenty-six thousand dollars for street cleaning and realized over twenty-nine thousand dollars from the sale of the manure collected. Despite this instance of profitable purifying, however, paid scavenging did not generally achieve great results. In those cases where private contractors were responsible for cleaning the streets, citizens often complained that they neglected other forms of rubbish and only collected the salable manure. Nor did a shift to public sanitation service improve things. Officials of post-Civil War years often reported that street dirt was becoming too mixed with other forms of litter to be sold as fertilizer. Moreover, whatever the salable quality of the street refuse, urban sanitation departments during the nineteenth century were notoriously inefficient. Vexed by graft and corruption, they were staffed by "old and indigent men," "prisoners who don't like to work," and "persons on relief."

Street cleaning, therefore, remained largely inadequate, and one is thus not surprised to discover that newspapers, diaries, and governmental reports abound with complaints about the problems created in the city by horse manure left in the public thoroughfares. Manure collected into unattended piles by the street cleaners bred huge numbers of flies and created "pestilential vapours." Offal was sometimes carried from wealthy residential neighborhoods and dumped in poor neighborhoods, where it was left to rot. Streets turned into virtual cesspools when it rained, and long-skirted ladies suffered the indignity of trailing their hems in liquefied manure. In London, ladies and gentlemen were aided in their navigation through a sea of horse droppings by "crossing-sweepers," but no such group appeared in more democratic American cities. Yet dry weather was no great improvement, for then there were complaints of the "pulverized horse dung" that blew into people's faces and the windows of their homes, and over the outdoor displays of merchants' wares. The coming of paved streets accelerated this problem, as wheels and hoofs ground the sun-dried manure against the hard surfaces and amplified the amount of dust.

And then there was noise. In many American cities, early paving consisted largely of cobblestones, on which the clopping and clanking of horses' iron shoes and the iron-tired wheels of carts and wagons created an immense din. Benjamin Franklin complained in the late eighteenth century of the "thundering of coaches, chariots, chaises, waggons, drays and the whole fraternity of noise" that assailed the ears of Philadelphians. Similar comments about urban noise were made by travellers in other cities. Attempts were made quite early to quiet the clamor. In 1747, in Boston, the town council banned traffic from King Street so that the noise would not distract the deliberations of the General Court. In 1785 New York City passed an ordinance forbidding teams and wagons with iron-shod wheels from the streets. In London good medical management required the putting of straw on the pavement outside sick people's houses to muffle the sounds of traffic, a practice undoubtedly followed in America. Yet the problem grew with the growing nation. As late as the 1890's a writer in *Scientific American* noted that the sounds of traffic on busy New York streets made conversation nearly impossible, while the author William Dean Howells complained that "the sharp clatter of the horses' iron shoes" on the pavement tormented his ear.

If the horse, by his biological necessities, created problems for the city, the city, in turn, was a harsh environment for the animals whose possession had once been the mark and privilege of nobility. The horse belonged to the open spaces and the battlefield. In an urban setting he was, with rare exception, a drudge. City horses were notoriously overworked. The average streetcar nag had a life expectancy of barely two years, and it was a common sight to see drivers and teamsters savagely lashing their overburdened animals. The mistreatment of city horses was a key factor in moving Henry Bergh to found the American Society for the Prevention of Cruelty to Animals in 1866. When released from harness, the working steed usually was led to a crowded and unsanitary stable without adequate light or air. Only the pleasure horses kept by the city's "swells" to drive handsome rigs in the park had access to the green fields enjoyed by their country cousins.

Many overworked, mistreated urban horses simply died in the city streets. Moreover, since asphalt-paved or cobbled streets were slipperier than dirt roads, horses often stumbled and fell. An unfortunate beast who broke a leg in this way was destroyed where it lay. (In order to minimize the risk of stumbles, some veterinarians recommended that city draft horses be shod with rubber-padded horseshoes, but few owners followed this advice.) A description of Broadway appearing in the *Atlantic Monthly* in 1866 spoke of the street as being clogged with "dead horses and vehicular entanglements." The equine carcasses added fearsomely to the smells and flies already rising in clouds from stables and manure piles. In 1880 New York City removed fifteen thousand dead horses from its streets, and as late as 1912 Chicago carted away nearly ten thousand horse carcasses. A contemporary book on the collection of municipal refuse advised that, since the average weight of a dead horse was thirteen hundred pounds, "trucks for the removal of dead horses should be hung low, to avoid an excessive lift." The complaint of one horse lover that "in the city the working horse is treated worse than a steam-engine or sewing machine," was well justified.

By the 1880s and 90s the immense population growth of American cities, the need for improved urban transportation to keep up with the geographic spread of communities, and a growing awareness of the need for better sanitation in the interest of public health, all emphasized the drawbacks of the horse as the chief form of urban locomotion and spurred a search for alternatives. The first major breakthrough came with the development of the cable car and the electric trolley car in the late 1880s. Traction companies were quick to substitute mechanical power for animal power on their streetcar lines. Writing in *Popular Science Monthly* in 1892, United States Commissioner of Labor Carroll D. Wright maintained that electric power was not only cheaper than horsepower, but also far more beneficial to the city from the perspective of health and safety. "The presence of so many horses constantly moving through the streets," wrote Wright somewhat ponderously, "is a very serious matter. The vitiation of the air by the presence of so many animals is alone a sufficient reason for their removal, while the clogged condition of the streets impedes business, and involves the safety of life and limb." While electric-powered transportation began to make inroads on the horse's domain, improvements in the gasoline engine made it clear that the automobile would soon be a viable alternative. Even the bicycle craze of the nineties reminded many that horseless commuting was possible over reasonable distances.

Horse lovers became defensive about the future of that quadruped. Writing in the *Chautauquan* in 1895, Robert L. Seymour maintained that while the "cheap horse" might be doomed, the "costly, good-looking horse, the horse of history, the heroic horse in action, will probably last long." Can you imagine, asked Seymour, "Napoleon crossing the Alps in a blinding snow storm on a bicycle or Alexander riding heroically at the head of his armies in a horseless carriage?" It is hard to blame Seymour for not having the prophetic gift to foresee tank commanders dashing ahead of their squadrons. A more fundamental error seems to have been made by a writer in *Lippincott's Magazine* who insisted that since "Americans are a horse-loving nation . . . the wide-spread adoption of the motor-driven vehicle in this country is open to serious doubt." Less romantic observers, however, embraced the possibility of the elimination of the horse with enthusiasm. When William Dean Howells' fictional traveller from the non-existent, utopian land of Altruria visited Chicago's World's Fair of 1893, he noted with pleasure that this metropolis of the future had "little of the filth resulting in all other American cities from the use of the horse."

During the opening years of the twentieth century the movement toward salvation by internal combustion continued to gather headway. Such popular journals as *Harper's Weekly*, *Lippincott's Magazine*, and the *Forum*, as well as more specialized periodicals like *American City*, *Horseless Age*, *Motor*, and *Scientific American*, were filled with articles extolling the automobile and the motor truck and disparaging the horse. There were several lines of attack. One of the most common was economic analysis, which argued, as did one writer in *Munsey's Magazine*, that "the horse has become unprofitable. He is too costly to buy and too costly to keep." Articles such as these computed the expense of the "horse cost of living" and compared it unfavorably to the expense of automobile upkeep. Other articles pointed out the advantages the motor truck had over the horse in hauling freight and in preventing traffic tie-ups by moving faster. One writer in *American City* noted that the good motor truck, which was immune to fatigue and to weather, did on the average of two and a half times as much work in the same time as the horse and with one-quarter the amount of street congestion. "It is all a question of dollars and cents, this gasoline or oats proposition. The automobile is no longer classed as a luxury. It is acknowledged to be one of the great time-savers in the world."

But a second and equally—if not more—convincing argument for the superiority of the motor vehicle over the horse rested on the testimony that the automobile was a better bet from the perspective of public medicine. "The horse in the city is bound to be a menace to a condition of perfect health," warned Dr. Arthur R. Reynolds, superintendent of the Chicago health department in 1901. Public health officials in various cities charged that windblown dust from ground-up manure damaged eyes and irritated respiratory organs, while the "noise and clatter" of city traffic aggravated nervous diseases. Since, noted *Scientific*

American, the motor vehicle left no litter and was "always noiseless or nearly so" (a judgment hard to understand if one has heard a primitive auto engine), the exit of the horse would "benefit the public health to an almost incalculable degree."

Also blamed on the horse were such familiar plagues as cholera and typhoid fever and intestinal diseases like dysentery and infant diarrhea. The reason why faithful dobbin was adjudged guilty was that such diseases were often transmitted by the housefly, and the favorite breeding place of the fly was the manure heap. In the late 1890s insurance company actuaries discovered that employees in livery stables and those living near stables had a higher rate of infectious diseases, such as typhoid fever, than the general public. Sanitation specialists pursued the question, and the first decade of the twentieth century saw a large outpouring of material warning of the danger of the infection-carrying "queen of the dung-heap," *Musca domestica.* The most obvious way to eradicate the "typhoid fly," as the carrier was called by L.O. Howard, chief of the Bureau of Entomology of the Department of Agriculture and a leader of a campaign to stamp out flies, was to eliminate the horse.

Writing in *Appleton's Magazine* in 1908, Harold Bolce entitled his article "The Horse vs. Health." In a thoroughgoing assault he blamed most of the sanitary and economic problems of the modern city on the horse and essayed to calculate the savings if all horses were replaced by automobiles and motor trucks. His figures were arrived at by an intriguing formula. According to Bolce, twenty thousand New Yorkers died each year from "maladies that fly in the dust" created mainly by horse manure. He estimated the monetary value to the community of these people's lives, plus the cost of maintaining hospitals to treat them, and laid the entire bill on the withers of the inoffensive horse. To this sum he added the cost of street cleaning and rubbish disposal. He also attributed a higher urban cost of living to the failure to use speedy motor trucks, instead of horses, in transporting goods. Finally he computed and added the costs of traffic congestion and reached a total of approximately one hundred million dollars as the price that New York City paid for not banning the horse from its streets. What fed Bolce's indignation was not so much hate of horses, perhaps, as dedication to progress. The horse, he maintained, represented one of the last stands of brute animal strength over applied science and, as such, had to go—Americans could no longer afford "the absurdities of a horse-infected city."

While no city ever took such drastic action as banning horses completely from its boundaries, many cities did eventually forbid them the use of certain streets and highways. But in the long run the horse's opponents triumphed without recourse to legislation. The number of horses in cities dropped sharply as the automobile and the motor truck rapidly gained popularity, although the number of horses in the nation stayed high until the 1920s (there were 20,091,000 horses reported in the 1920 census). As this happened, the benefits promised by motor-vehicle enthusiasts seemed to be initially realized. Streets were cleaner, particle pollution resulting from groundup manure and the diseases thereby produced were diminished, the number of flies was greatly reduced, goods were transported more cheaply and efficiently, traffic travelled at a faster rate, and the movement of people from crowded cities to suburbs was accelerated by the automobile. Events appeared to justify the spokesmen for the advantages of the motor vehicle over the horse.

And yet, as current difficulties resulting from the massive use of the automobile attest, the motor vehicle's proponents were extremely shortsighted in their optimistic faith that their innovation would not only eradicate the urban health problems created by the horse but would also avoid the formation of new ones. As the number of automobiles proliferated and such cities as New York and Los Angeles experienced smog conditions that were a serious hazard to public comfort and health, it became apparent that the automobile, too, was a major obstacle to humane metropolitan existence.

Are the problems of noise and air pollution created by thousands of cars and trucks "worse" than those, for which the horse was responsible? It is impossible to answer flatly. Altered environmental and demographic conditions in the city today, when judged beside those of a century or so ago, make specific comparisons between the horse and the automobile as polluters difficult at best. Aside from the disagreeable aesthetic effect created by horse manure, its chief impact upon public health seemed to come from wind-blown manure particles that irritated respiratory organs; from the reservoir furnished by the manure for disease spores, such as those of tetanus; and, most critically, from the fact that horse dung provided a breeding ground for the fly, proven by medical science to be the carrier of thirty different diseases, many of them acute. The pollution created by the automobile, on the other hand, is also aesthetically displeasing; and while it has not yet been firmly linked to any specific disease, it has primarily a chronic effect on health. The pollutants released by the internal-combustion engine irritate people's eyes and lungs, weakening their resistance to disease and worsening already present health problems. The immense number of automobiles in cities today has produced environmental difficulties that, unless soon dealt with, will generate problems that will dwarf those produced by horses in the cities of the past.

But the narrowness of vision of the early automobile advocates and their conviction that their machines would make urban life more tolerable, can be understood not as their failing alone. Most Americans, when informed of some technological advance that promises to alter their lives for the better without social cost, rush to embrace it. Second thoughts come later. Witness the apprehensions voiced presently over nuclear power plants after an initial flush of enthusiasm based on the hope that this cleaner and more efficient method of generating electricity would free us from dependence on dirty fossil fuels. We are only now learning to weigh the biological and other costs of new inventions with some caution. The career of the automobile has been one element in our education. Horses may be gone from city streets, but the unforeseen problems created by their successors still beset us.

Fire

Leon Stein

I intend to show Hell.
—DANTE: *INFERNO,*
CANTO XXIX:96

The first touch of spring warmed the air.

It was Saturday afternoon—March 25, 1911—and the children from the teeming tenements to the south filled Washington Square Park with the shrill sounds of youngsters at play. The paths among the old trees were dotted with strollers.

Genteel brownstones, their lace-curtained windows like drooping eyelids, lined two sides of the 8-acre park that formed a sanctuary of green in the brick and concrete expanse of New York City. On the north side of the Square rose the red brick and limestone of the patrician Old Row, dating back to 1833. Only on the east side of the Square was the almost solid line of homes broken by the buildings of New York University.

The little park originally had been the city's Potter's Field, the final resting place of its unclaimed dead, but in the nineteenth century Washington Square became the city's most fashionable area. By 1911 the old town houses stood as a rear guard of an aristocratic past facing the invasions of industry from Broadway to the east, low-income groups from the crowded streets to the south, and the first infiltration of artists and writers into Greenwich Village to the west.

Dr. D.C. Winterbottom, a coroner of the City of New York, lived at 63 Washington Square South. Some time after 4:30, he parted the curtains of a window in his front parlor and surveyed the pleasant scene.

He may have noticed Patrolman James P. Meehan of Traffic B proudly astride his horse on one of the bridle paths which cut through the park.

Or he may have caught a glimpse of William Gunn Shepherd, young reporter for the United Press, walking briskly eastward through the Square.

Clearly visible to him was the New York University building filling half of the eastern side of the Square from Washington Place to Waverly Place. But he could not see, as he looked from his window, that Professor Frank Sommer, former sheriff of Essex County, New Jersey, was lecturing to a class of fifty on the tenth floor of the school building, or that directly beneath

Reprinted from *The Triangle Fire*, (1962), Cornell University Press.

him on the ninth floor Professor H. G. Parsons was illustrating interesting points of gardening to a class of forty girls.

A block east of the Square and parallel to it, Greene Street cut a narrow path between tall loft buildings. Its sidewalks bustled with activity as shippers trundled the day's last crates and boxes to the horse-drawn wagons lining the curbs.

At the corner of Greene Street and Washington Place, a wide thoroughfare bisecting the east side of the Square, the Asch building rose ten floors high. The Triangle Shirtwaist Company, largest of its kind, occupied the top three floors. As Dr. Winterbottom contemplated the peaceful park, 500 persons, most of them young girls, were busily turning thousands of yards of flimsy fabric into shirtwaists, a female bodice garment which the noted artist Charles Dana Gibson had made the sartorial symbol of American womanhood.

One block north, at the corner of Greene Street and Waverly Place, Mrs. Lena Goldman swept the sidewalk in front of her small restaurant. It was closing time. She knew the girls who worked in the Asch building well for many of them were her customers.

Dominick Cardiane, pushing a wheelbarrow, had stopped for a moment in front of the doors of the Asch building freight elevator in the middle of the Greene Street block. He heard a sound "like a big puff," followed at once by the noise of crashing glass. A horse reared, whinnied wildly, and took off down Greene Street, the wagon behind it bouncing crazily on the cobblestones.

Reporter Shepherd, about to cross from the park into Washington Place, also heard the sound. He saw smoke issuing from an eighth-floor window of the Asch building and began to run.

Patrolman Meehan was talking with his superior, Lieutenant William Egan. A boy ran up to them and pointed to the Asch building. The patrolman put spurs to his horse.

Dr. Winterbottom saw people in the park running toward Washington Place. A few seconds later he dashed down the stoop carrying his black medical bag and cut across the Square toward Washington Place.

Patrolman Meehan caught up with Shepherd and passed him. For an instant there seemed to be no sound on the street except the urgent tattoo of his horse's hoofbeats as Meehan galloped by. He pulled up in front of 23 Washington Place, in the middle of the block, and jumped from the saddle.

Many had heard the muffled explosion and looked up to see the puff of smoke coming out of an eighth-floor window. James Cooper, passing by, was one of them. He saw something that looked "like a bale of dark dress goods" come out of a window.

"Some one's in there all right. He's trying to save the best cloth," a bystander said to him.

Another bundle came flying out of a window. Halfway down the wind caught it and the bundle opened.

It was not a bundle. It was the body of a girl.

Now the people seemed to draw together as they fell back from where the body had hit. Nearby horses struggled in their harnesses.

"The screams brought me running," Mrs. Goldman recalled. "I could see them falling! I could see them falling!"

John H. Mooney broke out of the crowd forming on the sidewalk opposite the Asch building and ran to Fire Box 289 at the corner of Greene Street. He turned in the first alarm at 4:45 P.M.

Inside the Asch building lobby Patrolman Meehan saw that both passenger elevators were at the upper floors. He took the stairs two steps at a time.

Between the fifth and sixth floors he found his way blocked by the first terrified girls making the winding descent from the Triangle shop. In the narrow staircase he had to flatten himself against the wall to let the girls squeeze by.

Between the seventh and eighth floors he almost fell over a girl who had fainted. Behind her the blocked line had come to a stop, the screaming had increased. He raised her to her feet, held her for a moment against the wall, calming her, and started her once again down the stairs.

At the eighth floor, he remembers that the flames were within 8 feet of the stairwell. "I saw two girls at a window on the Washington Place side shouting for help and waving their hands hysterically. A machinist—his name was Brown—helped me get the girls away from the window. We sent them down the stairs."

The heat was unbearable. "It backed us to the staircase," Meehan says.

Together with the machinist, he retreated down the spiral staircase. At the sixth floor, the policeman heard frantic pounding on the other side of the door facing the landing. He tried to open the door but found it was locked. He was certain now that the fire was also in progress on this floor.

"I braced myself with my back against the door and my feet on the nearest step of the stairs. I pushed with all my strength. When the door finally burst inward, I saw there was no smoke, no fire. But the place was full of frightened women. They were screaming and clawing. Some were at the windows threatening to jump."

These were Triangle employees who had fled down the rear fire escape. At the sixth floor, one of them had pried the shutters open, smashed the window and climbed back into the building. Others followed. Inside, they found themselves trapped behind a locked door and panicked.

As he stumbled back into the street, Meehan saw that the first fire engines and police patrol wagons were arriving. Dr. Winterbottom, in the meantime, had reached Washington Place. For a moment he remained immobilized by the horror. Then he rushed into a store, found a telephone, and shouted at the operator, "For God's sake, send ambulances!"

The first policemen on the scene were from the nearby Mercer Street Station House of the 8th Precinct. Among them were some who had used their clubs against the Triangle girls a year earlier during the shirtwaist makers' strike.

First to arrive was Captain Dominick Henry, a man inured to suffering by years of police work in a tough, two-fisted era. But he stopped short at his first view of the Asch building. "I saw a scene I hope I never see again. Dozens of girls were hanging from the ledges. Others, their dresses on fire, were leaping from the windows."

From distant streets came piercing screams of fire whistles, the nervous clang of fire bells. Suddenly, they were sounding from all directions.

In the street, men cupped their hands to their mouths, shouting, "Don't jump! Here they come!" Then they waved their arms frantically.

Patrolman Meehan also shouted. He saw a couple standing in the frame of a ninth-floor window. They moved out onto the narrow ledge. "I could see the fire right behind them. I hollered, 'Go over!'"

But nine floors above the street the margin of choice was as narrow as the window ledge. The flames reached out and touched the woman's long tresses. The two plunged together.

In the street, watchers recovering from their first shock had sprung into action. Two young men came charging down Greene Street in a wagon, whipping their horses onto the sidewalk and shouting all the time, "Don't jump!" They leaped from the wagon seat, tore the blankets from their two horses, and shouted for others to help grip them. Other teamsters also stripped blankets, grabbed tarpaulins to improvise nets.

But the bodies hit with an impact that tore the blankets from their hands. Bodies and blankets went smashing through the glass deadlights set into the sidewalk over the cellar vault of the Asch building.

Daniel Charnin, a youngster driving a Wanamaker wagon, jumped down and ran to help the men holding the blankets. "They hollered at me and kicked me. They shouted, 'Get out of here, kid! You want to get killed?'"

One of the first ambulances to arrive was in the charge of Dr. D.E. Keefe of St. Vincent's Hospital. It headed straight for the building. "One woman fell so close to the ambulance that I thought if we drove it up to the curb it would be possible for some persons to strike the top of the ambulance and so break their falls."

The pump engine of Company 18, drawn by three sturdy horses, came dashing into Washington Place at about the same time. It was the first of thirty-five pieces of fire-fighting apparatus summoned to the scene. These included the Fire Department's first motorized units, ultimately to replace the horses but in 1911 still experimental.

Another major innovation being made by the Fire Department was the creation of high-water-pressure areas. The Asch building was located in one of the first of these. In such an area a system of water-main cutoffs made it possible to build up pressure at selected hydrants. At Triangle, the Gansevoort Street pumping station raised the pressure to 200 pounds. The most modern means of fighting fires were available at the northwest corner of Washington Place and Greene Street.

A rookie fireman named Frank Rubino rode the Company 18 pump engine, and he remembers that "we came tearing down Washington Square East and made the turn into Washington Place. The first thing I saw was a man's body come crashing down through the sidewalk shed of the school building. We kept going. We turned into Greene Street and began to stretch in our hoses. The bodies were hitting all around us."

When the bodies didn't go through the deadlights, they piled up on the sidewalk, some of them burning so that firemen had to turn their hoses on them. According to Company 18's Captain Howard Ruch the hoses were soon buried by the bodies and "we had to lift them off before we could get to work."

Captain Ruch ordered his men to spread the life nets. But no sooner was the first one opened than three bodies hit it at once. The men, their arms looped to the net, held fast.

"The force was so great it took the men off their feet," Captain Ruch said. "Trying to hold the nets, the men turned somersaults and some of them were catapulted right onto the net. The men's hands were bleeding, the nets were torn and some caught fire."

Later, the Captain calculated that the force of each falling body when it struck the net was about 11,000 pounds.

"Life nets?" asked Battalion Chief Edward J. Worth. "What good were life nets? The little ones went through life nets, pavement, and all. I thought they would come down one at a time. I didn't know they would come down with arms entwined—three and even four together." There was one who seemed to have survived the jump. "I lifted her out and said, 'Now go right across the street.' She walked ten feet—and dropped. She died in one minute."

The first hook and ladder—Company 20—came up Mercer Street so fast, says Rubino, "that it almost didn't make the turn into Washington Place."

The firemen were having trouble with their horses. They weren't trained for the blood and the sound of the falling bodies. They kept rearing on their hind legs, their eyes rolling. Some men pulled the hitching pins and the horses broke loose, whinnying. Others grabbed the reins and led them away.

The crowd began to shout: "Raise the ladders!"

Company 20 had the tallest ladder in the Fire Department. It swung into position, and a team of men began to crank its lifting gears. A hush fell over the crowd.

The ladder continued to rise. One girl on the ninth floor ledge slowly waved a handkerchief as the ladder crept toward her.

Then the men stopped cranking. The ladder stopped rising.

The crowd yelled in one voice: "Raise the ladders!"

"But the ladder had been raised," Rubino says. "It was raised to its fullest length. It reached only to the sixth floor."

The crowd continued to shout. On the ledge, the girl stopped waving her handkerchief. A flame caught the edge of her skirt. She leaped for the top of the ladder almost 30 feet below her, missed, hit the sidewalk like a flaming comet.

Chief Worth had arrived at the scene at 4:46½, had ordered the second alarm to be transmitted at 4:48. Two more alarms were called, one at 4:55 and a fourth at 5:10.

In the first two minutes after his arrival, the Chief had assessed the situation. He directed his men to aim high water pressure hoses on the wall above the heads of those trapped on the ledge. "We hoped it would cool off the building close to them and reassure them. It was about the only reassurance we could give. The men did the best they could. But there is no apparatus in the department to cope with this kind of fire."

The crowd watched one girl on the ledge inch away from the window through which she had climbed as the flames licked after her. As deliberately as though she were standing before her own mirror at home, she removed her wide-brimmed hat and sent it sailing through the air. Then slowly, carefully, she opened her handbag.

Out of it she extracted a few bills and a handful of coins—her pay. These she flung out into space. The bills floated slowly downward. The coins hit the cobblestones, ringing as she jumped.

Three windows away one girl seemed to be trying to restrain another from jumping. Both stood on the window ledge. The first one tried to reach her arm around the other.

But the second girl twisted loose and fell. The first one now stood alone on the ledge and seemed oblivious to everything around her. Like a tightrope walker, she looked straight ahead and balanced herself with her hands on hips hugging the wall.

Then she raised her hands. For a moment she gestured, and to the staring crowd it seemed as if she were addressing some invisible audience suspended there before her. Then she fell forward.

They found her later, buried under a pile of bodies. She was Celia Weintraub and lived on Henry Street. Life was still in her after two hours in which she had lain among the dead.

William Shepherd, the United Press reporter and the only newspaperman on the scene at the height of the tragedy, had found a telephone in a store and dictated his story as he watched it happen through a plate-glass window. He counted sixty-two falling bodies, less than half the final total.

"Thud—dead! Thud—dead! Thud—dead!" Shepherd began his story. "I call them that because the sound and the thought of death came to me each time at the same instant."

As he watched, Shepherd saw "a love affair in the midst of all the horror.

"A young man helped a girl to the window sill on the ninth floor. Then he held her out deliberately, away from the building, and let her drop. He held out a second girl the same way and let her drop.

"He held out a third girl who did not resist. I noticed that. They were all as unresisting as if he were helping them into a street car instead of into eternity. He saw that a terrible death awaited them in the flames and his was only a terrible chivalry."

Then came the love affair.

"He brought another girl to the window. I saw her put her arms around him and kiss him. Then he held her into space—and dropped her. Quick as a flash, he was on the window sill himself. His coat fluttered upwards—the air filled his trouser legs as he came down. I could see he wore tan shoes.

"Together they went into eternity. Later I saw his face. You could see he was a real man. He had done his best. We found later that in the room in which he stood, many girls were burning to death. He chose the easiest way and was brave enough to help the girl he loved to an easier death."

Bill Shepherd's voice kept cracking. But he was first of all a newspaper reporter, and he steeled himself to see and to report what untrained eyes might miss.

He noticed that those still in the windows watched the others jump. "They watched them every inch of the way down." Then he compared the different manner in which they were jumping on the two fronts of the Asch building.

On the Washington Place side they "tried to fall feet down. I watched one girl falling. She waved her arms, trying to keep her body upright until the very instant she struck the sidewalk."

But on the Greene Street side "they were jammed into the windows. They were burning to death in the windows. One by one the window jams broke. Down came the bodies in a shower, burning, smoking, flaming bodies, with disheveled hair trailing upward. These torches, suffering ones, fell inertly.

"The floods of water from the firemen's hoses that ran into the gutter were actually red with blood," he wrote. "I looked upon the heap of dead bodies and I remembered these girls were the shirtwaist makers. I remembered their great strike of last year in which these same girls had demanded more sanitary conditions and more safety precautions in the shops. These dead bodies were the answer."

At 4:57 a body in burning clothes dropped from the ninth floor ledge, caught on a twisted iron hook protruding at the sixth floor. For a minute it hung there, burning. Then it dropped to the sidewalk. No more fell.

Coxey's Army

Page Smith

When the Chicago World's Columbian Exposition closed in the fall of 1893, the country slumped back into the depression; the magic illusion was dismantled, and hungry men and women roamed the city's streets or gathered to hear anarchists and socialists denounce capitalists. Samuel Gompers estimated that 3,000,000 men and women were unemployed countrywide. One alarming manifestation was the companies of tramps, numbering, it was estimated, tens of thousands, that roamed the country, begging or stealing food and terrorizing whole communities. James Weaver called particular attention to "vast armies of homeless tramps ever wandering alongside of vacant land held for speculation. . . ."

Congress could think of nothing better to do than fiddle with the tariffs again. Henry Adams described that body as "Poking the tariff with a stick to make it mad." "Winter is here," he wrote Hay, "and my perpetual miracle is that people somehow seem to go on living without money or work or food, or clothes, or fire. One or two million people are out of work; thousands of the rich are cleaned out to the last shoe-leather; not one human being is known to be making a living; yet on we go. . . . But it can't last."

One man had a notion. He believed in the eccentric idea that Congress not only could take actions to relieve the general distress but had the moral obligation to do so. In Massillon, Ohio, in the spring of 1894, Jacob Coxey planned a march on Washington to dramatize the plight of the unemployed millions and plead for some action on the part of the government to relieve suffering. Ray Stannard Baker, then a fledgling reporter for the *Chicago News-Record*, was assigned to report on Coxey's march.

Coxey was a prominent citizen of the little community, jack-of-all-trades, a farmer and horse breeder as well as the owner of a quarry that produced silica sand, a product used in making steel. He lived with his wife and daughter in a large, comfortable farmhouse which served as "General" Coxey's GHQ for the planning and organization of his projected march. A small, mild-looking, bespectacled middle-aged man with a straw-colored mustache, who had fought in the Civil War, he was a classic American type. Behind his innocuous exterior burned the ardent heart of a utopian reformer. A devout Christian, Coxey wished to see the United States at last converted into a true Christian commonwealth. Although he had certainly never read John Winthrop's "A Model of Christian Charity," he was animated by the same desire to redeem the times.

He had a most unlikely coadjutor in Carl Browne from Calistoga, California. Browne was a large, flamboyant man who dressed in fringed buckskins with silver-dollar buttons and sported a spectacular flowing beard parted in the middle. To Baker he looked like a salesman of Kickapoo Indian medicines. Browne handed Baker a card with his written signature and the words "The pen is mightier than the sword."

He also showed Baker a large portrait that he had painted of Jesus Christ, which bore a striking resemblance to Browne himself. He was a Theosophist, and he told the young reporter that when people died their souls and bodies went into separate reservoirs to make new human beings. He had within him a portion of the soul of Christ and of the Greek historian Callisthenes. Around the painting of Christ, Browne had written: "PEACE ON EARTH Good Will toward men! He hath risen!!! BUT DEATH TO INTEREST ON BONDS!!!"

Browne had painted a considerable array of banners and signs. One banner showed Coxey dosing "the sick chicken of honest labor" from a bottle of "eye-opener," the Coxey plan for the "resurrection of the nation." Other banners bore such slogans as "We workmen want work, not charity: how can we buy at the stores on charity and cast-off clothes?"

The two oddly assorted leaders informed the skeptical Baker that they intended to start from Massillon on Easter Sunday with 20,000 marchers and on May Day reach Washington and there present a petition to Congress demanding that something be done to relieve the distress of unemployed and destitute Americans. Coxey had received thousands of letters of encouragement and many contributions of money from individuals, labor unions, and Populist organizations. He called the projected march "a petition in boots."

To Baker's queries on how Coxey intended to feed his "army," the leaders replied with handbills which proclaimed: "Fall in, let everybody send or bring all the food they can . . . join the procession, you who have bring to those who have not. . . . We are acting from inspiration from on high. We believe that the liberty-loving people comprising this indivisible and undividable American Union will respond in such numbers to this call of duty that no hessian Pinkerton thugs . . . can be hired for gold to fire upon such a myriad of human beings, unarmed and defenceless, assembling under the aegis of the Constitution. . . ." Coxey quoted Elbert Hubbard's prophecy of an Armageddon where "the brute nature and immortal soul of man" would close "in final contest, which shall herald the dawning of the era of love and tenderness, when nations shall know the fatherhood of God and live the brotherhood of man."

While the preparations for the march went ahead, Mrs. Coxey gave birth to a baby, who was promptly named Legal Tender Coxey, and Browne gathered recruits in nearby towns by fiery speeches at torchlit rallies denouncing the "Money Power" and the "Octopus of the Rothschilds." Browne also composed a song for his enthusiastic listeners to sing to the tune of "After the Ball."

After the march is over,
After the first of May,
After the bills are passed, child,
Then we will have fair play.

Coxey and Browne found unwitting allies in the reporters who soon swarmed around Massillon, writing colorful and often mocking accounts of the preparations for the march. If more sophisticated readers smiled at the bizarre accounts, hungry and desperate men in cities and towns felt a surge of hope. Newspaper editorials that denounced the march as dangerous and revolutionary served only to heighten public interest in it and win more recruits for the army. One of the recruits was Dr. Cyclone Kirkland, a little man in a silk hat whose mètier was predicting hurricanes through astrology. He began writing an epic poem on the march in the style of the *Odyssey*. Kirkland told Baker it would be a "hummer in a cyclonic way." A black minstrel singer named Professor C. B. Freeman, who claimed to be the loudest singer in the world, had left his wife and children to "follow de Gen'l." Another recruit, who arrived by Pullman car, was "The Great Unknown"; he subsequently turned out to be "Dr." Pizarro, a traveling medicine man who was usually accompanied by a band of Indians. There was even a brass band, the "Commonwealth of Christ Brass Band—J. J. Thayer, Conductor."

The cynical reporters, sure that the march would never start, debated the idea of hiring 100 unemployed roustabouts from a nearby defunct circus to march for a day or so with Coxey and Browne so that their papers would at least have a story. But astonishingly, as Easter approached, grim, ragged men began to appear, dropping off freight trains, arriving in farmers' wagons or on foot. Soon there was indeed the nucleus of an army. The people of Massillon, doubtless pleased at their town's sudden fame, turned out to provide food and shelter for the recruits. At eleven o'clock on Easter morning Windy Oliver, the bugler, riding a horse with a red saddle, sounded attention. Browne, on one of Coxey's finest horses and wearing a dashing sombrero, joined the general at the head of the column, the Commonwealth of Christ Band struck up a tune, and the march began. At the head of the strange column rode Jasper Johnson Buchanan, a black man, carrying the United States flag. Conspicuous among the marchers was Hugh O'Donnell, one of the leaders in the Homestead strike.

The Three Graces—Faith, Hope, and Charity—were female relatives of Coxey's. Mrs. Coxey accompanied the march in a carriage with Legal Tender, and the general's son, Jesse, wore a blue and gray uniform, symbolizing the unity of North and South in the fight for social justice. A huge crowd had assembled to witness the beginning of the march, and the army, counting perhaps 400, set off for Canton, its first day's march, to the accompaniment of shouts of encouragement.

No one was more surprised by the spectacle than the newspaper reporters, themselves grown into a small army. "The whole enterprise had seemed preposterous; it couldn't happen in America," Ray Stannard Baker reflected. Other "armies" were recruited elsewhere around the country, some from as far away as California.

The reporters who had been covering the preparations for the march were convinced that it had to end in disaster because of the difficulty of supplying any considerable number of marchers with food, but, as Baker noted, "instead of beginning to disintegrate immediately, as we had anticipated, the army grew in numbers and at each stopping place the crowds were larger and more enthusiastic. . . . Coxey had started with only enough in his wagons for a day or two, but at each town where a stop was scheduled, there appeared an impromptu local committee, sometimes including the mayor and other public men, with large supplies of bread, meat, milk, eggs, canned goods, coffee, tea—a supply far more generous and varied than even Coxey and Browne had expected or imagined." It was clear that the good wishes and hopes of large numbers of ordinary Americans marched with Coxey's tatterdemalion band.

When the army reached Pittsburgh, a city often racked by labor troubles, the humbler citizens, many of whom had vivid memories of the Great Strikes of 1877, turned out in a tumultuous welcome. Bands, delegations of marchers from unions, schoolchildren, and socialists packed the streets to cheer the marchers and join in what took on the character of a victorious parade. "I shall never forget as long as I live," Baker wrote, "the sight of that utterly fantastic, indescribably grotesque procession swinging down a little hill through the city of Allegheny singing with a roar of exultation Coxey's army song to the tune of 'Marching Through Georgia.'"

> Come, we'll tell a story, boys,
> We'll sing another song,
> As we go trudging with sore feet,
> The road to Washington;
> We shall never forget this tramp,
> Which sounds the nation's gong,
> As we go marching to Congress.

Baker, increasingly sympathetic to the strange procession and its eccentric leaders, walked with the marchers and talked with them. "I had known just such men in my boyhood," he wrote. "To call them an army of 'bums, tramps, and vagabonds,' as some of the commentators were doing, was a complete misrepresentation. A considerable proportion were genuine farmers and workingmen whose only offense was that they could not buy or rent land . . . or find a job at which they could earn a living." Baker became convinced that "there could have been no such demonstration in a civilized country unless there was a profound and deep-seated distress, disorganization, unrest, unhappiness behind it—and that the public would not be cheering the army and feeding it voluntarily without a recognition, however vague, that the conditions in the country warranted some such explosion." He wrote to the editor of his paper: "It seems to me that such a movement must be looked on as something more than a huge joke. It has more meaning than either Coxey or Browne imagines." But the editor, reprinting Baker's letter as part of an editorial, drew from it conclusions opposite to those intended by his young correspondent. To the editor, "the continual turning of the people to Washington for aid . . . is pathetic and portentous. The country," he concluded, "is sick just to the extent that its people try to lean on the government instead of standing upright on their own feet."

The editor's view was shared by the great majority of middle- and upper-class urban Americans, who could discover little sympathy for the armies that threatened to converge on Washington with their demands for congressional action to relieve the widespread suffering. Coxey's Army and those auxiliary armies forming—by one journalist's calculations—in at least eleven different towns and cities aroused the never distant anxiety about the "dangerous classes" that was such a persistent element in the consciousness of the upper classes. John Hay professed to believe that revolution was just around the corner. Coxey and his army would soon be in Washington, and Hay hoped the mob would spare his house, as he wrote Henry Adams, "because it adjoins yours. You, of course, are known throughout the country as a Democrat and an Anarchist and an Unemployed. Your house will be safe anyhow; so you might as well stand on my steps while the army passes, and shout for 'Chaos and Coxey' like a man."

As the army approached Washington, it found the going increasingly arduous. There were cold spring rains and even snow to contend with. The residents of the towns through which the army passed were far less hospitable; food and fuel grew scarce; toll roads barred the marchers' way, and tolls were demanded for every "soldier" in the now-depleted force. Beyond Cumberland, Maryland, the roads were so bad that Coxey chartered canalboats on the Chesapeake & Ohio Canal at the charge for "perishable freight" of fifty-two cents a ton. For three days the army made its way down the canal past "the dog-woods and judas trees in bloom, and innumerable wild flowers on the hillsides." The marchers sunned themselves on the decks; the general hammered out "orders" and "resolutions" on a battered typewriter, and Browne wrote poems celebrating the great journey. At Williamsport, Maryland, the army debarked and was joined a few days later by two converging armies, one from Philadelphia, led by a man in a high silk hat named Christopher Columbus Jones.

At last, on a blisteringly hot day, the combined armies approached the Capitol itself, marching down Pennsylvania Avenue. Coxey's daughter Mame, dressed in red, white, and blue, on a handsome white horse and representing the goddess of peace, led the procession. Large crowds lined the streets, and the police were out in force to block any effort to invade the congressional chambers. In front of the Capitol Browne dismounted, and Coxey, leaving his carriage, kissed his wife to the cheers of the onlookers.

Browne then made a dash through the police lines, apparently with the intention of entering the Capitol. The police overtook him and clubbed him to the ground. Coxey, meanwhile, reached the steps of the Capitol, but before he could read his prepared address to the crowd, the police dragged him away, too. He was arrested and charged with walking on the grass. The marchers were scattered by mounted police, and the Commonwealth of Christ was no more.

Coxey's "Address of Protest" was read in Congress by a sympathetic Populist legislator. It declared that the Constitution guaranteed to all citizens the right to petition for redress of grievances. "We stand here to-day to test these guarantees. . . . We choose this place of assemblage because it is the property of the people. . . ." They were there to protest "the passage of laws in direct violation of the Constitution" and

to draw the eyes of the entire nation to this shameful fact. . . . Up these steps the lobbyists of trusts and corporations have passed unchallenged on their way to committee rooms, access to which we, the representatives of the toiling wealth-producers, have been denied. We stand here to-day in behalf of millions of toilers whose petitions have been buried in committee rooms, whose prayers have been unresponded to, and whose opportunities for honest remunerative, productive labor have been taken from them by unjust legislation, which protects idlers, speculators, and gamblers; we come to remind the Congress here assembled of the declaration of a United States Senator, 'that for a quarter of a century the rich have been growing richer, the poor poorer, and that by the close of the present century the middle class will have disappeared as the struggle for existence becomes fierce and relentless.'" In the name of justice "and in the name of the commonweal of Christ, whose representatives we are, we enter a most solemn and earnest protest. . . . We have come here through toil and weary marches, through storms and distresses, over mountains, and amid the trials of poverty and distress, to lay our grievances at the doors of our National Legislature and ask them in the name of Him whose banners we bear, in the name of Him who pleaded for the poor and oppressed, that they should heed the voice of despair and distress that is now coming up from every section of our country, that they should consider the conditions of the starving unemployed of our land, and enact such laws as will give them employment, bring happier conditions to the people, and the smile of contentment to our citizens.

If the Eastern newspapers were contemptuous of the remnants of Coxey's ragged army that reached Washington, they had many supporters in the Midwest and among workingmen and women. The *Topeka Advocate* observed: "These men have as much right to go to Washington and demand justice at the hands of congress as bankers, railroad magnates and corporation lawyers have to go and lobby for measures by which to plunder the public; and if their rights are not respected there will be trouble; rest assured of that. Let the powers that be beware how they treat the Coxey army." The *Wealth Makers*, published in Lincoln, Nebraska, noted apropos of Coxey's march: "For our part we wish that all the destitute, wretched, miserable millions of American citizens which unjust legislation has made, could camp around the Capitol at Washington and form an ever present conscience-arousing spectacle for our national lawmakers to face."

Annie Diggs, a Kansas Populist, urged the passage of legislation that would form the unemployed into an "industrial army" to be "employed on works of public improvements, such as canals, rivers, and harbors, irrigation works, public highways, and such other public improvements as Congress . . . shall provide."

In fact, the so-called good roads bill (also known as the Coxey Bill) was introduced into the Senate by William Alfred Peffer, a Kansas newspaper editor, turned Populist politician. The bill called for the printing of $500,000,000, the money to be used to employ the jobless on the construction and improvement of the "general county-road system of the United States." The pay should be not less than $1.50 a day for an eight-hour day, and "all citizens of the United States making application to labor shall be employed."

Three days later another Coxey Bill was proposed to allow any "State, Territory, county, township, municipality, or incorporated town or village" to issue noninterest-bearing bonds, the proceeds from which were to be used to make "public improvements."

Former President Benjamin Harrison took the occasion of an address to the Republican State Convention in Indiana to support protective tariffs, declaring: "The times are full of unrest, disaster, and apprehension. I believe today that all the tumult of this wild sea would be satisfied, as by the voice of Omnipotence, if the industrial and commercial classes of this country would know today that there would be no attempt to strike down protection in American legislation."

Larger than Coxey's Army was that of a thirty-two-year-old printer named Charles Kelley. Kelley's Industrial Army, recruited primarily in California, numbered some 1,500, among them Jack London. One of the "soldiers" was a young miner-cowboy named William Haywood, called Big Bill by his friends because of his size. Haywood remembered the "march" as one of the "greatest unemployed demonstrations that ever took place in the United States." At Council Bluffs, Iowa, Kelley's Army was turned out of the railroad cars that had brought them East and forced to exist as best they could in the rain while the people of the town brought them food. After a week they continued their march on foot, but hungry, weary, and discouraged, the "Industrial Army" melted away.

In Montana a group of 650 miners, led by "General" Hogan, captured a Northern Pacific train at Butte and ran it themselves. When a trainload of railroad deputies overtook them at Billings, there ensued a sharp fight in which the railroad men were routed. At this point troops were called up from a nearby Federal fort, and the train was surrounded. The men surrendered and were dispersed, a handful finally making their way to Washington.

Although fewer than 1,000 or so men of the various armies that set out for Washington arrived there and although their reception was unvaryingly cold—hostility mixed with ridicule—the episode was an unsettling one for the world's greatest democracy. For each of the ragged, hungry, and defiant men who reached the nation's capital in symbolic protest there were thousands who shared his bitterness and, perhaps more, his confusion and disillusionment, who wished to know what had happened to the dream of "liberty and justice for all." To a contemporary journalist named M. J. Savage, the marches were a symptom. "Symptoms," he wrote, ". . . mean always internal disturbance, they mean the possibility of diseases that may threaten the vitals."

Big Stick Abroad

John Milton Cooper

In contrast to his restraint in domestic policy, Theodore Roosevelt conducted a vigorous, assertive foreign policy during his first three years as president. Many contemporary observers and later historians have judged these years the high-water mark of American imperialism. Roosevelt frequently proclaimed himself an unabashed, unapologetic imperialist. The baldest statement of his convictions came in his December 1904 message to Congress, in which he enunciated what he had repeatedly said privately and in secret diplomatic messages. This was his Roosevelt Corollary to the Monroe Doctrine. "Chronic wrongdoing," he announced, "or an impotence which results in the general loosening of the ties of civilized society may in [North and South] America, as elsewhere, ultimately require intervention by some civilized nation, and in the western hemisphere the adherence of the United States to the Monroe Doctrine may force the United States, however reluctantly, in flagrant cases of such wrong-doing or impotence, to the exercise of an international police power." Even before becoming president, Roosevelt had repeatedly offered the motto of a West African tribe, "Speak softly and carry a big stick and you will go far," as the best guide to foreign policy. The "big stick" quickly became the emblem of his diplomacy.

Within a year of taking office, Roosevelt intervened in a major way in Latin American affairs. For several months during 1902, the president engaged in elaborate diplomatic maneuvers, partly public but mostly private, to block Germany from intervening in Venezuela to collect debts owed to German banks. Similar problems of large debts to European lenders later prompted him to exert pressures on Haiti and, starting in 1904, to establish an American financial protectorate over the Dominican Republic. Later in 1906, Roosevelt confirmed the purely formal character of Cuban independence by sending in troops to begin a three-year occupation. These actions lent substance to boasts in the United States that the Caribbean was an "American lake."

Nor did Roosevelt's settled beliefs in Anglo-American cooperation prevent him from asserting United States primacy on the North American continent. For at least a decade, Roosevelt had been convinced that Britain and the United States had no serious conflicts of

Reprinted from *The Pivotal Decades: The United States, 1900–1920*, (1990), W.W. Norton & Company.

national interest and instead shared a great mission as the chief representatives of the "English-speaking races." Such solidarity, however, did not stop him from pushing around the British and their former colonial dependents, the Canadians. In 1902 a long simmering dispute with Canada over the southeastern boundary of Alaska, which had been an American territory since its purchase from Russia in 1867, heated up again when new gold discoveries were reported in Alaska. The president sent additional troops to patrol the border areas claimed by the United States. The disputed lands were not rich or extensive—only a few hundred square miles of wilderness—but they seemed essential to both countries because they controlled access to the sea. Roosevelt meanwhile engaged in another bit of complicated public and private maneuvering to gain permanent cession of the territory to the United States. After repeatedly refusing arbitration, Roosevelt relented during the summer of 1903 and, with a great show of reluctance, agreed to permit an international tribunal settle the dispute. This allowed the Canadians apparently to save face, although they and the British together appointed only three judges to the panel, while the Americans also appointed three. Through his friends Senator Lodge and Justice Holmes, the president pressed the British to favor the American claims, which their representative eventually did. Although the Canadians were incensed at the outcome, Roosevelt's behind-the-scenes moves actually strengthened amity between the United States and Britain.

The single act of his presidency, in domestic and foreign affairs, for which Roosevelt always publicly professed greatest pride also came during 1903. No diplomatic move of any American president would do more to assert a dominant American stake in the Caribbean and Central America; at the same time, practically no action by any president ever did more to tarnish the United States's reputation for morality and straight dealing in the Western Hemisphere. This was Roosevelt's critical role in the armed insurrection of October 1903 that resulted in the secession of Panama from Colombia, and the cession to the United States of a swath of territory running through the middle of the new country. This territory came to be called the Canal Zone. It became the site of the inter-oceanic waterway and would remain under American rule for nearly all of the twentieth century.

Construction of a canal across Central America to link shipping on the Atlantic and Pacific Oceans fulfilled a fifty-year-old American dream. Ever since the United States had expanded to the Pacific, the need had existed to shorten the time and distance required for maritime shipping between the two coasts. The California Gold Rush in 1849 and the Alaskan gold strikes in the 1890s had repeatedly shown how costly, time-consuming, and dangerous it was to ship people and goods around South America's Cape Horn, or to transport them by land across the mountainous, jungled, yellow-fever-infested isthmus of Panama. The difficulties of maintaining and reinforcing fleets in the Pacific, even before the Spanish-American War, had demonstrated the strategic boon that an inter-oceanic waterway would provide to the United States Navy. Schemes for the construction of a canal had begun as early as the 1850s, and from 1879 to 1889 a French company, headed by Ferdinand de Lesseps, the builder of the Suez Canal, had tried and failed to dig a canal in Panama. This failure, together with reportedly gentler terrain and a chain of lakes in Nicaragua, prompted many canal advocates to favor a route there instead.

Diplomatic negotiations to secure a route for an American canal across Central America had dragged on for several years before 1903. The Panama route was finally chosen thanks in part to lobbying by investors in de Lesseps's company. American acquisition of the route would allow those investors not only to recoup their losses but also to realize profits of several million dollars. Further complications arose, however, when Colombia, of which Panama was then a part, refused to ratify a treaty ceding the territory and compensating the French investors. The Colombian government was holding out for a bigger payment. An infuriated Roosevelt demanded action. The United States then stationed naval vessels off the principal Panamanian ports, and Panama's secessionist revolt swiftly followed. Troops from the American vessels helped block Colombian attempts to quell the uprising. Furthermore, the State Department recognized newly independent Panama within hours of the revolt, and already had treaties to acquire the territory for the canal prepared for signing and swift ratification. The representative of the French investors was immediately appointed the minister of newly independent Panama to the United States, and he at once signed the treaty that granted the United States the canal route under the previous terms.

Roosevelt himself retained curiously mixed attitudes toward the Panama affair. The building of the canal, which was not completed until 1914, five years after Roosevelt left office, stood at the head of every list he made of his presidential accomplishments. This gigantic feat of engineering meshed perfectly with his appetite for grandeur and with the enthrallment of Americans and Europeans of that era with triumphs of technology. What better proof of human mastery over nature could be offered than the Panama Canal? It was a magic path between the seas that transported ships for fifty miles over mountain ranges and speeded them toward distant ports. For Roosevelt, the emotional high point of his presidency was his trip to Panama at the end of 1906 to inspect work on the canal. On the trip he became the first president to leave the United States while in office, and he revelled at witnessing the massive earth-moving and lock-construction projects. A widely circulated photograph taken of Roosevelt showed him in a white tropical suit at the controls of a huge steam shovel. Nothing depicted him better as an empire builder.

Yet Roosevelt more than once betrayed a trace of guilt over the way the route was acquired. At the first hint of possible American collusion in the Panamanian revolt, the president issued thunderous private denials in letters and monologues to his cabinet, and he leaked his version of the story to sympathetic reporters. After leaving office, he made frequent public declarations of his righteousness, including a lengthy section in his *Autobiography*, published in 1913. "From the beginning to the end," he avowed, "our course was straightforward and in absolute accord with the highest standards of morality." Furthermore, he charged, "it is hypocrisy, alike odious and contemptible, for any man to say both that we ought to have built the canal and that we ought not to have acted in the way we did." Those declarations, like earlier statements, had the overwrought quality that Roosevelt's language usually assumed when he was unsure of his moral ground. Elihu Root put his finger on the false note when, after a harangue to the cabinet on the subject of the canal, Roosevelt demanded to know whether he had defended himself adequately. "You certainly have, Mr. President," the secretary of state quipped. "You have shown that you were accused of seduction and you have conclusively proved that you were guilty of rape."

The activist diplomacy of Roosevelt's first term comprised more than bluster and assertiveness. Behind his overbearing public posture often lay more subtle, restrained, cautious dealings with other nations. Whereas Roosevelt bullied smaller, weaker countries, mainly in Latin America, he exercised caution and sensitivity toward nations of equal or greater power, especially in Europe. The mixed character of Roosevelt's diplomacy displayed more than an imperialist's disdain for inferiors and respect for peers. His warnings to Germany over Venezuela, acquisition of the Canal zone, and especially enunciation of the Roosevelt Corollary all sprang from a well-defined strategy of forestalling incursions by European powers in the Western Hemisphere. Roosevelt pursued that goal assiduously for the sake of both his country's security and the world's harmony and order.

With the 1904 presidential campaign on the horizon, Roosevelt became more active still in foreign affairs. At the same time, he became more assertive on the domestic front. "Our place as a nation is and must be with the nations that have left indelibly their impress on the centuries," he declared in May 1903. At home and abroad, Roosevelt urged Americans to tread arduous paths of righteousness and challenge. "I ask that this people rise level to the greatness of its opportu-nities. I do not ask that it seek the easiest path."

Meat Inspection:
Theory and Reality

Gabriel Kolko

In October, 1904, a young man named Upton Sinclair arrived in Chicago with a $500 stake from Fred S. Warren, editor of *The Appeal to Reason*. After seven weeks of interviews and observation in the stock yard area, Sinclair sent back stories to Warren on the working conditions, filth, and gore of the packing industry, and his novel *The Jungle* electrified the nation, spreading Sinclair's name far and wide and, finally, bringing the Beef Trust to its knees. The nation responded. Roosevelt and Congress acted by passing a meat inspection law, and the Beef Trust was vanquished. Or so reads the standard interpretation of the meat inspection scandal of 1906.

Unfortunately, the actual story is much more involved. But the meat inspection law of 1906 was perhaps the crowning example of the reform spirit and movement during the Roosevelt presidency, and the full story reveals much of the true nature of progressivism.

Alas, the movement for federal meat inspection did not begin with the visit of Sinclair to Chicago in 1904, but at least twenty years earlier, and it was initiated as much by the large meat packers themselves as by anyone. The most important catalyst in creating a demand for reform or innovation of meat inspection laws was the European export market and not, as has usually been supposed, the moralistic urgings of reformers. And since the European export market was more vital to the major American meat packers than anything else, it was the large meat packers who were at the forefront of reform efforts.

Government meat inspection was, along with banking regulation and the crude state railroad regulatory apparatus, the oldest of the regulatory systems. In principle, at least, it was widely accepted. The major stimulus, as always, was the desire to satisfy the European export market. As early as December, 1865, Congress passed an act to prevent the importation of diseased cattle and pigs, and from 1877 on, agents of the Commissioner of Agriculture were stationed in various states to report on diseases.

Reprinted from *The Triumph of Conservatism*, (1985), Free Press.

In 1879 Italy restricted the importation of American pigs because of diseases, and in 1881 France followed suit. Throughout the 1880s the major European nations banned American meat, and the cost to the large American packers was enormous. These packers learned very early in the history of the industry that it was not to their profit to poison their customers, especially in a competitive market in which the consumer could go elsewhere. For the European nations this meant turning to Argentine meat, to the American consumer to another brand or company. The American meat industry was competitive throughout this period, mainly because the level of investment required to enter packing was very small and because there were no decisive economies in large size. In 1879 there were 872 slaughtering and meat packing establishments, but there were 1,367 in 1889. Chicago in the late 1870s had established a municipal system of inspection, but it left much to be desired and was weakened over time. In 1880, after England banned the importation of cattle with pleuropneumonia, the livestock growers initiated a campaign for legislation designed to prevent the spread of the disease. The Grange and many state legislatures joined the movement, and in 1880 Rep. Andrew R. Kiefer of Minnesota introduced a bill to prohibit the transportation of diseased livestock from infected to clean areas. Similar bills designed to halt the spread of pleuropneumonia followed, but failed to gather sufficient support. In late 1882, however, exposés in the Chicago papers of diseased meat led to reforms in municipal inspection, and the major packers cooperated with the city health department to set up more examining stations to root out disease. Other cities also created inspection systems at this time, although they varied in quality.

Despite the failure of Congress to legislate on the matter, in 1881 the Secretary of the Treasury created an inspection organization to certify that cattle for export were free of pleuropneumonia. Such limited efforts and haphazard municipal inspection, despite packer support, were inadequate to meet exacting European standards. In March, 1883, Germany banned the importation of American pork, cutting off another major export market. Congress was forced to meet the threat to the American packers, and in May, 1884, established the Bureau of Animal Industry within the Department of Agriculture "to prevent the exportation of diseased cattle and to provide means for the suppression and extirpation of pleuropneumonia and other contagious diseases among domestic animals." Despite the research and regulatory activities of the bureau, which by 1888 cost one-half million dollars per year, the Department of Agriculture from 1885 on began appealing for additional federal regulation to help improve exports to Europe. Its major impetus was to fight European restrictions, not to aid the American consumer, and in doing so it effectively represented the interests of the major American packers who had the most to gain from the Department's success.

Rather than improving, the situation further deteriorated with a hog cholera epidemic in 1889 worsening the American export position. Congress acted to meet the challenge, and in August, 1890, responding to the pressure of the major packers, passed a law providing for the inspection of all meat intended for export. But since provision was not made for inspection of the live animal at the time of slaughter, the foreign bans remained in effect. Desperate, in March, 1891, Congress passed the first major meat inspection law in American history. Indeed, the 1891 Act was the most significant in this field, and the conclusion of the long series of efforts to protect the export interests of the major American packers. The Act provided that all live animals be inspected, and covered the larger part of the animals passing through interstate trade. Every establishment in any way involved in export was compelled to have a Department of Agriculture inspector, and violations of the law could be penalized by fines of $1,000, one year in prison, or both. Hogs were required to have microscopic examinations as well as the usual pre- and post-mortem inspections. The law, in brief, was a rigid one, and had the desired effect. During 1891 and 1892, prohibitions on importing American, pork were removed by Germany, Denmark, France, Spain, Italy, and Austria.

The Act of 1891 satisfied the health standards of European doctors, but greatly distressed the European packing industry. Slowly but surely the European nations began imposing new medical standards in order to protect their own meat industries. Major American packers failed to appreciate the retaliatory tactics of their foreign competitors, and protested to the Department of Agriculture, which pressured the Department of State into helping it defend the vital interests of the American meat industry. The government's meat inspection organization, in the meantime, gradually extended control over the greater part of the interstate meat commerce, and in 1895 was aided by another act providing for even stronger enforcement. In 1892 the Bureau of Animal Industry gave 3.8 million animals ante- and post-mortem examinations; it examined 26.5 million animals in 1897. It maintained 28 abattoirs in 12 cities in 1892, 102 abattoirs in 26 cities in 1896. The inspection extended to packaged goods as well, despite the rumors that American soldiers during the Spanish-American War were being served "embalmed meat" that damaged their digestive systems—rumors strongly denied by Harvey W. Wiley, the leading American advocate of pure food legislation. By 1904, 84 percent of the beef slaughtered by the Big Four packers in Chicago, and 100 percent of the beef slaughtered in Ft. Worth, was being inspected by the government; 73 percent of the packers' entire U.S. kill was inspected. It was the smaller packers that the government inspection system failed to reach, and the major packers resented this competitive disadvantage. The way to solve this liability, most of them reasoned, was to enforce and extend the law, and to exploit it for their own advantage. They were particularly concerned about the shipment of condemned live stock to smaller, non-inspected houses, and applied pressure on the bureau to stop the traffic. When the Association of Official Agricultural Chemists created a committee in 1902 to determine food standards for meat products, the major meat companies cooperated with the effort and agreed with the final standards that were created.

When Sinclair arrived in Chicago in late 1904 to do a story for *The Appeal to Reason* he was primarily interested in writing a series on the life of Chicago's working class. His contact with the local socialists led him to Adolph Smith, a medically qualified writer for the English medical journal, *The Lancet*, and one of the founders of the Marxist Social Democratic Federation of England. Smith proved to be of great aid to Sinclair, supplying him with much information. In January, 1904, Smith published a series of articles in *The Lancet* attacking sanitary and especially working conditions in the American packing houses. Smith's series was hardly noticed in the United States—certainly it provoked no public outcry. In April, 1905, *Success Magazine* published an attack on diseased meat and packer use of condemned animals. This article also failed to arouse the public, which was much more concerned with alleged monopoly within the meat industry than with sanitary conditions.

The inability of these exposés to capture the attention of the public was especially ironic in light of the unpopularity of the packers. Charles Edward Russell had just completed his series in *Everybody's Magazine* on "The Greatest Trust in the World," an exaggerated account that nevertheless did not raise the question of health conditions. The Bureau of Corporations' report on beef displeased the public, and made the Roosevelt Administration especially defensive about the packers. The Bureau of Animal Industry, at the same time, feared that attacks on the quality of inspection would reflect on the integrity of the bureau and damage the American export market—and advised against the publication of the *Success Magazine* article.

Roosevelt had been sent a copy of *The Jungle* before its publication, but took no action after it was released. The controversy over it was carried on for several months by J. Ogden Armour, Sinclair, and the press, and Roosevelt was dragged into the matter only after Senator Albert J. Beveridge presented inspection bill in May, 1906. In February, shortly before *The Jungle* received wide attention, the Department of Agriculture ordered the packers to clean up their toilet and sanitary conditions for workers, even though it had no legal power to do so. J. Ogden Armour, in early March, took to the *Saturday Evening Post* to defend government meat inspection. He pointed out that the Chicago packing houses had always been open to the public, and that the stockyards, for the past six years, had been in the process of total reconstruction. The large packers, Armour insisted, strongly favored inspection.

> *Attempt to evade it would be, from the purely commercial viewpoint, suicidal.* No packer can do an interstate or export business without Government inspection. *Self-interest forces him to make use of it. Self-interest likewise demands that he shall not receive meats or byproducts from any small packer, either for export or other use, unless that small packer's plant is also "official"—that is, under United States Government inspection.*
>
> *This government inspection thus becomes an important adjunct of the packer's business from two viewpoints. It puts the stamp of legitimacy and honesty upon the packer's product and so is to him a necessity. To the public it is insurance against the sale of diseased meats.*

Armour's reference to the small packers reflected his genuine concern with the increasing growth of competitors, the number of companies in the field increasing by 52 percent from 1899 to 1909. And since the six largest packers slaughtered and sold less than 50 percent of the cattle, and could not regulate the health conditions of the industry, government inspection was their only means of breaking down European barriers to the growth of American exports.

In March, at least, Roosevelt was not thinking of legislative reform in beef. Although he favored "radical" action, he told Sinclair in a discussion over socialism, "I am more than ever convinced that the real factor in the election of any man or any mass of men must be the development within his or their hearts and heads of the qualities which alone can make either the individual, the class or the nation permanently useful to themselves and to others." Roosevelt was ready to allow the triumph of personal conversion rather than legislation in March, but in April his alienation with the packers went somewhat further. In March, 1906, a District Court dismissed the Justice Department's case against the Big Four packers on the grounds that their voluntary production of evidence to the Bureau of Corporations in 1904, on which evidence the suit was heavily based, gave them immunity under the Fifth Amendment. On April 18, Roosevelt sent Congress a message denying the packers' contention that Garfield had promised them immunity—which he had—and calling for legislation denying immunity to voluntary witnesses or evidence. By May, when Beveridge brought in his proposed meat legislation, the unpopular and grossly misunderstood major packers were ready to welcome the retaliatory legislation against them.

Historians, unfortunately, have ignored Upton Sinclair's important contemporary appraisal of the entire crisis. Sinclair was primarily moved by the plight of the workers, not the condition of the meat. "I aimed at the public's heart," he wrote, "and by accident I hit it in the stomach." Although he favored a more rigid law, Sinclair pointed out that "the Federal inspection of meat was, historically, established at the packers' request; . . . it is maintained and paid for by the people of the United States for the benefit of the packers; . . . men wearing the blue uniforms and brass buttons of the United States service are employed for the purpose of certifying to the nations of the civilized world that all the diseased and tainted meat which happens to come into existence in the United States of America is carefully sifted out and consumed by the American people." Sinclair was correct in appreciating the role of the big packers in the origins of regulation, and the place of the export trade. What he ignored was the extent to which the big packers were already being regulated, and their desire to extend regulation to their smaller competitors.

In March, 1906, sensing the possibility of a major public attack on its efficiency, the Department of Agriculture authorized an investigation of the Chicago office of the Bureau of Animal Industry. Although the report of the inquiry admitted that the inspection laws were not being fully applied because of a lack of funds, it largely absolved its bureau. Soon after, realizing that the Department of Agriculture report was too defensive, Roosevelt sent Charles P. Neill, the Commissioner of Labor, and James B. Reynolds to Chicago to make a special report. Neill, an economist with no technical knowledge of the packing industry, and Reynolds, a civil service lawyer, had never been exposed to the mass slaughtering of a packing house, and like Sinclair were sensitive, middle-class individuals. Roosevelt regarded the Department of Agriculture report as critical, but he hoped the Neill-Reynolds report would vindicate the worst.

Senator Albert J. Beveridge, in the meantime, began drafting a meat inspection bill at the beginning of May, Drafts passed back and forth between Beveridge and Secretary of Agriculture James Wilson, and Reynolds was frequently consulted as well. Wilson wished to have poultry excluded from the law, and diseased but edible animals passed. By the end of May, when a final bill had been agreed upon, Wilson strongly defended the Beveridge proposal. The measure was submitted as an amendment to the Agriculture Appropriation Bill, and the big packers indicated at once that they favored the bill save in two particulars. They wanted the government to pay for the entire cost of inspection, as in the past, and they did not want canning dates placed on meat products for fear of discouraging the sales of perfectly edible but dated products. Save for these contingencies, the Beveridge Amendment received the support of their American Meat Packers' Association and many major firms. The packers' objections were embodied in the amendments to the Beveridge proposal made in the House by James W. Wadsworth, chairman of the Committee on Agriculture.

Roosevelt immediately opposed the Wadsworth amendments, and threatened to release the Neill-Reynolds report if the House failed to support his position. The House supported Wadsworth, and Roosevelt sent the report along with a special message to Congress on June 4. He must have had qualms as to what it would prove, for he hedged its findings by asserting that "this report is preliminary," and that it did not discuss the entire issue of the chemical treatment of meats. The report, the packers immediately claimed, reluctantly but definitely absolved them, but also "put weapons into the hands of foreign competitors."

The Beveridge Amendment passed the Senate on May 25 without opposition. To strengthen his position, Wadsworth called hearings of the Committee of Agriculture for June 6 through June 11. Two significant facts emerge from the testimony, both of which Wadsworth intended making. Charles P. Neill's testimony revealed that the sight of blood and offal, and the odors of systematic death, had deeply shocked the two investigators, and that they had often confused the inevitable horrors of slaughtering with sanitary conditions. Roosevelt had erred in sending to the slaughterhouses two inexperienced Washington bureaucrats who freely admitted they knew nothing of canning. The major result of the hearings was to reveal that the big Chicago packers wanted more meat inspection, both to bring the small packers under control and to aid their position in the export trade. Formally representing the large Chicago packers, Thomas E. Wilson publicly announced "We are now and have always been in favor of the extension of the inspection, also to the adoption of the sanitary regulations that will insure the very best possible conditions," including nearly all the recommendations of the Neill-Reynolds report. "We have always felt that Government inspection, under proper regulations, was an advantage to the live stock and agricultural interests and to the consumer," but the packers strongly opposed paying for the costs of their advantage. The packers opposed dating canned food because of its effects on sales, but had no objection to reinspection of older cans or the banning of any chemical preservatives save saltpeter.

Although segments of the press immediately assumed that the packing industry opposed regulation that presumably damaged their interests—and historians have accepted their version—most contemporaries, including Beveridge, knew better. Upton Sinclair was critical of the bill from the start, and called for municipal slaughter houses. On June 29, as the packers and livestock growers were urging passage of the Beveridge amendment with the government footing the expenses, Beveridge announced that "an industry which is infinitely benefited by the Government inspection ought to pay for that inspection instead of the people paying for it." The value of meat inspection for the export trade, Senator Henry C. Hansbrough of North Dakota declared, is obvious. What was wrong with the entire measure, Senator Knute Nelson pointed out, was that "the American consumers and the ordinary American farmer have been left out of the question. Three objects have been sought to be accomplished—first, to placate the packers; next, to placate the men who raise the range cattle, and, third, to get a good market for the packers abroad."

The battle that followed was not on the basic principle of a meat inspection law, but on the issue of who should pay for the cost of administering it and on the problem of placing dates on processed meat. During the committee hearings, Wadsworth asked Samuel H. Cowan, the lawyer of the National Live Stock Association, to prepare a bill with the modifications acceptable to the big packers. This he did, and it was rumored in the press that Roosevelt had given Cowan's efforts his tacit approval. If an agreement between Roosevelt and Wadsworth was, in fact, reached, it was surely secret, although the two men had at least two private discussions between June 1 and 15. On June 15 the President dashed off an attack on Wadsworth's bill that was intended for the press. Wadsworth, Roosevelt claimed, was working for the packers. "I told you on Wednesday night," Wadsworth answered, referring to their private conversation, "when I submitted the bill to you, that the packers insisted before our commit-tee on having a rigid inspection law passed. Their life depends on it, and the committee will bear me out in the statement that they placed no obstacle whatever in our way. . . ."

The House stood firm on its bill, and there was a stalemate for a week. Since an effi-cient inspection bill was to the interests of the packers, the *New York Journal of Commerce* announced on June 18, they should be willing to pay its costs. But the House conferees could not be made to budge on the issues of the government assuming the cost of inspection and the dating of cans and processed meats. Beveridge abdicated, and on June 30 the bill was signed by the President. The bill, George Perkins wrote J.P. Morgan, "will certainly be of very great advantage when the thing once gets into operation and they are able to use it all over the world, as it will practically give them a government certificate for their goods. . . ."

The most significant aspect of the new law was the size of the appropriation—3 mil-lion as compared to the previous peak of $800,000—for implementing it. The law provided for the post-mortem inspection of all meat passing through interstate commerce. In this respect, the law was a systematic and uniform application of the basic 1891 Act, but it still excluded intrastate meat. Indeed, even in 1944 only 68 per cent of the meat output was cov-ered by federal laws. The new law was unique insofar as it extended inspection to meat prod-ucts and preservatives, and determined standards for sanitation within the plants. The basic purpose of Sinclair's exposé, to improve the conditions of the working class in the packing houses, could have been achieved either through better wages or socialism. Although they now had cleaner uniforms at work, their homes and living conditions were no better than before, and if they became diseased they were now thrown out of the packing houses to fend for themselves. "I am supposed to have helped clean up the yards and improve the country's meat supply—though this is mostly delusion," Sinclair later wrote. "But nobody even pre-tends to believe that I improved the condition of the stockyard workers."

Yet historians have always suggested that Sinclair brought the packers to their knees, or that "The Greatest Trust in the World" collapsed before the publication of the Neill-Reynolds report. Given the near unanimity with which the measure passed Congress, and the common agreement on basic principles shared by all at the time, there is an inconsistency in the writing of historians on this problem. If the packers were really all-powerful, or actually opposed the bill, it is difficult to explain the magnitude of the vote for it. The reality of the matter, of course, is that the big packers were warm friends of regulation, especially when it primarily affected their innumerable small competitors.

In late August the packers met with officials of the Department of Agriculture to dis-cuss the problem of complying with the law. ". . . the great asset that you gentlemen are going to have," Secretary Wilson told them, "when we get this thing to going will be the most rigid and severe inspection on the face of the earth." According to the minutes of the meet-ing, the packers responded to this proposition with "loud applause" and not with a shudder. The purpose of the law "is to assure the public that only sound and wholesome meat and meat food products may be offered for sale," Swift & Co. and other giant packers told the public in large ads. "It is a wise law. Its enforcement must be universal and uniform."

Meat inspection ceased to be a significant issue during the remainder of the Progres-sive Era. Beveridge, for several years after the passage of the 1906 Act, tried to restore his defeated amendments, but he had no support from either Roosevelt or other important politicians. Secretary of Agriculture Wilson, among others, opposed Beveridge's efforts to have the packers pay for the expenses of inspection. The packers naturally resisted all attempts to saddle them with the costs, but strongly defended the institution of meat inspection and "the integrity and efficiency of the Bureau's meat inspection service." Despite the urging of the American Meat Packers' Association, which wanted action to eradicate tuberculosis and other diseases in livestock, the issue of meat inspection died.

House of Truth

Stuart Ewen

Eight o'clock in the evening, September 27, 1918. A brief interval between shows at a local movie house in Portland, Maine. As the house lights came on, Virgil Williams, a local bank manager known to many in the audience, rose determinedly from his aisle seat and strode toward the front of the theater. Then, in a voice that resonated beyond the last row of the auditorium, he began to address the 150 of his neighbors who had gathered that night to take in a couple of movies.

His words were fired by the Great War in Europe, a war that, for the past year and a half, had embroiled the lives of American servicemen. "While we sit here tonight, enjoying a picture show," he began deliberately, "are you aware that thousands and thousands of people in Europe—people not unlike ourselves—are languishing in slavery under Prussian masters?" Assuming an inflection of gravity, Williams continued.

If we are not vigilant, their fate could be ours.

Now, then, do you folks here in Portland want to take the slightest chance of meeting Prussianism here in America?

If not, then you'll have to participate in summoning all the resources of this country for the giant struggle. In addition to buying Thrift Stamps, andWar-Savings-Stamps to support our boys overseas, we must also hold fast the lines here at home.

To do this, we must remain alert. We must listen carefully to the questions that our neighbors are asking, and we must ask ourselves whether these questions could be subverting the security of our young men in uniform.

You have heard the questions:

Is this a capitalists' war?

Was America deliberately pushed into the war by our captains of industry, for money-making purposes?

Are the rich coining blood into gold while the poor are taking on the greater burdens?

Take heed. These questions are not innocent. They can not be ignored.

These are questions constantly whispered by German sympathizers, openly asked by many others who simply do not understand.

Our response to these questions is plain. Our democratic system of income tax insures that the rates paid by those who are most well-off are greater than those rates paid by Americans who are less well-off. Tell those who ask such questions, that all Americans *are sacrificing to defeat Prussianism*, to make the world safe for democracy.

When you hear such questions, take heed. Do not wait until you catch someone putting a bomb under a factory.

Report the man who spreads pessimistic stories, or who asks misleading questions, or who belittles our efforts to win the war. Send the names of such persons—even if they are in uniform—to the Department of Justice in Washington. Give all the details you can, with names of witnesses if possible. Show the Hun that we can beat him at his own game. For those of you who are concerned for your own, or your family's safety, I can assure you that the fact that you made a report will never become public. Make the world safe for democracy! Hold fast the lines at home!

As Williams concluded his brief but urgent speech, he turned to sit down. Members of the audience offered him a small round of applause and, within moments, lights dimmed and the picture show resumed.

At first glance, Williams's oration may appear to have been a fairly impulsive occurrence, a battle-charged sample of a town-meeting heritage native to New England. This, however, was not the case.

Williams's visit to the movies was part of a carefully synchronized national mission; as he spoke to residents of Portland that evening, thousands of other people in theaters across the United States were being issued similar messages of alarm. Williams, along with 75,000 others, was a lieutenant in a nationwide brotherhood known as the "Four-Minute Men," a group of local opinion leaders—mostly small-businessmen, lawyers, and other professionals—who had been rallied to maintain home-front support for U.S. military involvement in the First World War. Nearly 150,000 times each week, men like Williams would rise before their communities to preach the holiness of the American war effort, to condemn the heresy of antiwar opinion.

Despite its magnitude, the Four-Minute Men was but the tip of an even larger iceberg, only one aspect of an unparalleled publicity campaign being conducted by the U.S. Committee on Public Information (CPI), a vast propaganda ministry established by President Woodrow Wilson in April 1917, just one week after the United States had joined the European Alliance and had declared war on Germany.

The unprecedented creation of the CPI—a comprehensive propaganda bureau intended to mobilize and channel popular enthusiasm—reflected a general awareness of "public opinion" among business and political elites in the United States during this disquieting period. It also revealed a heightened sensitivity to a number of specific problems that American political leaders faced as they moved toward a declaration of war in 1917. Government officials presumed that the majority of Americans would accept the decision to go to war, but there were significant pockets of antiwar sentiment and potential resistance that were causing them serious concern.

First of all, as he stood for reelection in 1916, President Wilson had run on the slogan, "He kept us out of war." Only a few months later, in the spring of 1917, a large number of native-born, middle-class Americans continued to hold Wilson to this oath. Particularly in western states, where many people embraced isolationist attitudes, there was a belief that events in Europe were not America's concern.

Reflecting familiar patterns of xenophobia, there were also concerns about the loyalty of America's huge immigrant population. Beyond specific questions of German immigrants (Would their devotions lie with "the Hun"?) or of Irish Americans—who, on the whole, despised America's ally, the British—the dreadful reality of many immigrants' lives in America could not help but throw the allegiances of the foreign-born into question.

Millions from Eastern Europe and the "southern tier" of Italy, who had come to the United States "with the hope that they were coming to a land of promise," had been summarily "dumped into the Ghettos of the big cities." In spite of expansive oratory about America as the great and democratic "melting pot," there was the sobering recognition among officials—as the American war effort commenced—that for many immigrants, "the melting pot had failed to melt"; the "Land of Opportunity" had not delivered on its promises. The social strains and chronic industrial unrest that had marked the preceding decades only punctuated this potentially perilous fact.

"We let sharks prey on them, we let poverty swamp them, we did not teach them English," lamented George Creel, the Progressive journalist who would become the civilian director of the CPI. He, along with other watchful Washington insiders, believed that without a direct campaign to promote loyalty in immigrant communities, the foreign-born could not be counted on to embrace the American war effort.

Compounding these fears, there was an overt and articulate political opposition to the war, even before U.S. involvement. Working-class and radical organizations, pacifists, anarchists and many socialists, maintained that this was nothing but a "rich man's war." Ralph Chaplin—a prominent member of the Industrial Workers of the World (IWW)—typified this perspective when, in a 1914 poem, he dubbed the European war a "Red Feast," a gruesome blood purge in which the flesh of workers was being devoured by rats, maggots, and capitalist "Lords of War."

"Go fight you fools!" Chaplin taunted those who would serve up their lives to the grim European banquet that was now under way.

Tear up the earth with strife
And give unto a war that is not yours;
Serve unto death the men you served in life
So that their wide dominions may not yield.
Stand by the flag—the lie that still allures;
Lay down your lives for land you do not own,
And spill each other's guts upon the field;
Your gory tithe of mangled flesh and bone.
But whether in the fray to fall or kill
You must not pause to question why nor where.
You see the tiny crosses on that hill?
It took all those to make one millionaire.

By 1917, lessons such as Chaplin's had left a deep imprint on the thinking of many. Instructed by compelling visions of a "Red Feast," many workers found it easy to interpret

U.S. entry into the war as little more than a thinly veiled attempt to recover endangered Wall Street loans.

International events only encouraged governmental anxieties about organized working-class resistance. In Great Britain, attempts to rally popular support for the war were seen as deficient; large sectors of the English working class felt little harmony with the cause. "That the working classes have to a certain extent failed to develop a sense of national unity is obvious enough," observed Wilfred Trotter, an eminent British social psychologist, in 1916. Socialistic, egalitarian aspirations were multiplying, Trotter noted, and Britain was now "faced with the possibility of having to make profound changes in the social system to convince the working-man . . . that his interests and ours in this war are one."

Even more alarming, an earthshaking social revolution was in the process of unfolding in Russia. Working people were marching in the streets. The czar's army refused to fight for the allied cause and had then refused orders to shoot down protesting workers in Moscow and St. Petersburg. After February 1917, a weak interim government was succumbing to the weight of its own indecision, and a "proletarian" Bolshevik regime stood at the threshold of power. Such world historic contingencies only underscored the dread of social disorder and chaos that encircled the American decision to enter the war.

Sensing that middle-class public opinion was volatile and that a revolt of the masses was possible, a number of noteworthy social analysts began to lobby President Wilson, calling for the establishment of an ideological apparatus that would systematically promote the cause of war. One of these analysts was Arthur Bullard, a leading Progressive, who had been a student of Wilson when the president had been a history professor at Princeton.

Early in 1917, Bullard sent a copy of his recently published book, *Mobilising America*, to Wilson, hoping that the volume would influence the president's blueprints for war. Attuned to his era's belief in publicity as a "moral disinfectant" and its deep mistrust of secrecy, Bullard warned that installing conventional systems of governmental press control would be a mistake. Given perceptions of this as a "businessman's war," any overt policy of censorship would simply encourage deep-seated public suspicion.

Developing his plan from the lessons of Progressive journalism, Bullard argued that a flood of publicity would be key in rallying America to war. "Timid advisors will urge secrecy," he advised, "but the Government needs publicity. Nothing will do more to hearten us, to stimulate the mobilisation of Public Opinion, than knowledge of what is being done." The wisest road to pursue when war is declared, he recommended, was to dispatch a steady flow of information to the public at large.

> *First, last and all the time, the effectiveness of our warfare will depend on the amount of ardor we throw into it. . . . [T]he prime duty of our government, the first step in any mobilisation, must be the awakening of our interest. . . . [a] Call to Arms, which will electrify public opinion.*

To accomplish this goal, Bullard proposed that the government should "organise a publicity bureau, which would constantly keep before the public the importance of supporting the men at the front. It would requisition space on the front page of every newspaper; it would call for a 'draft' of trained writers to feed 'Army stories' to the public; it would create a Corps of Press Agents. . . . In order to make a democracy fight whole-heartedly," he resolved, "it is necessary to make them understand the situation." America must, Bullard concluded, organize "propaganda campaigns to make the struggle comprehensible and popular."

Bullard was fervent in this conviction:

By every means at its disposal our Government must strive to get us thinking together. For unless that is accomplished there is nothing but endless muddle before us, a welter of blunders, inefficiency and disgrace. We—the people of the United States—are the force back of the Government. Unless our Will to Win is passionate and determined, our Army and Navy will accomplish little.

On March 11, in a private letter to the president, Walter Lippmann seconded Bullard's recommendation. With U.S. involvement less than a month away, he exhorted Wilson to create an official government news bureau, an agency that would advertise the war as one "to make a world that is safe for democracy." In wartime, Lippmann added cryptically, it is necessary to nurture "a healthy public opinion."

On April 6, 1917, when the United States formally declared war, the issue of propaganda moved to the top of the president's agenda. On April 12, responding to an assignment from the president, Lippmann submitted a ground plan to Wilson, laying out specifics for a wartime "publicity bureau," a "clearinghouse for information on government activities" that would mobilize the propagandistic skills of artists, intellectuals, journalists, and other media professionals from around the country. Moving beyond a paradigm of publicity that was grounded in journalism, Lippmann's plan spoke of the need to rally a wide range of communications specialists, including people working in the "motion picture industry." Beyond propagating information, Lippmann suggested, the bureau should also direct a variety of relevant intelligence functions, "a monitoring of the foreign press . . . and the tracking down of 'rumors and lies' " that would undermine American morale.

Heeding these admonitions, on April 14, 1917, Wilson took action to "hold fast the inner lines," issuing Executive Order No. 2594, which decreed the establishment of the CPI. From within the government, the committee's membership included the secretary of state, the secretary of war, and the secretary of the navy. To head the CPI, Wilson appointed Creel, a well-connected Progressive journalist, as its civilian chairman.

In light of Wilson's unease about possible liberal opposition to the war, the appointment of Creel was ingenious and adroit. Beginning in Kansas, in the mid-1890s, Creel had been part of the founding generation of Progressive publicists, writers who built careers aiming their pens at governmental corruption and corporate excess. By 1910, he had acquired a national reputation as a top investigative journalist. Beyond his Progressive pedigree, Creel had also been an early champion of Wilson's run for the presidency in 1912; since then he had gained the president's notice and confidence.

Given the exigencies of the moment, Creel was precisely the kind of man Wilson needed to head a wartime publicity bureau. From a lifetime of experience, he understood "the importance of public opinion" in modern political life. Creel was also acquainted with an extensive community of Progressive journalists around the country; Wilson believed that Creel could bring these potential "opinion leaders" into the fold, to establish a visible link between liberal ideals and pursuit of the war. On the whole, Wilson's assumption was justified. When war was declared, an impassioned generation of Progressive publicists fell into line, surrounding the war effort with a veil of much-needed liberal-democratic rhetoric.

Most important, Creel had been a conspicuous critic of big business—and of pro-business propaganda—in the years directly preceding the war. (It was Creel, after all, who, in *Harper's* magazine, had written a scathing critique of the Rockefeller interests and of Ivy Lee's role as the Rockefeller family's mouthpiece following the Ludlow Massacre.) In a political milieu in which skepticism about a "capitalists' war" was rife, who better to place at the helm of a propaganda ministry than a man whose anti–big business credentials were immaculate.

In a number of ways the active collaboration between progressivism and the war effort made historical sense. By 1917, the aims of progressivism and the agenda of the CPI were not that far apart.

For some time, Progressives had articulated a vision of the future in which intellectuals and social technicians would come to lead a new and rational world order. In 1917, with one of their own—Woodrow Wilson—at the helm of government, many saw the war as an opportunity for America and American liberal values to frame the world's future.

Moreover, fears of revolt from below had haunted the Progressive imagination for some years. The desire to govern and guide public perception—in order to effect the social order— was hardly alien to the philosophy of progressivism. When the moment to lead the public mind into war arrived, the disorder threatened by antiwar sentiments—particularly among the lower classes—was seen as an occasion that demanded what Lippmann would call the "manufacture of consent."

Last, there was a bridge between the domestic objectives of progressivism and an aggressive approach to world affairs that had roots going back to the late nineteenth century. From the period leading up to the Spanish-American War, there were many politicians, businessmen, and Progressives who discerned a relationship between the United States' ability to assume the world stage as a political and economic power and its ability to generate an improved standard of living for the masses of people at home. As a generation of Progressives united around the war effort in 1917, many believed that the war—and its triumphal aftermath—would place the United States in an incomparable position to deliver on its timeworn pledge of prosperity for the many.

* * *

As director of the CPI, Creel brought an understanding of publicity to his post that had been nurtured by his experience as a Progressive publicist. Like many of his contemporaries, Creel had a finely honed awareness of the paths along which ideas were carried, and he applied this awareness expansively. The "House of Truth," as Creel called the CPI, was extraordinarily sophisticated and far reaching, providing an unequaled laboratory for pursuing local, national, and international publicity work.[17] With the assistance of advisers, Creel erected a publicity apparatus that, in scope and conception, transcended anything that had previously existed.

To some extent, the CPI built upon publicity strategies that had been evolving in the United States since the late nineteenth century, strategies that had come to the fore during the Progressive Era. In the Domestic Section of the CPI, for example, the Division of News channeled thousands of "official war news" press releases through the mails and along telegraph lines on a twenty-four-hours-a-day basis. Concurrently, the Foreign Section of the CPI, which maintained offices in over thirty countries, used naval radio transmitters to "pour a steady stream of American information into international channels of communication." Syndicated "human-interest" features were also distributed, aimed at those readers who skipped over the news columns.

In a move that extended beyond existing public relations practices, a direct effort was made to influence media aimed at immigrant populations. Developing contacts with six hundred foreign language papers—published in nineteen languages—the CPI made special appeals to a heterogeneous population whose loyalty was of special concern.

To "guide the mind of the masses" more directly, the CPI also began publishing its own newspaper, the *Official Bulletin*, in May 1917. Designed to set off a mental chain reaction, the *Official Bulletin*—with a circulation reaching 115,000—was targeted at public officials, other newspapers, and any other "agencies of a public or semi-public character equipped to disseminate the official information it will contain."

If the CPI elaborated on and extended the accumulated knowledge of public relations specialists, however, Creel was convinced that newspapers alone could not do the job at hand. To achieve the ideological mobilization of an entire nation and to sell America's vision of the war globally, an extensive fabric of persuasion would have to be knit.

This undertaking required an expansion of both the tools and occasions for publicity. To that time, print journalism had been seen, for the most part, as the primary medium for shaping public opinion. The power of the printed word had stood at the core of the publicist's faith. The CPI went beyond this premise; in its publicly subsidized laboratories, it experimented quantitatively and qualitatively with other forms of media.

Transcending the confines of traditional press agentry, the CPI constituted a more audacious approach to publicity than had previously existed. To sell the war to Americans, Creel believed, an all-encompassing fabric of perception—every moment of human attention—had to be mobilized. "How could the national emergency be met without national unity?" he inquired rhetorically. "The printed word, the spoken word, motion pictures, the telegraph, the wireless, posters, signboards, and every possible media should be used to drive home the justice of America's cause."

Though Creel was a journalist, his instincts for publicity were more familiar among people employed in the advertising industry. By 1917, advertising men were boastfully extolling the deftness with which they were able to induce resistant customers to purchase a growing variety of factory-produced consumer goods. Many in the industry also maintained that advertising techniques could also be used to sell social and political ideas and even to combat social discontent.

Given the evolution of American advertising by 1917, this conceit made some degree of sense. By this time, advertising was more than a simple description—truthful or not—of goods. In a seductive mix of words and images, advertising had begun to associate goods with the emotional lives—the needs, cravings, aspirations, and fears—of the consumers to whom it spoke.

Acknowledging the already considerable power of advertising in American society, by 1917 Creel was approaching the conclusion that "people do not live by bread alone; they live mostly by catch phrases." If advertising techniques could sell soap or face cream or biscuits, he reasoned, why not a war? "The work of the Committee was so distinctly in the nature of an advertising campaign," he explained some years later, "that we turned almost instinctively to the advertising profession for advice and assistance."

Following this intuition, the CPI conscripted the advertising forces of the country on behalf of the war effort. "By . . . one stroke of President Wilson's pen," Creel explained, "every advertising man in the United States was enrolled in America's second line, and from the very moment of their enrollment we could feel a quickening of effort, the intensification of endeavor." Under the leadership of William H. Johns, president of the American Association of Advertising Agencies and head of the George Batten advertising agency, the Advertising Division of the CPI generated hundreds of advertisements and bill-boards, at the same time pressuring newspapers around the country to donate free advertising space for the CPI.

If fact-oriented journalism had provided the model by which publicists sought to promote corporate interests and political intentions prior to the war, the CPI elevated the importance of advertising techniques and emotional appeals to a national political level. Coming out of a tradition of publicity that relied most heavily on the vehicle of words, the CPI ventured into constructing a language of images.

To supply illustrations for advertisements and for designing posters, the CPI deployed a Division of Pictorial Publicity, a brigade of volunteer artists, headed by Charles Dana Gibson—creator of the Gibson Girl and America's foremost commercial artist. In conjunction with this division, the Bureau of Cartoons published the *Weekly Bulletin for Cartoonists*, a newsletter sent to 750 newspaper cartoonists around the country, that contained "ideas and captions" that cartoonists were expected to provide drawings for.

Creel took particular pride in his ability to mobilize the graphic arts. Observing that "artists, from time immemorial" have often been seen as "an irresponsible lot," Creel declared that under the leadership of the CPI, "painters, sculptors, designers, illustrators, and cartoonists rallied to the colors with instancy and enthusiasm."

Perhaps most prophetically, and following Lippmann's initial recommendations on wartime publicity, the nascent movie industry of Hollywood was also drafted into the CPI's publicity apparatus under the Division of Films. In a number of significant ways this innovation made sense.

Movies were an extraordinarily charismatic and universal form of communication. Unlike printed matter, literacy was not a precondition of movies' ability to speak to an audience. In the era of silent films, in which a wordless language of gesture was used to tell a story, knowledge of English was similarly unnecessary. This was an especially serviceable feature in a society that housed such an enormous population of immigrants.

A visual rhetoric of filmmaking was also developing that extended film's potential as a medium of persuasion. Techniques of cinematography (camera movement, the conscious use of close-ups, medium- and wide shots, the expressive play of shadow and light) and editing (crosscutting, montage, and the use of dissolves) each provided captivating vehicles for leading the eye and mind toward specific ways of seeing a story unfold.

In 1917, as official plans for wartime propaganda were being laid, the bewitching eloquence of film—its peculiar capacity to induce an altered state of consciousness among audiences drawn from all classes—was widely recognized as one of the medium's most salient properties.

A sea change in the capacity to touch the inner life of an audience, to transfigure the physics of perception, is palpable in the following description of cinema that appeared in a popular encyclopedia of modern technological wonders, published in 1915.

> *Here, at last, is the magic of childhood—appearances, apparitions, objects possessed of power of movement and of intelligence. . . .*
>
> *For the motion picture does for us what no other thing can do save a drug. . . . It eliminates the time between happenings and brings two events separated actually by hours of time and makes them seem to us as following each other with no interval between them. Unconscious of this sixth sense of time, because it is so much a factor of our daily lives, ignorant of the fact that it is this and not our eyes alone which have been tricked, we leave the darkened theater with wonder in our hearts and admiration on our lips.*

Now, adding to the ability to capture a semblance of "reality" on film and to present social arguments through pictorial narratives, film was developing its own, unparalleled idiom of persuasion—a language that touched the recesses of inner life and spoke the uncanny vocabulary of dreams, permitting storytellers to enchant an audience silently with deep, psychologically charged ways of seeing.

Nowhere was the propagandistic potential of film more evident than in D.W. Griffith's *Birth of a Nation*, which had appeared in 1914. With enormous power, the film—which had war as its central theme—incited audiences into a frenzy of identification with racist Southern myths and contributed to the resurgence of the Ku Klux Klan. The film's ability to rally people to a cause provided a model for World War I propaganda.

To this point, the practices of publicity had been founded on the ability to communicate a semblance of news, of facticity. Now, from the intoxicating realm of entertainment, the medium of film had revealed a new, uncanny ability to transcend facticity for the purposes of persuasion, to reach a public on another, more emotional level.

Employing this powerful new tool—with all its suggestive implications—the CPI's Division of Films launched an unprecedented effort to deploy movies as implements of war. Under the division's direction, a number of feature films were produced for worldwide theatrical distribution: *Pershing's Crusaders, America's Answer, Under Four Flags,* and others, shown alongside more conventional Hollywood productions.

These propaganda films, however, were not directly produced by the CPI. Instead, the Division of Films maintained a "scenario department," which simply drafted general story outlines. These "scenarios" were then passed on to seasoned commercial film producers, whose job it was to introduce the magic of Hollywood, to ensure audience appeal.

Distribution also drew on Hollywood know-how. As films were completed, their distribution was overseen by George Bowles, "an experienced theatrical and motion-picture manager," who had "made a name for himself" distributing and promoting *The Birth of a Nation.*

On an international level, Hollywood's already considerable global allure was exploited as a wedge. To ensure the exhibition of CPI propaganda films around the world, movie producers were expected to attach a quid pro quo to their immensely popular feature films as they were exhibited around the world. As Creel explained it:

> Hollywood producers had to agree that no American entertainment films would be sold to any foreign exhibitor who refused to show the Committee's war pictures, and that none would be sold to houses where any sort of German film was being used. As exhibitors simply had to have our comedies and dramas . . . we soon had sole possession of the field. Much as they may have disliked our propaganda features, Douglass Fairbanks, Mary Pickford, and the Keystone Cops were a necessity.

Beyond news, advertising, posters, political cartoons, and feature films, the CPI exploited countless other avenues of publicity as well. Academics from around the country were enlisted to write "authoritative" pamphlets on behalf of the war. Exhibitions at state fairs and other expositions were also mounted. Over 200,000 slides, stereopticon images, and photographs were likewise produced for exhibition in schools, churches, and other community centers.

Overall, in terms of the evolution of twentieth-century publicity, the CPI was built around a conception of the mass media that had never before been applied. Looming over each individual division was a conception of the mass media that saw them as parts of an interwoven perceptual environment. It was the espoused goal of the CPI to impregnate the entire fabric of perception with the message of the war.

Along with its sweeping use of media, the CPI broke ground in another critical way. In 1898, Gabriel Tarde had speculated on a hookup that existed between an evolving mass media system and patterns of personal conversation. Under the stewardship of Creel, such speculations guided concrete policy. In its attempt to manufacture a comprehensive universe of discourse, the CPI implemented pragmatic strategies that were overtly calculated to shape and direct the private conversations of everyday people.

This idea stood behind the creation of the Four-Minute Men. More than just a circle of men established to deliver rousing speeches throughout the country, the CPI's Division of Four-Minute Men was the centerpiece in a strategy designed to shape attitudes within the frame of people's daily lives. Four-Minute Men were chosen from among people assumed to be local community leaders, primarily business and professional men. Speakers were chosen not because of their support of the war—this would be a given—but because of the accustomed influence they had exerted over their neighbors' points of view in other contexts. Bellwethers of local thinking, these men were enrolled, according to Creel, to provide guidance for conversation throughout the country, "to bring some order out of oratorical chaos."

If it was assumed that people in America's communities followed the viewpoints of their local leaders, local leaders, were simultaneously expected to echo the viewpoints of regional leaders (even more prominent business and professional men), and these men, in turn, were expected to follow leaders of the national organization. In short, the Division of Four-Minute Men was predicated on a hierarchical sociology of influence, a judgment that informal patterns of human interaction might be identified and exploited on behalf of the war.

On a weekly basis, this oratorical chain of command was administered through the *Four-Minute Man Bulletin,* an instructional newsletter that contained a "Budget of Materials," detailed guidelines for the speeches members would be expected to deliver in a given week. Issues of the bulletin introduced the general topic to be addressed each week: "Why We Are Fighting," "Unmasking German Propaganda," "Maintaining Morals and Morale," "The Danger to Democracy," and so forth. This theme was then divided into a five- to seven-part outline for the speech that was to be delivered. Specific information or ideas to be conveyed were also supplied. Samples of "typical speeches" were included as well. Speakers were encouraged to muster enthusiasm, and their performances were routinely monitored by local chairmen, who judged the competence of their delivery and offered suggestions for improvement. Those judged to be boring speakers were expeditiously removed from the Four-Minute Men speakers' circuit.

Together, these exercises ensured that in any given week, influential men throughout the country were addressing their neighbors with standardized speeches, covering identical topics, in a manner calculated to suggest spontaneity and evoke enthusiasm. Beyond simply dispensing a governmental line, Four-Minute Men were expected to get movie audiences to carry ideas and topics back into the community at large, to create what one bulletin characterized as "an endless chain of verbal messages."

If speeches were planned to instigate discussion, there was also concern that this discussion should remain governable. CPI leaders were wary about nourishing an atmosphere of impromptu "curbstone oratory." "It was imperative," reflected Creel, "to guard against the dangers of unrestraint."

As such, Four-Minute Men cautioned audiences to discuss weekly topics within proscribed limits of conversation, to avoid those contexts that might inadvertently further a climate of unrest. "Only where men meet naturally to talk and to listen, at the table, at social gatherings, at noon in the workshop, at night at home, is discussion in place," advised a weekly bulletin.

Augmenting the regular program for adults, which concentrated its efforts in movie theaters, the Division of Four-Minute Men also operated a youth group, the Junior Four-Minute Men, which focused on elementary and secondary schools. Speaking competitions for children were held, to be administered by teachers and principles whose loyalty was judged by their willingness to cooperate. The junior division also published the *National School Service Bulletin,* which provided teachers with topics for regular classroom discussion. Beyond putting America's educational system in uniform, these activities gave children topics that—it was expected—they would carry back into their homes.

Speakers also participated in an ideological policing function. Audiences were encouraged to identify, interrogate, and even report people in their communities who expressed antiwar sentiment.

To deal with potentially fractious communities, special brigades of speakers were deputized. African Americans—many of whom found it difficult to swallow the liberal rhetoric of the CPI while they were burdened by entrenched patterns of racism—were identified specifically as a troublesome group, in need of special attention. For example, in Brunswick, Georgia—where Jim Crow laws routinely subverted African Americans' rights—Alfred Wood, chairman of the "Regular Four-Minute Men," expressed worries that "colored people . . . seem particularly susceptible" to antiwar propaganda. Responding to this perceived problem,

Wood drafted William A. Perry, a "responsible and patriotic colored man," to serve as chairman of a new organization, the "Colored Four-Minute Men of Brunswick."

Within the purview of the CPI, every moment of human interaction became a suitable venue for publicity. Heated by the fires of war, the concept of public relations was moving beyond the borders of journalistic press agentry, attempting to encompass the ether of human relations itself. "Never before in history," wrote Charles and Mary Beard, "had such a campaign of education been organized; never before had American citizens realized how thoroughly, how irresistibly a modern government could impose its ideas upon the whole nation."

The dual role of the Four-Minute Men—as a localized propaganda agency and a nationwide organization for extinguishing opposition to the war—offers a microcosm of what was, in fact, a much larger truth encompassing the activities of the CPI: the wholesale smothering of ideas and outlooks that ran against the grain of the official story. Part and parcel of the committee's success in mobilizing America's intellectual and creative resources for war was the simultaneous establishment of an ambience of censorship, calculated to discourage or punish impure thought.

Writing in 1935, Harold Lasswell—one of America's leading students of propaganda—observed that "the high importance of coordinating propaganda with all other means of social control cannot be too insistently repeated." In the context of the First World War, while the CPI blanketed every nook and cranny of American life with liberal-sounding rhetoric, this formula was followed to the letter. A severe climate of suppression was being instituted throughout the United States.

In his public declarations Creel repudiated censorship and the squelching of opposition. "The work that is being carried on by the Committee on Public Information is not a censorship and never has been a censorship. It is a medium of expression," he maintained in 1918. Yet underneath this pledge of openness, an atmosphere of suppression was taking hold.

The legal framework for this suppression was provided by the Espionage Act—passed on June 15, 1917—which upheld the censorship of ideas considered injurious to the war effort. As widespread prosecutions took place, the carrot of "voluntary censorship" was continually toughened first, by the stick of the Espionage Act and then by the Sedition Act of 1918, "a statute which in effect made any criticism of the Wilson administration illegal."

"Under the general terms of the Espionage and Sedition acts," wrote the Beards, "newspapers were continually silenced by orders and prosecutions. Individual critics of the war and the Wilson program were rounded up by the government, often without warrants of arrest, hustled to jail, held incommunicado without bail, tried in courts where the atmosphere was heavily charged with passion, lectured by irate judges, and sent to prison for long terms—in one case an adolescent girl for twenty years."

To a large extent, the general climate of thought control was sustained by much of the ongoing work of the CPI: its repeated warnings that people must be "vigilant"; scrutinize their neighbors; listen in on others' conversations; and, if necessary, embrace the role of government informer.

More than a huge publicity apparatus, the CPI was the intrinsic outcome of new ways of thinking that had been percolating during the preceding decades. "The tossing about of symbols," noted one important analyst, became an increasingly serviceable "substitute for intellectual transaction." Amid the CPI, a decisive shift in the ways that publicists thought about the public and about shaping public opinion was revealed.

Whatever contradictions their actual practices may have contained, Progressive publicists— in the years preceding the war—had embraced Enlightenment notions about the work they were doing. They were seekers of "truth," exposers of "fact," exercisers of "reason." Proponents of corporate public relations, as has been seen in Ivy Lee and Theodore Vail, also couched their activities within an argot of facticity.

In public utterances about the CPI, it must be added, Creel—a dyed-in-the-wool Progressive—continued to do the same. "I do not believe that public opinion has its rise in the emotions," he wrote in 1918. "I feel that public opinion has its source in the minds of people, that it has its base in reason, and that it expresses slow-formed convictions rather than any temporary excitement or any passion of the moment."

Yet despite his ongoing protestations that "We have never made any appeal to the emotions," the record of the CPI points toward a considerably different conclusion.

Under the direction of Gibson, for example, the pictorial work of the CPI was routinely aimed at the heart, not the head. "One cannot create enthusiasm for the war on the basis of practical appeal," Gibson maintained. "The spirit that will lead a man to put away the things of his accustomed life and go forth to all the hardships of war is not kindled by showing him the facts." Artwork produced for the CPI, he concluded, must "appeal to the heart."

Posters and other CPI-sponsored imagery complied with Gibson's instruction. In a Red Cross poster produced for the CPI, a photomontage juxtaposed a giant, close-up image of a protective nurse/mother over a wide camera shot of a body-strewn battlefield. In a striking, avant-garde composition, the war's harvest of death was powerfully transformed into a metaphor for nurturing security.

In another Red Cross poster, a Pieta-like image of a nurse/Blessed Virgin was rendered, eyes raised to God, arms cradling a wounded, infant-Jesus-sized soldier in her arms. Beneath her the caption read: "The Greatest Mother in the World."

In yet another poster, a painterly portrait of a drowning mother and child, perishing as they sink beneath the surface of a dark green ocean, provided an emotive justification for the one-word mandate: "Enlist!"

Reinforcing such sentimental monuments to the American war effort, images of the enemy were built on a bedrock of fear, invoking an ineluctable climate of xenophobic paranoia. Many images portrayed an inscrutable enemy, lurking around every corner, threatening even the most apparently innocent circumstances. One CPI magazine ad, for example, displayed a picture of two women engaging in private conversation. Nearby, apparently combing through a newspaper, a man's eyes reveal that he is, in fact, eavesdropping on their conversation. Below the image was the caption "Spies and Lies" and a text that warned, "German agents are everywhere. . . . Do not become a tool of the Hun by passing on the malicious, disheartening rumors which he so eagerly sows. . . . You are in contact with the enemy today, just as truly as if you faced him across No Man's Land. In your hands are two powerful weapons with which to meet him—discretion and vigilance. Use them."

Another image depicted the enemy as a menacing spider wearing a German helmet, waiting to ensnare loose-lipped people in his web. "SPIES are LISTENING" announced the poster in resounding typography.

Still another image displayed a map of the United States, its geography renamed to offer a chilling picture of postwar America should the enemy be victorious. Now called "New Prussia," the familiar outline of the United States is studded with alien, Hun-inspired names: Heineapolis, Denverburg, Cape U Boat, the Gulf of Hate, and the like.

Reinforcing such terrifying visions of America's future, one macabre CPI poster displayed the Statue of Liberty "crumbling under German fire, with the burning ruins of New York City silhouetted against the background."

This approach became routine within the CPI. In the Budgets of Materials they received, for example, Four-Minute Men were continually schooled in the particular serviceability of emotional appeals. In Bulletin No. 39, William Ingersoll (director of the division) told speakers that beyond presenting "facts and details" to "satisfy the reasoning faculties of our audiences," Four-Minute Men must also "appeal to the feelings, in which we stir the sentiment and emotion and arouse the desire to DO something" on the part of an audience.

Elsewhere, in instructions for a speech on Liberty Bonds, the bulletin summarized the essence of an effective presentation, which was lifted directly from the nascent wisdom of advertising psychologists. "One idea—simple language—talk in pictures, not in statistics—touch their minds, hearts, spirits—make them want to win with every fiber of their beings—translate that desire into terms of bonds—and they will buy."

In spite of Creel's insistent denials, the "House of Truth" was perched not on a foundation of facts, but upon a swamp of emotions. As a vast laboratory experiment in the molding of public opinion, the CPI moved away from earlier, rationalistic models that had been defined primarily by journalism toward communications strategies that aimed ineffably for the gut. This shift was summarized ten years later, when Harold Lasswell summarized the lesson of World War I.

[A] new and subtler instrument must weld thousands and even millions of human beings into one amalgamated mass of hate and will and hope. A new flame must burn out the canker of dissent and temper the steel of bellicose enthusiasm. The name of this new hammer and anvil of social solidarity is propaganda. Talk must take the place of drill; print must supply the dance. War dances live in literature and at the fringes of the modern earth; war propaganda breathes and fumes in the capitals and provinces of the world.

As many among a generation of Progressive intellectuals flocked to serve as ideological emissaries for the CPI or lent their talents to other facets of the war mobilization, there were some who disapproved, seeing intellectual war service as a fickle betrayal of principles. Among them, it was Randolph Bourne, in a 1917 jeremiad entitled "War and the Intellectuals," who presented one of the most outspoken accounts of this metamorphosis.

Published barely two months after the United States had entered the war, Bourne's bleak epitaph for the abandoned social ideals of progressivism mourned that "it has been a bitter experience to see the unanimity with which the American intellectuals have thrown their support to the use of war technique." Progressives, who had once believed in the fertile powers of human reason, were now, according to Bourne, dealing with the American people as if they were "sluggish masses, too remote from the world-conflict to be stirred, too lacking in intellect to perceive their danger." From this vantage point, he continued, an intellectual legion of "socialists, college professors, publicists, new-republicans, [and] practitioners of literature, had assumed the iniquitous task of "riveting the war mind on a hundred million more of the world's people."

With bitter irony, Bourne mocked the conceit of these fallen idealists, men who had opened "the sluices" in order to "flood us with the sewage of the war spirit."

"War and the Intellectuals" was Bourne's funeral oration for the questioning social consciousness that had, in his estimation, marked prewar progressivism. Now, in the crucible of war, contemplative humanistic ideals were giving way to a fateful brand of cynicism. People who had once believed in the ability to use "creative intelligence" to bring about a more humane social order were becoming dutiful technicians of mass persuasion, craven manipulators of consent.

In many ways, Bourne's obituary for the critical spirit of progressivism was prophetic. Bourne's vision of liberal intellectuals becoming "servants of power" not only spoke to their role during the war, but, to a large extent, described what would become of them over the decade that followed.

Progressive intellectuals had customarily been critics of big business, of its greed, exploitativeness, and inherent corruption. During the war, however, as corporations buttressed and profited from the war effort, critiques of big business subsided, giving way to a more receptive view of corporate America. After the war, this view would persist for the most part. At the same time, a preoccupation with the need to adjust public attitudes and the search for techniques by which this adjustment might be achieved were also carried into the postwar period. This mix of sensibilities—a greater friendliness toward big business and increased attention to the importance of molding public opinion—animated the lives of a growing class of American intellectuals as they moved from war service back into civilian life.

While there continued to be intellectual dissidents during the twenties, those who complied with a new way of seeing would prove to be far more consequential to the future development of public relations thinking. Central to their perspective was a new understanding of who the public was and what were the most effective ways of influencing that public.

Before the war Progressive intellectuals had espoused the Enlightenment dictum that people—at least middle-class people—were essentially rational, capable of evaluating information and then of making intelligent decisions. In the context of the CPI, "public opinion" became something to be mobilized and managed; the "public mind" was now seen as an entity to be manufactured, not reasoned with.

The war had also elevated the function of unreason, of the "night mind," for people engaged in the business of shaping public opinion. Reflected within this shift was a transformed conception of human nature itself. In their discussions of the public—of people in general—Brahmins of public opinion, educated by the war, were becoming increasingly conversant with psychological aspects of human perception. In the citadels of the Enlightened

West, a naive faith in reason was beginning to fade from view. Publicists were beginning to look for unconscious or instinctive triggers that might be pulled to activate public passions.

Aligned with this search, publicists also began to broaden their understanding of the rhetorics of persuasion. If prior notions of publicity had been built on carefully constructed armatures of "fact," the CPI had unearthed the venerable power of symbols to inspire and sway the public's imagination.

Last, if preceding approaches to persuasion had focused on newspapers and periodicals as the primary arenas for forging public attitudes, the war had dramatized the existence of complex, interlocking networks of perception. In the context of the CPI, public relations moved beyond its myopic fixation on the printed page toward an increasingly sophisticated appreciation of the media environment overall and of the webs of influence that touch people in their everyday lives.

Within twenty-four hours of the Armistice, the CPI was summarily dismantled. In the aftermath of the war, it must be added, the reputations of Creel in particular and of Progressivism more generally suffered a decline, partly because of their roles in the promotion of the war. Yet the experiences gained in the CPI and its general lessons about the terrain of the public mind would inform the concerns of public relations specialists and affect the contours of American cultural life for decades to come.

"When Johnny Comes Marching Home"

Meirion and Susie Harries

Little though the Allies cared to acknowledge the fact, the United States emerged with credit from the Great War. American money, materials, and manpower had saved the Allies from near-certain defeat and built the platform from which the drive to victory could be made. But the cost was immense in money, ecological damage, a fragmented society, and the disillusion of a dream gone sour. And the most painful price was paid, cash on the nail, by the soldiers of the AEF.

The final total of American dead in the First World War was 75,658. Of these, 34,249 would be listed as killed in action—that is to say, they had died before receiving medical attention—while 13,691 had died of their wounds after receiving medical attention. The Marines had the highest percentage of casualties—four out of ten officers dead or wounded, three out of ten men. The 2nd Division had the highest aggregate of casualties (25,232) and the highest number of decorations, including seven Medals of Honor. (For the Army as a whole, the War Department ordered 511 miles of medal ribbon.)

In all, 23,937 men died of disease, the majority from influenza; many caught the disease in the trains taking them to their embarkation points or in the transports crossing to France; many more died without ever leaving the camps. And 3,681 died by suicide, murder, or accident.

Most of the battlefield dead were initially buried where they fell, hastily covered with earth by their comrades; shell holes were used as mass graves, topped by rough crosses or cairns of rubble with indications of the units involved, to attract the attention of the burial parties coming up behind. Amid the chaos, danger, and misery, the soldiers performed this service as carefully as they could; less than 2 percent of American dead remained unidentified.

Many of the dead were recovered from the battlefield graves after the war and reinterred in eight military cemeteries, one in Belgium, one in England, and six in northern France: 2,200 graves at the cemetery at Belleau, which took most of the dead from the Marne; 6,000 at the Oise-Aisne cemetery; 4,100 at Saint-Mihiel; 1,850 at the Somme cemetery;

Reprinted from *The Last Days of Innocence*, (1997), by permission of Random House, Inc.

1,500 at the Suresnes cemetery; 14,117 at the Meuse-Argonne cemetery at Romagne-sous-Montfaucon.

The mothers and fathers, sisters and brothers of the dead, if they were able to visit the cemeteries, found (and still find) them to be meticulously tended, dignified, peaceful places in the green French countryside. The evidence of the doughboys' suffering, the violence and the horror, was quickly tidied away and grassed over, though the landscape would be scarred for years to come. The human wreckage that came home was often harder to accept.

The wounded came home by the boatload, their numbers increasing all the time. Hoboken, New Jersey, one of the principal ports of disembarkation, received 169 casualties from France in February 1918; the total in July was 539. In September, once the system had processed the wounded from Belleau Wood and the Marne, Soissons, and the Vesle, 1,883 came home; in October, after Saint-Mihiel, it was 2,666; in November as the wounded poured in from the Meuse-Argonne, the figure was 3,474. During the relative calm of the armistice negotiations, 18,443 came home in December, and this monthly rate would be maintained through the spring of 1919.

Their wounds were specialities of the Western Front. To deal with an unusually high proportion of injuries to the face, typical of trench warfare, American dentists developed a new expertise and American physicians gave medical science the team approach to reconstructive facial surgery.

Gas gangrene was an occupational hazard of fighting over heavily manured agricultural land. Shrapnel carried dirt and scraps of clothing with it and was rarely traveling fast enough to exit; if a fragment lodged in a fleshy part of the body, the flesh closed behind it, shutting off the air and creating the ideal conditions for gangrene, which men rarely survived without amputation. More left arms were lost than right, as the left arm was generally unprotected while the soldier lay in position for shooting in the trench and wounds were aggravated by fragments of the wristwatch.

Injuries to the mind were less conspicuous than the empty sleeve or the artificial leg, but they disabled 69,934 American soldiers temporarily or permanently, and war trauma was still emerging in the late 1920s. In 1918, techniques for the diagnosis of mental illness were not sophisticated. The medical services at home, working under immense pressure, had tried to filter out the mentally unfit from units embarking for France, but often there had been no time to do more than simply ask organizational commanders for lists of "dull, queer or nervous men" in their units. Many cases of "feeblemindedness" slipped through, greatly complicating the task of doctors in France trying to distinguish the shell-shocked and traumatized from the sound but slow. Some were diagnosed as psychoneurotic when they simply had a mental age of less than ten; what life on the battlefield can have been like for them is hard to imagine.

The medical authorities had had no idea of the number of mentally ill casualties they should expect. The debarkation hospital in Newport News, Virginia, was proudly scheduled to open on November 17, 1918, with 30 beds for acute psychoses, 110 for neuroses. Unfortunately, already on October 13 the Aeolus had docked with a total of 127 psychoses and 39 neuroses, plus 55 epilepsies, 18 "feebleminded," and 3 diseases of the nervous system. There was no advance notice, and the ship arrived with its crew ravaged by flu. "Two patients hung themselves on the ship, one on the last day of voyage and one while the transfer from boat to train was going on. The ship, of necessity, carried these patients between decks without lights from sunset to sunrise."

To try to understand the nature and effects of the war, Eleanor Roosevelt made herself visit the mental ward of Saint Elizabeth's Hospital in Washington, D.C. To be allowed to talk to the men, she had to be locked into the ward, and she never forgot the time she spent with battle-shocked sailors, "some chained to their beds, others unable to stop shouting of the horrors they had seen."

For the physically disabled, the administration had the best of intentions. Treatment was becoming far more enlightened, with a heavy emphasis on reabsorbing the disabled into the community and helping them to become self-sufficient again. Therapy and vocational training were to be offered to the disabled man "to enable him to enjoy the freedom and happiness afforded by worldwide democracy for which he has given his all." The Red Cross Institute for Crippled and Disabled Men in New York selected six main trades as suitable for the rehabilitated: the manufacture of artificial limbs; oxyacetylene welding; mechanical training; monotype casting in printing establishments; motion-picture operation; and jewelry making. Corps of "cheer up men," who had overcome their disabilities with the right spirit, were to be attached to transports and hospitals; and the Red Cross Institute organized "cripple parties" to put the wounded in touch with "successful cripples."

America, courtesy of its Civil War, already led the world, in company with the Germans and Danes, in the manufacture of artificial limbs. Italian boys prayed to the Madonna for 'an American leg.' Experience taught that complicated prostheses tended to break, so American manufacturers placed function before appearance. They made artificial feet enlarged soles for the disabled agricultural worker needing to walk on plowed soil, as well as arms to which devices could be attached for grasping the reins of a horse, grips for turning a cream separator, or a hook to hold a plow handle.

In some trades, of course, such as sales, looks did count. There one might be given the more attractive, better-groomed "*bras de parade*," or "Sunday arm," whose use had otherwise "fallen into disfavor except as a luxury for dress occasions or for the use . . . of men in occupations where appearance is an important factor in economic efficiency." Artificial eyes remarked the medical officers, "do contribute greatly to availability in the labor market and to peace of mind," and there was some pressure on authorities to provide a type of cosmetic ear that had been developed by the French. "The wounded man leaves the hospital . . . taking with him the model of his ear and a jar of paste, tinted to match his complexion, and he can make himself a new ear when he needs one, which will be usually about every eight days."

The highly efficient War Risk Insurance plan introduced by the administration had made certain that the great majority of men were insured against disability. But when the time came to administer the payments going out, officials found some difficulty in gauging the degree of affliction. It was safe, they decided, to allot $100 a month for "the loss of both feet or both hands or both eyes, or . . . becoming helplessly and permanently bedridden"—though one could never be sure that some of the men with these disabilities might not be capable of earning a decent living: "A man who has lost both arms now runs one of the busiest newsstands in New York City. A man who lost two legs, one arm and four fingers of the remaining hand is a flourishing business man in a Western State." One must make an effort, they concluded, to discount "the feeling of compassion that will persist for any visible mutilation of the human body even if it is proved to the intellect that the portion of the body which has been lost is of no economic importance." For all the pious hopes that went into the program, in 1926 veterans of the Civil War were still getting more in pensions than men living on World War disability awards.

As for the survivors, those neither killed nor seriously wounded, at the Armistice 1,980,654 men were in Europe, in transit, or in Russia. Another 1,689,998 were in camp in America. Getting home was the only thought in most men's minds. Captain Harry Truman, the future President, had served his country during 1918 as an artillery officer in the ill-fated 35th Division, so badly mauled in the Exermont ravine. In January 1919, he was still stuck in France, his only hope being that "Woodie" might soon "cease his gallivantin' around and send us home at once and quickly." The AEF, in Truman's opinion, did not "give a whoop (to put it mildly) whether Russia has a Red Government or no Government; and if the King of the Lollipops wants to slaughter his subjects or his Prime Minister, it's all the same to us."

In the cold and mud of winter in northern France, the tension of war relaxed into purposeless military routine and discipline began to be sorely tested. Large numbers of men with previously blameless records went AWOL, ending up in Paris. Others shot the light fixtures out of their billets or picked off chickens in village streets. Fifty-one new companies of military police were created. Trains carrying supplies for the American occupation forces in Germany were looted by gangs of veterans; four soldiers were killed on separate occasions by the same low bridge while riding on the top of a railroad car. A French soldier was killed by an American truck driven, in the words of the court-martial report, "at exaggerated speed, at least 20 kph."

When the veterans finally did reach home, they looked for some recognition of what they had achieved, some understanding of what they had endured; but time after time they were disappointed. After the welcome parades, they returned to their hometowns—to find, very often, that their jobs were gone. The special employment offices simply could not cope with the lines of veterans looking for work; by May 1919, more than eight thousand officers alone had asked for help finding jobs. Former engineers, clergymen, accountants, teachers, clerks, physicians, attorneys, dentists, brokers, all had been squeezed out of their former slots in society. In the ranks, hundreds of thousands of blue- and white-collar workers found their old jobs filled, at least temporarily, by women or blacks.

All around them, men who had stayed at home in war industries commanded what seemed like remarkable wages. The returnees were faced with astonishing price rises—food, clothing, and home furnishing all at nearly double the prices they remembered—and a government that apparently grudged them any help in meeting the bills. The veterans of earlier wars could look to their war bonuses to give them a start in their new life. But this administration was determined to avoid the colossal expenditure of the past, and there was violent argument in Congress over the appropriate reward for veterans' services. Not until 1924 would any allocation of bonuses be finally agreed on, and no actual payments would be made until 1945.

Veterans' bitterness found its way into some of the best and most enduring writing of the period. Some older writers, such as Willa Cather, Edith Wharton, and others who had helped but not fought, still found it possible to revel in the romance of war, and the popular conceptions of heroism and adventure died hard. But for those who had been to Europe with the AEF or the ambulance services, such as John Dos Passos, e e cummings, and Ernest

Hemingway, a far more typical reaction was to find creativity in anger, cynicism, and a kind of licensed rebellion. The scarred veteran, it was felt, was entitled to speak his mind. The writing of Laurence Stallings, who had lost a leg after injuries received at Belleau Wood, was powered at this stage, before nostalgia took a hand, exclusively by rancor. In his novel *Plumes,* the protagonist is obsessed by the secret treaties signed by America's allies, all the time "trying to face the fact that he threw himself away [in] . . . a brutal and vicious dance directed by ghastly men. It was the tragedy of our lives that we had to be mutilated at the pleasure of dolts and fools."

In *Company K,* William March attacked one of the standard texts of the old value system in his grotesque burlesque of an official letter of condolence:

> *Your son Francis, died needlessly at Belleau Wood. You will be interested to hear that at the time of his death he was crawling with vermin and weak from diarrhea. . . . A piece of shrapnel hit him and he died in agony, slowly. . . . He lived three full hours screaming and cursing. . . . He had nothing to hold onto, you see: He had learned long ago that what he had been taught to believe by you, his mother, who loved him, under the meaningless names of honor, courage, patriotism, were all lies.*

Disillusionment about the war and anguish at its aftermath were not confined to the ranks. Woodrow Wilson spent a sick, introspective, lonely retirement until his death on February 3, 1924, at the age of sixty-seven, living long enough to see his vision of the postwar world in ruins. His son-in-law William McAdoo, the financial powerhouse of his administration, had disappointments of his own, failing three times to win the Democratic nomination. Herbert Hoover, in contrast, would achieve his better-disguised ambition and win the presidency, only to become one of the most heavily criticized presidents in American history. Newton Baker turned his back on the world of the Army and returned to his life as a lawyer, becoming more conservative with age. Josephus Daniels, on the other hand, emerged more vocally liberal than ever. A newspaperman once more, except for a stretch as the American ambassador to Mexico, he violently attacked the activities of the Ku Klux Klan in North Carolina, championed the League of Nations and the World Court, and transferred his loyalties to Franklin D. Roosevelt.

Of the administration's "enemies within," John Reed died of typhus in Moscow in 1920. He lay in state for seven days guarded by Red Army soldiers, and thousands of workers came out into the sleet and snow to watch his interment in the Kremlin wall. "Big Bill" Haywood also took refuge in Russia, to avoid the twenty-year jail sentence waiting for him at home. Initially hailed as a revolutionary hero, he was devastated to discover that the Comintern no longer favored the IWW, having higher hopes of working through the American Federation of Labor. He died in Moscow in 1929, in his own eyes a traitor to his lifelong cause.

Of the "enemies without," none faced war crimes trials. Ludendorff allied his fortunes with a corporal in the German Army who on Armistice Day was lying in a hospital, temporarily blinded by mustard gas. In 1923, Ludendorff appeared on the same platform as Adolf Hitler at a huge rally in Nuremberg and took part in the failed attempt to seize control of the government of Bavaria. Acquitted of treason, the Second Reich's former Supreme

Commander stood for the presidency of the new republic in 1925; he came last in a contest that was won by Hindenburg, the man whose name he had made famous.

Ludendorff's end was ultimately less miserable than that of Henri Pétain, who, as the eighty-four-year-old head of the French government in 1940, would seek terms from the Germans; sentenced to death as the principal Vichy traitor and collaborator, Pétain would be spared only because of his age.

Of America's generals, Peyton March was perhaps treated the worst. His acerbic style had made many enemies in Congress, and, humiliatingly, they refused to grant him permanent rank as a full general after the war. Not until 1954, at the age of eighty-eight, would this great soldier receive any official thanks—and then the tribute was carefully worded, referring to his "selfless and patriotic interest in the United States Army *since his retirement.*"

March being what he was, he would not have been hurt half as much by personal pettiness as by the damage inflicted on the army organization that he had helped to revolutionize. Around the globe, other governments and military leaders were digesting the lessons of a first World War—most obviously, the lesson that total war required preparation in time of peace. March handed over piles of documents to staff officers in the imperial Japanese Army who were anxious to study the American mobilization. His intention was that this evidence of American effectiveness should act as a deterrent: "When those trained Japanese General Staff officers saw precisely what the nation at war meant in men and material, and the rapidity with which we had achieved the results we did . . . there would be no more Japanese problem. . . . It was certain to my mind that Japan would never want to go to war with us." In fact, during the 1920s and 1930s, the Japanese would build elaborate mobilization machinery, listing the nation's resources down to the last chauffeur, which would enable them to go to war with anyone.

In March's own country, on the other hand, Congress deliberately turned its back on the need to prepare in peacetime. Civilian America now balked at funding a large defense establishment. The General Staff had proposed a modified system of universal military service, producing citizen reservists to take the place of the National Army and a greatly increased and professionalized regular army. Congress would have none of either proposal; by mid-1923, the U.S. Army would be down to 131,254 men, little bigger than it had been in April 1917. Only a newly created Industrial College served to remind officers of the intimate connection between the smokestacks and the front line.

Meanwhile, Pershing received the nation's gratitude, a permanent full general commission and the title "General of the Armies of the United States." He became Chief of Staff and won a Pulitzer Prize for his wartime reminiscences (which were sharply critical of March). From time to time he visited Paris and Michette, and late in life he married her. When World War II came, he was an invalid, confined to the Walter Reed veterans hospital, where the news of war was brought to him by the man his influence had made Chief of Staff: George C. Marshall.

Marshall had defeated another AEF general for the post: Hugh Drum, who had also consistently risen in the postwar army. Douglas MacArthur had already scaled the heights of the Chief of Staff's post. In that role, it had been his task in May 1932, on the orders of President Herbert Hoover, to face the anger of 17,000 AEF veterans who had marched on the Capitol to demand the immediate payment of the bonus, during the depths of the Great Depression. Much as he may have sympathized with their plight, MacArthur had no hesitation in moving on two thousand of the most stubborn with tanks and tear gas, crushing their camps, and scattering the protestors.

The smooth rapidity of MacArthur's rise throws into sharp relief the bumpy passage of Billy Mitchell, another of the most brilliant of the younger men under Pershing's command. For all his drive and inventiveness, Mitchell had been forced to watch the record of America's air service in the war being spoiled by the chaos at home. During the last three months of the fighting, the air forces had been losing planes faster than they were arriving in France. In all, 677 American pilots had died over all, 508 of them in accidents and 263 of those before they ever left America. For every 100 trained pilots who reached the front line, 33 were killed. But just as the war ended, the American air effort was beginning to hit its stride. Satisfactory planes were being built and pilots recruited in large numbers; the service had grown from a mere 1,395 officers and men to almost 200,000.

Mitchell had seen many of his theories vindicated, and he had made the case for equal status for the air service most convincingly. The service was officially recognized as being on a par with the other wings of the Army under the Army Reorganization Act of June 1920. Mitchell's mistake was in the lack of restraint with which he then harried both Army and Navy commanders to boost their airpower further. In September 1925, he told journalists that the crash of a naval air balloon was the inevitable outcome of the Navy's neglect of aviation; the Army, he added, was no better. He was promptly court-martialed for "conduct prejudicial to good order and military discipline" and seven other offenses. Found guilty, he resigned from the Army the following year.

Saddest of all, perhaps, was the fate of Major Charles Whittlesey. The agony of his "Lost Battalion" stayed with him; he was decorated for his astonishing bravery and endurance, but the burden of suffering he had imposed on his men was too much for him to bear. In 1926, eight years after leading the pathetic remnants of his unit out of their death trap in the Argonne Forest, he put his affairs in order and boarded a boat for Cuba. In mid-ocean he disappeared from the vessel, one more victim of this most terrible of wars.

"Fear Itself": Depression Life

Robert S. McElvaine

To most Americans who escaped the ravages of the Depression, as to almost all Americans today, the unemployed of the 1930s were part of a faceless mass. Many pitied them, some despised them, most tried to ignore them. Few attempted to understand them. Such an understanding must begin with the realization that they were individuals, not statistics. They were a diverse lot, with cleavages along racial, religious, ethnic, sexual, occupational, age, regional, and other lines. Some were proud, others beaten. Some were optimistic, others had lost all hope. Some blamed themselves, others cursed businessmen, politicians, the "system," or "the Interests." They were, to be sure, victims, but they were not *only* victims. In most cases they had no part in the cause of their suffering, but the ways in which they reacted to their plight form a large—although poorly understood—portion of the history of the Depression.

Here I try to follow anthropologist Clifford Geertz's prescription for cultural analysis. "A good interpretation of anything," Geertz has said, "takes us into the heart of that of which it is the interpretation." "Mass unemployment," Cabell Phillips has noted, "is both a statistic and an empty feeling in the stomach. To fully comprehend it, you have to both see the figures and feel the emptiness." The principal goal is to go into the center of the Depression experience and attempt to feel the emptiness; in short, to blend social and intellectual history through an excursion into the minds of working-class Americans.

Undoubtedly the main reason that this topic has been so long neglected is the difficulty of approaching it. Working people are largely absent from the traditional types of historical documentation. Yet many sources do exist. The Depression and its effects upon its victims proved to be an irresistible subject for many sociologists and psychologists in the 1930s. The resulting contemporary investigations are also extremely valuable sources of information. The most important kinds of evidence are those that bring us into contact with individual working-class people of the Depression era. Several varieties of such personal

Source: Chapter Eight, "'Fear Itself:' Depression Life," by Robert S. McElvaine, reprinted from *The Great Depression, America 1929–1941*, 1993, Random House, Inc.

sources are extant. Field investigators sent out by the Federal Emergency Relief Administration and, later, the Works Progress Administration, to report back to Federal Relief Administrator Harry Hopkins on conditions and attitudes among the poor provide us with a wealth of information. The fact that we receive our impressions of working-class thought through the eyes and words of middle-class investigators should make us cautious. Even so, the reports add much to our understanding. Interviewers hired by the WPA Federal Writers' Project collected thousands of personal histories from "ordinary" Americans in the late thirties. These, too, are a significant addition to our knowledge of working-class culture.

The most useful source of direct contact with the people of the thirties is the immense collection of letters that were addressed to public figures, especially to Franklin and Eleanor Roosevelt. These communications bring us into direct contact with more than 15 million Depression-era Americans, a majority of them laborers, clerks, and farmers. By weaving together the various types of evidence and using one kind as a check on the indications found in another, we can begin to understand the lives and values of American workers in the Great Depression. What follows is a composite of the Depression experience, using the words of Depression victims from all these sources.

For those workers who had enjoyed at least a taste of prosperity in the 1920s, the initial blow of the Depression was crushing. The twenties had seen the traditional middle-class American values, which taught that success and failure went to those who deserved them and which stressed acquisitive individualism, spread widely among workers. Such workers had been pleased to think that their modest accomplishments in the twenties were the result of their selection—whether by Calvin's God or Darwin's Nature depended upon one's viewpoint—for success. Like the Republican party, which had taken credit for good times and hence found it difficult to escape blame for bad times, Americans who had claimed responsibility for personal gains found it difficult not to feel guilty when confronted with failure.

A widespread attitude of the unemployed early in the Depression was: "There must be something wrong with a fellow who can't get a job." *Sure, I've lost my job, but I'm still a worthy provider. Work will turn up soon.* Every morning up before dawn, washed, shaved, and dressed as neatly as possible. To the factory gates, only to find a hundred others already there, staring blankly at the sign: NO HELP WANTED. The search then became more feverish. One day in 1934 a man in Baltimore walked twenty miles in search of a job. "I just stopped every place," he said, "but mostly they wouldn't even talk to me." *Perhaps an employment agency? A long wait, but it will be worth it to get a job. At last a chance.* The questions: name, age, experience. Yes, well, we'll see what we can do, but there are already more than a hundred men in our files with similar backgrounds, and most of them are younger than you. Employers can be choosy, you know. It's a buyer's market. Why hire a man who is over forty, when there are plenty of unemployed men still in their twenties? Business has to be efficient, after all. "A man over forty might as well go out and shoot himself," said a despairing Chicago resident in 1934.

Gradually those over forty, though fit physically, began to *feel* old and *look* and *act* poor. Keeping up the appearance necessary to secure employment, particularly of the white-collar variety, became increasingly difficult. As an Oklahoma woman put it in a letter to Eleanor Roosevelt in 1934, "The unemployed have been so long with out food-clothes-shoes-medical care-dental care etc-we look pretty bad-so when we ask for a job we don't get it. And we look and feel a little worse each day—when we ask for food they call us bums—it isent our fault . . . no we are not bums." Yet, "with shabby suits, frayed collars, worn shoes and perhaps a couple of front teeth gone," men *looked* like bums. "We do not dare to use even a little soap," wrote a jobless Oregonian, "when it will pay for an extra egg a few more carrots for our children."

As the days without finding a job became weeks, the weeks months, and the months years, it came to be more difficult even to look for work. ". . . You can get pretty discouraged and your soles can get pretty thin after you've been job hunting a couple of months," a Minnesota Depression victim pointed out. First you came to accept the idea of taking a job of lower quality than you thought you deserved. Then you began to wonder just what you did deserve. It came finally, for some, to be a matter of begging. "For God's sake, Mister, when are you going to give us work?" "How," asked the daughter of a long-unemployed man, "can you go up and apply for a job without crying?"

Modern industrial society does not provide a place or position for a person; rather, it requires him to make his own place—and to strive to better it. This is taken to be the measure of one's individual worth. Americans had been brought up on the belief that meaningful work is the basis of life. Without such work, people felt they had no reason for being. "Drives a man crazy," said a seventy-five-year-old former knifemaker, "or drives him to drink, hangin' around." One must, as a St. Louis man said in 1933, "get the job to keep his mind and body whole."

Community attitudes toward the unemployed sometimes added to the feelings of guilt, shame, inferiority, fear, and insecurity. Many of those who remained employed made it plain that they believed that "something is wrong with a man who can't support his family." "Taxpayers" complained of paying for the upkeep of "thieves and lazy, immoral people," "no good for nothing loafers," "human parasites," and "pampered poverty rats."

Although some of the unemployed successfully resisted the psychological effects of such verbal attacks, others were likely to hear internal as well as external voices telling them that they were to blame for their plight. "I'm just no good, I guess," a Houston woman told a caseworker in 1934. "I've given up ever amounting to anything. It's no use." "I'd kinda like to think I could get a job and hold it," an Oklahoma WPA worker said at the end of the Depression.

As scant resources ran out, self-blame often grew into the shame of having to seek assistance. In some areas, people "would almost starve rather than ask for help." Indeed, some of their fellow citizens expected no less from them. "I have had too much self respect for my self and Family to beg anything," wrote a North Carolina man in 1933. "I would be only too glad to dig ditches to keep my family from going hungry." But there were no ditches to be dug. For many, there seemed "little to look forward to save charity," with all the stigma that implied. The loss of one's "good standing" was a matter of great concern. The thought of seeking charity was "very distasteful and humiliating."

Desperation began to take over. For many, nighttime was the worst. "What is going to become of us?" wondered an Arizona man. "I've lost twelve and a half pounds this last month, just thinking. You can't sleep, you know. You wake up about 2 A.M., and you lie and think." When you could sleep, bad dreams were likely. Worry and fear became dominant. Sometimes you would look at your children and wonder what would happen to them. Sheer terror would suddenly overcome you. Some say you appear to be shell-shocked; others tell you that you look like a frightened child. And well you should, because at times that's just the way you feel. Often you cry like a youngster; you try to do it privately, but you know the children hear you at night.

Of course you try to forget. For some, alcohol was a means of escape. It was not much help when you were hungry, though. "It's funny," a nineteen-year-old in Providence said. "A lot of times I get offered a drink. It seems like people don't want to drink alone. But no one ever offers me a meal. Most of the time when I take a drink it makes me sick. My stomach's too empty."

An alternative to drinking was withdrawal from social contacts. Convinced that you are a failure, you try to avoid your friends, fearing that they will look upon you with scorn or, what is sometimes worse, pity. Thus you are unlikely to find out that many of your friends have also fallen victim to the Depression. In this small, hothouse world, self-blame, shame, and self-pity bloom magnificently.

As desperation grows worse the choices narrow. "My children have not got no shoes and clothing to go to school with," a West Virginia man complained in 1935, "and we havent got enough bed clothes to keep us warm." You resort to using old coats in lieu of blankets. *What can be done? What of the children? They are cold and hungry, but* "to do anything desperette now they would never live down the disgrace." "What is a man to do?" You face "a complete nervous breakdown as a result of being idle. . . . What is the next move for a desperate man? To commit some crime in this time of need?" When "all else has failed," one must do something. Is it wrong to steal coal to keep your family warm? Survival becomes the goal, the justification. Much like the slaves of the Old South, some Depression victims developed a distinction between *stealing* (from a fellow sufferer) and what the slaves had called *taking* (what you need and can convince yourself is rightfully yours because its possessor has exploited you or others like you). To some, it was acceptable to get "busy" and bring "home some extra money," as the wife of a Michigan WPA man put it. "I'd steal if I had the guts," declared a Rhode Island boy.

If not crime, what? How long can I take it? Is there no hope? Perhaps the only thing left is to "end it all." If no one will help, "than [*sic*] I will take my life away," said a Detroit woman in 1935. Suicide at times "seemed the only solution." "The Atlantic calls from our shores that there is plenty of room for us," a Massachusetts woman proclaimed. Suicide would be the ultimate admission of defeat, but it might appear "as the best way out," as it did to a New York woman who stated, "I am not a coward but good Lord it is awful to stand helpless when you need things." "Can you be so kind as to advise me as to which would be the most human way to dispose of my self and family, as this is about the only thing that I see left to do," a Pennsylvania man inquired in 1934. "No home, no work, no money. We cannot go along this way. They have shut the water supply from us. No means of sanitation. We can not keep the children clean and tidy as they should be."

Relatively few, of course, actually took the fatal step, but many Depression victims appear to have considered it. An FERA investigator in New York City reported late in 1934 that "almost every one of her clients" had "talked of suicide at one time or another." The programs of the New Deal may have persuaded some that life might still hold some hope. "You have saved my life," a New Jersey woman wrote, referring to assistance she had received from the Home Owners' Loan Corporation. "I would have killed myself If I would have lost my house."

Sometimes the decision of whether to seek assistance was a question of socially determined sex roles. An Italian man in Massachusetts, for instance, threatened to kill himself, his wife, and children because he was about to lose his house. It was unacceptable for *him* to ask for help. His wife saved the day by appealing to a neighbor for a loan. The bulk of the help-seeking letters of the thirties were written by women to Eleanor Roosevelt. What was inappropriate behavior for most men—"begging"—was proper for women, either because women were believed to be naturally weak or because a mother seeking help was not showing weakness, but playing her accepted role.

Thousands of the down-and-out, almost all of them women, wrote to Mrs. Roosevelt asking for old clothes. Americans facing adversity clung to their traditions and pride as long as possible, but the Depression forced many to set aside the former and swallow the latter, lest they have nothing at all to swallow. Clothing was considered an area of female responsibility. "Please do not think this does not cause a great feeling of shame to me to have to ask for old clothing," an Iowa woman wrote to the First Lady in 1936. "I am so badly in need of a summer coat and under things and dresses. oh don't think that it is not with a effort I ask you to please send me anything you may have on hand in that line which you don't care to wear yourself." "I can sew and would only be too glad to take two old things and put them together and make a new one," wrote a desperate Philadelphia woman. "I don't care what it is, any thing from an old bunch of stockings to an old Sport Suit or an old afternoon dress, in fact. Any-thing a lady 40 years of age can wear."

Although men were more plentiful among writers asking for direct financial assistance than among those seeking clothing, women appear to have outnumbered men in this category as well. Men might be as pleased as women to receive help, but their expected sex role made it more difficult for them to ask. To do so would be further admission of failure as a provider.

That so many wrote to the Roosevelts seeking help was indicative of the views most Depression-era workers had of the First Family. Such people often saw FDR in a fashion much like the European peasant who, as Oscar Handlin put it, thought "of the religious figure of the sanctified King as his distant protector who, if only he were told, would surely intercede for his devoted subjects." Letters to Roosevelt echoed this attitude. "You honor sir and your royalty. Majesty," began a 1935 letter to the President from an incapacitated black man in Georgia. When he heard Roosevelt speak over the radio in 1932, a Kansas man said, it seemed "as though some Moses had come to alleviated us of our sufferings."

The special relationship between the Roosevelts and the downtrodden made it possible to think that asking for help from that source was somehow different from seeking charity. One might even convince oneself that a modicum of independence was being preserved if help came from one's "personal friends" in the White House. Grasping at hope, a woman could ask Mrs. Roosevelt to intercede with the manager of a contest "and ask him kindly to give me a prize."

When the hope for prizes and direct assistance from the "royal family" flickered out, little was left but to apply for the dreaded dole. Any savings you once had were either lost in bank failures or long since used up. You have asked friends and relatives for a little help more times than is likely to keep them friendly. The grocer has allowed your bill to go up, but now he has said that he can do no more. Pay some of it or go hungry. By now you have been hungry—*really* hungry—for several days. A twelve-year-old boy in Chicago summed it up in a letter: "We haven't paid 4 months rent, Everyday the landlord rings the door bell, we don't open the door for him. We are afraid that will be put out, been put out before, and don't want to happen again. We haven't paid the gas bill, and the electric bill, haven't paid grocery bill for 3 months." *Something* must be done. Survival being prerequisite to independence, the latter must be sacrificed, if only temporarily. So at last it is that painful walk to the local school, which houses the relief office.

You walk by a number of times, trying to get up the nerve to go in. What if your children—or their friends—see you? Finally, it can be delayed no longer. *Why is that policeman there?* Surely *you* have recently felt like breaking something; maybe others are also on the verge of destructive acts. Still, seeing that uniform and gun does not make you any more comfortable. You tell the clerk what you are there for. You are mumbling. Speak up! he says, impatiently. (He is on relief, too, and has few qualifications and little training for the delicate position he holds.) You finally make yourself understood. (*What* else *would you have been there for? Why did he even have to ask?*) Take a seat. Your name will be called.

The "intake" room is crowded. You sit down, focusing your gaze on one of the holes in your shoes. After a while your eyes, thoughtlessly moving about, make contact with those of another applicant. He looks away as quickly as you do. *How can so many people be failures? . . . What's taking them so long? Do they think I have all day? . . . Come to think of it, I guess I do. What a failure I am! . . . The stink in this place is awful!*

Two hours later you realize that your name is being called—for the second time. You rise slowly and go over to the desk. The questions bother you. *Yes, four months since we paid the rent. Yes, we have been evicted before. No, we lost the car months ago. The radio? It's paid for, and it isn't worth enough to keep us fed for a week. Can't we keep it? That's all?* You can go home and wait. An investigator will visit you in a few days. More questions, more embarrassment, further degradation. Pauperization, that's what it is. *How did this happen?* You have become "something anonymous who will presently be more or less fed." *What's that? It may be several weeks before we get any help? How do we eat in the meantime? If we had anything at all left, I wouldn't be here now.*

The shame persists, but eventually it may give way to despair and, then, apathy, particularly among those on direct relief. "Why the Hell should I get up in the morning, lady?" asked a youth of twenty. "What am I going to do with all these days? . . . I've been looking for a job for four years. I've had two. Five months in all. After a while you know it ain't getting you anywhere. There's nothing for us!" Many were bewildered. An FERA investigator described Americans in 1934 as being "terrifyingly patient." "They are sick, mentally and physically," a New York Home Relief Bureau supervisor had said of Depression victims a year earlier. "They have given up even trying to look for work. The majority have become so apathetic that they accept without questioning us whatever we give them, no matter how pitifully inadequate it is or how badly administered."

Such dole recipients were variously characterized as listless, "sinking into indifference," lethargic, and "too docile, too much licked to put up any fight." One FERA investigator described providing relief for such people as "a kind of desperate job like getting the wounded off the battlefield so that they can die quietly at the base hospital."

Apathy, too, was a stage, one beyond which many of the unemployed moved after the New Deal had taken root. Sooner or later those sets of eyes in the relief office would meet. One would see "that there were other fellows who didn't look such a bad sort or low mentality in the same fix he was." It made you feel a little better. "Bit by bit," an FERA investigator reported from Bethlehem, Pennsylvania, late in 1934, "these men discovered that it was bolstering their morale to swap experiences and reactions and to realize that their situation was the result of a social condition, not a personal failure." And if the government had accepted responsibility for providing relief, the problem must not be the fault of the individual.

For such people, resentment began to displace self-blame and apathy. If it is not your fault, why should you suffer the indignities of the relief system? Relief "clients" began to object to the young college women who often served as caseworkers. (Not always without reason. One in California visited "her clients in a very elegant riding costume—breeches, top boots, crop, and all!") "We get work from the Relief as the little young folks thinks we need it," complained a Georgia woman. "They have always been used to plenty. Don't know how hard it is for folks like us."

Among the common criticisms of relief was that recipients were treated as children: given food orders instead of cash, instructed by nutrition experts, investigated by "busybodies," and generally "regimented." "Why should it be 'dished' out to us like we were *little children*, and tell us exactly what every cent should be spent for?" asked a Californian. People who had "always managed to raise their children and feed them without advice from the outside" were unenthusiastic about such lectures. They wanted to be on their own, to have cash to buy what and where they chose, to spend it on beer every now and then, if they so desired. Although relief recipients had already become far more dependent than most of them wished to be, they wanted to retain as much independence as possible, even within the relief system.

What gave relief "clients" the chance to reassert their independence was the opportunity for work relief, first with the CWA and later with the WPA. Self-respect could finally begin to return. When a New York relief investigator told a man who had been receiving grocery orders that there was a CWA job for him, she related, "He grabbed me, swung me right up off the floor, and hugged me." When he went to work, the man left an hour earlier than necessary.

People on WPA jobs spoke with heartfelt conviction about their preference for this type of assistance. "My pride took an awful beating when I had to apply for relief," a fifty-one-year-old Minneapolis man recalled in 1940, "but I feel different about this [WPA]. Here I am working for what I'm getting." "It means," a woman said of the WPA, "that I can look people in the eye because I'm not on a dole . . . it isn't like relief. Being on relief just breaks you all up." Another man spoke of the WPA enabling him "to sleep nights instead of lying awake thinking of desperate things I might do."

By 1935 the attitude of many Depression victims toward relief had changed. Complaints increased. Shame over being on public assistance was replaced in some by anger at the smallness of payments and at relief administrators. A Muncie, Indiana, housewife expressed the latter view when she wrote, "Those in charge of relief have never lain awake at night worrying about unpaid rent, or how to make a few groceries do for the seemingly endless seven days. . . ." "It is always," she continued, "the people with full stomachs who tell us poor people to keep happy."

In the mid-thirties many of the unemployed concluded that relief simply amounted to Depression victims getting what was rightfully theirs. Social workers were reporting as early as 1934 that some people seemed to think "that the Government actually owes it [relief] to them." Lorena Hickok called such recipients "gimmies." Some, an Iowa relief administrator wrote, had "adopted a more demanding attitude" and were "willing for the government to see them through." People on public assistance in Salt Lake City developed a slang of their own. Significantly, they referred to the FERA as "Santa Claus." In many places, groups of angry unemployed people gathered at relief offices and harassed the administrators with their demands for better treatment. Within the context of a basically dependent situation, relief recipients were finding means by which to express their independence.

Whatever the changes in attitudes toward relief and dependence as the Depression continued, the psychological problems for the unemployed remained devastating. For many Americans who avoided the ravages of the Depression, it became an article of faith that relief recipients irresponsibly had children for whom they could not provide. Some conservatives charged that relief women had babies in order to qualify for higher payments. Even FERA investigators were not above accepting such notions. "On the relief rolls," wrote Martha Gellhorn in 1934, "it is an accepted fact that the more incapable and unequipped (physically, mentally, materially) the parents, the more offspring they produce." "Apparently," she concluded in another report, "the instinct of self-preservation is not very well developed in the working class American."

For the victims, however, the problem was far more complex. Some social workers excused poverty-ridden, hopeless young women who had illegitimate children, because "their lives are so empty that they fall prey to anything which offers momentary escape from the horror of their lives." Although this view was not without some validity, the problem was more complicated. For many "forgotten women" of the thirties, the question of intercourse, birth control, and having children were among the most gnawing of the Depression years. The wife of a Massachusetts WPA worker (and mother of his eleven children) voiced one aspect of the difficulty: "Ya know down at the Catholic Charities they tell ya your not supposed ta have children if you're on the W.P.A. An' in the church they tell ya you're not supposed ta do anything about it. An' they say you're supposed ta live with your man. Now what's a woman gonna do?"

Even for women without religious qualms about birth control sexual questions caused anguish. A woman in the San Joaquin Valley haltingly told Lorena Hickok of something "that had nearly driven her crazy" and that "she knew was one of the worst problems of women whose husbands are out of work." Almost no one in such circumstances *wanted* to have babies, but "here you are, surrounded by young ones you can't support and never knowing when there's going to be another. You don't have any money to buy anything at the drugstore. All you have is a grocery order. I've known women to try to sell some of their groceries to get a little money to buy the things needed."

This still did not describe the depth of the problem, however. "I suppose," the woman continued, "you can say the easiest way would be not to do it. But it wouldn't be. You don't know what it's like when your husband's out of work. He's gloomy and unhappy all the time. Life is terrible. You must try all the time to keep him from going crazy. And many times—that's the only way."

Pleasure in the Depression was, to be sure, often limited to such inexpensive pastimes. In many places, meat and fruit were rarities. One woman bought a dozen oranges with part of her husband's first CWA check. "I hadn't tasted any for so long," she explained, "that I had forgotten what they were like!" People were gloomy. "I know a party that has got a radio + spends some of his money for beer," a Vermont woman wrote to President Roosevelt. Her family was not so fortunate: "We don't have no pleasure of any kind."

The absence of pleasure sometimes produced family problems. "What about the children who's parents can't give their children the little things in life such as a cone of cream or a 1 *cts* piece of candy or a soft drink once a week," asked a Kentuckian. "Who will get the blame for this neglect The father of course. . . . Do you think it is right that we poor never have the pleasure of a show or a trip back home. Just stay at home and watch others have all the fun good eats fine automobiles town houses, country homes. . . ." Other family problems grew out of the quest for pleasure on empty pocketbooks. "Half the men you have Put to work taken their maney When they get Paid an spends it for whiskey," a Nashville woman complained to FDR. "If my husban new that I wrote this he would kill me," she added in a postcript.

The lack of money, work, and self-esteem caused even greater family troubles. Unemployment upset the traditional roles of father, mother, and children. Since the father's position was based upon his occupation and his role as provider, the loss of his job was likely to mean a decline in his status within the family. The man who was without a position was, well, without a position. It was he who was supposed to provide independence for the family. Having little to do, unemployed men hung around home much of the time. In doing so, they infringed upon the sphere of the wife. If the husband blamed himself for his loss of income, the wife might try to encourage him. At first most did. But as hardships grew, and as the man sitting by the kitchen stove began to irritate his wife, the latter was increasingly likely to see, and point out, faults in her mate. And as his resentment and guilt expanded, he was apt to find more in his wife's actions that displeased him. Quarrels became more numerous.

Being "on relief" stigmatized an entire family, but most especially the father. Male dominance was endangered in the Depression. It asserted itself in odd ways. In some cases, most family resources were devoted to obtaining clothes for the man. "The women," it was concluded, "can stay inside and keep warm, and the children can stay home from school." There were cases, however, where a father was obliged to share his son's clothes. "They're all we've got now," said a North Dakota farmer. "We take turns wearing 'em." The symbolism for the breadwinner must have been apparent.

The traditional role of the mother is far less dependent than that of the father on the family's status in the outside world. The Depression was, accordingly, less harmful to mothers' positions inside their families. John Steinbeck said it well in *The Grapes of Wrath*: "Woman can change better'n a man,' Ma said soothingly. 'Woman got all her life in her arms. Man got it all in his head.'" Some women simply took over for their unemployed husbands. In one case, a man first learned of his wife's decision to rent another house "when he came home to find the furniture had been moved." But mothers' roles were also upset by the economic breakdown. Distribution of relief commodities, Chicago social workers pointed out, "deprived the housewife of the privilege of shopping and in a sense destroyed their responsibility as housewives." Nor was it easy for "a mother to hear her hungry babe whimpering in the night and growing children tossing in their sleep because of knawing plain HUNGER," as an Oregon woman put it. "I have laid many a night & cried my self to sleep when I think of what I have to work with," wrote a Pennsylvania mother.

People did their best to maintain traditional roles. If a woman must work for her family to survive, so be it. The reemergence of a family economy of pooled resources was one means of maintaining family independence. "But soon's the men get goin' the wife's through," a Portuguese fisherman in Massachusetts said. "She stays home then. Yes ma'am, we like our wives to be home." Of course spouses who continued to cooperate during the Depression helped each other make it through with a minimum of upheaval. "We got enough ta get along on, and we got each other. That should be enough ta make any body happy," declared a shoe machinery worker. For all the problems, in fact, available evidence indicates that the families of many unemployed men continued to operate under the direction of the traditional head, with little apparent change in internal status. The principal effect of the Depression on internal family relationships, in fact, was to exaggerate the qualities and tendencies already present. The additional strain was often too much for weak families to withstand, but strong relationships usually weathered the hard times successfully.

Discrimination against women in employment became worse with the Depression. It was easy to assert that women were taking jobs that otherwise would go to male heads of households. Norman Cousins stated this argument in its most simplistic form in 1939: "There are approximately 10,000,000 people out of work in the United States today; there are also 10,000,000 or more women, married and single, who are jobholders. Simply fire the women, who shouldn't be working anyway, and hire the men. Presto! No unemployment. No relief rolls. No depression." Those who made such statements usually had little interest in facts, but most women who worked outside the home during the Depression clearly did so out of necessity. They supported themselves and their families just as did male "breadwinners." Such was the case not only with single women, but also with most working married women, whose husbands were either unemployed or paid too little to provide for their families. Nonetheless, campaigns against hiring married women were common in the 1930s. Fully 77 percent of the school districts in the United States would not hire married women to teach; 50 percent of them had a policy of firing women who married.

Despite the prejudice against women—especially married women—working, their numbers in the work force actually increased, both absolutely and as a percentage of all workers, during the Depression. In 1930, women had represented 24.3 percent of all workers; in 1940, 25.1 percent of the work force was female. Similarly, the proportion of women workers who were married increased in the face of Depression-era discrimination, from 28.8 percent at the beginning of the decade to 35 percent at its end. This seemingly remarkable development resulted from several causes.

Most women who sought employment, before as well as during the Depression, did so because the economic realities of American life obliged them to work. Most families in this country have aspired to an "American standard of living," which has always been ill defined, but is something clearly above mere subsistence. Early in the present century it was not possible for working-class families to reach that level on the wages of one adult male. The income of the father was often supplemented by the wages of children. As child labor declined, wives filled the resulting gap in family income. The living standards of most families improved in the 1920s. When the Depression hit, even those families that did not *need* the wife's extra income in an absolute sense, needed it if they were to stay close to the standard that they had enjoyed during prosperity. As husbands lost their jobs, had their wages cut, or became increasingly fearful that they *might* become unemployed, wives who had not previously worked outside the home sought jobs. Here was a distinct—and often overlooked—irony of the Depression: as jobs became much more difficult to find, far *more* people began looking for work. One estimate held that 2.5 million more people were in the work force in 1937 than there would have been had there been no depression. Most of these new workers were women, so one reason that more women found jobs in the thirties was simply that more sought them.

This might seem to support the claim that women were displacing men from jobs, but another reason for the increase in female workers refutes that argument. Women lost proportionately fewer jobs than men precisely because their types of employment were *not* considered interchangeable. There existed many positions that were identified as "women's work": domestic service, primary education, many clerical and social service jobs. Such situations remained available to women regardless of how many men were out of work. The Depression itself placed women in a relatively better position for obtaining work—poorly paid, of course—than men. "[I]deas that once had consigned women to inferior places in the labor force," historian Alice Kessler-Harris has pointed out, "now preserved for them jobs that menfolk could not get." The economic collapse hit hardest just those sectors of the economy (especially heavy industry) that had barred women workers. The fields in which women were most likely to be employed suffered a lesser decline and, as in the case of clerical work (in the new government agencies), social services, and education, actually grew under the impact of the New Deal. A 1940 study found that in the five most depressed industries women represented only 2 percent of the employees. In the employment categories with the smallest drop in employment, on the other hand, women held 30 percent of the jobs. In a strange sense, women might be said to have benefited from past employment discrimination against them.

Before we become too envious of women workers during the Depression, though, it is well to remember what sort of jobs were reserved for them and what they were paid. At the end of the decade fully one-fifth of all women who worked for wages were employed as domestic servants. Live-in maids in the mid-thirties earned less than $8 per week in New York City, the highest-paying locality in the country. Other women workers were better paid, but not by much. One-fourth of the NRA codes permitted lower rates of pay for women than men. The federal government not only allowed discrimination, it practiced it. Men on WPA projects were paid $5 per day; women received only $3.

Women workers during the Depression also had to face increased psychological pressures. Antagonism from male workers and from wives who remained at home was intensified by the general mistaken belief that women were taking jobs from men. And at a time when their traditional nurturing role seemed especially needed in the home, women who were obliged to work for wages carried a particularly heavy burden of guilt. One study placed the blame for "truancy, incorrigibility, robbery, teenage tantrums, and difficulty in managing children" on the "mother's absence at her job."

Given all the obstacles working wives faced during the Depression, it is not surprising that many people came to associate employment of women outside the home with harsh, undesirable economic conditions. In the thirties an ideal came to be formed among many Americans—women as well as men—of what American family life ought to be like. It was summed up in the answer the vice president of a United Auto Workers local made to a 1939 complaint a union member's wife had made about married women working. "Some day, Dear Sister, I hope we will reach that economic ideal where the married woman will find her place in the home caring for children, which is God's greatest gift to women and her natural birthright," Mike Mannini wrote. Here was an example of a very important part of the origins of what Betty Friedan later called "the feminine mystique." The return of the wife and mother to her "natural" sphere came during the Great Depression to be a goal, the achievement of which would be a sign of the return of "good times."

In those families where there was turmoil during the Depression, the children often suffered. Fathers (and mothers) might take out their frustrations on the children. As the effects of unemployment, shame, and worry became noticeable in parents, children grew more anxious. "The children all seem to be so excitable and high-strung these days," said a New York settlement house kindergarten teacher. "I can't help thinking it's due to the distress at home."

Why do we live like this, a child would wonder. *Things used to be better. We're not even clean anymore. Mama says the relief doesn't give enough for soap. And the bedbugs. In our old house we never had anything like that!* What's wrong with Daddy? Times are hard, they say, but "all the other little girls are getting Easter dresses." "Our friends have skates and we are not able to buy them." *Surely it's not Daddy's fault; he's the greatest. Why, he's been on relief longer than the other kids' fathers—that's* something.

How can you go to school when the other kids know your family has been evicted before and people are saying your father's not paying the rent now? *Why should* I *be the one who has* "to put a piece of cardboard in the sole of my shoe to go to school"? All the questions in a young mind. "My father he staying home. All the time he's crying because he can't find work. I told him why are you crying daddy, and daddy said why shouldn't I cry when there is nothing in the house. I feel sorry for him. That night I couldn't sleep."

The special times that usually bring joy to children and parents were often the hardest to bear during the Depression. Christmas could be particularly painful. "My little children talking about Santa Claus," a Texas father wrote to the President in 1934, "and I hate to see Xmas come this time because I know it will be one of the dullest Xmas they ever witnessed." A Virginia mother described a similar problem. "My little boy was speaking of Santa Claus 'He says why is it most children gets pretty toys and so many seems like they are rich and we so poor' This made tears come in my eyes," she said. "Then I told him if we are ever lucky enough to get work we will try to get him something pretty. I have to tell him of some happy day which may come."

While many adults compared Franklin Roosevelt to Lincoln, Moses, or Jesus, for some children the President was Santa Claus. Two Rhode Island boys, for instance, wrote their annual Christmas letter in 1935, but mailed it to Washington rather than the North Pole. They wanted bicycles or microscope-chemistry sets. Other children who sought gifts from the jolly man in the White House were more practical. "We have no one to give us a Christmas presents," wrote a ten-year-old Ohio girl, "and if you want to buy a Christmas present please buy us a stove to do our cooking and to make good bread." Such were the holiday thoughts of some children in 1935.

Although the children of the thirties lived through the same economic hardship as their parents did, it meant different things to the new generation. For one thing, children were largely free from the self-blame and shame that were so common among their elders. Obviously economic problems were not the fault of a child. He could rest assured that *he* had not failed. Adults might have botched things up; perhaps Dad was a failure, but few children felt any personal guilt. The Depression's most significant psychological problem was generally absent in the young.

The hardships many families faced in the thirties led children to assume greater responsibilities at an earlier age than has been customary in the years since World War II. It has been said with accuracy that there were no working-class "teenagers" in the 1930s. The generation had no time for an irresponsible, prolonged adolescence. Challenges had to be met. Often children (especially boys) were called upon to supplement meager family incomes by working after school (or in place of school). When mothers found it necessary—and possible—to get jobs, older children (especially girls) were given the responsibility of looking after their younger brothers and sisters.

Although the loss of any appreciable portion of one's childhood is tragic, there were some compensations for the youth of the thirties. The work thrust upon children in the Depression was likely to instill in them what industrial society commonly considers to be virtues: dependability, self-reliance, order, awareness of the needs of others, and practice in managing money. To the extent that the Depression furthered the development of such qualities in the young, it had a strikingly different effect on the children than on their elders. Ironically, the same family hardship that might weaken the self-reliance of a father could strengthen that quality in his child.

If being a child in the thirties was difficult, but at least on occasion rewarding, being a young adult presented problems with few compensations. Americans have always been future-oriented. If things were not quite perfect at the moment, just wait for tomorrow or next year. This attitude has been especially associated with the young.

In this as in so much else, however, the 1930s were different. Not that optimism did not survive, at least below the surface. Throughout the Depression, the slightest good news was sufficient to activate the latent hopefulness in some Americans. The creation of the CWA and the implementation of the corn loans brightened the outlook in Iowa to the point that an Irish man shouted, "In another 20 days we'll be out of the depression!" In the late spring of 1934, Lorena Hickok temporarily convinced herself that "people are in a pretty contented, optimistic frame of mind. They just aren't thinking about the Depression any more," she said, displaying at least as much optimism as she thought she detected in others. Speaking of the reaction of drought-stricken Colorado ranchers to two cloudbursts, she said, "Funny how people will cheer up if given half a chance!" "If only they will be patient, circumstances will work themselves out, and every-thing will be O.K.," a Wisconsin woman wrote in 1935. Even after a full decade of depression, WPA workers could be found in 1940 expressing faith in the future. "My idea," said an Oklahoma laborer, "is that all this is just a temporary thing, but it'll give us a chance to get another start if jobs will just pick up."

Despite the persistence of such attitudes in some quarters, though, the future looked bleak to many in the thirties. When asked "what his hope for the future was," an ex-truck driver gave a typical answer in 1934: "I just don't know." In the same year, Oklahoma relief recipients were said to "no longer have the 'chin up' attitude." Rather, they "lived in constant fear of what the next day or next week would bring." Young people simply had "nothing to look forward to." Many of the young—at just the stage in life in which the future often appears limitless—were nearly without hope during the Depression years. Older people, FERA investigator Martha Gellhorn pointed out, could "remember an easier life, a less stringent world." They refused "to believe that the end had inevitably come." "But," Gellhorn declared, "these young people have grown up against a shut door."

What hope could the future hold for the young adult of the thirties? Marriage and raising a family appeared out of the question. The CCC was all right for a while, but it was hardly a career. Work relief meant survival, but it offered no chance for advancement and no training for a "real" job. How could you get interested in it? Horatio Alger stories were fine in the old days, but what now? The traditional formula was work, save, succeed; but now you could not even reach step one. It appeared that "we shall never have good times again," we were "permanently licked." It was hard to disagree with the sobering conclusion that "it would be a cinch to run a war these days, with a good many of the world's young men having nothing better to do anyhow than get shot, and at least fed for a bit beforehand, and busy. . . ."

For most, of course, unemployment had to end sometime. The offer of a "real job" often brought tears of joy. "This will be our last week on relief," wept the wife of a skilled worker in Joplin, Missouri, after her husband obtained employment. "Next week we shall be able to take care of ourselves again." Unfortunately, such joy was often short-lived. Long unemployment had taken its physical and psychological toll. People became "nervous, muscularly soft and unconfident of their ability to do the work they formerly did." On a new job, they were so fearful of "making mistakes that they make mistakes and are promptly fired," reported a Chicago settlement official in 1934.

The Great Depression was, of course, an economic disaster for most Americans, but black people suffered a disproportionate share of the burden. The old and true saying that blacks are the last hired and the first fired cut both ways during the Depression. Unemployment in the "prosperity decade" had been much higher among blacks than whites. "The Negro was born in depression," Clifford Burke told Studs Terkel. "It only became official when it hit the white man."

As layoffs began in late 1929 and accelerated in the following years, blacks were often the first to get pink slips. By 1932 black unemployment reached approximately 50 percent nationwide. As with women, some undesirable jobs had long been reserved for blacks. But such jobs became less undesirable when no other work was to be found. Although women's work generally remained just that in the Depression, the same was not the case with some traditionally "Negro occupations." Whites demanded that blacks be discharged as domestic servants, garbage collectors, elevator operators, waiters, bellhops, and street cleaners. A group of whites in Atlanta adopted the slogan "No Jobs for Niggers Until Every White Man Has a Job." A poorly educated Georgia woman spoke for many whites when she wrote to the President in 1935: "negroes being worked ever where instead of white men it dont look like that is rite." A year earlier a white clerk in Marianna, Florida, said in the wake of a lynch mob attack on a store that employed blacks, "A nigger hasn't got no right to have a job when there are white men who can do the work and are out of work." The number of lynchings in the United States rose from eight in 1932 to twenty-eight, fifteen, and twenty in the three succeeding years. A Depression-era study showed a positive correlation between the number of lynchings in the Deep South and economic distress. "Dust had been blown from the shotgun, the whip, and the noose," a *New Republic* article reported in 1931, "and Ku Klux practices were being resumed in the certainty that dead men not only tell no tales but create vacancies."

Those blacks who were able to keep their jobs suffered great hardship as well. A 1935 investigation in Harlem indicated that skilled workers there had experienced a drop of nearly 50 percent in their wages since the onset of the Depression. The lack of employment opportunities in northern cities cut down the extraordinary rate of black migration from the rural South, but more than 400,000 blacks did make the journey in the Depression decade. If jobs were not available in the North, at least there was not as much discrimination in the administration of relief as in the South. The continuing heavy migration of blacks into cities where they could vote, in states with large representation in the electoral college, was a political fact of growing importance.

The political influence of blacks had been minuscule since the end of Reconstruction. They voted in overwhelming majorities for the Republican Party, which had come to take the "Negro vote" for granted. The Grand Old Party offered blacks little more by 1930 than the grand old platitudes of Abraham Lincoln, Thaddeus Stevens, and Charles Sumner. The Democrats, however, offered still less. The Democrats had *never* seated a single black delegate at any national convention prior to the New Deal. A few blacks were selected as alternates in 1924, but at the 1928 Democratic National Convention in Houston, the black alternates were seated in an area separated by chicken wire from the white delegates and alternates. Here was a perfect symbol of the racial attitudes of the party.

If there was little cause for blacks to hope for much from the Democratic party, there was not much more reason for optimism about the party's candidate in 1932. Like most northern Democrats, Franklin D. Roosevelt had never said anything about race that might upset southern party leaders. He went along without complaint when President Wilson ordered the institution of a complete Jim Crow system in the Navy. In 1929, FDR issued a public denial that he had eaten lunch with blacks. Both Roosevelt's administration in Albany and his 1932 campaign staff were devoid of blacks. Despite their suffering from the Depression, blacks voted for Hoover by greater majorities against Roosevelt in 1932 than they had against Smith four years before.

Yet a decade later Swedish sociologist Gunnar Myrdal wrote in his classic study of American race relations, *An American Dilemma*, that Roosevelt's presidency had "changed the whole configuration of the Negro problem." Few today would disagree with this assessment. The civil rights revolution that reached fruition in the 1960s had its origins in the Depression years. A number of factors converged to bring about this remarkable result.

In the early New Deal no direct steps were taken toward easing the plight of black Americans. To advocates of legislation to improve race relations, Roosevelt argued, with considerable justification, that pushing such bills would destroy the support of southerners in Congress needed to pass recovery legislation vital to all Americans, black as well as white. "First things come first, and I can't alienate certain votes I need for measures that are more important at the moment by pushing any measures that would entail a fight," Roosevelt said in 1933. "I've got to get legislation passed by Congress to save America," FDR explained to Walter White, the national secretary of the National Association for the Advancement of Colored People. "The Southerners by reason of the seniority rule in Congress are chairmen or occupy strategic places on most of the Senate and House committees. If I come out for the anti-lynching bill now, they will block every bill I ask Congress to pass to keep America from collapsing. I just can't take that risk."

Thus the legislation of the First Hundred Days concentrated on the immediate economic crisis, leaving the specific concerns of blacks unaddressed. The National Recovery Administration's effects on blacks were symptomatic of the impact of the early New Deal on that segment of the population. More than a hundred NRA codes established regional wage differentials under which southern workers (which in many instances meant blacks, because of the job classifications) were paid less than people doing the same work elsewhere. The Blue Eagle did not even cover the occupations in which most blacks were employed: farm labor and domestic service. Eighteen NRA codes included what one NAACP official called the "grandfather clause of the NRA." It established wage scales for types of labor based upon what wages had been at a certain date in the past. Obviously this perpetuated pay discrimination based on racial distinctions in job classifications. And in those instances where NRA codes *did* enforce equal pay for workers of either race, the result was often that blacks lost their "advantage" of working for less and were replaced by whites. Black newspapers had their own versions of what NRA stood for, including "Negro Run Around" and "Negroes Rarely Allowed."

For blacks, the Agricultural Adjustment Administration served mainly to reduce their incomes (which they could stand much less than could their large landholding white neighbors), and force black landowners into tenancy, tenants into sharecropping, and many blacks off the land entirely. These effects were extremely significant. Some 40 percent of all black workers in the United States during the Depression years were farm laborers or tenants. A 1934 investigation estimated the average annual income of black cotton farmers of all types at under $200. The AAA was not the *cause* of such deplorable conditions, but it continued them without improvement and in some cases made the problems worse.

Most early New Deal programs included the ideal of decentralized administration or "grass-roots democracy." (No one in the thirties, as far as I am aware, used the term "New Federalism.") Much could be said for the concept in the abstract. In practice, however, it meant that local elites controlled the federal programs in their areas. "[T]he releaf officials here," a black resident of Reidsville, Georgia, wrote to President Roosevelt in 1935, ". . . give us black folks, each one, nothing but a few cans of pickle meet and to the white folks they give blankets, bolts of cloth and things like that." A Georgia official confirmed a discriminatory policy: "There will be no Negroes pushing wheelbarrows and boys driving trucks getting forty cents an hour when the good white men and white women, working on the fields alongside these roads can hardly earn forty cents a day." Relief payments to blacks in Atlanta averaged $19.29 per month, while white relief clients in the same city received $32.66, nearly 70 percent more. A black person in Hattiesburg, Mississippi, summed up the effect of local control in an eloquent, if nearly illiterate, letter to FDR: "i wish you could See the poor hungry an naket half clad's at the relief office an is turned away With tears in their eyes Mississippi is made her own laws and dont treat her destituted as her Pres. had laid plans for us to live."

The need for change should have been obvious. In the 1920s, American popular culture was blatantly racist. Movies portrayed blacks as shiftless, stupid, and laughable. Radio joined in in 1928 with *Amos 'n' Andy*, a series in which white actors spoke the parts of black characters who fit all the white stereotypes of blacks. By 1929, *Amos 'n' Andy* was radio's most popular program, heard by about 60 percent of all radio listeners. Other broadcasts in the decade made frequent use of "darky" jokes. Amusement parks advertised games in which whites could "Hit the Coon and Get a Cigar." Optimists seeking signs of improvement were hard pressed for examples. Perhaps it was a significant reform when *The New York Times* began, early in 1930, to spell "Negro" with a capital "N." Early in the New Deal, though, at least one official of the Federal Housing Administration was still in the habit of telling "darky" and "coon" stories in public speeches. (Administration leaders soon stopped the practice, although it did not die forever, as Nixon-Ford Agriculture Secretary Earl Butz demonstrated in the early 1970s.)

The shift in the attitude of the federal government toward race relations was in large part the work of a few dedicated integrationist reformers, white and black. Unquestionably, the person most responsible for beginning the change in the attitude of the federal government toward blacks was Eleanor Roosevelt. Mrs. Roosevelt had shown no particular concern or understanding for the problems of blacks before her husband became president. But her empathy for the downtrodden led her quite naturally to take up the cause of blacks. She was shocked at the uproar that followed her having lunch with a black woman in Florida in 1933.

In 1927, Eleanor Roosevelt met Mary McLeod Bethune, a black woman who had risen from a sharecropper's family of seventeen children to found Bethune-Cookman College in Florida. The friendship between these two women continued over the ensuing years, and as a result Mrs. Roosevelt's understanding of black problems expanded greatly. She recommended Mrs. Bethune as an assistant to Aubrey Williams at the National Youth Administration, and under the leadership of Williams, a dedicated white liberal from Alabama, and the influence of Bethune, the NYA became a model of government assistance for blacks.

The First Lady also became friendly with Walter White, the first black national secretary of the NAACP. With the guidance of Bethune and White, Eleanor Roosevelt became the leading white advocate of racial integration in the United States. As such, she found herself the target of virulent abuse from white racists. One of the harshest was the ditty that put the following words in the President's mouth, speaking to his wife:

You kiss the niggers,
I'll kiss the Jews,
We'll stay in the White House
As long as we choose.

Eleanor Roosevelt's concern for black people was a reflection of her larger attitude of compassion, which in turn meshed with the values of cooperation that were becoming popular among the American people during the Depression years. The "day of selfishness," Mrs. Roosevelt declared in a 1934 speech to a conference on black education, was over; "the day of working together has come, and we must learn to work together, all of us, regardless of race or creed or color. . . . We go ahead together or we go down together." Seen in this light, the emerging values of the American people seemed to point toward racial coopera-tion. But it was not so simple. A move toward racial harmony—admittedly, a very *small* move—was not the only possible effect of the Depression on racial attitudes. A glance at contemporary events in Germany is sufficient to remind us that hard times can cause an intensification of racial and religious animosity. The increase in lynching in the American South in those years indicates that such a potential existed in the United States as well. Senator Theodore Bilbo of Mississippi was one of those Americans who thought the Nazis had the right idea. "Race consciousness is developing in all parts of the world," Bilbo declared in 1938. "Con-sider Italy, consider Germany. It is beginning to be recognized by the thoughtful minds of our age that the conservation of racial values is the only hope for future civilization. . . . The Germans appreciate the importance of race values."

That the United States in the Depression moved in the direction of the values of com-passion and cooperation pointed to by Eleanor Roosevelt, rather than toward the "race val-ues" outlined by Senator Bilbo (who sought a $1 billion congressional appropriation in 1939 to deport all blacks to Africa), was the result of more than Depression-bred concepts of justice, as important as they certainly were. The push given the President and his policies by Mrs. Roosevelt, Mrs. Bethune, Walter White, Harold Ickes, Will Alexander, the southern white Methodist minister who became head of the Farm Security Administration, Aubrey Williams of the NYA, and Clark Foreman, a young white Georgian who became FDR's special assistant on the economic status of Negroes, was of great importance. So was pressure from the Communist party and the CIO, both of which were in the forefront of the quest in the thir-ties for a larger degree of racial equality. In addition, significant pressure came from blacks themselves, both politically and in terms of organization, demonstrations, and even rioting.

The chronological proximity of President Roosevelt's shift to more forceful opposition to racial discrimination with the only major race riot of the decade, that in Harlem in 1935, may have been coincidence. Be that as it may, the growing importance of black voters in national politics surely was directly related to FDR's move to include blacks in his new Demo-cratic coalition. Black voters began their historic desertion of the Republican party in 1934, *before* the Roosevelt administration had done much specifically for them. In the midterm elec-tions of 1934, a majority of black voters cast their ballots for Democrats for the first time. That year Arthur Mitchell became the first black Democrat ever to win a seat in Congress, when he upset incumbent black Republican Oscar De Priest in a Chicago district. Mitchell won using the slogan "Forward with Roosevelt." The fact that Roosevelt at least attempted to prohibit discrimination in some federal programs and that his administration provided sig-nificant amounts of relief for blacks were enough to end three-quarters of a century of Repub-lican allegiance. "Let Jesus lead you and Roosevelt feed you," a black preacher advised his congregation in 1936.

In that year, the dramatic shift in black political support was unmistakable. "Abraham Lincoln," the Baltimore *Afro-American* reminded its readers, "Is Not A Candidate in the Pre-sent Campaign." Franklin Roosevelt was, and he won an incredible 76 percent of the black vote, roughly reversing the outcome of four years earlier. The change in black voting was more decisive than that of any other group in 1936. As with working-class whites, many blacks who had never voted before were sufficiently impressed with the New Deal to cast their first ballots for Roosevelt. Even in the rural South, many blacks were by this time getting to participate in elections of a sort for the first time, as they voted in AAA referendums on such issues as crop limitations. A new political awareness and hope began to dawn among southern blacks. "They's talked more politics since Mistuh Roosevelt been in than ever befo'," one southern black said of other blacks in his area. "I been here twenty years, but since WPA, the Negro sho' has started talkin' politics."

Unsurprisingly, some Democrats did not welcome the new black members of their party. When a black minister rose to give the invocation at the 1936 Democratic National Convention in Philadelphia, Senator Ellison D. "Cotton Ed" Smith of South Carolina was horrified. "By God, he's as black as melted midnight!" Smith gasped. "Get outa my way. This mongrel meeting ain't no place for a white man!" Smith stormed out of the convention. It was the first time there had been reason for any southern delegate to walk out of a Democratic convention since 1860, but the South Carolinian's action was a foretaste of the future, not a dim reflection of the past. Some southern delegates bolted the Democratic conventions again in 1948 and 1964, as the party gave them considerably more provocation than a black minister's prayer. Senator Smith insisted that he had no objection to "any Negro praying for me, but I don't want any blue-gummed, slew-footed Senegambian praying for me *politically*." As he later embellished the story for the white folks down home, Smith said that as he left the convention, "it seemed to me that old John Calhoun leaned down from his mansion in the sky and whispered in my ear, 'You did right, Ed.'"

The attitude of such southern reactionaries as "Cotton Ed" Smith to the Democratic alliance with blacks indicates the last critical factor in the Depression-era association between liberalism and the quest for racial justice. Early in the Roosevelt administration, such vehement racists as Theodore Bilbo and John Rankin of Mississippi and Martin Dies of Texas supported the New Deal. But as southern fears grew that Roosevelt was moving toward the twin horrors of socialism and racial equality, racism and economic conservatism became intertwined. Southern conservatives combined red-baiting and race-baiting in their struggle against Roosevelt and his liberal economic policies. Charging that the President sought a second Reconstruction, southern racists created a climate in which racism was plainly identified with conservatism. For economic liberals, this provided one more incentive to come out strongly for greater equality between the races. Racism, particularly as it came increasingly to be associated with fascism and Hitler in the late thirties, was a powerful weapon to use against conservatives. In the 1930s, for the first time since the 1870s, reforms for blacks took their clear place on the liberal agenda. The groundwork was laid, but the "second Reconstruction" so dreaded by such conservative southern senators as Virginia's Carter Glass and North Carolina's Josiah Bailey would not come until a quarter century later.

Although obviously severely limited, the improvements for blacks during the Depression were discernible. In May 1935, as the "Second New Deal" was getting under way, President Roosevelt issued Executive Order 7046, banning discrimination on projects of the new Works Progress Administration. Discrimination continued, but the WPA proved to be a godsend for many blacks. In the later thirties, between 15 and 20 percent of the people working for the agency were black, although blacks constituted less than 10 percent of the national population. This, of course, was a reflection of how much worse off blacks were than whites, but the WPA did enable many blacks to survive. More than that, even minimum WPA wages of $12 a week were *twice* what many blacks had been earning previously.

Harold Ickes's Public Works Administration provided to black tenants a more than fair share of the public housing it built. The PWA went so far as to construct several integrated housing projects. PWA construction payrolls also treated blacks fairly. Some 31 percent of PWA wages in 1936 went to black workers. Ickes first made use of a quota system requiring the hiring of blacks in proportion to their numbers in the local work force. This precedent was followed again (at least in theory) by the wartime Fair Employment Practices Commission and in the civil rights legislation and court decisions of the 1960s and 1970s.

Other foundations were also laid in the New Deal for later victories in the civil rights movement. Roosevelt's Attorney General Frank Murphy created the Civil Rights Section in the Justice Department in 1939. Two years earlier, FDR appointed NAACP attorney William Hastie as the first black federal judge in American history. Robert Weaver, who had just completed a Ph.D. in economics at Harvard, was appointed in 1933 with Clark Foreman to advise the President on black economic problems. Almost a quarter century later, Lyndon Johnson named Weaver as the first black Cabinet member. Roosevelt himself was advised by a group of black leaders who came to be known in the press as his "Black Cabinet." It was, in fact, something considerably less than the name implied, but such an advisory group went far beyond anything any previous president had done in the area. By 1941 the number of blacks in regular (as opposed to WPA) government jobs exceeded their percentage in the population as a whole. But what may have been FDR's most significant legacy to the civil rights movement involved several white appointees. Seven of Roosevelt's eight choices for the United States Supreme Court were advocates of civil rights for blacks. (James F. Byrnes of South Carolina was the exception.) The Roosevelt Court set the stage for the Warren Court of the fifties and sixties.

The New Deal did more for blacks than provide hope for the future. There were measurable improvements at the time. Most telling was the increase in life expectancy at birth. During the 1930s this statistic rose from 63 to 67 years for white women, 60 to 62 for white men, 49 to 55 for black women, and 47 to 52 for black men. While blacks still trailed far behind their white counterparts in this key indicator of health and well-being, they narrowed the gap in the Depression years. The New Deal also helped bring about a drop in black illiteracy, from 16.4 percent at the beginning of the decade to 11.5 percent at the end.

Two well-known incidents late in the Depression symbolized both the gains blacks had made and how far they had yet to go. When, in March 1939, the Daughters of the American Revolution refused to allow black contralto Marian Anderson to give a concert in the organization's Constitution Hall in Washington, administration officials arranged for Miss Anderson to give a free concert at the Lincoln Memorial. An integrated crowd of more than 75,000 attended the event, and more than two-thirds of those asked in a nationwide Gallup poll how they felt about Eleanor Roosevelt's resignation from the DAR in protest over the organization's racist policy approved the First Lady's stand. Little more than a decade before, at the dedication of the Lincoln Memorial, blacks were segregated in a roped-off section across a road from white spectators. A notable change in white attitudes had taken place in the interim.

Less than two years after the Anderson performance, as American industry geared up for war production, A. Philip Randolph, the socialist president of the Brotherhood of Sleeping Car Porters, launched the March on Washington Movement (MOWM). The plan was to stage a massive black march on the capital to press for desegregation of the armed forces and equal opportunity in defense industries. The MOWM was, as historian Richard Dalfiume has said, "something different in black protest." The New Deal had begun a change in the American racial climate, but it had done so in such a way that blacks had been left dependent on whites in the government. Some blacks, like Randolph, were ready by 1941 to insist on doing things for themselves, on making their own gains. The New Deal approach, Ralph Bunche argued, was "in its very nature" a "defeatist attitude, since it accepts the existing patterns while asking favors and exceptions within them." The MOWM amounted to a public notice that some blacks wanted to stop asking for favors and start confronting injustice on their own. The threat of the march was sufficient to lead FDR to issue his famous Executive Order 8802, creating a Fair Employment Practices Commission to investigate charges of discrimination in defense-related industries. In exchange for this, Randolph agreed to call off the march. As it happened, the FEPC in World War II was not very effective and Randolph's militant approach declined. But another precedent had been set, and two decades later Randolph's March on Washington at last took place. Randolph was there to hear Martin Luther King, Jr., deliver his stirring "I Have a Dream" speech.

The rebirth of that dream of true racial equality, which had been crushed with the end of Reconstruction in the 1870s, was the real achievement of the New Deal years in race relations. The dream, of course, remained only that. Black expectations were raised and white liberals were enlisted in the cause. Little of substance had been accomplished by 1941 in bringing about equal rights for blacks, but the seeds of the Black Revolution of the fifties and sixties had been sown.

The Bonus Army Invades Washington

Edward Robb Ellis

Walter W. Waters was too young and too stubborn to take defeat without putting up a good fight. By early May, 1932, he was one of 12,000,000 unemployed people in the United States. Waters lived in Portland, Oregon, and had worked as foreman in a canning factory until he lost his job through no fault of his own. That had been a year and a half ago, and he had been unable to find any other work since. Now his home and car had been repossessed, his money had run out, and he ached as he saw his wife and two small daughters suffer. His wife was a tiny blonde weighing only 93 pounds.

Waters was a thirty-four-year-old veteran, tall and handsome, restless and dynamic, his thick blond hair pushed back from his forehead. Never in his Army experience had he been an officer, but he liked to wear smart officer's boots and breeches, and he carried a cane. As a private he had skirmished along the Mexican border with Pershing, and as a sergeant attached to the 146th Field Artillery he had fought several battles in France. Glory lay behind him. Now, about the only thing he could call his own was a piece of paper known as an adjusted service credit certificate—a soldier's bonus. Flipping this back and forth in his strong fingers, Waters decided that he wanted action and he wanted it now!

During World War I the American doughboys had been paid $30 a month while in uniform, and when they were discharged, each got $60 in cash and a ticket home. But while they were saving democracy at about $1 a day, shipyard workers and munitions makers on the prosperous home front were earning $90 a week and strutted around in silk shirts. Furthermore, when the federal government took over the nation's railroads during the war, it had adjusted the pay of railway employees.

In 1919 the American Legion had broached the idea that since the soldiers had been paid so poorly, they, too, should get adjusted compensation. Subsequently, both houses of Congress passed a compensation bill, but it was vetoed by President Harding. The measure was revived, passed again by the House and Senate, but again it was vetoed—this time by President Coolidge. However, in 1924 both branches of the Congress passed the bill over Coolidge's veto, and it became the law.

On January 1, 1925, about 3,500,000 veterans received adjusted compensation certificates. Not money—just pieces of paper. These certificates were like paid-up twenty-year endowment insurance policies paying 4 percent interest compounded annually. Each veteran was credited with $1 a day for each day's service within the United States and $1.25 for each day served abroad. A man entitled to, say, $400 would get about $1,000—in the year 1945.

By 1931, though, with Depression blighting the land, members of the American Legion pressured its executive committee so hard that the Legion finally asked for immediate payment of the certificates. With other demands being made on it the federal government finally decided on a compromise measure. While veterans still could not cash their certificates in full, the government agreed to lend them half the face value of their bonuses at 4½ percent interest. Even this failed to satisfy the veterans. As more and more of them lost their jobs and homes, they demanded the full and immediate payment of all certificates.

Representative Wright Patman, a Democrat from Texas who had been a machine gunner during the war, urged the House of Representatives to pass a bill calling for the immediate payment of all certificates by issuing $2.4 billion in flat money. Flat money is paper currency that is declared legal tender by law. It does not represent specie, such as gold or silver. It is not based on specie. It contains no promise of redemption.

Patman's opponents screamed that this would result in inflation. Denying this charge, Patman replied: "We don't expect to start out on any wild program like Germany did. We are willing to tie to a 40 percent gold basis." He went on to say that there was still $4 billion in gold in the Treasury, that this was enough to support the $10 billion in currency, but even so there was only $5.5 billion in paper money circulating throughout the country. To print another $2.4 billion, Patman declared, would leave the nation safely below the danger mark.

President Hoover disagreed. Banks were failing; cash was being hoarded; stock prices were plummeting. Besides the cry for the soldiers' bonus, the President was beset by a variety of proposals to induce inflation and provide unemployment benefits. He declared that "the urgent question today is the prompt balancing of the budget. When that is accomplished, I propose to support adequate measures for relief of distress and unemployment."

Governor Roosevelt also disagreed with Patman, saying: "I do not see how, as a matter of practical sense, a government running behind two billion dollars annually can consider the anticipation of bonus payment until it has balanced the budget."

Walter W. Waters of Portland knew little and cared less about budget balancing and national finances. He knew he was suffering needlessly and he wanted something done about it. He liked what Patman said about the Reconstruction Finance Corporation: "The millions released to the R.F.C. went to the big boys by way of New York. The millions involved in the full-payment bonus bill will go to the little fellow, into every nook and corner of the nation. It will take money not now in circulation and put it into circulation. It will mean increased revenue to the government."

Waters was struck by a remark made by President Hoover about "the locust swarm of lobbyists who haunt the halls of Congress." Lobbyists? Waters grinned to himself and slapped his cane against his boots. He told other Portland veterans that it might be a good idea to get some of the boys together and go to Washington to lobby for passage of the Patman bill, which was bottled up in the House Ways and Means Committee. Why not? It was worth a try. Anything was better than a guy sitting around on his can waiting for total disaster. The vets had their rights. Why not agitate for them?

His listeners nodded and passed along the word, and soon Waters was addressing ever larger groups, speaking forcefully like the born leader he was. March on Washington! March on Washington! Jobless men pinched their chins in thought, scratched their stubbled cheeks, mulled over the idea, then beat calloused hands together in applause. On May 10, 1932, the day that Patman began collecting signatures on a petition to get his bill out of committee, the Oregon veterans organized themselves into a quasi-military outfit.

They dubbed themselves the Bonus Expeditionary Force. They donned faded uniforms or parts of uniforms—high-collared tunics, canvas leggings, khaki caps. They promised not to drink any booze, forswore panhandling and proclaimed themselves true Americans—not radicals. There were 300 of them, and when they turned their collective pockets inside out, they found they had less than $30 in cash among them. The nation's capital lay more than 3,000 miles to the east. How were they to get there?

By riding the rails, they decided. So they hopped freight trains out of Portland and rode into one sunrise after another. At first they went unnoticed by the national press, much concerned at this time by the discovery of the Lindbergh baby's body, but after the BEF reached East St. Louis, Illinois, it burst into headlines. That was on May 21. When the Oregon travelers swarmed aboard a Baltimore & Ohio freight, railway officials ordered the engineer not to start the train. Cursing, the veterans piled off, slipped out of town, waited until the train was in slow motion, fell upon it, uncoupled cars, cut air lines and soaped the tracks so the engine wheels would slip. Illinois National Guard units were called out to restore order, and this "Battle of the B. & O." focused the attention of the American people on the Bonus Expeditionary Force. The veterans forgot their resolve not to accept charity when East St. Louis townspeople—some sympathetic, some fearful—gave them 200 pounds of sausages and lent them enough trucks to carry them out of town and all the way across Illinois.

Governor Paul V. McNutt of Indiana was so apprehensive about the invasion of his state by this shabby little army that he also gave them trucks to whisk them through, asking only that they promise not to move en masse through Indiana on their way back home. And so, that May, 1932, while Mayor Jimmy Walker of New York City fought for his political life in a witness chair, while Nazis chased Communists around Berlin, while 224 New York families were homesteaded on farms to grow their own food, the Oregon veterans accepted handouts and free rides, moving steadily on trucks across Ohio, West Virginia, Pennsylvania and Maryland. The evening of May 28 they bedded down on the floor of a skating rink in Cumberland, Maryland, only one day away from the capital. By this time Walter W. Waters had won the title of regimental commander of the BEF, the University of Chicago's department of economics had declared that the bonus would not restore prosperity, and federal officials were worrying about the imminent invasion.

At last, on Sunday, May 29, 1932, the Oregonians rolled into Washington, D.C., riding in sixteen trucks, shouting jubilantly, waving American flags and a banner that said: GIVE US A BONUS OR GIVE US A JOB. Chills ran up the spines of Washingtonians when Waters announced that he and his men were ready to stay there until 1945, if necessary, to get cash payment for their certificates. To the surprise of the West Coast veterans, they found that about 1,000 other veterans had preceded them to the national capital. Publicity about the BEF, plus legislative pressure to pass the Patman bill, had attracted other ex-servicemen there, and still more were on their way.

Who were they? They were former soldiers and sailors. They were the unemployed. They were white and black. They were blue-collar workers and white-collar workers. In the recent past they had slumped in barbershops and on front porches, in Legion posts and in grocery stores, staring at their hands, their idle hands, and they had mumbled and muttered and then lifted their voices and their faces and decided to go to Washington. It ain't good for a fella to sit around with no work to do. Man's gotta right to what's his, that's fer dang sure! This here Congressman from Texas—what's his name? Patman—maybe Patman got the right idea. Let's drop in at Washington and sort of help him along a little.

They were the jobless truck driver from Philadelphia, once with the Fifteenth Engineers, his wife holding the only job in the family and supporting the kids. They were the coal miner from Morgantown, West Virginia, proud of his record in the Rainbow Division, out of work the past eighteen months, a grown man getting pocket money from his paw and maw. They were the Pole from Chicago, a veteran of the Thirty-ninth Division, unemployed for three years, his wife dead, their kids with his mother, a man who had moaned while sleeping in flophouses. They were the idle steelmetal worker from Columbus, Georgia, once an infantryman with the First Division, now three years behind in his debts.

As warriors they had known violence, as Depression victims they now knew despair, and Walter W. Waters of Portland, Oregon, tall in his boots with more than 3,000 miles under his dusty belt, looked out over them and said in a voice of brass: *"We are going to stay here until the veterans' bill is passed!"*

Washington trembled.

* * *

Within the previous six months the capital had endured two smaller unemployment marches, the first led by Communists, the second by a Catholic priest from Pittsburgh. People with long memories recalled that back in 1894, on the heels of an earlier depression, a rich businessman named Jacob Coxey had herded 1,200 ragged and jobless men from Ohio to Washington to clamor for road-building projects and public works to relieve unemployment. In none of these cases had there been any rioting but now, as thousands of more veterans spilled into the capital, apprehension grew.

District of Columbia affairs were run by a three-man board of commissioners appointed by the President. Laws were enforced by Major General Herbert B. Crosby, the district commissioner in charge of police matters, through Pelham D. Glassford, superintendent of the metropolitan police department, and his 660 cops. Glassford, who had taken office the previous November, totally lacked police experience. When a reporter asked about his qualifications as chief of police, Glassford grinned and replied: "Well, I've been arrested—once for driving through a red light and once for speeding on a motorcycle." His flippancy was deceptive. A man of high intelligence, Glassford had buckled down to a cram course in criminology and abnormal psychology.

The son of an Army officer, he was born in New Mexico, met Douglas MacArthur when both were West Point cadets, served as a soldier in the Philippines and Hawaii and along the Mexican border, fought in France during World War I, and at the age of thirty-four became the youngest brigadier general in the AEF. After the war he worked as a San Francisco reporter, as a circus sign painter, as pinch hitter for a barker, and then took up residence in Washington to study art. Zestful and fearless, fair-minded and friendly, Glassford was known to all his many friends as "Happy."

The day that Waters arrived in Washington he met Glassford and was so impressed that he wrote: "Here was certainly no hard-boiled disciple of the old police school. In him the human element was above the law." Glassford, who kept a diary, noted "Waters' blue eyes in which there sometimes burned an almost fanatical gleam." The two men sat on the grass together, the police chief letting the veterans' leader do most of the talking. Glassford later said: "I agreed, of course, with their determination to be lawabiding and orderly. . . . As I listened to this first group, I suddenly realized that what was ahead of me was not a mere local police job. It was national. From all over the United States ex-soldiers were heading for Washington and what would be the result? I didn't know. Nobody knew. . . . I told the commissioners that the few hundred men already in Washington were only the advance guard of what might turn out to be a huge army and I wanted to be told how they wanted it handled. Imagine my surprise when it was suggested to me that I treat these men as indigents, pass them along to the Salvation Army or any other charity organization that would feed them, and then make them move on as rapidly as possible."

Through Washington there spread a rumor that 1,000,000 veterans would descend on the capital. Those already present banded together and adopted the name first used by the Oregon contingent—the Bonus Expeditionary Force—and elected Waters their commander in chief. Glassford had greeted the bonus marchers so pleasantly that the grateful men named him their secretary-treasurer. This position enabled the police chief to keep in constant touch with the veterans and to kid and cajole them into keeping the peace.

Despite the fears of district residents, Washington's crime rate actually dropped while the bonus army was in town. Newspaperman Mark Sullivan wrote: "To go out among them was to recognize instantly their complete harmlessness. A child or a lost pocketbook would be safer among them than among any average cross-section of a city population." Correspondent Floyd Gibbons described the veterans as "at all times law-abiding and orderly." Will Rogers wrote: "They hold the record for being the best behaved of any fifteen thousand hungry men assembled anywhere in the world. Just think what fifteen thousand clubwomen would have done to Washington even if they wasn't hungry. The senate would have resigned and the President committed suicide."

Exactly how many veterans finally gathered in Washington? No one will ever know for sure. BEF leaders claimed 80,000, but this figure is far too high. Glassford probably was closer to the mark when he estimated the peak number at 22,000. Even so, this was but a tiny fraction of the 3,500,000 veterans living in the United States. Glassford also believed that there were never more than 300 Communists among the bonus marchers. When a reporter asked him whether he considered all the bonus marchers dangerous, he replied: "Dangerous? No—except the danger of gradual rust and rot which attacks those with no occupation and no incentive. These are just middle-aged men out of a job."

And so they were, for the most part, but Secret Service agents were already infiltrating their ranks, for Communists were trying to take over the movement.

* * *

About a year earlier American Communists had demanded immediate payment of the bonus. Then, in December, 1931, the Reds had led a hunger march to Washington to agitate for jobs, a minimum wage and national unemployment insurance. For two days 10,000 jobless persons paraded through the streets, picketed the White House and chanted slogans such as: "The Hoover program—a crust of bread on a bayonet!" They tried to provoke incidents, but Glassford's policy of gentle firmness kept the situation from getting out of hand.

The failure of the December demonstration frustrated Red leaders in New York and Moscow, but now, with the coming of spring, peaceful and patriotic Americans had stolen their thunder by staging a middle-class march on Washington. The Communists had been caught off guard, and this worried Earl Browder, who had succeeded William Z. Foster as head of the American Communist Party. A Comintern representative now hastened from Moscow to the United States with an urgent directive. Browder and other Red leaders were ordered to: (1) take the bonus army leadership away from Waters and his commanders; (2) establish the National Provisional Bonus March Committee of the Workers' Ex-Service-men's League: (3) trick the veterans into hating the federal government; (4) provoke riots that might result in a massacre of the veterans; (5) use the consequent resentment to increase membership in the Communist Party; (6) above all, try to touch off a revolution.

While a Communist secret board of strategy remained at the Red headquarters in New York, a party front organization was opened in Washington at 905 I Street, NW. Presiding over this National Provisional Bonus March Committee was Emanuel Levin, a former Marine, a Communist candidate for the California Assembly in 1928 and now editor of the *Daily Worker.* The task of trying to take the bonus army away from Waters was given to John Pace of Detroit. Also a former Marine, Pace had joined the Communist Party in 1931 after losing his contracting business.

As this Communist plot slowly uncoiled, unsuspecting veterans kept streaming into Washington from every corner of the nation. Besides being jobless and penniless, they were almost aimless. Walter W. Waters himself said that "not one man in twenty really expected to get the bonus." The *New Yorker* magazine observed that the BEF "was something more than a lobby; it was the expression of men's desire to huddle together when their courage is gone." In his book *The Lean Years,* Irving Bernstein wrote: "This bonus march might well be described as a flight from reality—a flight from hunger, from the cries of the starving children, from the humiliation of accepting money from worn, querulous women, from the harsh rebuffs of prospective employers." A welfare worker said: "Their real demand was for security, and in their bewilderment and confusion they seem to have reverted to the old army ways and to the earlier institutional situation where shelter and food are provided."

President Hoover tried to ignore the presence of the veterans, refusing time and again to receive any of their leaders. Governor Roosevelt announced that he would arrange to get the fare for any New York bonus marcher who cared to come home. No official of the federal government or the District of Columbia cared to assume responsibility for either sheltering the veterans or evicting them. The sole exception was Police Chief Glassford, but he lacked orders, funds or food. In his opinion, the crisis boiled down to the alternative of feeding them or fighting them—and he had no stomach for fighting men with whom he had soldiered.

His chief's cap on his head, his gold badge pinned to his white shirt, wearing dun-colored breeches and puttees, Glassford mounted his blue motorcycle to chug here and there on errands of mercy. Breezily he begged funds from the rich and comfortable, besides spending $733 of his own money on the men he called his friends. He cajoled his cops into staging a boxing match and donating the net receipts of $2,500 to the veterans. He pried a donation out of Jimmy Lake, proprietor of the Gayety burlesque house. From the National Guard he obtained the use of secondhand pup tents.

One of the richest women in Washington—and in all the world, for that matter—was Mrs. Evalyn Walsh McLean. She owned the fabled $2 million Hope diamond, was heiress to a mining fortune, reigned as Washington's society queen and lived in a vast $1 million estate called Friendship on the northwest edge of the district. Her husband, Edward B. McLean, was proprietor of the Washington *Post* and the Cincinnati *Enquirer.*

Seldom seen without her jewels, she wore huge horn-rimmed spectacles that made her look half-astonished, half-inquisitive. Feverishly devoted to the pursuit of pleasure, Mrs. McLean confessed that for a time she had been a morphine addict. During one of her wild parties at Friendship the scene was surveyed by Senator William E. Borah, who then commented bitterly: "This sort of thing is what brings on a revolution."

Mrs. McLean watched as the families of the bonus marchers joined them in the national capital, and her first reaction was one of anger "because I felt that crowd of men, women and children never should have been permitted to swarm across the continent."

Later, though, after reading in the newspapers that they were starving, she decided in the middle of one night to help them. She also felt that her son Jock should see this chapter in American history. Taking him along, she drove to a camp and got out of her car to talk to the veterans.

"Have you eaten?" she asked one man.

He shook his head from side to side.

Just then Mrs. McLean was approached by Police Chief Glassford, whom she knew. Glassford said: "I'm going to get some coffee for them."

Mrs. McLean cried: "All right! I'm going to Child's."

It was 2 A.M. when she and her son walked into the restaurant. When a waiter came to take their order, she asked: "Do you serve sandwiches? I want a thousand. Oh! And a thousand packages of cigarettes."

"But, lady—"

"I want them right away! I haven't got a nickel with me, but you can trust me. I am Mrs. McLean."

After feeding some veterans that night, Mrs. McLean went the following day to see John Barton Payne, head of the Red Cross, whom she also knew. Despite her barrage of words, she was unable to persuade him that the bonus army was part of a national crisis with which the Red Cross was morally obligated to deal. Barton did promise her a little flour, which she accepted. Next, she visited local headquarters of the Salvation Army, finding girls hard at work doing all they could to help the veterans. Their harried officer told Mrs. McLean that what the men most needed was a big tent to serve as headquarters for registering newcomers, so she ordered one delivered from Baltimore. Time and again she went out among the bonus marchers, giving them clothing, books and radios.

At last Mrs. McLean succeeded in getting Walter W. Waters to visit her at her estate. He showed up with his wife, who had just reached Washington dressed as a man, her tiny feet encased in shiny boots. She was tired and dirty after her long bus trip from Oregon. Mrs. McLean led the exhausted woman upstairs and into the guest bedroom her father had designed for use by King Leopold of Belgium, urged her to lie down and ordered a maid to draw a bath.

"You get undressed," the hostess suggested, "and while you sleep I'll have all your things cleaned and pressed."

"Oh, no! Not me! I'm not giving these clothes up. I might never see them again!"

However, she did agree to rest awhile. Mrs. McLean then joined Waters, who said: "I'm desperate! Unless these men are fed, I can't say what won't happen to this town!"

That evening, with Waters standing by her chair, Mrs. McLean phoned her friend Charles Curtis, the Vice President of the United States. Urgently she said: "These men are in a desperate situation, and unless something is done for them, unless they are fed, there is bound to be a lot of trouble."

Vice President Curtis told Mrs. McLean that he would call a secret meeting of Senators, but nothing came of it.

* * *

Glassford turned for help to his old friend Douglas MacArthur, the Army chief of staff, and MacArthur lent the bonus marchers some of the Army's rolling kitchens. These made it possible to feed the men for only seven cents a day, but this infuriated one Congressman, who took the floor of the House to warn: "If they come to Washington, sit down and have three meals furnished them free every day, then God knows what will happen to us! . . . If the government can feed those that are here, then we can expect an influx that will startle the whole country." The rolling kitchens rolled away.

Some veterans took over empty buildings within the federal triangle just northwest of the Capitol, while others grouped together in camps in and around the city. Ultimately, there were twenty-two BEF billets. The largest was Camp Anacostia, located on swampland south of the Capitol near the confluence of the Potomac and Anacostia rivers, on the southern bank of the Anacostia, stretching from the Anacostia Bridge south to Bolling Field. From this site the ragged campers could see the Capitol dome with its bronze statue called "Freedom."

The men were free to exist as best they could. Many used cardboard to patch their shoes; some had no shoes at all. They wore old army caps, tattered trousers, wash-faded denim shirts and other odd garments. They scrounged through city dumps to collect old newspapers, cardboard boxes, tin cans, tar-paper roofing, egg crates, packing cases, hunks of tin and the carcasses of abandoned cars. Sweating in the humid heat of Washington, they made huts out of this junk.

The veterans picked weeds from the edge of the river and wove them through chicken wire and old bedsprings to improvise beds. One man slept in a coffin set on trestles; another in a barrel filled with grass; a third in a piano box. They gagged at sewage flowing just a few feet away, swatted at flies and mosquitoes. The surgeon general of the United States warned of the danger of an epidemic, so the bonus marchers appointed their own sanitary officer. In the soft marshy ground they dug latrines which they called Hoover villas.

And when they had finished putting up their miserable shanties and torn tents, they stuck American flags here and there, muttering in disgust because they had been disowned by both the American Legion and the Veterans of Foreign Wars. Feverish men lay in one tent with a cynical sign saying: THE LAME, SICK AND LAZY. Breezes shook a poster promising: "Don't cry, little girl, I will come back home." Sick and hungry, dirty and deprived, falling back on half-remembered habits to ward off chaos, these middle-aged men fell asleep and came awake to the sound of a bugle, sucked in bellies to drill before visitors, asked for passes to leave camp.

And waited.

The Communists announced that the veterans would hold a "monster demonstration" in the streets of Washington, but when only 160 men showed up at the staging area, the demonstration was called off. Glassford heard from a Washington reporter that the Communists, despite all their efforts, were making almost no impression upon the bonus marchers. On June 10 John Pace arrived at the head of a small unit of Detroit Communists. This was so heartening to the Reds already present that on that same evening 200 of them attacked Camp Anacostia. The radicals got the worst of it, however, the Washington *Herald* reporting: "Husky buddies from the Texas plains vied with lanky New Englanders for the privilege of 'going to work' on the Communists." When Glassford got to the scene, he found the Reds cowering in a corner of the camp, trying to use their arms to ward off blows. He and his cops pulled the angry veterans off the Communists, led them off the grounds and marched them to the relative safety of a vacant lot some distance away.

Washington, a city of 486,000 population, had 19,000 of its own residents who were without work. The need for jobs for local people, the lack of proper facilities to care for them and now the presence of a growing army of veterans—all this created a strain too great to be handled. Glassford wired all forty-eight state governors, urging them to try to keep more veterans from converging upon the capital. He also begged Congressional leaders to end the crisis by bringing the bonus bill to a vote.

The Patman bill was discharged from committee and debated in the House, which was mostly Democratic. All the Representatives knew that every bonus seeker and everyone influenced by a bonus seeker would vote against the Congressman who voted against the bonus. Congressman Edward E. Eslick, a sixty-year-old Democrat from Tennessee, died of a heart attack while arguing in favor of paying the compensation. The next day, June 15, the House passed the Patman bill, 209 to 176. Most Democrats favored it, while most Republicans opposed it.

By this time delegates to the Republican National Convention had gathered in Chicago to nominate a Presidential candidate, and some Chicago veterans noisily invaded convention rooms. Despite this disorder, Herbert Hoover was renominated. Some wishful-thinking veterans felt that Hoover would not dare veto the bill if it reached his desk in this election year of 1932. The measure was sent to the Senate Finance Committee, which reported against it. Now the entire Senate met to consider the issue. If Senators rejected the bill, what would the veterans do? Some members of the administration were so frightened that they wanted to mount machine guns on the roof of the Capitol, but this horrified Glassford so it was not done. On June 17 the Senate opened debate.

With the fate of the BEF trembling in the balance, agitators raced through various camps shouting: "On to the Capitol! On to the Capitol! Over the bridges, comrades! The Senate is going to defeat the bonus bill! Everybody to Washington!" A local newspaper called this "the tensest day in the capital since the war."

Groups of ragged, menacing men pushed their way into the Capitol Building and stretched out on the marble floors of corridors. Guards eyed them uneasily and uncertainly, afraid to touch them for fear of sparking a riot. Most of the bonus marchers—perhaps 10,000 strong—assembled in the plaza fronting on the Senate chamber, squatted on stone steps, sprawled on green grass, muttered and sang and dozed and stirred restlessly all afternoon long and into the evening. Within the Senate the debate dragged on. Every now and then a Senator would tiptoe to a window, peek down on the multitude, anxiously shake his head, creep back into the chamber.

The legislators' apprehension was openly voiced by Republican Senator Hiram Johnson of California, an old man in a baggy blue serge suit with white piping on his vest. Johnson prophesied: "This marks a new era in the life of our nation. The time may come when this folderol—these trappings of government—will disappear, when fat old men like you and me stop making speeches to sleepy galleries and be lined up against a stone wall."

Outside the fear-soaked chamber, out in the plaza, the tall and lean and sunburned Walter W. Waters stood waiting, flicking his cane against his boots. A reporter asked him: "What's going to happen when these men learn of the defeat of the bill? It's going to be swamped, you know." To the reporter's surprise, Waters replied: "Nothing will happen."

But who could be sure?

Darkness fell. Out of a door of the Capitol came an elderly man with a sharp nose, pale and shrewd eyes—Senator Elmer Thomas, an Oklahoma Democrat who favored the Patman bill. An acre of eyes locked on this slim figure and followed it as Thomas stepped up to Waters and whispered into his ear. Waters' jaw muscles tightened. Then, when the Senator had finished whispering, Waters climbed onto a pedestal at the edge of the Capitol steps and spread out his arms.

"Comrades!"

His voice was low and tired. The veterans scrambled to their feet, babbling and shouting. Waters waggled his outstretched arms and at last got silence—silence as menacing as a razor's edge.

"Comrades! . . . I have bad news for you. Prepare yourselves for a disappointment, men! . . . The bonus has been defeated . . . sixty-two to eighteen. . . ." (Another sixteen Senators had abstained from voting.)

"*Booooooooo-oooo-oooo!*"

The sound, like an artillery barrage, rose and rolled and rumbled throughout the plaza. Then the men stood in stunned silence. They did not seem to breathe. Fists clenched. Muscles were rigid against ragged sleeves. For a split second Waters looked uncertain, fearful. Near him stood Elsie Robinson, a middle-aged newspaper columnist with a furrowed face. She whispered to Waters: "Tell them to sing 'America'!"

Waters shouted: "Let's sing 'America,' men—and then go back to your billets!"

Snatching caps off their heads, the dazed and disappointed veterans sang as ordered. At the end of the song there came cries: "North Carolina—fall in here! . . . New Mexico—over here!" Soon the shapeless crowd fell into patterns as the men formed platoons and began tramp-tramp-tramping out of the plaza and back to their encampments. Half an hour later silence swathed the plaza. Senators wiped their brows and went home.

Some disgusted veterans—the police said 1,000, the BEF said 200—now started drifting away from Washington. Fifteen thousand or more remained, however, and these diehards tried to cheer up one another by chanting: "Stay until 1945!" Actually, those who stayed were not really sure what to do next. Some resented the seemingly casual way in which their leader had accepted the Senate's decision. John Pace, the Communist agitator from Detroit, tried to use this dissension to wrest power from Waters. The veterans wrangled among themselves so ferociously that the BEF almost fell apart. In three days two new leaders were elected, but then Waters staged a coup, regained his title of commander in chief and won dictatorial authority.

Waters now began talking about organizing a paramilitary force like the Nazi storm troopers and the Italian Blackshirts, naming it the Khaki Shirts of America and demanding "reform" of the American government. He demanded rigid obedience and took to saluting his men with the stiff-arm gesture of Mussolini. When some veterans objected, Waters bellowed: "I'll do what I want to do whether you like it or not, and those that don't can get the hell out of the BEF! I'm going to be hard-boiled!"

"Hot Waters," as some now called him, believed that what this country needed was a hard core of 100 percent Americans to serve as a shield against Communism. As Waters heated and hardened, Glassford watched in dismay, scribbling in his diary that the BEF leader "saw 'Red' a little too strenuously." But Waters kept on roaring that he would do things his own way "if I have to detail five hundred MP's!"

He already had his own self-proclaimed "military police," a band of more than 300 men under the immediate command of a colorful character named W. D. Atwell. When the police chief accused Atwell of throwing seven Communists into the river, Atwell snarled: "Sure, I did! They needed a bath!" Under orders from Waters and Atwell, kangaroo courts sentenced Red leaders to fifteen lashes across the back with belts, destroyed their leaflets and booted them out of camp.

The bonus marchers had their own five-cent newspaper, *The B.E.F. News*, which now flailed radicals and the rich alike. It warned that wealthy people were "making it easier for the Reds to add to their ranks." It shrilled: "Eyes front—not left!"

With the widening of the split between Red activists and other veterans, Earl Browder proclaimed from New York: "The Bonus revolutionary force in Washington is the significant beginning of the mass struggle against the deepening consequence of the crisis." The Communists' secret board of strategy, together with the representative of the Comintern, distributed a quarter-million copies of a manifesto. In bold type it screamed: ONLY MASS ACTION WILL WIN BONUS FIGHT!

John Pace, stepping up his activities, led radicals and others into the center of Washington, to a spot three blocks from the Capitol Building, to an area bounded by Third and Fourth Streets, NW, and Missouri and Pennsylvania Avenues. There they took over four abandoned buildings that already housed some veterans. These red-brick half-demolished structures, owned by the Treasury Department, were scheduled to be torn down completely to make space for a new project. District Commissioner Crosby now accused Glassford of dereliction of duty by failing to enforce an ordinance banning the use of buildings that lacked sewers. Crosby told Glassford to evict the squatters. Glassford told him that this would result in a riot, and then the Army or National Guard would have to be called out. A crisis of this kind, Glassford told all three commissioners, would threaten the safety of everyone in the city. He pleaded with the commissioners to confer with the disgruntled veterans, but they refused.

As the situation worsened in Washington, the Democratic National Convention opened in Chicago. Governor Roosevelt was so sure he would win the Presidential nomination that he began drafting his acceptance speech, sitting in his Albany office in shirtsleeves, smoking one cigarette after another. A fellow Democrat, Senator Huey Long of Louisiana, called him long distance and coaxed him to come out for immediate payment of the bonus. Roosevelt said he did not favor the bonus. Huey Long rasped: "Well, then, you're a gone goose!" But the Senator was wrong. Roosevelt won the nomination on July 1.

In Washington the bonus marchers were so low on food that Waters flew to New York City, where he managed to get a donation of one ton of supplies. On the Fourth of July the veterans paraded through the streets of the capital, but instead of the 20,000 BEF members claimed by Waters, a mere 5,000 or less trudged forlornly behind two buglers and a single drummer. This turnout was so disappointing that at last even Waters confessed that perhaps the bonus army might as well dissolve and its members leave for home.

Taking shape at this time were plans to make it easy for them to get out of town. Glassford had been negotiating with railroads for cheap fares, and both the Pennsylvania and Baltimore & Ohio lines had offered the veterans a one-cent-per-mile rate for a ride home. President Hoover had asked Congressional leaders to introduce a joint resolution authorizing the Veterans Bureau to spend $100,000 for this kind of transportation. Some veterans said they might take this money if it were offered to them, but others shouted that they wanted meal tickets, not train tickets.

BEF morale was low when 700 California veterans arrived in Washington under the leadership of Roy W. Robertson of Los Angeles. While serving in the Navy, Robertson had broken his back in a fall from a bunk, and he still wore a back brace and a clamp on his head. A bluff and arrogant man, he scorned both the Communists and the men loyal to Waters. During his only conference with Waters, he snapped: "We came to Washington to petition Congress, not to picnic!" The night the Californians arrived they slept on the lawn of the Capitol, and the next morning they boldly walked into the House Office Building to shave and wash.

This was the beginning of an ominous demonstration. The militant West Coast veterans, joined by others, started marching in single file back and forth in the Capitol plaza. They called their demonstration a Death March because of the imminent adjournment of Congress. Back and forth, day and night, in sunshine and in rainfall, occasionally booing President Hoover, the men marched, marched, marched, until they unnerved Vice President Curtis.

Charles Curtis was a political hack; one cynic said that Curtis thought the Trinity consisted of the Republican Party, the high tariff and the Grand Army of the Republic. As a Senator from Kansas he had accepted money to endorse Lucky Strike cigarettes, and upon assuming the Vice Presidency, he had become the target of ridicule by insisting on preferred protocol for his half sister, Dolly Curtis Gann. President Hoover did not think highly of Curtis.

Eager to quash the demonstration in front of the Capitol, Curtis called out the Marines. They arrived from the navy yard in something less than military style, for they rode trolleys and taxicabs. Police Chief Glassford took one look at them and exploded. Getting in touch with Curtis, he roared that he alone was responsible for law and order in the District of Columbia—with the sole exception of the President of the United States. He shouted that he was fed up with "hysterical meddlers." After slamming down the phone, Glassford found a Senator who was willing to call the White House and ask the President whether he would take responsibility for summoning the Marines. Hoover replied that he would not. The Marines were withdrawn.

But on July 14 some blustering veterans invaded the Vice President's office, and another tremor of fear rolled across Washington.

The next day the hazardous situation was discussed at a conference held in the office of General Douglas MacArthur. Among those present were ranking Army officers and Glassford. According to the police chief, MacArthur said flatly that the Army would not be used against the bonus marchers "unless directed by the President." Vice President Curtis sent word to the conferees that he wanted the Capitol grounds completely cleared of demonstrators. Glassford argued that this would aggravate matters. After further discussion, Glassford agreed to a compromise—only the plaza in front of the Capitol would be cleared. His cops managed to herd back the veterans without any trouble, but the Death March continued at a greater distance from the Capitol Building.

That same day, Hoover cut his Presidential salary by 20 percent. Independently wealthy, Hoover never used any of his public salaries for personal purposes, giving them instead to charity. His Cabinet members also reduced their salaries by 15 percent so there could be no complaint by federal employees, whose wages had been slashed by 8¼ percent.

That same day, too, acceding to the President's request, Congress appropriated $100,000 to get the BEF out of town. Now the Veterans Bureau could advance each veteran the price of a railway ticket home, plus 75 cents a day for food during the trip. The sum given each man represented a loan without interest; if it were not repaid, it would be deducted from his bonus—if and when he got it. Glassford hopped onto his motorcycle and chugged through the camps and shantytowns, handing out copies of a letter in which he urged the men to accept the government's offer. Many of them balked. Why go back home when no homes or jobs awaited them? Why not stick close to the seat of power and fight to the finish? Besides, the veterans groused, Hoover's offer of a lift out of town was his first official acknowledgment that they even existed.

Agreement on this last point came from Walter Lippmann, who wrote in his column: "Mr. Hoover does not shrink from holding conferences and issuing statements. How can he justify the fact that he never took the trouble to confer with the bonus marchers?" Historian Arthur M. Schlesinger, Jr., has pointed out: "The President himself had ample time in these weeks to receive Jim Londos, the heavyweight wrestling champion, delegations from Eta Upsilon Gamma Sorority and from the Baraca Philathea Union, adolescent winners of essay contests and other dignitaries; but audiences were denied to the leaders of the B.E.F."

Only a few hundred veterans took the tickets and departed for home, leaving behind thousands of resentful men. Tension tightened. *The B.E.F. News* whipped up emotions: "A dog in the gutter will fight to feed its pups," but for three years "you have cringed and fawned and begged for crumbs. . . . Why stand you thus, when all is within your power? Are you truly curs and cowards? Or are you men?"

On July 16, the day Congress was due to adjourn, the bonus army took up vigil at opposite ends of Pennsylvania Avenue. About 17,000 men gathered near the Capitol Building. A small group approached the White House, clamoring to get inside to talk to the President, but they were turned away. Numbering only about 50 men, they stayed as close to the White House grounds as possible. They knew it was customary for the President to go to the Capitol on the final day of each session to sign bills and watch the closing ceremonies. Hoover had announced he would make this short trip, and for two hours a limousine waited at the White House door.

Outside the Capitol, "Hot Waters" climbed onto a portico and shouted to his massed men: "You've got to keep a lane open for the white-collar birds so they won't rub into us lousy rats! We're going to stay here until I see Hoover!"

Hours passed, night came, and still the President failed to leave the White House. Commissioner Crosby was so worried about Hoover's safety that he ordered Glassford to tighten security at the White House and in the surrounding area. No gathering of large groups. No demonstrations. Cops to be responsible for Pennsylvania Avenue and all approaches, except from the south. Park police to patrol the East and West Executive Avenues and the southern approach. White House gates shut and chained. And Crosby told Glassford: "In the event of a call for federal troops, responsibility shall pass to the commander thereof."

Three hundred armed soldiers had been assembled inside the nearby Munitions Building, although few persons knew it at the time. Now the police went into action, driving veterans away from the vicinity of the White House and jailing three of them. All pedestrians and cars were chased off Pennsylvania Avenue and adjacent streets. If these thoroughfares had not been cleared instantly, reporters were told, the President would have called out the Army.

But veterans and spectators backed away from the White House, Hoover sat tight, Waters and his legion waited in vain, Congress adjourned, and at last the bonus army drifted disgustedly away from the Capitol. This crisis had been weathered—but what next?

The administration decided to step up its pressure against the veterans. During the previous weeks the Treasury Department had made no overt objection to the fact that veterans had occupied its four vacant buildings within the federal triangle. Now, however, an assistant secretary of the treasury ordered Glassford to oust the squatters so that wrecking crews might finish demolition of the buildings. The police chief recognized this as a ruse, for he also was told that the BEF would be chased out of all its camps. The worried Glassford consulted with the district commissioners, but they seconded what he called "this sudden and drastic change of policy." Glassford went to Waters and begged him to tell his men to take the railway tickets and go home; Waters refused.

On July 26 an emergency conference was held by administration leaders, Red Cross officials and BEF representatives. Commander in chief "Hot Waters" had his chief of staff and attorney at his side as he faced the others—the first confrontation they had been given with any federal official other than Glassford. The meeting lasted five hours.

One of the participants was Secretary of War Patrick J. Hurley, a picturesque and fearless loudmouth. One day during the bonus troubles he had attended a barbecue held by Washington correspondents, had shown off a toy that roared like a bull, had slapped reporters on their backs and cried: "I like my beef raw!" After this emergency meeting, Waters quoted

Hurley as saying: "You and your bonus army have no business in Washington! We are not in sympathy with your being here. We will not cooperate in any way with your remaining here. We are interested only in getting you out of the district. At the first sign of disorder or bloodshed in the B.E.F., you will all get out—and we have plenty of troops to get you out!"

Another man who took part in the conference was Chief of Staff Douglas MacArthur—handsome and brilliant, rigid and imperious. Harold L. Ickes once said: "MacArthur is the type of man who thinks when he gets to heaven, God will step down from the great white throne and bow him into His vacated seat." Mistakenly believing that the Communists had seized leadership of the BEF, MacArthur had referred to the veterans as "traitors," "the enemy" and "the mob."

The general paced the floor most of the time during the long conference. As it broke up, Waters turned to him and asked: "If the troops should be called out against us, will the B.E.F. be given the opportunity to form in columns, salvage their belongings, and retreat in orderly fashion?" According to Waters, MacArthur replied: "Yes, my friend. Of course!"

Waters now realized that the government meant business. The next day he called together his 182 group commanders and warned them that one false step would bring out the Army. If an attempt was made to evict any of the veterans, Waters said, they were to offer "absolutely no resistance." He suggested that the men occupying the federal buildings withdraw to Camp Bartlett on Alabama Avenue, SE. At Glassford's request, this 32-acre estate had been lent to the BEF by its owner, John H. Bartlett, a former governor of New Hampshire and former assistant postmaster general. About 1,000 veterans were already billeted in Camp Bartlett, which Waters now called the last resort of the BEF.

While Waters was talking to his men, Hoover was talking to his own assistants, Hurley and MacArthur among them. Hoover said that order could be restored in Washington only if "disturbing factions" were driven from the center of town. He specified, however, that he did not want them chased out of the entire district. As the President later explained: "I did not wish them driven from their camps, as I proposed that the next day we would surround the camps and determine more accurately the number of Communists and ex-convicts among the marchers."

The afternoon of that July 27 Glassford summoned Waters to the office of the district commissioners. Although Waters had been in the capital eight weeks, he had not met the commissioners—and he did not meet them now. They sat in an inner office, Waters sat in an anteroom, and Glassford acted as an envoy, shuttling back and forth between them and him. Waters chuckled: "It isn't every ex-sergeant that can have an ex-general for messenger boy." At issue was the question of when Waters had to pull his men out of the four old government buildings. After much bickering by proxy, he was told the deadline was Monday, July 31. Three days of grace.

At 4:57 A.M. the following day, Thursday, July 28, 1932, the sun rose in a cloudless sky over the city, and a soft breeze blew from the southwest. By 9 A.M. the mercury had risen to 81 degrees, foretelling another of those sultry summer days for which the capital is noted. Shortly after 9 A.M. a bugle blast called veterans to a meeting in an improvised theater in the middle of the 300 block of Pennsylvania Avenue, a block containing the four disputed buildings. Waters took the rostrum and pleaded with the men to leave the area and take up new quarters in Camp Bartlett. Just then Glassford's secretary walked onto the stage and handed

Waters a paper. This was a Treasury Department order demanding the evacuation of the armory—one of the four buildings—by ten o'clock that morning. Not three days of grace. Minutes. Waters read the order aloud, then roared: "You've been double-crossed!" Despite his own anger and chagrin, though, he redoubled his arguments about the advantages of Camp Bartlett. They could settle down there for a long siege. The sullen veterans heckled their leader.

When he could make himself heard, Waters asked: "Will you move or won't you?"

"No! No! No!"

This chant broke up the meeting and the men straggled out into the sunshine, grumbling.

At 10 A.M. Glassford arrived at the head of a force of 100 policemen in white shirts. The cops swiftly strung a rope around the armory and then took up positions at eight-foot intervals inside this thin barrier. Waters kept on begging his men to leave peacefully. Glassford ordered them out. They refused to evacuate the place. Six treasury agents walked up, each protected by a pair of cops. These agents, the policemen and Glassford himself entered the ground floor of the armory.

The first-floor veterans put up no fight and were led outside, one after another. One woman, smiling broadly, emerged on the arm of a treasury agent. Cheers arose from the 1,500 bonus marchers who waited outside, some of them sitting on a pile of rocks.

Now, with the ground floor cleared, agents and cops climbed to the second floor. There they met their first resistance. A black veteran lay on the floor. Agents asked him to get up. He refused. Three patrolmen grabbed him, and although he tried to fight back, they half dragged, half carried him downstairs and out to a patrol car. On that second floor the cops found a big basket filled with bricks, which they thoughtfully removed. Then they cleared the floor of all veterans, who walked out of the building carrying their belongings in boxes, bundles and pails.

A hundred Texas veterans held the third floor, and they yelled that they would have to be carried out. So far, except for the scuffle with the black veteran, the eviction had been a fairly good-natured affair. But now, with the arrival of 3,000 angry veterans from Camp Marks, the mood soured. Men in overalls and dirty shirts started throwing rocks and bricks at the cops. Stolidly, the authorities charged the third-floor Texans, drove them down the stairs, pushed them into the open, shoved them into paddy wagons.

By 11:50 A.M. the last man had been ousted from the armory.

Three minutes later Attorney General William D. Mitchell ordered the immediate evacuation of all veterans from all federal property in the District of Columbia. As the temperature rose, so did tempers. At 12:17 P.M. the police learned that thousands of veterans from billets throughout the district were approaching lower Pennsylvania Avenue. In the avenue's 300 block wrathful veterans continued to mill around the roped-off armory. About thirty-five of them tried to push past the rope and police line to get back into the building. They were brought up short at the barrier. Another hail of bricks and stones fell on the cops, who retaliated by clubbing anyone within arm's length. The police chief's badge was torn off his shirt. A cop who tried to protect Glassford was knocked down and kicked unconscious.

Glassford roared: "Be peaceful, men! Be peaceful! You may have killed one of our best officers!"

"Hell! A lot of us were killed in France!"

Glassford yelled: "Come on, boys! Let's call an armistice for lunch!"

Laughs. Cheers. In five minutes the battle was over.

Glassford raced back to the office of the district commissioners to report that the first building had been repossessed by the Treasury Department. He warned his superiors, though, that the veterans were becoming so ugly that it would be unwise to attempt any more evacuations that day. Ignoring his advice, misrepresenting his attitude, the commissioners sent the President a message asking that the Army be called out. Glassford felt then, as well as later, that it was a mistake to summon the Army. But he had been shorn of much of his authority. Governmental wheels began to turn. Hoover told War Secretary Hurley to send the Army into action. Hurley conveyed this order to Chief of Staff MacArthur.

As he sped back to the federal triangle, Glassford did not know about this order. In the 91-degree heat, thousands of veterans and hundreds of cops shifted from foot to foot and eyed one another uneasily. Some veterans argued among themselves about what to do next.

At 1:25 P.M. two veterans began scrapping on the second floor of a squatter-occupied building at Pennsylvania Avenue and Third Street. Glassford told four of his cops to break up the fight. As they got near the second floor, they were attacked. One officer was knocked down the steps. Another had his head bashed in with a garbage can. A third was about to be slugged with a brick when the fourth cop drew his gun and fired.

Glassford's head jerked up when he heard the shot. "Don't shoot!" he screamed up the staircase.

Too late. In the melee above Glassford's head a penniless Chicago veteran named William J. Haska was drilled through the heart, while mortal wounds were inflicted upon Eric Carlson of Oakland, California. The veterans outside the building had heard the gunfire, and as the police left, they had to run a gauntlet of missiles. Four cops were injured and had to be rushed to a hospital.

This second disturbance of the day was also brief, if bloodier. Walter W. Waters blamed the trouble on John Pace and his Communist followers. Moments after peace was restored Glassford learned from a reporter that troops were on their way.

To the press War Secretary Hurley had given copies of his reply to the district commissioners: "In response to your information that the police of the district were overwhelmed by an organized attack of several thousand men, and were unable to maintain law and order, I complied with your request for aid from the army to the police."

This was not at all what Glassford had told the commissioners.

Hurley's statement was published in early editions of afternoon papers, so now every veteran in the district knew that the Army had been called out. Hordes of excited men swarmed out of their camps and headed for the federal triangle, where the next action seemed most likely to occur.

It had been 2:55 P.M. when Hurley told MacArthur that Hoover wanted to use troops. The general asked the secretary to put this order in writing, and Hurley did. The order did not require MacArthur to take personal command of the operation, but he never shirked his duty—as he saw it. A few days earlier MacArthur had said to a fellow officer: "If the President gives me orders to act, I would not give this distasteful and disagreeable job to any other officer of the United States Army. If anything should go wrong, it will [*sic*] be the kiss of death for that officer's future."

The fifty-two-year-old general had a forty-one-year-old aide named Dwight D. Eisenhower. When Major Eisenhower heard that MacArthur planned to take active command in the field, he had the audacity to object. If the affair turned into a riot, Eisenhower argued, it would be highly inappropriate for the chief of staff to get involved. MacArthur curtly disagreed. Declaring that the issue was maintenance of federal authority in the district, the general barked that there was "incipient revolution in the air!"

In 1932 military officers wore civilian clothes in Washington because the Hoover administration did not want too many uniforms visible in the streets. MacArthur was wearing a white linen suit when he got the word to act. Now, ordering Eisenhower into uniform, he said he was going to his own quarters to change. As MacArthur strode out of his office, Joseph Baird of the United Press fell into step with him. The reporter asked if he might accompany the general. MacArthur said: "Sure—but you'll have to ride home with me first." Baird rode in MacArthur's big black army car out to Fort Myer, where the general lived with his elderly mother. There MacArthur changed into riding boots and spurs, flared whipcord breeches and a jacket ornamented with eight rows of ribbons and medals.

When he got back to his office, he found Eisenhower uniformed and wearing a Sam Browne belt. A colonel told MacArthur that the President forbade any troops to cross any bridge spanning the Anacostia River; Hoover did not want the veterans followed into any of their camps far from the center of the city. MacArthur paid no attention to the colonel's words. Noticing this, another general repeated the Presidential order. Eisenhower later recalled: "In neither instance did General MacArthur hear these instructions. He said he was too busy and did not want either himself or his staff bothered by people coming down and pretending to bring orders."

MacArthur called out a total of almost 1,000 soldiers. They constituted the second squadron of the Third Cavalry from Fort Myer; the third battalion of the Twelfth Infantry from Fort Howard; and six tanks from the first tank platoon from Fort Meade. About 4:30 P.M. this force rendezvoused just south of the White House.

Several historic firsts were in the making: It was the first display of armed force by the United States Army since the American expedition to Siberia had been withdrawn in 1920. It was the first time in American history that federal troops had been summoned by a President to attack American citizens in their national capital. It was the first time soldiers used gas masks in warfare in their own country. It was the first use of newstyle tanks.

With the deepening of this fateful afternoon, throngs of curious veterans, file clerks, secretaries, Congressmen, women shoppers and out-of-town sightseers gathered in and near the federal triangle. They sat and they dozed; they chatted and they strolled in the sun; they bought popcorn and lemonade from sidewalk vendors. They mopped their brows and fanned themselves, for the temperature still stood at 91 degrees. At 4:45 P.M. their heads whipped toward the southeast as they heard the clanking and rumbling of an approaching military force.

It came from around a corner of the White House and advanced on the pavement of Pennsylvania Avenue. Four cavalry troops, each horseman holding a drawn saber that glinted in the sunshine. Six tanks bristling with machine guns. Behind the tanks, trotting on the double, foot soldiers wearing steel helmets, tear-gas grenades jiggling from belts, fixed bayonets at the ready.

From the three disputed buildings still held by the veterans, the men gazed down upon this show of military might—and hooted. Other veterans stood on the ground in front of their ramshackle huts along the block and jeered the boyish-looking soldiers: "Yellow! Yellow!" A prankster tied a white handkerchief to a wire and poked it through a slit in one of the tanks. Onlookers laughed.

The cavalrymen, their faces blank, deployed along the north side of the avenue and halted. A black veteran pranced back and forth in front of them, waving a big American flag. Two troopers raised curved swords in salute. The others were impassive as they sat their horses. Then a command rang out. The troopers waved their sabers and charged the crowd. Men, women and children screamed and fled. Some ran along the pavement. Others cut through vacant lots, tripping over debris. Swords flashed. Horses reared, pawing the air. People who had fallen to the ground twisted desperately to roll out of the way of the hooves.

Most soldiers acted with restraint, but a few—through fear or inexperience or self-importance—were violent. A man in civilian clothes bellowed his resentment at this attack by Americans on Americans. A cavalryman cried: "We hate this worse than they do—but they brought it on themselves!" A spectator shouted: "The American flag means nothing to me after this! The American flag means nothing to me after this!" General MacArthur started toward him and barked: "Put that man under arrest if he opens his mouth again!"

One mounted man was about to ride down a flag-carrying veteran when an officer threw up his hand, screaming: "No, no, no!" However, other cavalrymen used the flats of their swords to whack fleeing veterans across their shoulders. A few frenzied horse soldiers cut off the ear of one veteran, stabbed another in the hip and slashed a teen-age boy across the arm. For no rational reason, one trooper threw a tear-gas bomb into a telephone booth where a reporter was on the line with his city room.

This cavalry charge drove most of the people back a distance of several blocks.

Meanwhile, the infantrymen wheeled and advanced across an empty lot toward the three veteran-held buildings and the crowd still massed in front of them. They executed this maneuver so fast that the people had no time to break and run. As the soldiers closed in, the people in front shrank back. Those in the rear, trying to relieve the pressure on them, pushed forward. As a result, the whole group was immobilized in the face of the advancing soldiers.

An officer snapped an order. The uniformed men halted, stepped back a pace, jerked gas masks from their packs, tugged the masks onto their faces, snatched grenades from their belts and lobbed them into the middle of the crowd. Everyone panicked. The tear-gas bombs exploded softly: *Pfuttt-pfuttt-pfuttt!* Here and there a veteran snatched up a hot can and threw it back at the soldiers. Some bombs accidentally fell into front yards jammed with Negro women and children. One bounced onto the porch of a home, and two little girls keeled over, choking and screaming.

The southwest breeze blew the sickly-sweet gas into the faces of thousands of sightseers and federal employees, soldiers and veterans, reporters and photographers. Glassford and MacArthur were among those gassed. Except for the soldiers wearing gas masks, everyone else choked, coughed, vomited, wept and wobbled away.

The infantrymen drove the hacking veterans from all three buildings and chased them out of the 300 block of Pennsylvania Avenue. Then, joined by cops, they moved methodically through the flimsy billets along the avenue, tearing down American flags, using torches to set fire to huts and shacks and tents. One woman begged for permission to run into her shanty to get a suitcase, but a soldier growled: "Get out of here, lady, before you get hurt!" And put the torch to her miserable home. Horsemen formed lines along the block to keep outraged veterans from interfering with this official arson. It was finished by 6:05 P.M.

Congressman Fiorello H. LaGuardia had been following these events by means of a teletype machine in his office in the House Office Building. The more he read, the angrier he grew. At last, his face flushed, he ran out of his office and slapped a paper onto the desk of an assistant, Ernest Cuneo. "What do you think of *that?*" LaGuardia shrilled.

Cuneo saw at a glance that it was a draft of a telegram to the White House. It said: BEANS IS BETTER THAN BULLETS AND SOUP IS BETTER THAN GAS . . . F. LAGUARDIA. Cuneo, a graduate of Columbia University, automatically replied: "You've got to say 'Beans *are* better than bullets' or 'A bean *is* better than a bullet.' " LaGuardia screamed at his aide: "The capital in flames and *you* talk *grammar!* Wise guy!" But the New York Congressman corrected his wire before sending it to President Hoover.

That evening the soldiers herded veterans down one street after another, past shantytown after shantytown, down toward the southeast. They kept bombarding the bonus marchers with tear-gas bombs, and the tattered and tired men retaliated by hurling bricks and stones at the uniformed youths. Men on both sides were hurt. Hospitals began receiving dozens of people suffering minor injuries.

By 7:15 P.M. every bivouac in the city had been evacuated and burned. An hour later 200 harried veterans fled from the District of Columbia and sought shelter in the open fields of Virginia. Nervous officials of that state announced they had been promised military aid in the event of trouble.

Now, disobeying President Hoover's order, MacArthur commanded his troops to pursue the raggle-taggle bonus seekers across the Anacostia Bridge. His belief that the veterans were Communist-dominated had been augmented by word that some veterans in outlying camps had armed themselves with weapons. MacArthur snapped: "I will not permit my men to bivouac under the guns of traitors!"

Eisenhower, who disagreed with his superior's judgment, later wrote of the veterans: ". . . most of them, after their arrival on Pennsylvania Avenue, however misled they may have been by a few agitators, were quiet and orderly. They insisted upon enough discipline within their ranks to guard against lawlessness or collapse into mob anarchy."

Colonel Edmund W. Starling, chief of the Secret Service, also disagreed with MacArthur and sided with Eisenhower, saying: "Our agents were among them, keeping us informed of the number of radicals in every group, and checking on the influence they had with the men. Generally speaking there were few Communists, and they had little effect on the men's thinking."

Many years later, after quitting the Communist Party, John Pace testified that there were no more than 100 Communists in the BEF. Pace added that "the active party group—party faction, that we knew were reliable party members—would number no more than twenty-five."

But MacArthur had made up his mind, and on that dreadful day of July 28, 1932, he told Glassford: "We are going to break the back of the B.E.F.!"

* * *

MacArthur's intentions were so clear that veterans ran to their camps on the south side of the Anacostia River to lead their women and children to safety. Seeing a woman at Camp Anacostia, one veteran shouted to her husband: "For God's sake—get her out of here! There'll be shooting in a few minutes!" The wife wailed: "I won't go! If he's going to be killed, I'm going to stay here and be killed with him!" Most women and youngsters, however, straggled out of the cantonment and up nearby Good Hope Hill, where they waited and watched and wept.

Since Anacostia was the largest of all the BEF camps, they expected it to be attacked by the main body of troops. So, from various parts of the city, with mingled motives, veterans streamed into Anacostia. Those without hope collected their few belongings and departed toward the south. Others, spurred by anger, began building a barricade of old autos and trucks around a part of the campsite. A few hotheads strode about carrying rifles, and others boasted of weapons buried in the ground nearby. Reporters were told to get the hell out of the place unless they wanted to be lynched.

As MacArthur's troopers clattered toward the illuminated Anacostia Bridge, district citizens by the thousands gathered on the span and near it, eager to see what might happen. The advancing military force was led by policemen, who pushed spectators to the southeast end of the bridge to clear a path for the soldiers. The people fell back as ordered, but it was obvious from their muttered comments that they sympathized with the veterans, the unseen veterans who huddled and waited in the darkness below the bridge, in the flatland of the camp.

MacArthur had decided on his battle plan: His tanks would crash through the car-and-truck barrier along the north side of Camp Anacostia. This done, he would send in trucks equipped with floodlights to light the battleground, attack with bayonet-brandishing foot soldiers, back them up with cavalrymen and with lorries mounting machine guns. Because of the soft breeze still wafting from the southwest, his men would have to don gas masks again when they threw grenades at the veterans. A reserve force of 3,000 soldiers was heading for the city to be thrown into combat if necessary.

"Hot Waters" rushed to the camp and raced here and there, begging the veterans to forget about resistance, pleading with them to leave peacefully while there still was time. "I don't want any more bloodshed!" Waters cried. Glassford also showed up, his white shirt wet with sweat, and rode his motorcycle around the site, yelling to the men to get out before they got massacred.

MacArthur sent word that he wanted to parley with the camp commander, W. D. Atwell. Waving a white shirt as a flag of truce, Atwell walked alone onto the broad parade ground to confer with the general, who had been given safe-conduct inside the camp. The general said he had orders to evacuate Camp Anacostia and would give the veterans one hour to leave. Earlier in the evening Atwell had urged his men to dig up their guns and fight. At the end of his brief conference with MacArthur, however, Atwell cried: "Give way, boys, give way! They've got the tanks and you haven't got a chance in hell!"

At 10 P.M. the troops attacked. Leaving the high ground at the southeast end of the bridge, they descended into the dark flatlands below. First the black hulks of tanks, their grinding gears blanking out the chirps of crickets. Then the trucks laden with floodlights, thudding and crunching over the rough terrain. Next the foot soldiers, sweating in their jackets and puttees, heavy shoes squishing in marshland, slogging forward anxiously, bayonet-tipped carbines held in slippery wet hands, moving single file along the dim riverbank. Behind them they heard the comforting purr of lorries and the metallic jangle of harnesses as horses picked their way down the steep embankment and into the camp.

All went as planned. The tanks broke through the flimsy barricade, opening a path for the trucks. *Click-click-click!* The huge floodlights punched blue-gray hazy holes through the black night. In this instant glare stood row upon row of tents and lean-tos. The lights pinned long shadows to the feet of all the angrily dancing veterans who dared to stay and fight. Then tear-gas bombs were thrown at these men, who cursed and shook their fists and retreated. They gave ground, weeping their fury, as they went down, disorganized and outnumbered, under a military force the like of which they had seen on the battlefields of Europe.

When the veterans broke and ran, the soldiers lit torches, long flaming brands, ran from hut to hut and tent to tent, peered in to make sure no one was left inside, then set fire to each dwelling. *Whoosh!* A pillar of flame arose from the camp platform that had been used for speechmaking and boxing matches. *Whoosh!* A second column of fire snaked into the night sky as the torch was put to the big gospel tent.

In their sullen retreat the veterans felt they might as well bring down the whole damned place in ruins, so they themselves began setting fires. One man dashed about begging for matches and ran to an edge of the billet to burn everything he could find.

The breeze had died down, so the smoke rose straight toward the heavens as flames snapped and stuttered, eating their way through Camp Anacostia. Over the national capital the sky seemed to hemorrhage. The bloody stain could be seen through the windows of the Lincoln Study in the White House, where President Hoover sat conversing with Seth Richardson, an assistant attorney general, and with Henry M. Robinson, a California banker and lawyer. Near the President stood his chief bodyguard, Colonel Starling, who stared at the crimson horizon and thought that the sight was shameful.

High and higher still licked the lemon-tipped flames until their glow could be seen from many miles away. In that twitching light, faces seemed to appear, vanish, reappear in the erratic sequence of an old-time movie. The fleeing veterans had been careful not to burn the National Guard pup tents that Glassford had got for them, but the soldiers put the torch to everything—the tents and huts and shanties and crates and beds—until the crazy-quilt camp sagged into ashes and hot metal, until the only things silhouetted against the glare were iron bedsteads looking like muted harps.

By midnight all was over. After two months, the Bonus Expeditionary Force had been driven from the national capital—but at what cost?

The police had killed two veterans. The Army had not fired a single bullet, but swords and gas had taken their toll. An eleven-week-old baby was gassed so severely that he later died. An eight-year-old boy was left partially blinded by gas fumes. More than 1,000 people felt the effects of the gas grenades. Sixty-three persons were injured. A total of 135 persons were arrested. And the Hoover administration suffered a fatal loss of prestige, one historian declaring that the BEF "goaded President Hoover into committing political suicide."

Chief of Police Glassford declared he had not reported that the situation was beyond the control of the police and that he had not asked for troops. Major Eisenhower felt sorry for the dispersed veterans. Governor Roosevelt shuddered and shook his head in sorrow. Mrs. Eleanor Roosevelt recoiled from the news in horror. Newscaster Lowell Thomas called the affair a "tragic spectacle." Senator Hugo L. Black of Alabama denounced the Army attack as "unnecessary and ill-timed." Norman Thomas said that Hoover's decision to use the troops was due to "a bad case of nervous irritation mixed with fear." Senator William E. Borah of Idaho was too embittered to say anything.

About 11 A.M. on the day after the "Battle of Camp Anacostia," General MacArthur went to the White House to make a personal report to President Hoover and War Secretary Hurley. The two of them, according to MacArthur, "expressed gratification at what had been accomplished." There seems to be no evidence that the President rebuked his chief of staff for exceeding his authority, for disobeying a Presidential order, by stampeding the veterans out of the District of Columbia. Instead, Hoover gave the press this comment: "A challenge to the authority of the United States government has been met, swiftly and firmly. After months of patient indulgence, the government met overt lawlessness as it always must be met if the cherished processes of self-government are to be preserved. We cannot tolerate the abuse of Constitutional rights by those who would destroy all government, no matter who they might be. Government cannot be coerced by mob rule. . . ."

The B.E.F. News managed to publish an edition on July 30, and half the front page was taken up with a cartoon of Hoover wearing the Capitol on his head like a Prussian helmet, while his face was painted with a spiked mustache that made him resemble Kaiser Wilhelm of Germany. But the newspaper, like the veterans themselves, faded from the scene.

By early August some 9,000 confused bonus marchers milled aimlessly about Johnstown, Pennsylvania, whose mayor had given them a refuge despite the protests of some citizens. A woman offered to give them 25 acres of land in Maryland for use as a permanent colony, but Walter W. Waters realized that the game was up. When he urged the veterans to disband and go home, they did so—having irrevocably changed the nation. The nature of this change was summarized by Thomas L. Stokes, a United Press reporter who had witnessed the smashing of the BEF in Washington. Stokes wrote:

"This, I said to myself, may be the end of this country as we know it. The United States Army turned on to American citizens—just fellows like myself, down on their luck, dispirited, hopeless. My mood was one of despair. It was an experience that stands apart from all others in my life. So all the misery and suffering had finally come to this—soldiers marching with their guns against American citizens."

The New Deal: The Conservative Achievements of Liberal Reform

Barton J. Bernstein

Many American historians in the past have praised the Roosevelt administration for its non-ideological flexibility and for its far-ranging reforms.

Recalling the bitter opposition to welfare measures and restraints upon business, many liberal historians have emphasized the New Deal's discontinuity with the immediate past. For them there was a "Roosevelt Revolution," or at the very least a dramatic achievement of a beneficent liberalism. . . . Rejecting earlier interpretations which viewed the New Deal as socialism or state capitalism, they have also disregarded theories of or of corporate liberalism. The New Deal has generally commanded their approval for such laws or institutions as minimum wages, public housing, farm assistance, the Tennessee Valley Authority, the Wagner Act, more progressive taxation, and social security. For most liberal historians the New Deal meant the replenishment of democracy, the rescuing of the federal government from the clutches of big business, the significant redistribution of political power. Breaking with laissez faire the new administration, according to these interpretations, marked the end of the passive or impartial state and the beginning of positive government, of the interventionist state acting to offset concentrations of private power, and affirming the rights and responding to the needs of the unprivileged.

From the perspective of the late 1960s these themes no longer seem adequate to characterize the New Deal. The liberal reforms of the New Deal did not transform the American system; they conserved and protected American corporate capitalism, occasionally by absorbing parts of threatening programs. There was no significant redistribution of power in American society, only limited recognition of other organized groups, seldom of unorganized peoples. Neither the bolder programs advanced by New Dealers nor the final legislation greatly extended the beneficence of government beyond the middle classes or drew upon the wealth of the few for the needs of the many. Designed to maintain the American system, liberal activity was directed toward essentially conservative goals. Experimentalism was most frequently limited to means: seldom did it extend to ends. Never questioning private

Reprinted from *Towards a New Past*, (1970), Pantheon Books.

enterprise, it operated within safe channels, far short of Marxism even of native American radicalisms that offered structural critiques and structural solutions.

All of this is not to deny the changes wrought by the New Deal—the extension of welfare programs, the growth of federal power, the strengthening of the executive, even the narrowing of property rights. But it is to assert that the elements of continuity are stronger, that the magnitude of change has been exaggerated. The New Deal failed to solve the problem of depression, it failed to raise the impoverished, it failed to redistribute income, it failed to extend equality and generally countenanced racial discrimination and segregation. It failed generally to make business more responsible to the social welfare or to threaten business's preeminent political power. In this sense, the New Deal, despite the shifts in tone and spirit from the earlier decade, was profoundly conservative and continuous with the 1920s.

The 1920s properly interpreted by focusing on the continuation of progressive impulses, demands often frustrated by the rivalry of interest groups. Through these years while agriculture and labor struggled to secure advantages from the federal government, big business flourished. Praised for creating American prosperity, business leaders easily convinced the nation that they were socially responsible, that they were fulfilling the needs of the public. Benefitting from earlier legislation that had promoted economic rationalization and stability, they were opponents of federal benefits to other groups but seldom proponents of laissez faire.

In no way did the election of Herbert Hoover in 1928 seem to challenge the New Era. An heir of Wilson, Hoover promised an even closer relationship with big business. . . . As Secretary of Commerce, Hoover had opposed unbridled competition and had transformed his department into a vigorous friend of business. Sponsoring trade associations, he promoted industrial self-regulation and the increased rationalization of business. He had also expanded foreign trade, endorsed the regulation of new forms of communications, encouraged relief in disasters, and recommended public works to offset economic declines.

By training and experience, few men in American political life seemed better prepared than Hoover to cope with the depression. Responding promptly to the crisis, he acted to stabilize the economy and secured the agreement of businessmen to maintain production and wage rates. Unwilling to let the economy "go through the wringer," the President requested easier money, self-liquidating public works, lower personal and corporate income taxes, and stronger commodity stabilization corporations. . . .

But these efforts proved inadequate. The tax cut benefitted the wealthy and failed to raise effective demand. The public works were insufficient. The commodity stabilization corporations soon ran out of funds, and agricultural prices kept plummeting. Businessmen cut back production, dismissed employees, and finally cut wages. . . . Blaming the collapse on European failures, he could not admit that American capitalism, had failed. When prodded by Congress to increase public works, to provide direct relief, and to further unbalance the budget, he doggedly resisted. Additional deficits would destroy business confidence, he feared, and relief would erode the principles of individual and local responsibility. Clinging to faith in voluntarism, Hoover also briefly rebuffed the efforts by financiers to secure the Reconstruction Finance Corporation (RFC). Finally endorsing the RFC, he also supported expanded lending by Federal Land Banks, recommended home-loan banks, and even approved small federal loans (usually inadequate) to states needing funds for relief. In this burst of activity, the President had moved to the very limits of his ideology.

Restricted by his background . . . he stopped far short of the state corporatism urged by some businessmen and politicians. With capitalism crumbling he had acted vigorously to save it, but he would not yield to the representatives of business or disadvantaged groups who wished to alter the government. He was reluctant to use the federal power to achieve through compulsion what could not be realized through voluntary means. Proclaiming a false independence, he did not understand that his government already represented business interests; hence, he rejected policies that would openly place the power of the state in the hands of business or that would permit the formation of a syndicalist state in which power might be exercised (in the words of William Appleman Williams) "by a relatively few leaders of reach functional bloc formed and operating as an oligarchy. . . .

. . . Using the federal government to stabilize the economy and advance the interests of the groups, Franklin D. Roosevelt directed the campaign to save large-scale corporate capitalism. Though recognizing new political interests and extending benefits to them, his New Deal never effectively challenged big business or the organization of the economy. In providing assistance to the needy and by rescuing them from starvation, Roosevelt's humane efforts also protected the established system: he sapped organized radicalism of its waning strength and of its potential constituency among the unorganized and discontented. Sensitive to public opinion and fearful of radicalism, Roosevelt acted from a mixture of motives that rendered his liberalism cautious and limited, his experimentalism narrow. . . .

Roosevelt's response to the banking crisis emphasizes the conservatism of his administration. . . . Entering the White House when banks were failing and Americans had lost faith in the financial system, the President could have nationalized it—"without a word of protest," judged Senator Bronson Cutting. . . . To save the system, Roosevelt relied upon collaboration between bankers and Hoover's Treasury officials to prepare legislation extending federal assistance to banking. So great was the demand for action that House members, voting even without copies, passed it unanimously, and the Senate, despite objections by a few Progressives, approved it the same evening. "The President," remarked a cynical congressman, "drove the money-changers out of the Capitol on March 4th—and they were all back on the 9th."

Undoubtedly the most dramatic example of Roosevelt's early conservative approach to recovery was the National Recovery Administration (NRA). It was based on the War Industries Board (WIB) which had provided the model . . . to limit competition through industrial self-regulation under federal sanction. As trade associations flourished during the decade, the FTC encouraged "codes of fair competition" and some industries even tried to set prices and restrict production. Operating without the force of law, these agreements broke down. When the depression struck, industrial pleas for regulation increased. After the Great Crash, important business leaders including Henry I. Harriman of the Chamber of Commerce and Gerard Swope of General Electric called for suspension of antitrust laws and federal organization of business collaboration. Joining them were labor leaders, particularly those in "sick" industries—John L. Lewis of the United Mine Workers and Sidney Hillman of Amalgamated Clothing Workers.

Designed largely for industrial recovery, the NRA legislation provided for minimum wages and maximum hours. It also made concessions to prolabor congressmen and labor leaders who demanded some specific benefits for unions—recognition of the worker's rights to organization and to collective bargaining. In practice, though, the much-heralded Section 7a was a disappointment to most friends of labor. . . . To many frustrated workers and their disgusted leaders, NRA became "National Run Around." The clause, unionists found, "had the practical effect of placing NRA on the side of antiunion employers in their struggle against trade unions. . . . [It] thus threw its weight against labor in the balance of bargaining power." And while some far-sighted industrialists feared radicalism and hoped to forestall it by incorporating unions into the economic system, most preferred to leave their workers unorganized or in company unions. . . .

Not only did the NRA provide fewer advantages than unionists had anticipated, but it also failed as a recovery measure. It probably even retarded recovery by supporting restrictionism and price increases, concluded a Brookings study. Placing effective power for code-writing in big business, NRA injured small businesses and contributed to the concentration of American industry. It was not the government-business partnership as envisaged by Adolf A. Berle, Jr., nor government managed as Rexford Tugwell had hoped, but rather, business managed, as Raymond Moley had desired. . . .

Viewing the economy as a "concert of organized interests," the New Deal also provided benefits for farmers—the Agricultural Adjustment Act. Reflecting the political power of larger commercial farmers and accepting restrictionist economics, the measure assumed that the agricultural problem was overproduction, not underconsumption. Financed by a processing tax designed to raise prices to parity, payments encouraged restricted production and cutbacks in farm labor.

With benefits accruing chiefly to the larger owners, they frequently removed from production the lands of sharecroppers and tenant farmers, and "tractored" them and hired hands of the land. In assisting agriculture, the AAA, like the NRA, sacrificed the interests of the marginal and the unrecognized to the welfare of those with greater political and economic power.

In large measure, the early New Deal of the NRA and AAA was a "broker state." Though the government served as a mediator of interests and sometimes imposed its will in divisive situations, it was generally the servant of powerful groups. "Like the mercantilists, the New Dealers protected vested interests with the authority of the state," acknowledges William Leuchtenburg. But it was some improvement over the 1920s when business was the only interest capable of imposing its will on the government. While extending to other groups the benefits of the state, the New Deal, however, continued to recognize the pre-eminence of business interests.

The politics of the broker state also heralded the way of the future—of continued corporate dominance in a political structure where other groups agreed generally on corporate capitalism and squabbled only about the size of the shares. Delighted by this increased participation and the absorption of dissident groups, many liberals did not understand the dangers in the emerging organization of politics. They had too much faith in representative institutions and in associations to foresee the perils—of leaders not representing their constituents, of bureaucracy diffusing responsibility, of officials serving their own interests. Failing to perceive the dangers in the emerging structure, most liberals agreed with Senator Robert Wagner of New York: "In order that the strong may not take advantage of the weak, every group must be equally strong." His advice then seemed appropriate for organizing labor, but it neglected the problems of unrepresentative leadership and of the many millions to be left beyond organization.

In dealing with the organized interests, the President acted frequently as a broker, but his government did not simply express the vectors of external forces. The New Deal state was too complex, too loose, and some of Roosevelt's subordinates were following their own inclinations and pushing the government in directions of their own design. The President would also depart from his role as a broker and act to secure programs he desired. As a skilled politician, he could split coalitions, divert the interests of groups, or place the prestige of his office on the side of desired legislation.

For millions suffering in a nation wracked by poverty, the promises of the Left seemed attractive. Capitalizing on the misery, Huey Long offered Americans a "Share Our Wealth" program—a welfare state with prosperity, not subsistence, for the disadvantaged, those neglected by most politicians. "Every Man a King": pensions for the elderly, college for the deserving, homes and cars for families—that was the promise of American life. Also proposing minimum wages, increased public works, shorter work weeks, and a generous farm program, he demanded a "soak-the-rich" tax program. Despite the economic defects of his plan, Long was no hayseed, and his forays into the East revealed support far beyond the bayous and hamlets of his native South. . . . More challenging to Roosevelt was Francis Townsend's plan—monthly payments of $200 to those past sixty who retired and promised to spend the stipend within thirty days. Another enemy of the New Deal was Father Coughlin, the popular radio priest, who had broken with Roosevelt and formed a National Union for Social Justice to lead the way to a corporate society beyond capitalism.

To a troubled nation offered "redemption" by the Left, there was also painful evidence that the social fabric was tearing—law was breaking down. When the truckers in Minneapolis struck, the police provoked an incident and shot sixty-seven people, some in the back. Covering the tragedy, Eric Sevareid, then a young reporter, wrote, "I understood deep in my bones and blood what fascism was. . . . Elsewhere, in textile mills from. Rhode Island to Georgia, in cities like Des Moines and Toledo, New York and Philadelphia, there were brutality and violence, sometimes bayonets and tear gas.

Challenged by the Left, . . . Roosevelt turned to disarm the discontent. . . . Harry Hopkins and the . . . [New Dealers] were not radicals: they did not seek to transform the system, only to make it more humane. They too, wished to preserve large-scale corporate capitalism, but unlike Roosevelt or Moley, they were prepared for more vigorous action. Their commitment to reform was greater, their tolerance for injustice far less. Joining them in pushing the New Deal left were the leaders of industrial unions, who, while also not wishing to transform the system, sought for workingmen higher wages, better conditions, stronger and larger unions, and for themselves a place closer to the fulcrum of power.

The problems of organized labor, however, neither aroused Roosevelt's humanitarianism nor suggested possibilities of reshaping the political coalition. When asked during the NRA about employee representation, he had replied that workers could select anyone they wished—the Ahkoond of Swat, a union, even the Royal Geographical Society. As a paternalist, viewing himself (in the words of James MacGregor Burns) as a "partisan and benefactor" of workers, he would not understand the objections to company unions or to multiple unionism under NRA. Nor did he foresee the political dividends that support of independent unions could yield to his party. Though presiding over the reshaping of politics (which would extend the channels of power to some of the discontented and redirect their efforts to competition within a limited framework), he was not its architect, and he was unable clearly to see or understand the unfolding design. . . .

Responding to the threat from the left, Roosevelt also moved during the Second Hundred Days to secure laws regulating banking, raising taxes, dissolving utility-holding companies, and creating social security. Building on the efforts of states during the Progressive Era, the Social Security Act marked the movement toward the welfare state, but the core of the measure, the old-age provision, was more important as a landmark than for its substance. While establishing a federal-state system of unemployment compensation, the government, by making workers contribute to their old-age insurance, denied its financial responsibility for the elderly. The act excluded more than a fifth of the labor force leaving, among others, more than five million farm laborers and domestics without coverage.

Though Roosevelt criticized the tax laws for not preventing "an unjust concentration of wealth and economic power," his own tax measure would not have significantly redistributed wealth. Yet his message provoked an "amen" from Huey Long and protests from businessmen. Retreating from his promises, Roosevelt failed to support the bill, and it succumbed to conservative forces. They removed the inheritance tax and greatly reduced the proposed corporate and individual levies. The final law did not "soak the rich." But it did engender deep resentment among the wealthy for increasing taxes on gifts and estates, imposing an excess-profits tax (which Roosevelt had not requested), and raising surtaxes. . . .

Those historians who have characterized the events of 1935 as the beginning of a second New Deal have imposed a pattern on those years which most participants did not then discern. In moving to social security, guarantees of collective bargaining, utility regulation, and progressive taxation, the government did advance the nation toward greater liberalism, but the shift was exaggerated and most of the measures accomplished far less than either friends or foes suggested. . . .

Nor were so many powerful businessmen disaffected by the New Deal. Though the smaller businessmen who filled the ranks of the Chamber of Commerce resented the federal bureaucracy and the benefits to labor and thus criticized NRA, representatives of big business found the agency useful and opposed a return to unrestricted competition. In 1935, members of the Business Advisory Council—including Henry Harriman, outgoing president of the Chamber, Thomas Watson of International Business Machines, Walter Gifford of American Telephone and Telegraph, Gerard Swope of General Electric, Winthrop Aldrich of the Chase National Bank, and W. Averell Harriman of Union Pacific—vigorously endorsed a two-year renewal of NRA. . . .

Roosevelt could attack the "economic royalists" and endorse the TNEC investigation of economic concentration, but he was unprepared to resist the basic demands of big business. While there was ambiguity in his treatment of oligopoly, it was more the confusion of means than of ends, for his tactics were never likely to impair concentration. Even the antitrust program under Thurman Arnold, concludes Frank Freidel, was "intended less to bust the trusts than to forestall too drastic legislation." Operating through consent degrees and designed to reduce prices to the consumer, the program frequently "allowed industries to function much as they had in NRA days." In effect, then, throughout its variations, the New Deal had sought to cooperate with business.

Though vigorous in rhetoric and experimental in tone, the New Deal was narrow in its goals and wary of bold economic reform. . . .

Usually opportunistic and frequently shifting, the New Deal . . . ran out of fuel . . . because it ran out of ideas. Acknowledging the end in 1939, Roosevelt proclaimed, "We have now passed the period of internal conflict in the launching of our program of social reform. Our full energies may now be released to invigorate the processes of recovery in order to preserve our reforms. . . .

The sad truth was that the heralded reforms were severely limited, that inequality continued, that efforts at recovery had failed. Millions had come to accept the depression as a way of life. A decade after the Great Crash, when millions were still unemployed, Fiorello LaGuardia recommended that "we accept the inevitable, that we are now in a new normal." "It was reasonable to expect a probable minimum of 4,000,000 to 5,000,000 unemployed," Harry Hopkins had concluded. Even that level was never reached, for business would not spend and Roosevelt refused to countenance the necessary expenditures. "It was in economics that our troubles lay," Tugwell wrote. "For their solution his [Roosevelt's] progressivism, his new deal was pathetically insufficient. . .

Clinging to faith in fiscal orthodoxy even when engaged in deficit spending, Roosevelt had been unwilling to greatly unbalance the budget. Having pledged in his first campaign to cut expenditures and to restore the balanced budget, the President had at first adopted recovery programs that would not drain government finances. Despite a burst of activity under the Civil Works Administration during the first winter, public works expenditures were frequently slow and cautious. Shifting from direct relief, which Roosevelt (like Hoover) considered "a narcotic, a subtle destroyer of the human spirit," the government moved to work relief. . . . By 1937 the government had poured enough money into the economy to spur production to within 10 percent of 1929 levels, but unemployment still hovered over seven million. Yet so eager was the President to balance the budget that he cut expenditures for public works and relief, and plunged the economy into a greater depression. While renewing expenditures, Roosevelt remained cautious in his fiscal policy, and the nation still had almost nine million unemployed in 1939. After nearly six years of struggling with the depression, the Roosevelt administration could not lead the nation to recovery, but it had relieved suffering. In most of America, starvation was no longer possible. Perhaps that was the most humane achievement of the New Deal.

Its efforts on behalf of humane *reform* were generally faltering and shallow, of more value to the middle classes, of less value to organized workers, of even less to the marginal men. In conception and in practice, seemingly humane efforts revealed the shortcomings of American liberalism. For example, public housing, praised as evidence of the federal government's concern for the poor, was limited in scope (to 180,000 units) and unfortunate in results. It usually meant the consolidation of ghettos, the robbing of men of their dignity, the treatment of men as wards with few rights. And slum clearance came to mean "Negro clearance" and removal of the other poor. Of much of this liberal reformers were unaware, and some of the problems can be traced to the structure of bureaucracy and to the selection of government personnel and social workers who disliked the poor. But the liberal conceptions, it can be argued, were also flawed, [for] . . . Liberalism was elitist. Seeking to build America in their own image, liberals wanted to create an environment which they thought would restructure character and personality more appropriate to white, middle-class America.

While slum dwellers received little besides relief from the New Deal, and their needs were frequently misunderstood, [Blacks] as a group received even less assistance—less than they needed and sometimes even less than their proportion in the population would have justified. Under the NRA they were frequently dismissed and their wages were sometimes below the legal minimum. The Civilian Conservation Corps left them "forgotten" men—excluded, discriminated against, segregated. In general, what the [Blacks] gained—relief, WPA jobs, equal pay on some federal projects—was granted them as poor people, not as [Blacks]. To many black men the distinction was unimportant, for no government had ever given them so much. "My friends, go home and turn Lincoln's picture to the wall," a [Black] publisher told his race." That debt has been paid in full. . .

Even less bold than in economic reform, the New Deal left intact the race relations of America. Yet its belated and cautious recognition of the black man was great enough to woo Negro leaders and even to court the masses. One of the bitter ironies of these years is that a New Dealer could tell the NAACP in 1936: "Under our new conception of democracy, the Negro will be given the chance to which he is entitled. . . . "But it was true, Ickes emphasized that "The greatest advance [since Reconstruction] toward assuring the Negro that degree of justice to which he is entitled and that equality of opportunity under the law which is implicit in his American citizenship, has been made since Franklin D. Roosevelt was sworn in as President. . . ."

It was not in the cities and not among the Negroes but in rural America that Roosevelt administration made its (philosophically) boldest efforts: creation of the Tennessee Valley Authority and the later attempt to construct seven little valley authorities. Though conservation was not a new federal policy and government-owned utilities were sanctioned by municipal experience, federal activity in this area constituted a challenge to corporate enterprise and an expression of concern about the poor. A valuable example of regional planning and a contribution to regional prosperity, TVA still fell far short of expectations. The agency soon retreated from social planning. . . . Fearful of antagonizing the powerful interests, its agricultural program neglected the tenants and the sharecroppers.

To urban workingmen the New Deal offered some, but limited, material benefits. Though the government had instituted contributory social security and unemployment insurance, its much-heralded Fair Labor Standards Act, while prohibiting child labor, was a greater disappointment. It exempted millions from its wages-and-hours provisions. So unsatisfactory was the measure that one congressman cynically suggested, "Within 90 days after appointment of the administrator, she should report to Congress whether anyone is subject to this bill." Requiring a minimum of twenty-five cents an hour ($11 a week for 44 hours), it raised the wages of only about a half-million at a time when nearly twelve million workers in interstate commerce were earning less than forty cents an hour.

More important than these limited measures was the administration's support, albeit belated, of the organization of labor and the right of collective bargaining. Slightly increasing organized workers' share of the national income, the new industrial unions extended job security to millions who were previously subject to the whim of management. Unionization freed them from the perils of a free market.

By assisting labor, as well as agriculture, the New Deal started the institutionalization of larger interest groups into a new political economy. Joining business as tentative junior partners, they shared the consensus on the value of large-scale corporate capitalism, and were permitted to participate in the competition for the division of shares. While failing to redistribute income, the New Deal modified the political structure at the price of excluding many from the process of decision making. To many what was offered in fact was symbolic representation, formal representation. It was not the industrial workers necessarily who were recognized, but their unions and leaders; it was not even the farmers, but their organizations and leaders. While this was not a conscious design, it was the predictable result of conscious policies. It could not have been easily avoided, for it was part of the price paid by a large society unwilling to consider radical new designs for the distribution of power and wealth.

In the deepest sense, this new form of representation was rooted in the liberal's failure to endorse a meaningful egalitarianism which would provide actual equality of opportunity. It was also the limited concern with equality and justice that accounted for the shallow efforts of the New Deal and left so many Americans behind. The New Deal was neither a "third American Revolution," as Carl Degler suggests, nor even a "halfway revolution," as William Leuchtenburg concludes. Not only was the extension of representation to new groups less than fullfledged partnership, but the New Deal neglected many Americans—sharecroppers, tenant farmers, migratory workers and farm laborers, slum dwellers, unskilled workers, and the unemployed Negroes. They were left outside the new order. As Roosevelt asserted in 1937 (in a classic understatement), one third of the nation was "ill-nourished, ill-clad, ill-housed. . . .

The Twisting Path to War

Stephen Ambrose and Douglas Brinkley

> *I hate war.*
> FRANKLIN DELANO ROOSEVELT

The United States felt fairly secure in the world of 1938. Neither of the great totalitarian political forces of the century, Fascism nor Communism, was a threat. So long as Britain and France continued to stand against Hitler and the Nazis, the United States had nothing to fear militarily from Germany. Elsewhere, anti-Communism was triumphing in Spain, while in central and eastern Europe governments hostile to the Soviet Union continued to contain Communism.

On the other side of the world the United States, in combination with the British, French, and Dutch, still ruled the Pacific. American control of Hawaii and the Philippines, Dutch control of the Netherlands East Indies (N.E.I., today's Indonesia), French control of Indochina (today's Laos, Cambodia [Democratic Kampuchea], and Vietnam), and British control of India, Burma, Hong Kong, and Malaya gave the Western powers a dominant position in Asia. Japan, ruled by her military, was aggressive, determined to end white man's rule in Asia, and thus a threat to the status quo. But Japan lacked crucial natural resources, most notably oil, and was tied down by her war in China.

On the great land mass connecting Europe and Asia, Russia was relatively weak and non-expansive. In the Middle East and Africa, European colonialism dominated. In Latin America, American economic imperialism guaranteed cheap raw materials for American industries and a dependable market.

The United States in 1938 saw no pressing need to play any great role in the world. Isolationism reigned in the Congress, reflecting a national mood. The Nye Committee, conducting a Senate investigation, had "proved" that Wall Street had dragged the United States into World War I. The aftermath led many to believe that entering World War I had been a mistake—so many as to make disarmament and neutrality the dominant factors in American foreign policy in the 1920s and 1930s.

The attitude of the President himself reinforced isolationism. Unlike Winston Churchill, Hitler, or the Japanese leaders and unlike his cousin Theodore Roosevelt, Franklin D. Roosevelt saw neither glory nor romance in war, nor did he feel that it strengthened the national fiber. If not a pacifist, FDR was certainly no militarist. On a number of occasions he declared, with deep emotion, "I hate war."

American foreign policy in 1938 was to support the status quo, but only through vaguely worded statements. Roosevelt, Secretary of State Cordell Hull, and a majority of the American people did not want a German domination of Europe or a Japanese domination of Asia, but neither were they ready to do much to stop it. Least of all were they willing to improve the armed forces so that the United States could threaten to punish aggression.

In mid-March of 1939 Hitler's armies overran Czechoslovakia. Roosevelt failed to support a Senate resolution that would have repealed the arms embargo (required in case of war by the neutrality acts of the mid-thirties) and allowed American industries to sell war goods to France and Britain on a cash-and-carry basis. Although FDR and a majority of the people had declared that their sympathies lay with the democracies, they had also demonstrated to Hitler that in the immediate future he had nothing to fear from the United States. On August 23, 1939, Hitler announced the Nazi-Soviet Pact, which provided for the division of Poland between Russia and Germany and relieved Germany of the nightmare of a two-front war. On September 1, 1939, the Nazis struck Poland; two days later Britain and France declared war on Germany, and World War II was under way.

Americans split sharply over the question of how to react. Isolationists resisted any steps that might lead to aid for the democracies, fearing that the United States would thereby become so committed to an Allied victory that, as in 1917, she would be drawn into war against her will. Interventionists, meanwhile, wanted to abandon neutrality and give military aid to Britain and France. Roosevelt took a middle ground. In a speech to a special session of Congress, FDR declared four times that his policy was designed to keep the United States out of war. He then asked for repeal of the embargo on arms and approval of a cash-and-carry system. Congress agreed in November 1939.

Cash-and-carry symbolized much that was to follow. It aligned the United States with the democracies, reiterated American concern and friendship for Western Europe, and made it clear that the country would resist any attempt to upset the balance of power in Europe. But it also indicated that the United States was unwilling to pay a high price to stop Hitler. America would sell arms to the democracies as long as the democracies picked them up and carried them off. America was taking uncommonly large risks by not doing more.

Just how great those risks were, Roosevelt knew as did few others in the world. On October 11, 1939, world-renowned physicist Albert Einstein, a Jewish refugee from the Nazis, warned FDR that the Germans were working on the problem of harnessing atomic energy into a bomb. If Hitler got an atomic bomb, he would surely conquer Europe. Roosevelt was impressed by Einstein's message. He conferred privately with key congressional leaders and together they started the Manhattan Project. This secret project was designed to build an atomic bomb capable of being dropped from an airplane, and to get it built before Hitler could complete his own plans.

The Manhattan Project was the beginning of the marriage between science and government in the United States, and thus one of the most important legacies of World War II. It was also the first use of extreme secrecy about government activities, justified on the grounds of national security. In the case of the Manhattan Project, most members of Congress did not even know where the funds they had appropriated were going.

But although Roosevelt was willing to act decisively in the race for an atomic bomb, there was otherwise a distinct limit on the American contribution to stopping Hitler. After German armies overran Poland in the fall of 1939, a period of stagnation set in on the western front. Americans called it a "phony war" and saw no pressing reason to strain themselves to build up their stength. FDR increased the regular army from 210,000 to 217,000 and asked for an army budget of $853 million, which the Congress cut by nearly 10 percent. These paltry figures constituted an announcement to Hitler that the United States did not intend to fight in Europe in the near future.

The German spring offensive of 1940 brought forth a tough verbal but limited practical response from the United States. The President asked for a supplemental appropriation to raise troop strength to 255,000; Congress, after hearing Army Chief of Staff George C. Marshall's desperate appeals, raised the force to 375,000. The Nazis, meanwhile, rolled on. On May 15 the new British Prime Minister, Winston Churchill, urgently requested forty or fifty American destroyers to protect Britain's Atlantic supply line. Churchill called it a matter of "life or death." Roosevelt was reluctant to act. On June 5, with the fall of France imminent and Britain about to be left standing alone, he told a Cabinet official that it would require an act of Congress to transfer the destroyers to England and implied that he was not ready to ask for such a bill.

He was ready to speak out. On June 10, 1940, the President told the graduating class of the University of Virginia that the United States would follow "two obvious and simultaneous courses," extending to France and Britain "the material resources of this nation" and speeding up the development of these resources so that the American armed forces could be strengthened. The speech was hailed by interventionists in the United States as setting a new course, but the French quickly discovered its limits. On June 14 French Premier Paul Reynaud appealed to Roosevelt to send American troops to Europe in France's hour of need. Roosevelt refused. Even had he wanted to act, he had no troops available to send overseas. Within the week the French signed an armistice with Germany.

The fall of France was a shattering blow. No one had forecast it. The United States now faced an entirely new situation. No longer could the nation comfortably expect that the British and French would stop the Germans. The British, standing alone, might survive, although even that was questionable, but would never be able to roll back the Nazis by themselves. The best-disciplined and most highly educated and productive nation in Europe now dominated the Continent. The balance of power was gone. Hitler posed no immediate military threat to the New World, but if he could conquer England and get control of the British fleet, then overrun Russia—suddenly real possibilities—he would command the greatest military might the world had ever known. What could happen then was anyone's guess, but it was becoming increasingly apparent that it behooved Americans to do something more than sit by and watch. Hitler could be stopped and some kind of balance could be restored in Europe only if others came to Britain's aid.

Isolationism was obviously an obstacle to forthright presidential action, but FDR had an inner conflict that reflected the public confusion. He was very much of his time and place, sharing general attitudes on the mistake of entering World War I. In a famous campaign speech in Boston on October 30, 1940, FDR declared: "And while I am talking to you mothers and fathers, I give you one more assurance. I have said this before, but I shall say it again and again and again: Your boys are not going to be sent into any foreign wars."

Neither, it seemed, was a great deal of American equipment. The British still obtained supplies only on a cash-and-carry basis and they lacked the destroyers necessary to protect the convoys transporting those goods they could afford to purchase. On July 21, 1940, Churchill made another eloquent plea for destroyers: "Mr. President, with great respect I must tell you that in the long history of the world this is a thing to do *now*." The British were losing merchant shipping in the Battle of the Atlantic in appalling numbers, the Battle of Britain was reaching its peak, and the German General Staff was preparing plans for an invasion of the British Isles. The President allowed private groups to work out the details of a destroyer-for-bases deal, which eventually (September 2) gave the British fifty overage American destroyers in return for rent-free bases on British possessions from Bermuda to British Guiana.

There was, meanwhile, a growing tension between the War Department and the White House. General Marshall reasoned that the only way to defeat Hitler was to fight and defeat the German army in northwestern Europe. To do that Marshall needed a mass army; to get that he needed conscription. But given the tenor of Roosevelt's third-term campaign, there was no possibility that the President could give public support to a conscription bill.

Congress proved more willing to act than the President. Private groups, led by Republicans Henry L. Stimson and Elihu Root, Jr., persuaded Congressmen favoring intervention to introduce a selective-service bill in both houses of Congress. Roosevelt remained aloof, but he did give General Marshall permission to support the bill; the President also helped by appointing Stimson, an interventionist, Secretary of War. In late August of 1940, Congress authorized the President to call the Natonal Guard and other reserves to active duty for one year, and on September 16 it provided for selective service for one year. Both measures limited the employment of troops to the Western hemisphere.

In November 1940 Roosevelt won the election. Churchill, among others, thought that the reelected President would be willing to assume a more active role in the struggle against Hitler. The Prime Minister sent FDR a lengthy and bleak description of the British situation, emphasizing that his nation was running out of money. Cash-and-carry would no longer suffice, for "the moment approaches when we shall no longer be able to pay cash for shipping and other supplies."

Roosevelt responded sympathetically. On December 7, 1940, he called in the press, outlined the British dilemma, and said he believed that "the best defense of Great Britain is the best defense of the United States." Seeking to avoid the mistakes of Woodrow Wilson and the long controversy over World War I war debts, Roosevelt said he wanted to simply lend or lease to England the supplies she needed. He compared his scheme to the idea of lending a garden hose to a neighbor whose house was on fire.

In a radio address to the nation a few days later, Roosevelt justified lend-lease as essential to national security. If England fell, "all of us in the Americas would be living at the point of a gun." He said the best way to keep the United States out of the war was to "do all we can now to support the nations defending themselves against attack by the Axis." He declared again that he had no intention of sending American boys to Europe; his sole purpose was to "keep war away from our country and our people." He would do this by making America the "great arsenal of democracy."

The isolationists were furious. They charged that lend-lease was a most unneutral act, placing the United States squarely on the British side. Senator Robert Taft found the idea of loaning military equipment absurd. He said it was rather like loaning chewing gum: "Once it had been used, you didn't want it back."

By early March 1941, however, the Administration had overcome the opposition, and the lend-lease bill went through Congress with an initial appropriation of $7 billion. Secretary Stimson correctly called it "a declaration of economic war." But it was hardly enough to sustain a Britain on the defensive, much less give Hitler cause for concern.

What was needed was a more extensive American involvement. Realizing this, Roosevelt declared an Atlantic neutrality zone that extended almost to Iceland, ordering the Navy to patrol the area and report the location of German submarines to the British. In April 1941 American troops moved into Greenland. In July, following Hitler's invasion of Russia, his first big mistake, American troops occupied Iceland, which released British troops for the Middle East, and the U.S. Navy began escorting convoys as far as Iceland. By September the U.S. Navy was fully at war with Germany in the Atlantic. When a German submarine fired a torpedo at the American destroyer stalking it, FDR brazenly denounced the "rattlesnakes of the Atlantic" for the supposedly unprovoked act and ordered the Navy to shoot on sight at all German submarines they encountered. In October FDR persuaded Congress to remove nearly all restrictions on American commerce; henceforth, American merchant vessels could carry goods to British ports. He also extended lend-lease to Russia.

Roosevelt's tone, in public and private, was by November of 1941 one of unrestrained belligerency. German advances to the gates of Moscow made it impossible to underestimate the threat. Roosevelt seems to have reasoned that Hitler could not long permit American ships to transport goods to Britain. The Germans would have to order their submarine captains to sink the American vessels. FDR could then overcome isolationist opposition in Congress and obtain a declaration of war.

Whether he was right or not will never be known. It is clear that by December 1941 American foreign policy in Europe had failed to make any significant contribution to stopping—much less overcoming—Hitler. In retrospect, the steps the President and Congress took to protect American interests in Europe were halting and limited. Everything hinged on Russia and Britain. If they kept going, America could—eventually—supply them with the tools and men to do the job. The United States, in the meantime, was taking great risks.

The American ship of state was drifting, without a rudder or power, in a storm. The world's greatest industrial democracy could not stem the tide of Fascism. Roosevelt's caution was so great that in September 1941, when the original selective service bill ran out and had to be repassed if the soldiers already partly trained were to be retained in the Army, he refused to pressure Congress, either privately or publicly. Working behind the scenes, General Marshall was able to get the draft bill passed—by one vote. Even this left the U.S. Army ridiculously small (1.6 million men) if the nation ever intended to play a role in the conflict raging in Europe.

Fortunately for the United States, the British and Russians held out against Germany, making it possible for America to later exert her power to help win the war. Fortunately, too, the Japanese solved Roosevelt's problem of how to get fully involved in the war.

Japan was the aggressor in the Pacific, as Mussolini was in the Mediterranean and Hitler was in Europe. Since the mid-thirties, Japan had been involved in a war of conquest in China.

From the beginning the United States had protested, but because FDR had not supported his demands with action, the Japanese ignored him.

The overall Japanese program called for Asia for the Asians (although some Asians were going to be more equal than others). The Japanese proposed to substitute themselves for the white rulers in China, Indochina, Malaya, Burma, the Philippines, and the N.E.I. It was essential to the Japanese that they control these areas if Japan were to be a great power, for despite her human resources Japan was almost devoid of critical raw materials, especially oil, which was available in Southeast Asia.

The American colony of the Philippines lay directly athwart the Japanese proposed line of advance. Whether correctly or not, the Japanese were convinced that the United States would never allow them to advance into Malaya or the N.E.I. without striking against their lines of communications. More fundamentally, they believed that the United States would never willingly allow them to become a great power and would consistently oppose their advance southward. Thus, although the Japanese realized that they were doomed if they goaded the United States into war and the United States chose to fight it to a finish, they felt they were also doomed without war. "Japan entered the war," a prince of the Japanese imperial family later wrote, "with a tragic determination and in desperate self-abandonment."

The fall of France in 1940 and Britain's preoccupation with Germany opened the door to Southeast Asia for Japan. Bogged down in her war with China, Japan decided to overcome her crippling shortage of oil through a program of southward expansion. Only the Soviet Union and the United States were potentially strong enough in the Pacific to interfere; Japan moved politically to minimize these threats. In the late summer of 1940 she signed a five-year nonaggression pact with the Soviets, an agreement that Stalin, fearing Hitler, was happy to sign.

Japan also entered into the Tripartite Pact with the Germans and Italians, a defensive alliance that pledged mutual support if any one of the three signatories were attacked. The German invasion of Russia in June 1941 opened new possibilities for Japan, and a great debate within Japan ensued. Should Japan take advantage of Russia's desperate position vis-à-vis Germany and attack the Soviets through Siberia? Some military leaders thought so. Others argued that because of Hitler's involvement in Russia, Germany no longer posed so much of a threat to England; this strengthened the Anglo-American position in the Pacific because Churchill was now free to send part of the fleet from the home isles to Britain's Asian colonies (as he in fact did do in 1941). Japan, therefore, should seek to reach an agreement with the United States, making such concessions as were necessary to stave off war. Still others held out for the long-planned conquest of Southeast Asia.

Roosevelt listened in on the debate through the medium of MAGIC,* the code name applied to intercepted and decoded Japanese messages, and characterized it as "a real dragdown and knock-out fight . . . to decide which way they were going to jump—attack Russia, attack the South Seas [or] sit on the fence and be more friendly with us." The decision was

---

*While the Americans were listening in on the Japanese, the British had broken the German code (they called their system ULTRA) and the Germans had broken the British code. And while the Japanese were decoding American messages, the Russians were reading Japanese radio traffic. On balance the Americans got more useful information from MAGIC and the British from ULTRA than the Axis got from their monitoring systems.

to reject war with Russia and instead move south immediately, meanwhile trying to avoid war with the United States by carrying on negotiations as long as possible. The first step was the unresisted occupation of French Indochina, which gave Japan possession of air and naval bases stretching from Hanoi to Saigon.

The U.S. Navy did not wish to provoke the Japanese. It wanted time, not only to bring about Hitler's defeat but also to build a first-class striking force. The Chief of Naval Operations, Admiral Harold R. Stark, advised the President to do nothing when the Japanese moved into French Indochina. But whatever the military realities, FDR also had political realities to deal with. The polls indicated that nearly 70 percent of the people were willing to risk war in the Pacific rather than let Japan continue to expand. FDR froze all Japanese assets in the United States. The British and Dutch supported his move. The effect of the freeze was to create an economic blockade of Japan. She could not buy oil, steel, or other necessities without Roosevelt's permission.

The embargo made it clear to the Japanese that they either had to pull back from Indochina and China and thereby reach an agreement with the United States that would provide them with access to oil, or go to war. The one slim hope remaining was that America's fear of a two-ocean war would impel Roosevelt to compromise. From August until November 1941, the Japanese sought some form of acceptable political compromise, all the while sharpening their military plans and preparations. If the diplomatic offensive worked, the military offensive could be called off, including the planned attack on the U.S. fleet at Pearl Harbor.

In essence, the Japanese demanded from the United States a free hand in Asia. There were variations through a series of proposals, but the central points always included an Anglo-American promise not to "meddle in nor interrupt" a settlement between Japan and China, a recognition of Japan's "special position" in French Indochina, an agreement not to reinforce Singapore and the Philippines, and a resumption of commercial relations with Japan, which included selling oil.

Although the Americans were willing to go part way to compromise, they would not consider giving the Japanese a free hand in China. Since it was precisely on this point that the Japanese were most adamant, conflict was inevitable. Neither side wanted war in the sense that each would have preferred to gain its objectives without having to fight for them, but both were willing to move on to a showdown. In Japan it was the military who pressed for action, over the protests of the civilians, while in America the situation was reversed. Prime Minister Fumimaro Konoye of Japan resigned in October when he was unable to secure military approval of a partial with-drawal from China in order to "save ourselves from the crisis of a Japanese-American war." His successor, General Hideki Tojo, was willing to continue negotiations with the United States, but only until late November. If no progress was made by then, Japan would strike.

In the United States, Roosevelt stood firm, even though his military advisers strongly urged him to avoid a crisis with Japan until he had dealt with Germany. Secretary Hull made one last effort for peace, suggesting on November 21 that the United States should offer a three months' truce. Japan might have accepted, but Chiang Kai-shek, the Chinese leader, protested vehemently, and Roosevelt would not allow Hull to make the offer. "I have washed my hands of the Japanese situation," Hull told Stimson on November 27, "and it is now in the hands of . . . the Army and Navy."

A little over a week later, on Sunday, December 7, 1941, the Japanese launched their attack, hitting Pearl Harbor, the Philippines, Malaya, and Thailand.* They soon added the N.E.I. to the list. On December 8 the Anglo-Americans declared war on Japan, but the United States still had no more reason to go to war with Germany than it had had on December 6, so even in the excitement over Pearl Harbor, FDR did not ask Congress for a declaration of war on Germany. All earlier war plans had assumed that the United States and the United Kingdom would concentrate their efforts against Germany; suddenly it seemed that the war would take an entirely unexpected course, with the Americans fighting only the Japanese. On December 11 Hitler ended the uncertainty by declaring war on the United States.**

The United States was finally at war with the Axis. The status quo in Europe and in Asia had been challenged and was being upset. America had been unable to preserve it short of war. The need now was to defeat the Axis on the field of battle, a task of staggering proportions but one that carried with it great opportunities for the extension of American power and influence. The United States was quick to grasp them, even while saving the world from the unimaginable horror of being ruled by Hitler and the Japanese Army.

---

*One of the most persistent myths in American history is that FDR knew the attack on Pearl Harbor was coming but refused to give the commanders in Hawaii advance notice. In fact, Washington gave the military in Hawaii plenty of warning about the imminent outbreak of hostilities. There was no specific warning about an attack on Pearl Harbor because no one imagined the Japanese were capable of such a daring raid. MAGIC was no help because the Japanese fleet maintained radio silence.

**An inexplicable action. No one has ever explained why Hitler did it. He was not required to do so by the terms of the Tripartite Pact; he did not discuss his actions with his own military leaders or foreign office, nor indeed with anyone else. Thus Hitler, after a long string of successes, made two fatal errors between June and December of 1941—the invasion of Russia and the declaration of war against the United States.

Mauthausen

Robert H. Abzug

After the unimaginable sights of Ohrdruf, Buchenwald, Dachau, and the others, it would be hard to believe that some new level of horror might be reached. Yet on May 5, as the American 11th Armored Division and other units reconnoitered along the Danube in the environs of Linz, Austria, they found at the "mother" concentration camp of Mauthausen and such satellite camps as Gusen, Ebensee, and Gunskirchen, new histories and varieties of death and degradation. Indeed, Mauthausen and its branches had a reputation among prisoners, from Dachau in the West to Auschwitz in the East, as the camp to avoid at all costs.

The history of Mauthausen dated from 1938, when Heinrich Himmler sought to expand the economic base of the SS by exploiting slave labor in the extractive and manufacturing industries. He needed new camps and new business opportunities. Soon after the *Anschluss* that made Austria a part of Germany, he chose a site near the village of Mauthausen which offered a combination of attractive features. The future camp would be built next to the Wienergraben, a municipal quarry which was a principal supplier of paving stones for Vienna and other cities and thus had a secure economic future. The quarry was located in isolated farm country, but near enough to Linz to be useful. Mauthausen also was a stop on a railway line, thus easing both transport of stone and labor.

By July 1938 prisoners from Dachau were leveling the ground for a complex planned to cover almost four square miles, more than a square mile of which was quarry. Three months later the first inmates arrived, about a thousand German political prisoners with a sprinkling of others. A year later the prisoner population had grown over two and a half times; SS statistics listed, among the major groups, 688 political prisoners, 143 Jehovah's Witnesses and other religious objectors, 51 homosexuals, 930 asocials (a catchall category), and 946 criminals. This last category was of particular importance, for German criminals supplied the SS with cruel prisoner-taskmasters who sometimes exceeded the Nazis themselves in sadism. As the years passed, the camp kept expanding its barracks and administrative facilities.

Reprinted from *Inside the Vicious Heart: Americans and the Liberation of Nazi Concentration Camps*, (1985), Oxford University Press.

Mauthausen shared with other concentration camps the usual array of atrocities: medical experiments, exterminations, torture, and the rest. But what set it apart from other camps—in fact what gave it its damning reputation among prisoners at Dachau, Buchenwald, and even Auschwitz—was its quarry. Stone cutting and hauling is an arduous occupation in the best of circumstances but, under the supervision of the SS, work at the Wienergraben became torture almost beyond belief. Slave laborers in the quarry had a life expectancy of between six weeks and three months, and that was the case only if an unplanned punishment did not get in the way. Though pneumatic tools were used and blasting was sometimes employed to loosen stone, most of the labor was with pick and axe. As for moving stone from the quarry, prisoners hauled heavy chunks of granite on their backs up 186 steep and narrow steps that connected the camp to the quarry.

The quarry was the site of not only impossibly hard work, but also unspeakable sadism. Hundreds of Dutch Jews were forced to jump to their deaths from the high cliff overlooking the quarry floor, a cliff which in the grim humor of the inmates became known as the "parachutists' wall." In one instance, the SS orchestrated a blasting operation that made even jaded prisoners tremble. The Nazi officer in charge ordered an Italian Jew known to have a beautiful voice to stand atop a rock mound and sing the "Ave Maria." As he sang, charges were laid around the rocks. In midsong the officer pressed the plunger and blasted both the Jew and the rocks. Every day at the quarry brought new and novel forms of death.

In addition, Mauthausen was one of the few camps in the West to employ its gas chamber regularly. At first a mobile gas van shuttled back and forth between the main camp and Gusen sub-camp. On each trip it killed thirty prisoners, and apparently was in constant use. By December 1941 a permanent gas chamber, one that could hold about 120 prisoners at a time, seems to have been put in operation. It was small by Nazi standards, and when large transports earmarked for extermination arrived at Mauthausen, most persons were sent to the larger facilities at nearby Hartheim Castle. It is estimated that between 1942 and 1945 a total of about 10,000 persons were executed in Mauthausen's gas chamber, at Hartheim Castle, and in the vans.

As with the other camps, conditions at Mauthausen began to get even worse after 1943 with the movement of prisoners west from Poland. Mauthausen, because of the geographical proximity of Hungary, was particularly affected by the late but efficient roundup of that country's Jews. Especially after the evacuation of Auschwitz in December 1944, the Nazis sent thousands of Hungarian Jews to Mauthausen and its sub-camps. Marched through the winter with little clothing or food, those that survived to enter the camp gates were in desperate physical and psychological condition.

In short, Mauthausen doubled as a profitable enterprise for the DEST (Deutsche Erd-und Steinwerke, or German Earth and Stone Works) and an alternative method of extermination to meet the SS's other goals. One estimate puts total deaths at Mauthausen between 1938 and 1945 at about 55,000, this out of a total prisoner population of about 185,000. But even these statistics are conservative, since they do not adequately take into account the reuse of prisoner numbers (more than one death occurring as represented by a prisoner number), the deaths of thousands of prisoners, especially at the end of the war, who were shipped to Mauthausen and died, and the number of prisoners at Mauthausen who were never properly registered.

Nor does the human destruction that Mauthausen spawned appear in its true magnitude if one limits oneself to the "mother" camp alone, for radiating out of the main camp was an extensive system of brutal sub-camps. This kind of proliferation of labor camps was common enough in the system—Buchenwald, Dachau, and other centers had their own satellite operations—but none contained a more consistently cruel set of sub-camps than Mauthausen. The major ones were Gusen and Ebensee. Gusen, founded in 1940, was an independent camp until 1944, when it came under the umbrella of Mauthausen. Six kilometers west of the mother camp, it too specialized in quarry work. Inmates at Gusen and its sub-camps also built underground armaments factories for production of machine guns and other weaponry, as well as fuselages for Messerschmidt aircraft. In 1945 Gusen became an end-destination for death marches from other camps, and death lists from the Gusen camps add up to over 38,000. Ebensee was created in 1943 to provide labor for the construction of underground factory tunnels, but by 1945 had become a grisly center for dying transported prisoners. In all there were close to fifty camps, big and small, that operated within Mauthausen's sphere of administration. They supplied labor for a wide variety of SS and privately owned industries, and were spread all over Austria.

As Allied troops swept across most of Germany in March and April 1945, the SS had to decide what to do with Mauthausen. At first Himmler's order was to turn it over to the Allies intact, but that was soon countermanded by more sinister plans to destroy the camp, sub-camps, and the prisoners that were left. The second plan was never put into operation. In late April, Nazi Commandant Zereis handed over administration of the camp to a captain in the Vienna police, leaving a small group of SS to help guard the camp. Underground groups in Mauthausen proper as well as at Gusen quickly began sabotage and resistance operations, but the sad fact was that what was needed most—food, medicine, clothing, and final liberation—had to await the arrival of American forces some days later. Until then the camps festered in dirt and disease. Thousands of prisoners died. Conditions were especially appalling among the latest transported prisoners. These men and women had survived Auschwitz, Dachau, and forced marches—only to perish at Mauthausen in the final week of the war.

It was, above all, these last arrivals that shocked the Americans as they entered Mauthausen and its sub-camps on May 5 and the days that followed. The knowledge that such camps existed, that in the previous month thousands of GIs had seen similar scenes, did nothing to lessen the impact. Here were human beings—dead, close to death, wandering in a haze, starved and beaten into a chilling sameness—naked and semi-naked and in any case stripped of all the things we rely upon to identify someone as human. Here the Americans responded in much the same way their fellow soldiers had in other camps. There seemed to be no limit to how bad conditions could get, only to how one could react. "When you see them," one GI remembered, "there is nothing to distinguish them, you know. Shaved heads and sunken cheeks . . . there is no way, it is hard to even see them as human. Under the circumstances you try to avoid seeing them too much. It is too hard to do. It is too hard to handle."

Indeed Mauthausen, like the other camps, was the stuff of which nightmares are made. George E. King was probably not alone in feeling victimized by his very presence in the camp, even as a liberator. He described one of his dreams: "You are the captured. And you go through this agonizing labor of trying to escape. In these cases you are always moving in slow motion, as if you were up to your hips in mud . . . you are making a maximum effort to run, but you are just barely moving . . . ." The fear of becoming one of the prisoners; assuaging guilt over not being one by joining the imprisoned in one's dreams; being tortured by the memory of all that surrounded one—these were some of the dreadful themes that only sometimes surfaced in the conscious or even dream world of the liberator.

Those Americans who entered Mauthausen, like GIs at other camps, sometimes exhibited strongly contradictory urges to remember and to forget. Franklin Clark felt he must photograph what he saw, and he wanted his wife to see the pictures as well. When he sent them to her, he asked her to burn them. "I didn't want them around," he recalled. "I didn't even want to be reminded of them." Yet finally he kept them.

Others seemingly had no conflict about remembering their experience and informing others. Like the Seventh Army at Dachau, the 71st Division, which liberated the sub-camp of Gunskirchen, published a small pamphlet of text, photographs, and drawings to convince those who read it of the reality of the experience: *The Seventy-First Came . . . to Gunskirchen Lager.* Gunskirchen Lager had been the destination for transports of Hungarian Jews, who once totaled 17,000 at the sub-camp. Only 5000 were alive when the 71st came upon the site. In one barracks there were 2600 people. "Filth all over," read the report of one medical doctor. "No water, no heating, no light, no food. About 500 bodies lying in the area. The living bodies were skin and bones. People full of lice and dirt."

Capt. J.D. Pletcher described Gunskirchen the morning of its discovery:

"Of all the horrors of the place, the smell, perhaps, was the most startling of all. It was a smell made up of all kinds of odors—human excreta, foul bodily odors, smoldering trash fires, German tobacco—which is a stink in itself—all mixed together in a heavy dank atmosphere, in a thick, muddy woods, where little breeze could go. The ground was pulpy throughout the camp, churned to a consistency of warm putty by the milling of thousands of feet, mud mixed with feces and urine. The smell of Gunskirchen nauseated many of the Americans who went there. It was a smell I'll never forget, completely different from anything I've ever encountered. It could almost be seen and hung over the camp like a fog of death.

As we entered the camp, the living skeletons still able to walk crowded around us and, though we wanted to drive farther into the place, the milling, pressing crowd wouldn't let us. It is not an exaggeration to say that almost every inmate was insane with hunger. Just the sight of an American brought cheers, groans, and shrieks. People crowded around to touch an American, to touch the jeep, to kiss our arms— perhaps just to make sure that it was true. The people who couldn't walk crawled out toward our jeep. Those who couldn't even crawl propped themselves up on an elbow, and somehow, through all their pain and suffering, revealed through their eyes the gratitude, the joy they felt at the arrival of Americans."

We were taken through the crematoriums—and one of the attendants of the crematorium swore to us that he had seen several bodies put in there alive. We looked in the crematorium and there were piles of ashes and bones inside. And outside of the crematoriums, the bodies were stacked like firewood—like hides and carcasses you see hanging of half a cow in a butcher shop—the spine, you could count every vertebra in the spine and every rib and these were the dead, but the living looked exactly like them. The living that were walking around were so gaunt; their heads were shaven; they had sores on their bodies. Some were walking around naked in a daze; others had blankets wrapped around them held together by a belt and their facial features were normal size, but everything else was completely out of proportion.—Bert Weston on conditions at Ebensee

The situation at Ebensee was hardly better. Bodies, ashes, the living dead riddled the compound, and even those who could stand sometimes just collapsed and died. One liberator recalled giving showers to the survivors and watching one collapse from the shock of the water.

The conditions at Mauthausen and its satellite camps were so bad that every day hundreds continued to die from exhaustion, dehydration, starvation, typhus, and tuberculosis. Americans witnessed these crushing scenes of death and human degradation even as millions of men and women safe in America danced wildly in the streets in celebration of V-E Day. The prisoners presented their own victory ceremony, with Allied officials and camp inmates present. The liberators at Mauthausen cheered, though with the muting knowledge of human carnage all around them. As for the liberated, some celebrated, others tried, and still others hardly knew what happened before they perished.

A Good Way to Pick a Fight

Charles L. Mee, Jr.

On April 12, 1945, Franklin Roosevelt died, and soon afterward Vyascheslav M. Molotov, the Russian foreign minister, stopped by in Washington to pay his respects to Harry Truman, the new President. Truman received Molotov in the Oval Office and, as Truman recalled it, chewed him out "bluntly" for the way the Russians were behaving in Poland. Molotov was stunned. He had never, he told Truman, "been talked to like that in my life."

"Carry out your agreements," Truman responded, "and you won't get talked to like that."

That's a good way to talk, if you want to start an argument. . . .

In Europe, Germany surrendered to the Allies on May 8. On May 12, Prime Minister Winston Churchill sent Truman an ominous cable about the Russians: "An iron curtain is drawn down upon their front," Churchill said, and, moreover, "it would be open to the Russians in a very short time to advance if they chose to the waters of the North Sea and the Atlantic." On May 17, Churchill ordered his officers not to destroy any German planes. In fact, Churchill kept 700,000 captured German troops in military readiness, prepared to be turned against the Russians.

That, too, is a good way to behave if you are looking for trouble. . . .

Joseph Stalin said little: he did not advance his troops to the Atlantic, but he planted them firmly throughout eastern Europe and, in violation of previous agreements with the British and Americans, systematically crushed all vestiges of democratic government in Poland, Hungary, Czechoslovakia, Bulgaria, Rumania, Yugoslavia, and Finland. In truth, not quite: the Finns had managed to salvage a few bits and scraps of democratic usage for themselves. At dinner one night in the Kremlin, Andrei Zhdanov, one of Stalin's propagandists, complained that the Russians should have occupied Finland. "Akh, Finland," said Molotov, "that is a peanut."

And that, too, is a nice way to behave, if you are trying to stir up a fight. . . .

Most people, most of the time, want peace in the world, and they imagine that most politicians, being human, share the same wishes. At the end of a war, presumably, the desire

Reprinted from *American Heritage*, vol.28, August 1977.

for peace is most intense and most widely shared. Lamentably, that is not always the case. At the end of World War II the Russians, as Churchill remarked, feared "our friendship more than our enmity."

The Russians had both immediate cause and long-standing historical reasons for anxiety.

"From the beginning of the ninth century," as Lous Halle, a former State Department historian, has written, "and even today, the prime driving force in Russia has been fear. . . . The Russians as we know them today have experienced ten centuries of constant, mortal fear. This has not been a disarming experience. It has not been an experience calculated to produce a simple, open, innocent, and guileless society." Scattered over a vast land with no natural frontiers for protection, as Halle remarks, the Russians have been overrun "generation after generation, by fresh waves of invaders. . . . Lying defenseless on the plain, they were slaughtered and subjugated and humiliated by the invaders time and again."

Thus the Russians sought to secure their borders along eastern Europe. The czars attempted this, time and again: to secure a buffer zone, on their European frontier, a zone that would run down along a line that would later be called the Iron Curtain.

Yet, at the end of World War II, Stalin's fears were not just fears of outsiders. World War II had shown that his dictatorship was not only brutal but also brutally inept; he was neither a great military leader nor a good administrator; and the Russian soldiers returning from the Western Front had seen much evidence of Western prosperity. Stalin needed the Cold War, not to venture out into the world again after an exhausting war, but to discipline his restless people at home. He had need of that ancient strategem of monarchs—the threat of an implacable external enemy to be used to unite his own people in Russia.

Churchill, on the other hand, emerged from World War II with a ruined empire irretrievably in debt, an empire losing its colonies and headed inevitably toward bankruptcy. Churchill's scheme for saving Great Britain was suitably inspired and grand: he would, in effect, reinvent the British Empire: he would establish an economic union of Europe (much like what the Common Market actually became); this union would certainly not be led by vanquished Germany or Italy, not by so small a power as the Netherlands, not by devastated France, but by Great Britain. To accomplish this aim, unfortunately, Churchill had almost nothing in the way of genuine economic or military power left; he had only his own force of persuasion and rhetoric. He would try to parlay those gifts into American backing for England's move into Europe. The way to bring about American backing was for Churchill to arrange to have America and Russia quarrel; while America and Russia quarreled, England would—as American diplomats delicately put it—"lead" Europe.

Truman, for his part, led a nation that was strong and getting stronger. Henry Luce, the publisher of the influential *Time* and *Life* magazines, declared that this was to be the beginning of "the American Century"—and such a moment is rarely one in which a national leader wants to maintain a status quo. The United States was securing the Western Hemisphere, moving forcefully into England's collapsing "sterling bloc," acquiring military and economic positions over an area of the planet so extensive that the United States did not practice Keynesian economics during the 1930's. It was not Roosevelt's New Deal that ran up the enormous federal deficit or built the huge, wheezing federal bureaucracy of today. War ran up the deficit; war licked the depression; war made the big federal government. In 1939, after a decade of depression, after the Civilian Conservation Corps, the Public Works Administration, the Civil Works Administration, the Agricultural Adjustment Act, the Social Security Act, and all the rest of the New Deal efforts on behalf of social justice, the federal budget was $9 billion. In 1945 it was $100 billion.

American prosperity was built upon deficit spending for war. President Truman knew it, and maintained deficit spending with the Cold War. Eventually, with the Truman Doctrine and the Marshall Plan, the encouragement of American multinational companies, and a set of defense treaties that came finally to encompass the world, he institutionalized it. The American people might find this easier to damn if they had not enjoyed the uncommon prosperity it brought them.

In October, 1944, Churchill visited Stalin in Moscow. The need then, clearly, was for cooperation among the Allies in order to win the war—and it appeared at the time that the cooperativeness nurtured during the war could be continued afterward. Each had only to recognize the other's vital interests. Churchill commenced to outline those interests to be recognized for the sake of the postwar cooperation.

"I said," Churchill recalled, "'Let us settle about our affairs in the Balkans. Your armies are in Rumania and Bulgaria. We have interests, missions, and agents there. Don't let us get at cross-purposes in small ways. So far as Britain and Russia are concerned, how would it do for you to have ninety per cent predominance in Rumania, for us to have ninety per cent of the say in Greece, and go fifty-fifty about Yugoslavia?'"

Churchill wrote this out on a piece of paper, noting, too, a split of Bulgaria that gave Russia 75 per cent interest, and a fifty-fifty split of Hungary. He pushed the piece of paper across the table to Stalin, who placed a check mark on it and handed it back. There was a silence. "At length I said, 'Might it not be thought rather cynical if it seemed we had disposed of these issues, so fateful to millions of people, in such an offhand manner? Let us burn the paper.' 'No, you keep it,' said Stalin."

Such casual and roughshod "agreements" could hardly be the last word on the matter; yet, they signified a mutual recognition of one another's essential interests and a willingness to accommodate one another's needs—while, to be sure, the smaller powers were sold out by all sides. At this same time, in October, 1944, Stalin and the Soviet Union gained complete control of the internal affairs of the ex-Nazi satellites in eastern Europe. As a briefing paper that the State Department prepared in the spring of 1945 for President Truman said, "spheres of influence do in fact exist," and "eastern Europe is, in fact, a Soviet sphere of influence."

In short, the stage was set for postwar peace: spheres of influence had been recognized; a tradition of negotiation had been established. Yet, the European phase of World War II was no sooner ended than symptoms of the Cold War began to appear. The Big Three no longer needed one another to help in the fight against Hitler, and the atomic bomb would soon settle the war against Japan.

Toward the end of May, 1945, Harry Hopkins arrived in Moscow to talk with Stalin, to feel out the Russians now that the war in Europe had ended, and to prepare the agenda for discussion at the Potsdam Conference that would be held in Germany in mid-July. The United States had a problem, Hopkins informed Stalin, a problem so serious that it threatened "to affect adversely the relations between our two countries." The problem was, Hopkins said, Poland: "our inability to carry into effect the Yalta Agreement on Poland."

But, what was the problem? Stalin wanted to know. A government had been established there, under the auspices of the occupying Red Army, a government that was, naturally, "friendly" to the Soviet Union. There could be no problem—unless others did not wish to allow the Soviet Union to ensure a friendly government in Poland.

"Mr. Hopkins stated," according to the notes taken by his interpreter, Charles Bohlen, "that the United States would desire a Poland friendly to the Soviet Union and in fact desired to see friendly countries all along the Soviet borders.

"Marshal Stalin replied if that be so we can easily come to terms in regard to Poland."

But, said Hopkins, Stalin must remember the Declaration on Liberated Europe (signed at the Yalta Conference in February, 1945) and its guarantees for democratic governments; here was a serious difference between them; Poland had become the issue over which cooperation between Russia and America would flourish or fail.

Evidently Stalin could not understand this demand; apparently he could not believe that Americans were sincerely so idealistic. Did not America, after all, support a manifestly undemocratic dictatorship in Franco's Spain? "I am afraid," Averell Harriman, the U.S. ambassador to the Soviet Union, cabled home to Truman, "Stalin does not and never will fully understand our interest in a free Poland as a matter of principle. He is a realist in all of his actions, and it is hard for him to appreciate our faith in abstract principles. It is difficult for him to understand why we should want to interfere with Soviet policy in a country like Poland, which he considers so important to Russia's security, unless we have some ulterior motive."

And indeed, Russia's sphere of influence was recognized, it seemed, only so that it might serve as a bone of contention. Poland, Czechoslovakia, Bulgaria, Rumania, Hungary, all became bones of contention. It is not clear that any one of the Big Three deeply cared what happened to these eastern European countries so long as the countries served as useful pawns. Hopkins insisted that Stalin must recognize freedom of speech, assembly, movement, and religious worship in Poland and that all political parties (except fascists) must be "permitted the free use, without distinction, of the press, radio, meetings and other facilities of political expression." Furthermore, all citizens must have "the right of public trial, defense by counsel of their own choosing, and the right of habeas corpus."

Of course, Stalin said, of course, "these principles of democracy are well known and would find no objection on the part of the Soviet Government." To be sure, he said, "in regard to the *specific* [italics added] freedoms mentioned by Mr. Hopkins, they could only be applied in full in peace time, and even then with certain limitations."

In the latter two weeks of July, 1945, the Big Three gathered at Potsdam, just outside of Berlin, for the last of the wartime conferences. They discussed the issues with which the war in Europe had left them, and with which the war in the Far East would leave them when it came to an end. They discussed spheres of influence, the disposition of Germany, the spoils of war, reparations, and, of course, eastern Europe.

At one of the plenary sessions of the Potsdam Conference, they outlined the spheres of influence precisely, clearly, and in detail during a discussion of the issue of "German shares, gold, and assets abroad." To whom did these items belong? What, for instance, did Stalin mean when he said "abroad"?

Stalin: ". . . the Soviet delegation . . . will regard the whole of Western Germany as falling within your sphere, and Eastern Germany, within ours."

Truman asked whether Stalin meant to establish "a line running from the Baltic to the Adriatic." Stalin replied that he did.

Stalin: "As to the German investments, I should put the question this way: as to the German investments in Eastern Europe, they remain with us, and the rest, with you . . ."

Truman: "Does this apply only to German investments in Europe or in other countries as well?"

Stalin: "Let me put it more specifically: the German investments in Rumania, Bulgaria, Hungary, and Finland go to us, and all the rest to you."

Foreign Minister Ernest Bevin: "The German investments in other countries go to us?"

Stalin: "In all other countries, in South America, in Canada, etc., all this is yours. . . ."

Secretary of State James Byrnes: "If an enterprise is not in Eastern Europe but in Western Europe or in other parts of the world, that enterprise remains ours?"

Stalin: "In the United States, in Norway, in Switzerland, in Sweden, in Argentina [general laughter], etc.—all that is yours."

A delegation of Poles arrived at Potsdam to argue their own case before the Big Three. The Poles, struggling desperately and vainly for their land, their borders, their freedoms, did not seem to understand that their fate was being settled for reasons that had nothing to do with them. They wandered about Potsdam, trying to impress their wishes on the Big Three. "I'm sick of the bloody Poles," Churchill said when they came to call on him. "I don't want to see them. Why can't Anthony [Eden] talk to them?" Alexander Cadogan, Permanent Undersecretary for Foreign Affairs, found the Poles at Eden's house late one night and "had to entertain them as best I could, and went on entertaining them—no signs of A. He didn't turn up till 11:30. . . . So then we got down to it, and talked shop till 1:30. Then filled the Poles (and ourselves) with sandwiches and whiskies and sodas and I went to bed at 2 A.M." Altogether, it had been an agreeable enough evening, although in general, Cadogan confided to his diary, he found the Poles to be "dreadful people. . . ."

Germany, too, provided a rich field for contention. The answer to the German question became a simple but ticklish matter of keeping Germany sufficiently weak so that it could not start another war and yet, at the same time, sufficiently strong to serve as a buffer against Russia, or, from Russia's point of view against the Western powers. To achieve this delicate balance, the Big Three haggled at Potsdam over a complex set of agreements about zones of authority, permissible levels of postwar industry, allocation of resources of coal and food-stuffs, spoils of war, reparations, and other matters. The country as a whole was divided into administrative zones in which Allied commanders had absolute veto powers over some matters, and in other respects, had to defer to a central governmental council for measures to be applied uniformly to Germany.

Out of all these careful negotiations came the astonishing fact that Germany was established as the very center and source of much of the anxiety and conflict of the Cold War. How this could have happened is one of the wonders of the history of diplomacy. The discussions and bargaining at Potsdam among Churchill, Truman, and Stalin, and among the foreign ministers, and on lower levels, among economic committees and subcommittees, is maddeningly tangled, but, once all of the nettlesome complexities are cleared away, the postwar arrangement for Germany can be seen with sudden and arresting clarity. The Big Three agreed to have a Germany that would be politically united—but, at the very same time, economically divided. They agreed, then, to create a country that could never be either wholly united nor entirely divided, neither one Germany nor two Germanies, but rather a country that would be perpetually at war with itself, and, since its two halves would have two patrons, would keep its two patrons in continuous conflict. Whether this postwar arrangement for Germany was intentional or inadvertent, it was certainly a diplomatic tour de force. In 1949, with the formation of the West German and East German governments, the contradictions of the Potsdam policy became overt.

Eastern Europe, Germany, and the atomic bomb were the three most striking elements of the early Cold War. It was while he was at the Potsdam Conference that President Truman received news that the test of the bomb at Alamogordo had been successful. By that time the bomb was no longer militarily necessary to end the war against Japan; the Japanese were near the end and were attempting to negotiate peace by way of their ambassador to Moscow. After the bomb was dropped, Truman would maintain that it had avoided the invasion of the Japanese mainland and so saved a million American lives. But was that true?

General Henry (Hap) Arnold, chief of the Army Air Forces, said, before the atomic device was dropped on Japan, that conventional bombing would end the war without an invasion. Admiral Ernest J. King, chief of U.S. naval operations, advised that a naval blockade alone would end the war. General Eisenhower said it was "completely unnecessary" to drop the bomb, and that the weapon was "no longer mandatory as a measure to save American lives." Even General George Marshall, U.S. chief of staff and the strongest advocate at that late hour for the bomb's use, advised that the Japanese at least be forewarned to give them a chance to surrender. Diplomats advised Truman that he need only have Russia sign his proclamation calling for Japanese surrender; the Russians had not yet declared war against Japan, and so the Japanese still had hopes that the Russians would help them negotiate peace: if Russia signed the proclamation, the Japanese would see that their last chance was gone and would surrender. None of this advice was followed.

After the war, the United States Strategic Bombing Command issued a study confirming the advice Truman had been getting before he gave the order to drop the atomic bomb: "Japan would have surrendered even if the atomic bombs had not been dropped, even if Russia had not entered the war, and even if no invasion had been planned or contemplated." Then why was it dropped? Admiral William Leahy, Truman's top aide, was unable to offer the puzzled British chiefs of staff a better explanation than that it was "because of the vast sums that had been spent on the project," although he commented that in using the bomb, the Americans "had adopted an ethical standard common to the barbarians of the Dark Ages."

However that may be, its use must have been chilling to Stalin, doubly chilling if Stalin realized that the United States had used the bomb even when it was not militarily necessary. Indeed, according to Secretary of State James Byrnes, that was the real reason why the bomb was used after all—"to make Russia," as he said, "more manageable in Europe." Perhaps it is because that constituted a war crime—to kill people when it is not militarily necessary is a war crime according to international accord—that Truman insisted to his death, and in obstinate defiance of all other opinon, that it was militarily necessary.

The bomb may have been dropped, too, in order to end the war against Japan without Russian help. The Russians had promised to enter the war in the Far East exactly three months after the war in Europe ended—which it did on May 8. Truman's aim was not merely to end the war against Japan, but to end it before August 8.

When word reached Potsdam that the atomic bomb had been successfully tested, Truman was enormously pleased. When the news was passed along to Churchill, the prime minister was overcome with delight at the "vision—fair and bright indeed it seemed—of the end of the whole war in one or two violent shocks." Churchill understood at once that "we should not need the Russians," and he concluded that "we seemed suddenly to have become possessed of a merciful abridgment of the slaughter in the East and of a far happier prospect in Europe. I have no doubt that these thoughts were present in the minds of my American friends."

The problem was what to tell the Russians. Presumably, as allies of the Americans and British, they needed to be told of this new weapon in which Truman and Churchill placed such tremendous hopes. Yet, if the Russians were told, they might rush to enter the war against Japan and so share in the victory. "The President and I no longer felt that we needed [Stalin's] aid to conquer Japan," Churchill wrote. And so Stalin must be told about the existence of the bomb—and at the same time he must not be told. In short, Truman and Churchill decided, Stalin must be informed so casually as not to understand that he was being informed of much of anything.

On July 24, after one of the sessions of the Potsdam Conference, Truman got up from the baize-covered table and sauntered around to Stalin. The President had left his interpreter, Charles Bohlen, behind and relied on Stalin's personal translator—signifying that he had nothing important to say, just idle, end-of-the-day-chit-chat.

"I was perhaps five yards away," Churchill recalled, "and I watched with the closest attention to the momentous talk. I knew what the President was going to do. What was vital to measure was its effect on Stalin. I can see it all as if it were yesterday."

"I casually mentioned to Stalin," Truman wrote in his memoirs, "that we had a new weapon of unusual destructive force. The Russian Premier showed no special interest. All he said was that he was glad to hear it and hoped we would make 'good use of it against the Japanese.'"

"I was sure," Churchill said, "that [Stalin] had no idea of the significance of what he was being told . . . his face remained gay and genial and the talk between these two potentates soon came to an end. As we were waiting for our cars I found myself near Truman. 'How did it go?' I asked. 'He never asked a question,' he replied."

According to the Russian General Shtemenko, the ploy worked: the Russian Army staff "received no special instructions" after this meeting. According to Marshal Georgi K. Zhukov, commander of the Russian zone of occupation in Germany, Stalin returned from the meeting and told Molotov about Truman's remarks. Molotov "reacted immediately: 'Let them. We'll have to talk it over with Kurchatov and get him to speed things up.' I realized they were talking about research on the atomic bomb."

Whatever the case, whether Stalin realized what he had been told at the time, or only in retrospect, the nuclear arms race began, in effect at Potsdam, on July 24, 1945, at 7:30 P.M.

Distrust, suspicion, anxiety, fear—all were intensified at Potsdam, and to them were added harshness and provocation, from all sides. During the next few months the agreements that had been reached were violated, or used as the bases for accusations of duplicity and bad faith. Many of the questions raised at Potsdam had been postponed and delegated to a Council of Foreign Ministers that was established to deal with these questions, and new ones, as they arose. The first meeting of the council was set for September, 1945. James Byrnes, before he left Washington to attend the meeting, had chatted with Secretary of War Henry Stimson. "I found that Byrnes was very much against any attempt to cooperate with Russia," Stimson noted in his diary. "His mind is full of his problems with the coming meeting of foreign ministers and he looks to have the presence of the bomb in his pocket, so to speak, as a great weapon to get through the thing. . . ." The British Chancellor of the Exchequer, Rt. Hon. Hugh Dalton, asked Foreign Minister Ernest Bevin how things were going, once the meeting started. "Like the strike leader said." Bevin replied, "thank God there is no danger of a settlement."

Not everyone was so quick or so eager to encourage the start of the Cold War. Henry Stimson was very much the elder statesman in 1945; he had spent more than fifty years in assorted government positions, and he foresaw dread consequences in Truman's developing policies toward Russia. Stimson had long thought that America should be tough with the Soviet Union, but he now believed that toughness was turning into harshness and harshness into provocativeness. In a memo that he wrote Truman in the autumn of 1945, he focused his thoughts around one of the most vexing problems of the post war world:

". . . I consider the problem of our satisfactory relations with Russia as not merely connected with but as virtually dominated by the problem of the atomic bomb. Except for the problem of the control of that bomb, those relations, while vitally important, might not be immediately pressing. . . . But with the discovery of the bomb, they became immediately emergent. These relations may be perhaps irretrievably embittered by the way in which we approach the solution of the bomb with Russia. For if we fail to approach them now and merely continue to negotiate with them, having this weapon rather ostentatiously on our hip, their suspicions and their distrust of our purposes and motives will increase. . . .

"The chief lesson I have learned in a long life is that the only way you can make a man trustworthy is to trust him; and the surest way to make him untrustworthy is to distrust him and show your distrust."

Men like Stimson—and Henry Wallace, then Secretary of Commerce—were allowed, or forced, to resign. Others, those who tended to believe in an aggressive attitude toward Russia, were spotted, and promoted—young men such as John Foster Dulles and Dean Rusk. George Kennan, then in the American embassy in Moscow, was discovered after he sent a perfervid 8,000-word cable back to Washington: "We have here a political force committed fanatically to the belief that with U.S. there can be no permanent modus vivendi, that it is desirable and necessary that the internal harmony of our society be disrupted, our traditional way of life be destroyed, the international authority of our state be broken. . . ." In his memoirs, Kennan says that he now looks back on his cable "with horrified amusement." At the time, however, he was ideal for Truman's use, and he was recalled from Moscow and made chairman of the State Department's Policy Planning Committee, or as the *New York Times* called him, "America's global planner."

At Potsdam, the Big Three had all agreed to remove their troops from Iran. They set a deadline of March 2, 1946, and, as the deadline approached, the British announced that they would be leaving. The Russians, however, let it be known that they were somewhat reluctant to leave until they had made an agreement with the Iranians for an oil concession, and, regardless even of that agreement, Stalin rather thought he would like to withdraw only from central Iran and keep some troops in northern Iran. Not all these matters were immediately clarified and so, on March 1, 1946, Stalin announced that Russian soldiers would remain in Iran "pending clarification of the situation."

President Truman, meanwhile, invited Winston Churchill to deliver an address in March, 1946, at Fulton, Missouri: "A shadow has fallen upon the scenes so lately lighted by the Allied victory," said the former prime minister. "Nobody knows what Soviet Russia and its Communist international organization intends to do in the immediate future, or what are the limits, if any, to their expansive and proselytising tendencies. . . . From Stettin in the Baltic to Trieste in the Adriatic [the line, as Churchill neglected to mention, to which he and Truman had agreed at Potsdam], an iron curtain has descended across the Continent. Behind that line lie all the capitals of the ancient states of Central and Eastern Europe . . . in what I must call the Soviet sphere. . . . This is certainly not the Liberated Europe we fought to build up. Nor is it one which contains the essentials of permanent peace."

In Moscow, a well-rehearsed Russian reporter quizzed Stalin.

Question: "How do you appraise Mr. Churchill's latest speech in the United States?"

Stalin: "I appraise it as a dangrous act, calculated to sow the seeds of dissension among the Allied states and impede their collaboration."

Question: "Can it be considered that Mr. Churchill's speech is prejudicial to the cause of peace and security?"

Stalin: "Yes, unquestionably. As a matter of fact, Mr. Churchill now takes the stand of the warmongers, and in this Mr. Churchill is not alone. He has friends not only in Britain but in the United States of America as well."

During the winter of 1946–47, a succession of snowstorms hit Britain. Coal was already in short supply; factories had already closed for lack of fuel that winter. With the blizzards came rationing, first of electricity and then of food; finally heat was cut off. Britain, as Louis Halle wrote, "was like a soldier wounded in war who, now that fighting was over, was bleeding to death." The empire was at last dying.

In Washington, on February 21, 1947, a Friday afternoon, First Secretary H. M. Sichel of the British embassy delivered two notes to Loy Henderson at the State Department. Until that moment, Britain had been the principal support for the economy of Greece and the provider for the Turkish Army. The first of Sichel's notes said that Britain could no longer support Greece; the second said Britain could no longer underwrite the Turkish Army, "What the two notes reported," Halle observed, "was the final end of the *Pax Britannica*."

The following week, on February 17, Truman met with congressional leaders in the White House. Undersecretary of State Dean Acheson was present at the meeting, and Truman had him tell the congressmen what was at stake. Acheson spoke for ten minutes, informing the legislators that nothing less than the survival of the whole of Western civilization was in the balance at that moment; he worked in references to ancient Athens, Rome, and the course of Western civilization and freedoms since those times. The congressmen were silent for a few moments, and then, at last, Senator Arthur Vandenberg of Michigan, a prominent Republican who had come to support an active foreign policy, spoke up. All this might be true, Vandenberg said; but, if the President wishes to sell his program to the American people, he would have to "scare hell out of the country." It was at that moment that the Cold War began in earnest for the United States.

It would be nice to be able to say that one nation held back from the nattering and abusiveness, that one seemed reluctant to start a conflict with its former allies, that one tried to compose the differences that had predictably arisen at the end of the war, that this one was the first to make a provocative move or charge and that one was last—but in truth all three leaped into the fray with such haste and determination that the origins of the Cold War are lost in a blur of all three sides hastening to be first in battle.

It is difficult to know the effects the Cold War had upon the Russian people in these years. But America paid heavy costs. When a nation has an actively internationalist, interventionist foreign policy, political power in that country tends to flow to the central government, and, within the central government, to the executive branch. That there was, in recent times, the creation of an "imperial presidency" in the U.S. was no quirk or happenstance; it was the natural outgrowth of the Cold War. From the imperial presidency, from the disorientation of the constitutional system of checks and balances, Watergate, proteiform and proliferating spy organizations, the impotence and decadence of Congress—all these were almost inevitable. That is why George Washington, a profoundly sophisticated man, advised Americans to avoid foreign entanglements; and that is why Americans who prize their freedom have always been a peace-loving people.

The Middle East: From Collaboration to Control

Gabriel Kolko

Reconciling its desire for cooperation with the British in political and military affairs in the Middle East with its increasingly aggressive efforts to win mastery over the area's oil was the Truman Administration's principal dilemma in the region before and especially after the outbreak of the Korean War. Given its coolness at this time toward Israel, which pursued a neutralist foreign policy and still purchased arms from the Soviet bloc, there were none of the political barriers to closer relations with the Arab states that emerged in the 1960s. Since 1947, London and Washington had explicitly pledged that their Near East policies would not only be mutually supporting but also that they would cooperate to exclude political or commercial challenges from other nations—in effect, to close the open door through which the United States was walking. At the beginning of 1950 this alliance was again renewed formally.

The Korean War strongly reinforced the centrifugal tensions inherent in the Anglo-American alliance because the subsequent world economic boom and rearmament greatly increased oil's economic and strategic importance, and the British in July 1950 drastically diminished their potential military utility when they informed Washington that in the event of a war with Russia they would concentrate their defenses in and around the Suez Canal and Egypt—writing off most of the region. This made its relations with Egypt the key to its future power in the area. More vital yet, by 1950 the Near East's oil reserves were already equivalent to all the rest in the world combined and double those in the United States—and this vast wealth was largely in British concessions. "Control of this source of energy," the State Department's experts advised in September, "important in peace and war, is a desirable goal in itself. . . . The U.S. Government should seek maximum development in U.S. owned concessions."

The single most important issue during the early 1950s to determine who would control the region's oil was the difference between competing oil interests over the division of profits and royalties among themselves and the key oil-producing nations. In 1948 U.S. companies in Venezuela were compelled to pay fifty-fifty, an unprecedented share, and Saudi Arabia soon demanded the same from its American firms—upsetting the area's stability in ways that were to prove far-reaching to the British, who were paying much less. The State Department endorsed the fifty-fifty split for the entire area and thereby gravely undercut their ally's position. Should there be a sharp diminution of Britain's role, the State Department's experts concluded at the end of 1950, "The Arab States are all oriented towards the West in varying degrees, opposed to communism, and generally successful at present in minimizing or suppressing existing Communist activities. . . ." The main risk to the West came from "ultra-nationalist elements." This force was primarily hostile to the British and French, they reasoned, and it was the United States' association with them that also risked isolating it, leaving the nationalists masters of the area. How much longer the Americans could afford politically, economically, or even militarily to cooperate closely with Britain was very much in doubt as the liabilities of the alliance began to outweigh an independent strategy.

At the end of 1950 the NSC began a study "possibly to reorient somewhat our political, economic, and military programs in the . . . area." Britain had abdicated the primary defense responsibilities in the region, it felt, leaving U.S. bases and interests in Saudi Arabia and the Gulf exposed. Roles and obligations had become very confused because, as the NSC concluded in February 1951, British power was "declining" politically and in every other domain as well. During early 1951 both the CIA and all U.S. diplomats working in the region agreed that Britain had been fatally weakened, could not defend Western interests adequately, and was less devoted to genuine equality with America than assuming the role of a "senior" partner. "Oil is the most important single factor in United States relations with the area," the diplomats concluded, and most of the internal Communist problems required only stronger "police controls." Stability would come most quickly if British oil firms would raise royalties to U.S. standards with the Saudis.

This growing general confrontation between the United States and Britain for hegemony in the region continued simmering throughout 1951, the inexorable logic of U.S. power and ambitions and Britain's eclipse, but Dean Acheson is nonetheless partially justified in his later recollection that "in an unplanned, undesired, and haphazard way American influence had largely succeeded French and British in that part of the world." Abstractly, Washington unquestionably opposed the total elimination of Britain's strength and authority and still preferred a regional alliance. The problem was that every one of its concrete steps undercut the British so that their ability and incentive to play their assigned role diminished with every year. During 1951 the increasingly tense allies quibbled over whether an American should be appointed NATO commander in the Mediterranean, swinging the Pentagon behind those who believed Britain's value was sinking. As the British "diddled," in Acheson's term, their adamancy infuriated America's leaders, and at the end of 1951 the NSC began groping for "a new basis and a new kind of relationship with the Middle Eastern states" that took into account "the declining ability of the U.K. to maintain and defend Western interests in the Middle East." The dilemma, as U.S. advisers argued from this point onward, was that America by itself still retained much goodwill in the region, and restive, largely middle-class and officer-led nationalism was anti-British but also anti-Soviet. The rapid demise of British power and the hesitancy of the United States to help fill the vacuum created instability that might lead to a loss of American access to oil and to neutralism—all without any Russian action. Whatever the short-term gains of the alliance with Britain, they concluded, in the long run the U.S. would be best off not identified with it. With the gap between its initial postwar premises and realities too wide to ignore, the Truman Administration now began to move more aggressively into the space Britain's weaknesses had created.

While it left the final resolution of the crisis emerging in Iran to its successors, in Egypt, the very place the British planned to concentrate their regional strength, the Truman Administration actively defined events when fighting between British and Egyptian forces broke out at the end of January 1952 after the British dismissed Cairo's demand that they withdraw their troops from the canal zone, thereby threatening to create uncontrollable xenophobic anti-Western upheavals. The immediate object of its efforts was the key nationalist officers, who were ready to deal with Kermit Roosevelt, head of the CIA operation, for their own ends. Roosevelt convinced King Farouk, whose past role as Britain's vassal was more of a liability for the United States than his notorious corruption and orgies, to fire the ministers on whom his power depended and replace them with General Naguib el-Hilali as prime minister. But Farouk could not be reformed, and in May the U.S. embassy and the CIA decided to help remove him, the last bastion of British influence, in order to reorganize the chaotic, corrupt nation. On July 22–23 a coup took place, with Naguib as its nominal head but in reality as a front for a group of colonels led by Gamal Abdel Nasser. The United States always knew that Nasser would be the true power behind the throne, but in Acheson's words, the "change appeared to us as mildly encouraging."

The United States immediately began to deal directly with Nasser and helped him to consolidate power by sending him advisers, including former Nazi generals to assist him to modernize his army. A "private understanding that the preconditions for democratic government did not exist and wouldn't exist for many years" had been reached with Nasser beforehand, since the United States wanted a period of discipline to purge the nation of inherited faults, a State Department consultant on Egypt later recalled, and for several more years Washington felt satisfied with its first major action in implementing its new Middle Eastern policy. For practical purposes, the United States had virtually displaced British influence in the nation strategically most important to it in the Middle East. It had also helped decisively to bring Nasser to the head of a vital state, the consequences of which Americans scarcely predicted.

The Iranian Crisis

All that Britain had left of major significance in the Middle East after the Egyptian coup was its claim to the control of the Iranian oil fields, and by 1951 even this had become tenuous. Indeed, from Britain's viewpoint it was soon to become apparent that the United States was intent on pushing it aside there as well, though in fact U.S. policy and actions were exceedingly convoluted because in that extremely complex local environment the Truman Administration sought to apply its increasingly schizophrenic policy of both fostering Britain's military presence and supplanting its influence in the region.

Iran after 1945 was a thoroughly anti-Russian state, and the young Shah was committed to encouraging a greatly increased U.S. role in the area both to offset British and Soviet strength and to modernize the army, on which his power depended. More important, Iran was going through a deep political and economic crisis that pitted the Shah against rising urban middle-class elements who also wished rather vaguely to modernize Iran along conventional Western bourgeois lines. Whatever their differences, both tendencies agreed that money was essential to bail Iran out of its nearly bankrupt condition and that the Anglo-Iranian Oil Company (AIOC), which had the concession on its oil and was owned by the British Admiralty, should provide much more of it. This national consensus transcended the immediate political rivalries in the long run, but after 1949 politics obscured this reality as factions sought to exploit the nationalist euphoria the oil issue provoked. From the U.S. viewpoint, however, both sides were anti-Communist, and the only real issue initially was the future of British power—which, in any event, it increasingly saw as in eclipse.

When the U.S. oil firms during 1950 agreed to give Saudi Arabia a fifty-fifty split on its oil, American officials had predicted that the Iranians, who had been negotiating terms with the AIOC since mid-1949, would increase their demands also. A coalition of nationalist groups in the Majlis (parliament), led by Dr. Mohammed Mossadegh, throughout 1950 made oil the all-consuming issue in Iranian politics—one the wily, opportunistic Mossadegh was prepared to exploit. He was a European-educated, aristocratic landlord who was both an anti-Communist and devoid of any social reform program. The fact that he wished to aid mainly the urban middle classes also meant that Mossadegh had no mass base unless he could appeal to a nationalism whose main obsession was English domination. It was for good reason that Americans on the scene thought he was capable of playing a useful role. By November 1950, when Mossadegh's committee in the Majlis called for nationalization of the AIOC, the State Department was furious with the British for ignoring its appeals to make concessions and defuse the issue. When the British in early 1951 finally agreed to fifty-fifty to forestall nationalization, it was too late, and after the assassination of the moderate prime minister on March 7 the Majlis proceeded to nationalize the AIOC, the next month electing Mossadegh prime minister.

The British responded haughtily to Iranian demands from the inception, spurning even their right to have simple information on AIOC's operations, and by March 1951 the U.S. ambassador in Tehran, Henry F. Grady, thought their representatives "self-righteous and arrogant." Their aloof disdain, cast in the purest imperialist tradition, continued until the end, but the entire U.S. government was hostile toward the British, and it was only the loyal support of the American oil companies for the AIOC that prevented an even sterner official policy. The Pentagon, above all, feared that Iran would be pushed into neutralism. The geopolitical implications of this as well as the loss of oil seemed far more crucial to the military than Britain's interests. No American official favored allowing what they saw, in Acheson's words, as "the unusual and persistent stupidity" of the British to damage the United States' standing in the region, and after the AIOC nationalization Washington advised London to accept the principle but to be certain they controlled the new company's administration and output. By May U.S. priorities, in order of importance, were to prevent armed conflict between the British and Iranians, which might then bring the Russians into the north of Iran but at the least destroy the position of the entire West in the region, to keep Iran on the side of the West, sustain the flow of oil, and, last, protect the sanctity of concession rights in Iran and the world. Mossadegh, the State Department knew, was anti-Russian, and they moved to shape his policies in ways the British justifiably deemed hostile. In July, Averell Harriman was sent to Tehran and London to mediate, which the British quite correctly saw as encouraging the Iranians to remain adamant until U.S. pressure forced them to make concessions. But American action was calculated, above all, to prevent Britain from using boats and land forces it had positioned in the gulf, and in this it succeeded. Mossadegh himself came to the United States the following fall and convinced Washington that a compromise was possible and that the failure to reach one was largely Britain's responsibility.

Its options exhausted and the British adamant, given the context of other regional problems the United States resolved to move toward a more independent Middle East policy, but it was reluctant at the same time to undercut the British completely in Iran as well as in Egypt. Increasingly unhappy with this stand, for much of early 1952 the United States publicly supported the British position, reducing its economic aid to Iran and halting military aid entirely. By July, with the Iranian economy in disorder and discontent strengthening the following of the Communist Tudeh Party, the United States was ready to press again for a compromise. During protracted negotiations it offered Iran a one-hundred-million-dollar advance if it accepted an arrangement that would have allowed U.S. firms to handle its oil, thereby convincing Mossadegh that he could play America against Britain—and causing the British to complain bitterly to Washington. As antitrust impediments to the U.S. oil giants entering Iran were removed, smaller U.S. companies were allowed publicly to buy Iranian oil to buoy up the bankrupt nation slipping quickly down a precipice that carried, in Acheson's words, "the gravest risk of having Iran disappear behind the Iron Curtain and the whole military and political situation in the Middle East change adversely to us." In November a thoroughly worried White House decided to make available one hundred million dollars to buy Iranian oil, in addition to American loans and private purchases, if Britain would agree to a settlement. Mossadegh, no less afraid of the turmoil within his nation and eager to hold on to American goodwill, seemed in Washington's opinion most conciliatory, but the British refused to consider the matter and so no progress was made.

The British, as the Administration feared, would make no concessions to Mossadegh because they wished to see his government removed, a goal they fixed upon no later than the fall of 1951. They believed that Mossadegh had no mass base and that rather than head off the Tudeh he would increasingly have to rely on it for support in the streets as he rode roughshod over opposition, which was precisely what his opportunism caused him to do. The British solution was for the Shah's position to be strengthened, along with that of the military, which was his main base of power. In November 1952, certain the Democrats would be defeated in the election and that nothing more should be done before they could determine the Republican mood, the British approached Kermit Roosevelt of the CIA and proposed a joint effort to overthrow Mossadegh. Roosevelt informed them the Democrats would reject the idea but that the Republicans might prove receptive, and so London bided its time.

For the new Republican Administration the question of Iran posed two challenges. The most obvious one, to which most attention has been paid, was the nature of the Mossadegh regime, which was in early 1953 both politically and economically in a grave internal crisis. By that time he had managed to alienate many of his earlier middle-class followers and, isolated, he did indeed turn to the Tudeh for support in the streets—where a great deal of activity was now occurring. Mossadegh was unwilling to compromise with the British but unable to bring them to heel, so the Eisenhower Administration, which favored an activist

CIA policy of preventive measures against deviant regimes, had no hesitation tentatively to authorize a joint project with the British to overthrow Mossadegh.

Even more important, however, was the new Administration's plans for Britain's future role in the region, and here the president shared completely the view of his predecessors that collaboration as equals was no longer useful. The partnership of World War Two could not be reactivated, Eisenhower noted in his diary in early January 1953 after berating Churchill personally on his handling of Iran. Nationalism was on the march, and for the United States to be associated too closely with British resistance to it would allow Russia to exploit the movement. Whatever the outcome of prior consultations, Eisenhower believed, "It will be far better for us to proceed independently toward the solution of knotty problems." It would be one thing to work with the British to throw Mossadegh out of office but quite another to give them what they wanted afterward.

While plotting for a possible CIA coup went forward, the United States and Britain continued to disagree on the same Iranian problems that had separated them under the Democrats, and for exactly the same reasons. The renewal of aid, sending U.S. technicians and equipment to maintain Iran's refineries to supply their new Japanese and Italian customers—all these possibilities kept the Anglo-Americans divided until June 22, when Washington gave the coup scheme its final approval. The decision to act was based on the fact that Mossadegh in his bid to take total power was losing followers, had alienated deeply the military, and in order to create leverage for his new goals had set loose street mobs whom he could not, ultimately, control.

The coup itself succeeded not because of the CIA's cunning but because Mossadegh had managed to alienate most of those with power while remaining incapable of organizing those, principally the masses, who had none. For while the relatively small Tudeh could bring numbers out on the streets, it was unable to defend a demagogic aristocrat who had no social program. The coup scenario began on August 12 when the Shah, who was already on his way out of the country, issued a decree firing Mossadegh, which merely led to the arrest of a few of the Shah's supporters. While Mossadegh's forces hesitated, the army spontaneously took over the Tehran streets in a pro-Shah coup of its own even as the CIA was ordering its plan aborted as a failure. The Mossadegh regime had been a house of cards, likely soon to fall in any case, and when the CIA reactivated its operation the demise of Mossadegh was a matter of a few days—he ending in jail while the Tudeh's leaders were rounded up for execution or prison. But it was one thing for Washington to help the British throw Mossadegh out of office, quite another to help them to get back their oil.

The problem was that no one in Iran favored Britain's return, the Shah above all because the keystone of his foreign policy before and surely after this period was to align Iran with the United States. Mossadegh's failure was not due to his anti-British stance, much less to his advocacy of nationalization, but to his political style and ineptness. The British saw all this quite clearly, realizing that America could easily replace not only its future influence in Iran but also, more important, its control of oil. As early as November 1951, to forestall these risks, they had offered the United States participation in Iran's fields once they were returned, but Washington demurred and waited for a more opportune time. The issue involved the basic question of the ambiguous relationship between the two nations as friends and rivals in the Middle East, and since the Democrats and Republicans shared one view on it, it was a matter of prime significance when the need to negotiate the oil dispute arose after August 1953.

Roosevelt, acting officially, had told the Shah that his cooperation in the coup left him "under *no* obligation. Not on petroleum, nor on anything else." The State Department, which had removed antitrust obstacles to American firms participating in Iranian oil, in September 1953 began approaching U.S. oil giants to discuss a new company that might buy out AIOC. The oil companies hesitated, and the British complained. But neither the Iranians nor the British would settle, and a forty-five-million-dollar U.S. grant to Iran in September allowed the former some leverage. At the end of 1953 the NSC, aware that the new regime looked to America for "counsel and aid," concluded that the danger of communism in Iran would return should the oil revenues not start flowing. It gave the British until July 1954 to settle, or the Americans would arrange to sell Iran's oil independently. The United States was ready to consult with London but not to allow it to veto essential action.

The Iranians wisely hired the former chairman of Texaco to advise them, while Washington's own representative to the negotiations, Herbert Hoover, Jr., had worked for major American oil firms. The talks went badly, and by early spring Dulles was furious, and both he and the Administration believed the British "do not have [a] very good title." They thought the British were attempting to get twice as much as was fair, but after bitter disputes and threats an accord was finally reached in August. Its main provisions left a nominally nationalized oil company that granted a new Western firm full rights to manage its output and prices with a fifty-fifty split in profits. Even the Shah disliked this arrangement, but he could do nothing about it. Ostensibly to provide the new firm with access to a world market from which Iranian oil had been barred and supplanted for four years, five U.S. giants were each given 8 percent interest in the firm—or 40 percent combined—in return for 32 million pounds immediately and 182 million pounds over the next twenty years. It was the best that the British, who came close to ending with nothing from both Mossadegh and then the Americans, could get—and they appreciated this full well. As for the Iranians, their fragile interlude with parliamentary politics had come to an end, with an absolute monarchy emerging in its place. The Americans, for their part, now had political hegemony in Iran and a large interest in its oil. A major shift in the overall balance of power in the region had occurred, and the extent to which it would continue remained an open question in Anglo-American relations. Unresolved, too, was the issue of what obligations as well as rewards for the United States came with its rapidly evolving replacement of British power.

The Middle Eastern Conundrum

The Middle East after the Second World War was undergoing a profound and accelerating transition away from its diverse traditional political and social orders, which made it not only inherently unstable but also exceedingly complex for the United States to relate to. These changes generally undermined Britain's historic domination of the region and were inevitable regardless of anything America might do. No portion of the Third World was as socially and politically complicated as the vast zone stretching from Iran to the eastern Mediterranean. Ultimately these dynamics had far less to do with the role of internal Communist parties—which were mainly inconsequential—than in any other area. This fact alone meant that U.S. policies focused much more on the positions and interests of its British and French allies than elsewhere, making Anglo-American, rather than U.S.-Soviet, relations far more significant. Within this context American decision makers had to deal with the social dynamics of the very real but still uneven pace of change in each of the zone's countries. And while the United States was able to gain successes for itself, eventually it, too, was to discover that the labyrinthine forces operating in the region transcended its ability to control.

The Middle East's political and class structures alone guaranteed instability. The traditional elites of the area comprised the monarchies, which ruled ten of the seventeen nations from Morocco to Pakistan in 1951, and a commercial bourgeoisie that was overwhelmingly made up of ethnically marginal elements: Jews, numerous Christians from diverse sects, Greeks, Palestinian Muslims who were recent migrants, and the like. These local capitalists had no loyalty to the nation in which they lived, were highly mobile, and both their commercial basis and intrinsic marginality made them incapable of introducing major industrial economic innovations that might modernize the agrarian societies they exploited. British power, to a great extent, depended on such traditional political and economic constituencies, and by 1945 what Manfred Halpern has called a "new middle class" had begun to challenge the inherited orders in most Middle Eastern states.

The class origins of this rising new element guaranteed that its dominant ideological expression would be nationalistic, and while this made largely anti-British sentiment axiomatic, at the same time it also assured that unlike the rest of the Third World, Marxism's influence would be negligible. Generally the children of professionals, state functionaries, or officers rather than the petit bourgeois or landed elite, they, too, pursued these occupations. Ready and capable to exploit the masses politically, the latter remained as unrepresented and invisible in the changed politics of the area as under the traditional rulers. While many from this new middle class entered the officer corps, whose growth was more rapid than that of the civilian sectors and whose ranks did not attract sons of the traditional elite, their ideas merely paralleled those of their peers not in the army but of the same social background, and the military was the product and instrument of the new elite rather than the reverse. Both were well trained, administratively talented, and proponents of modernization in ways that undermined radically the power of the traditional rulers. Their access to guns made them capable successfully to aspire to power, and despite the failure of most of the thirty military coups since 1930, by 1962 the military already ruled five of these countries and the monarchies had been reduced to six in number. This admixture of tradition, embodying Islam as well as monarchical societies, anti-Marxism, and a rising middle class's syncretic ideologies all defined the development of the region in ways that were altogether unique.

Perhaps most disorienting to the United States was this ascendent class's rhetoric, which concocted doctrines that were often both confused and confusing. Ultranationalist, it also tended to be committed to a strong state economic sector because the ephemeral nature of the local commercial bourgeoisie historically had required, even in reactionary states, that capital investments come primarily from the government—or no one. But whatever the rhetoric, such middle-class leaders were and have been eminently conservative in administering various forms of state capitalism. At the same time, their relationship to Islam has been uncomfortable and often ambiguous, not the least because Islam alone had the potential to reach the masses in ways that Marxist parties have been incapable of doing.

In the 1950s, such dynamic changes in the Arab world were quickly undermining the historic monarchical and traditional foundations of British domination, thereby opening the way for the entry of American influence. During 1951, indeed, State Department Middle East analysts had begun to study this new middle class, and many regarded it as a positive element against the atavistic forces that Britain had sustained for generations. The fact that it was both anti-Soviet as well as anti-British made support for it enticing, but other American experts doubted that aligning unreservedly with them was the best way to advance U.S. interests, if only because Washington also was ready uncritically to sustain royalist regimes in Saudi Arabia and the Gulf that acceded to its desires. In the end, as Iran demonstrated, American policy proved almost as convoluted as modernizing Arab nationalism itself, opportunistically exploiting nationalism and the new middle classes against the USSR and Britain while never precluding working with reactionary elements. Such self-serving pragmatism explains why virtually every British leader who has written about U.S. policy in the region in the 1950s has bitterly portrayed it as primarily anti-British both in motive and in consequence.

It was in this context that the United States backed Nasser during his first years in power and avoided a too-close identification with British plans in the area. American approval did not include significant economic and military aid until November 1954, immediately after Egypt made a statement of support for the West and signed an agreement with Britain governing the removal of British troops in the Suez Canal Zone but also allowing them to return in case of war. Nasser had also removed Naguib from the presidency during November, and Nasser was desperate to consolidate his domestic following lest he, too, lose a grip on power. Foreign aid was indispensable toward that end. But he refused to get drawn into the diverse proposals for a regional military pact the British began to sponsor and that Washington regarded with mixed feelings.

The British themselves saw a military alliance of "northern tier" states bordering the USSR as a way of bolstering their interests in the region at a time when their forces were being reduced dramatically. A treaty between Turkey and Iraq was signed in February 1955, and London tried to get the United States to join, believing that the success of what was to become the Baghdad Pact required it. While Pakistan and Iran joined the wholly innocuous symbolic gesture on Britain's part, the United States adamantly refused to become more than an observer.

Dulles was extremely irritated at the aggressive, unilateral British leadership in producing the alliance, however hopelessly impotent it was, though in principle he favored anti-Soviet treaties. Nasser, on the other hand, had made it abundantly clear that while he was pro-Western he also intended being neutral in the Cold War insofar as pacts were concerned. The British-led alliance of the region's reactionary states offended his mounting nationalistic pretensions in the area. At this time Dulles and the Administration were convinced that he was justified. As British foreign secretary Selwyn Lloyd later described it, Dulles did not want "to incur the hostility of Nasser and those in other Arab states who thought as Nasser did." It had become clear after 1950 that the mounting economic and political tension between Britain and the United States would also lead to profound differences on how to relate to rival factions within states as well as to the larger forces of an exceedingly fluid nationalism and middle-class-inspired change growing in importance throughout the region. This emerging Anglo-American conflict of interests and strategies in an increasingly unstable setting produced the context for the final elimination of British power in the Middle East that was to occur with the Suez crisis of November 1956.

The Suez Crisis and the End of British Power

By 1956 U.S. policy in the Near East was firmly committed to replacing British hegemony over the region with its own, and the Administration's immediate estimates of how they might help to accomplish this primary objective tended to color profoundly its responses to the emerging forces of nationalism, the new middle class, and even neutralism. Notwithstanding a division within the American government on how to react to these destabilizing factors in the Arab world, even those who were hostile toward the ideas Nasser best typified—and they were the majority in high places—were ready opportunistically to deal with them whenever a gain could be made. The question of Russia, much less Communism, within the Arab nations was not a major concern to the United States before 1957.

Everyone in Washington from late 1954 until the spring of 1956 knew that Nasser was most concerned with consolidating his precarious domestic position, and they repeatedly (and correctly) interpreted his foreign policy and efforts to obtain aid in this light. Nearly all of the United States' specialists wanted to see Nasser survive, and its ambassadors to Cairo throughout this period shared the view that if American aid was not forthcoming the risk of a return to the old order—and British supremacy—was reasonably great. They also understood that the large majority of the region's educated Arabs and the new middle class were neutral in the Cold War, the implications of which were initially far greater for Britain than for the United States.

Nasser's confidence that he could parlay a neutralist foreign policy, mainly anti-British in emphasis, to get both aid for his domestic goals as well as to buttress his pretensions to lead the Arab world's foreign policy was greatly reinforced when he received a desperately needed $40 million American economic aid grant in November 1954 despite his refusal to meet U.S. demands on regional defense matters. He knew, too, that the new American ambassador in Cairo, Henry Byroade, was urging the State Department to give him military aid on his own conditions and indeed represented him as the best bet in the long run against both Britain and Russia. Washington was less certain of this and delayed a twenty-million-dollar military aid grant. In the summer of 1955 Nasser let it be known that unless the United States acted quickly he would get arms from the Soviet bloc. However angry the Administration was when Egypt announced a large purchase of arms from Czechoslovakia on September 27, given Saudi Arabia's political and financial support for Nasser at this time it could not turn against him. Both the British and American governments understood perfectly well that Nasser was attempting, in British foreign secretary Harold Macmillan's words, to "induce both the West and the Soviets to bid up each other's price." Dulles, too, shared the view that "it is a risk we are taking but . . . we have to."

The outcome was that both Britain and America decided to up the ante by funding the huge Aswan dam irrigation project to forestall rumors that the USSR might sponsor it if they hesitated, and London was especially eager to do so because it thought that Russians working on the Aswan enterprise might extend Soviet influence to Africa for the first time. In mid-December the British and Americans, in conjunction with the World Bank, offered Egypt four hundred million dollars for the Aswan scheme—a gesture that not only greatly assisted Nasser in consolidating power at home but also confirmed his belief that an independent foreign policy and playing the East against the West paid far greater dividends than slavish support for either.

Thus encouraged, Nasser overextended his hand and deeply offended the U.S. government, which nevertheless retained an ambiguous attitude toward his regional nationalist aspirations. On one hand, as Selwyn Lloyd accurately described it, "there was in many American hearts a dislike of colonialism, a resentment of any authority left to us from the great days of our Empire, and a pleasure, only half-concealed, at seeing us done down." On the other, as Dulles confided, "we are sympathetic with whatever action Nasser reasonably takes to emphasize genuine independence of Egypt," but there was a limit, and it was reached when Cairo recognized China on May 16, 1956.

Egypt's gesture alienated the Administration deeply, but even more important it galvanized the Taiwan and Israel lobbies in Congress into a common bloc able to halt the funds for Aswan. The Americans had never been enthusiastic about Aswan, the British had pushed them into it, and with a presidential election just four months away, the United States on July 19 unilaterally canceled the Aswan Dam loan. Dulles, Robert Murphy later recalled, "never told explicitly why he acted so abruptly," and "the effects of summarily withdrawing the Aswan offer had not been weighed carefully in advance." It was the British, who were informed officially of the decision only a few hours before the public announcement and never consulted as to their advice, who now had to confront the quite predictable consequences, the least of which was that the Soviet Union agreed to fund the project. For Nasser could not afford, either at home or in the Arab world, to remain passive. Quite predictably, he seized and nationalized the Suez Canal a week later. The British reaction, as Anthony Nutting, who was to resign as minister of state for foreign affairs over Suez later wrote, "bordered on panic and hysteria." Suez was essential to Britain's lifeline to the Persian Gulf, Asia, and the Pacific, and given Britain's dramatic decline since 1945, it simply could not afford patiently to absorb such a decisive blow to its position in the world economy. Having already begun aggressively to undermine the remaining governments in the region friendly to it, Nasser had militarily and politically assaulted Britain's imperialist pretensions as well.

Many participants have already produced detailed accounts of the Suez crisis, but Prime Minister Anthony Eden's judgment that "The course of the Suez Canal crisis was decided by the American attitude toward it" is unquestionably accurate. From its inception, the British problem was that they did not know what Washington's policy really was, and they naïvely misread its initial opposition to the nationalization of the canal as approval for the increasingly forceful actions they and the French were to consider. But even before Dulles flew to London on July 31 and gave the British and French encouragement that Nutting called "unwise and dangerous," and appeared ready also to isolate Nasser, Dulles and Eisenhower had concluded that the Anglo-French desire to act strongly was symbolic: for the French it was their worries about its "grave repercussions in North Africa," and for the British "their position in other countries." Given the election pending, the Republicans were also resolved not to appear as defenders of "French colonialism." Dulles, by contrast, never felt he had committed the United States to joint action with its allies. Until September 3, in any case, the British believed that Washington would support eventual Anglo-French use of force if peaceful efforts failed, as they consistently did during August in large part because of lackadaisical American support for all the alternatives being offered. U.S. insistence on a negotiated resolution of the dispute from that time onward, the British justifiably argued, reinforced Nasser's obduracy—but by early September Dulles was ready to downplay the Suez's importance and in early October publicly admitted there were fundamental differences between his government and its allies. The White House would not identify too closely with colonialism. The alliance, Dulles stated in so many words, would be united on purely European questions only.

As the election drew closer, the Administration created more and more obstacles for its allies, the effect of which was to harden Nasser's position. When Israel attacked Egypt on October 29 as the first stage of the Anglo-French invasion of the canal zone, Eisenhower and Dulles were furious and reiterated, more forcefully than ever, that they do "not want to be associated with them in the Arab world," unanimously condemned the attack, and presented a UN Security Council resolution against the use of force that the British and French vetoed. The election aside, the Administration feared that Nasser would be driven into the Russian camp in some vital way at the very moment the Soviet invasion of Hungary had caused Moscow's international prestige to collapse. No less important, they were angered that their European allies had failed to consult them, thereby challenging U.S. hegemony over them in matters crucial to itself, a point Eden was made to understand explicitly. America's cynicism after a long chain of unrelated actions, Eden recounts, had ended a true partnership, leaving "only the choice of parting, or a master and vassal relationship. . . ."

The British had been all too slow to learn about their American associates, whom they had distinctly underrated, but Suez was the final lesson in their decade-long schooling in the Middle East. On December 3, they, the French, and the Israelis were compelled to agree to withdraw their forces from Egypt. The last half of 1956 represented the nadir of Anglo-American relations in the postwar period and the final demise of Britain's historic position in the Middle East. It meant also that the United States would define the West's role in the area without the intermediary role of Britain to insulate it from those unstable new forces of nationalism now coming to fruition. Everything the United States had done in the Near East since 1945 had worked toward imposing its hegemony, and Washington always comprehended the direction of its broad policy; it did not, however, envision its ultimate consequences for its own obligations—and risks.

The American position, Britain's leaders believed then and afterward, was treacherous, having created a crisis without consultation. They saw the U.S. diplomats working on the region as "anti-British" in some cases, with a "mixture of anti-colonialism and hard-headed oil tycoonery," or as callously concerned only with their own interests—which in 1956 meant, at least for Eisenhower, not doing anything that could cost him the forthcoming election. Dulles, at best, was neutral toward the fate of his closest allies, and he and Eden, who resigned as prime minister because of the crisis, "were to end up"—as Nutting phrased it—"as the bitterest of enemies." American leaders, for their part, believed that Eden "had not adjusted his thoughts to the altered world status of Great Britain," and many regarded him as "slippery." "The material interest of the United States was not identical with that of either France or the United Kingdom," Murphy later observed, and "Eisenhower was determined not to have the United States used as a cat's paw to protect British oil interests."

The Eisenhower Doctrine and the New Middle East Equation

The Suez crisis led to the termination of the already tattered Anglo-American alliance in the Middle East and the U.S. assumption, for practical purposes, of the virtually complete Western self-appointed responsibility for regulating the affairs of the area, and it was the first time since 1945 that a major Third World region shed European domination entirely and allowed an open field to the Americans. Neither in Asia nor Africa had such a fundamental transfer of authority yet occurred, and the main explanation for it was both the triumph of the United States' aggressive oil policy, which gave it a unique incentive to succeed, and widespread forces of nationalism, which by undermining British power greatly eliminated the main barrier to America's triumph. U.S. priorities still stressed a Europe-first, NATO-oriented global policy. But while this vision was an inhibition to its ambitions in Asia and Africa, in the Middle East it chose to ignore the restraints that such a commitment might have created in order to exploit the weaknesses of its most important European ally. And since the stakes were economic rather than strategic, for the Soviet Union in no way threatened the area, the materialist foundations of Washington's policy were revealed in a quite incontrovertible manner.

The problem after Suez, obviously, was that just as Arab nationalism had earlier posed a threat to Britain, the United States now had to attempt to control and shape Arab nationalism's and Islam's complex, diverse, and mercurial nature and avoid assuming the role of its new principal enemy. This task became, and remains more than ever, one of the great postwar challenges confronting the United States, one that was the inevitable outcome of its own desire for economic domination and initially had virtually nothing to do with countering the USSR.

At the end of 1956 both Dulles and Eisenhower perceived the magnitude of the new power equation in the Middle East, and without consulting the experts in the State Department, the Pentagon, or the CIA, who later deemed it an incomprehensible error, decided to proclaim the so-called Eisenhower Doctrine. During January 1957 the president discussed it with members of Congress and then asked them to pass a joint resolution. In it the president was authorized to assist nations of the region economically as well as to use U.S. armed forces "to secure and protect the territorial integrity" of any nation requesting help "against overt armed aggression from any nation controlled by international communism." "The United States appears as the self-appointed policeman and patron of the Middle East," as a staunch defender of its mission explained it. The problem, which greatly embarrassed those in Washington dealing with the region, was that the resolution was aimed at Nasser, who was not by any criterion a Communist. The only challenge the U.S. confronted in 1957 came from the very same forces it had exploited to remove Britain's influence.

"For a variety of reasons," Dulles coyly told the Senate, "certain Western European nations" could no longer deter Communist aggression. When pressed, the State Department had to admit that no state in the region was under "international communist" domination, nor was there any imminent danger of a Communist coup. There was, nonetheless, Dulles warned, now "the most serious threat that we have faced over the past 10 years." Nasser and Arab nationalism, the Administration's principal concerns, were the real objectives of the new doctrine and the main obstacles to the consolidation of U.S. power. Toward the end of the hearings, when former ambassador Jefferson Caffery testified, he wryly noted that Nasser had outlawed the Communist Party and put its leaders in jail. Nasser was ambitious, of course, but "when I was there, he was extremely, extremely cooperative." The Middle East, obviously, was a very complex place.

For much of 1957 and 1958 the United States worked energetically at making an enemy out of a former friend. And for the first time, in a self-fulfilling prophecy, it produced a political vacuum that indeed now made it possible for the Russians to play a much more important role in the area's geopolitics. If stability were the criterion of success, neither Nasser nor the U.S. Army could provide it, for virtually every nation in the region with any degree of literacy was in the process of change, internecine political struggles, cabals, and much else. In Lebanon there was no end to the age-old struggle among the many Christian and Muslim sects, which was intensifying again. Even in Jordan, the British were cut off as arms suppliers and Egypt, Syria, and Saudi Arabia became King Hussein's protectors. At the beginning of 1957 a pro-Egyptian element in the Syrian Army and in the middle-class, socialist, but very anti-Communist Baath Party came to power, soon to be challenged once again by the antireform, conservative Independent Party, which began successfully to outflank it by calling for better relations with and aid from the USSR—initiating a successful policy in August 1957 of exploitation of the Cold War that has kept Syria well supplied, and thoroughly non-Communist, to this day.

Nasser's influence in Syria and the entire Arab world mounted precisely because he had defied the Anglo-French and profited from the Cold War to augment aid to Egypt enormously. As the leadership of these Arab-speaking nations found that their domestic political struggles could not be resolved, they increasingly began to search for allies among their neighbors, and while pan-Arabism was one expression of this, collaboration among rightist regimes was another. While Syria represented the main challenge to the United States in 1957, causing Turkey and Iraq to threaten to partition it, the Eisenhower Doctrine did not prevent a continuous imbroglio within and among most of the Arab states: wars between Muscat and Oman in July 1957, Buraimi and Saudi Arabia at the same time, the rupture of the Jordan-Egyptian alliance in November, the mythical merger of Syria and Egypt into the United Arab Republic by February 1958, to be followed by an equally fictitious confederation of Jordan and Iraq the following March.

In a word, Britain's demise with Suez, the triumph of Nasser (with American aid), and the subsequent outpouring of Arab nationalism—and intrigues—created a far greater instability than the area had ever known. The vacuum the consistent American undermining of the British position since 1945 had created in the Near East had to be filled quickly or the U.S. victory would be chimerical at best and finally open the region to much greater Soviet participation in its geopolitics. The United States won its primacy in the Middle East at a time and in a fashion that presented it with incalculable problems and challenges, not the least of which was the perpetuation of its image as a nation with the power and wisdom to achieve the hegemony that had eluded its predecessors. But the sheer economic importance of the region guaranteed that Washington would make every effort to succeed in this vaguely defined and elusive objective.

The Eisenhower Administration convinced itself by the spring of 1958 that it must act soon to reverse the disorder spreading throughout the region. This time, because King Hussein of Jordan was among those Washington considered threatened, the British were consulted, and after serious sectarian fighting broke out in Lebanon in early May, largely in response to Christian president Camille Chamoun's effort to consolidate his power in the precariously balanced country, the United States announced on May 17 that if asked it would send troops to Lebanon. Planning for the operation with the British began immediately. Assurance of American salvation removed the incentive for Chamoun to negotiate with his numerous domestic rivals and guaranteed that turbulence in Lebanon would continue. As Dulles freely admitted, the "political situation in Lebanon is not simple . . . it is extremely confusing."

While the political troubles throughout the region were far more of a concern to Washington than the Lebanon crisis, more important yet was the Administration's intense, morbid obsession over its credibility in the area should friendly regimes, as Dulles put it, "think we lost our nerve and those govts will probably run to cover" by compromising with Nasser. Indeed, by mid-June Dulles had come to the pessimistic conclusion that "If we go in it will turn Arab sentiment against us. If we don't all the Arab countries which have pro-Western governments will be overthrown . . . they will in any rate." On July 14 there was a military coup in Iraq that destroyed the pro-British monarchy, and Eisenhower concluded that "it looks now as if you have a solid Arab world against us because Jordan can't stick." To save the non-Arab nations on the edges of region, in his opinion, was perhaps as much as could be attained.

In a situation where its political objectives were extremely vague and from which the United States could only lose politically, when the first of its fourteen thousand troops landed peacefully in Lebanon on July 15, accompanied by atomic artillery, many in the Pentagon were skeptical about the outcome of such a palpably quixotic undertaking. Both Eisenhower and Dulles constantly reiterated that the political goal, at least primarily, was "to demonstrate in a timely and practical way that the United States was capable of supporting its friends." The Iraqi revolution provided a politically necessary justification as a convenient afterthought, but it was entirely a coincidence rather than a cause. Credibility was the cause, and as U.S. soldiers found there was no one to shoot at and settled down comfortably on the beaches, the Administration's reasoning began to appear both highly dangerous and politically irrelevant. Dulles immediately had second thoughts and worried that the United States might "get bogged down like the Br in Suez and have to pull out."

While British troops entered Jordan on July 17 and reinforced Hussein's power, events in Iraq escaped both America's and Nasser's control. Meanwhile, as the first U.S. troops were being withdrawn, by late August Dulles concluded that "the heart of the Arab world" was being lost to the United States. The remaining soldiers were out of Lebanon by the end of October. The United States had not quite reenacted Suez, but it left Lebanon with its credibility far more tarnished than it had been at the beginning of the adventure, its position in the Arab world seriously damaged, and its capacity to guide events there in the manner it had hoped fatally undermined. Ultimately the most important lesson of its Lebanon debacle was that "credibility" as a symbolic mode of calculating its actions indeed had a powerful hold over America's leaders even in a situation where it knew that political realities preordained any action to be ridiculous or profoundly dangerous. In Lebanon it proved to be the former, but the fact that it possessed both unlimited weapons and political ambitions became an almost hypnotic fixation from this time onward, with credibility requiring extremely high-risk American policies and actions lest the leaders in Washington had to acknowledge that in a world of dynamic social, political, and economic forces, U.S. military strength and foreign policy goals were somehow pathetically irrelevant. Lebanon revealed this, but also that America's aspirations contained a demonic, irrational capacity consciously to ignore realities on behalf of obsessions such as credibility, which now had a life and force of their own in shaping its foreign policy.

The problem, which the Administration soon acknowledged in private, was that the complexity of Arab politics, whether within each nation or among them, transcended any outside state's capacity to master, and that the United States might be just as much a victim of the region's social and political dynamics as the British had been. It was obvious, too, that while Nasser's influence had risen, largely because British and American actions made him the region's only hero, he too was incapable of dominating the area's political currents. This was graphically revealed when Egypt's relations with Iraq began to deteriorate dramatically, so that on March 12, 1959, Nasser denounced General Abdul Karim Kassim's regime as "a Communist reign of terror." Kassim, as the CIA itself admitted publicly in April 1959, was surely not a Communist; he refused to allow Communists in the government, and Russia itself seemed to have no control over them and was urging Kassim, who was now demanding economic and military aid Moscow could scarcely afford, to pursue a much more cautious line on oil nationalization than the local Communists were advocating. Iraq emerged as one of many national political mutations in the Arab world, each with its specific character and originality and quite beyond the control of either the United States or the Soviet Union, much less Nasser, who was merely the first and most charismatic leader of the army-backed new middle classes coming to power in the Arab world. All the two superpowers could be certain of doing was to pay handsomely for their pretensions to meddle into the affairs of the most mercurial, and dangerous, of all the Third World's regions as the Arab states began with mounting success to play one against the other while pursuing their own independent foreign policies.

The confusion and folly of its position soon compelled the Eisenhower Administration to return discreetly to its earlier strategy of treating Nasser as a useful, potentially cooperative force in the region. In March 1958 he intensified his repression against his own Communists, and on July 1 the first U.S. aid agreement since Suez was signed, for a mere eight million dollars. By the time the Eisenhower Administration left office, however, Nasser could boast of having received three hundred million dollars in American aid from it. Nothing more revealed the sheer pragmatism and opportunism that guided American policy throughout the 1950s, for Nasser was in fact a barrier to a Communist movement that loomed immeasurably larger in American imaginations than in reality. He had served Washington's purposes well against Britain. If he was a frustration to its mastery of the politics of the region, he was nonetheless only one of many in a part of the world in which instability and politics were synonymous. The Administration sensed full well that it could go no further in the Middle East after 1958, despite the elimination of British interests, and that the better part of wisdom was to exploit the handsome advantages it had gained for its oil companies—and hope for the best.

Eisenhower later recalled that the region stabilized after 1958 and ceased to distract him, and Communists took power nowhere. In one crucial sense, however, the transfer of the dominant role in the Middle East from Britain to America throughout the 1950s, with all of its rich assets as well as obvious liabilities, was possible so quickly and easily because the Republican Administration was not friendly to Israel, and privately it was hostile—a fact the entire Arab world both understood and greatly appreciated. Congress, despite Dulles's and Eisenhower's resentment, was quite ready to give Israel modest amounts of economic aid in the form of grants and loans, largely because of the Zionist bloc's skill in mobilizing both Congress' ethnic voting coalition and the Democrats. But having triumphantly projected U.S. power into the region, it remained a very open question whether the Democrats, who were for political reasons obligated to be much friendlier to Israel, could avert the shoals of the Arab-Israeli conflict in the same manner, and if the U.S. policy in the region, after such great successes, could avoid becoming hostage to the quixotic fluctuations in American politics.

The Middle East: Toward Protracted Crisis

The Middle East in the decade after 1958 had moved from being one of Washington's principal concerns to a relatively minor place, largely because the comparative stability in the region gave it little to think about contrasted to its growing preoccupations elsewhere. But none of the basic political or economic elements in the area changed, and U.S. policy also remained constant. No state had become Marxist, the British were still present as a minor but useful partner, and not until Israel's lightning surprise attack against its neighbors in June 1967 did the Middle East once again begin to pose serious challenges to the United States. The Six-Day War rekindled the fires of Arab nationalism and initiated an arms race that permitted the Soviet Union to play a far greater role in the region than ever.

U.S relations with Israel, friendly but also relatively discreet until then, became increasingly close after 1968, when Washington agreed to supply it with advanced weapons and share intelligence. However complicating this growing intimacy, even more significant was Britain's decision in December 1967 to withdraw all its forces from the Persian Gulf area by the end of 1971, for it raised fundamental strategic and economic issues. After 1950 America had desired to supplant Britain's economic and political domination, but not to the extent requiring it alone to assume all responsibility for policing and directing the entire vast area—an undertaking its intervention in 1958 had shown to be very precarious at best. Now its triumph over the British left it with major concerns and, potentially, obligations it could scarcely afford given its vast distractions in Asia and elsewhere. This challenge confronted the Nixon Administration in 1969.

The White House, fully aware of its vast international commitments and eager to avoid more, resolved that preventing a vacuum of power into which Soviet influence could move should be the responsibility of its key surrogates in the region. Iran and, later, Saudi Arabia were both anxious to play such a role. Although the State Department preferred to view the main dangers as those arising from nationalism and the Arab-Israeli conflict rather than the Cold War with Russia, both Nixon and Kissinger ignored its sophisticated rejection of conventional wisdom and defined policies by themselves, with global politics usually their primary concern. Given the enormous American stakes in the area, one that purely local nationalist forces might also endanger, the assertion of American power was essential regardless of any role the Soviets might or might not play. With the five U.S. major oil companies alone controlling half of the output of the Middle Eastern and Libyan fields, the stakes involved had immense value at a time when world demand for oil was rising far more quickly than supplies and when prices had already begun to climb sharply. Washington never contemplated at the inception of it whether its strategy of relying on surrogates was likely to be a solution to its problems or increase them because of its additional need to defend and stabilize its proxies.

It was the United States' decisive tilt toward Israel after 1967 that made possible the USSR's growing leverage in the Middle East, for the Arab nations that Israel threatened most were unable to obtain all the arms that they desired elsewhere. This fact alone greatly complicated America's policy insofar as it believed, as did Kissinger, that its credibility was also involved whenever Soviet weapons in the hands of non-Communists threatened to defeat U.S. arms in the hands of its friends. This expanded credibility doctrine, which the United States applied during the India-Pakistan crisis in 1971, revealed that while the Nixon Administration would pursue a surrogate strategy, it would be quite as ready as its predecessors also to intervene directly in the area, usually confronting the USSR at the same time, and ultimately remain unable to exercise self-control. This dual-track approach toward conflict in the region was not calculated well in advance but was initially a visceral reaction to immediate events. This was first revealed for the Nixon Administration during the Jordanian crisis of September 1970, and it has remained the fundamental, and dangerous, contradiction as well as the premise of U.S. Middle Eastern policy since then.

Since 1968 Nasser had energetically tried to increase Soviet aid and advisers to his nation, and by 1970 had succeeded to a greater extent than ever before. In the summer of 1970, Nasser and King Hussein decided to move against the radical elements of the Palestine Liberation Organization stationed in both their nations but primarily in Jordan. The now familiar tragic imbroglio in the Arab world broke out when Hussein on September 15 began to stamp out the PLO and when Syria sent tanks and troops to protect them. At this point, in constant touch with and supporting Hussein, Washington announced the dispatch of aircraft carriers and other ships into the eastern Mediterranean and alerted its airborne troops. And while Kissinger warned the bewildered Russians that they would be held responsible should their Syrian "client" not withdraw, the United States also urged the Israelis to prepare to invade if required to save Hussein. Israel in turn demanded and got a U.S. promise to intervene should it become the target of a Soviet or an Egyptian attack. Reassured, Israel mobilized, and on September 23 the thoroughly frightened Syrians, probably under Soviet pressure as well, began to leave Jordan. A major war had been averted. And after trying desperately to keep the conflict from escalating, Nasser died of a heart attack on September 28.

The Jordan crisis, coming just as the British were leaving the region, reinforced the United States' commitment to Iran as its principal ally in the Persian Gulf, and while the containment of the Soviet-armed radical Iraqis was Tehran's primary responsibility, it was also to assure that radicals not undermine the Gulf states. This reliance "on the central importance of Iran to the safeguarding of the American . . . interest in the oil region of the Persian Gulf," as President Jimmy Carter's national security adviser later described it, was to continue until 1978, when the Shah's eagerness to spend vast sums on arms and his pro-Americanism led to his undoing and to a historic new challenge to the United States.

Israel, meanwhile, became the Administration's principal but not exclusive surrogate in the territory immediately surrounding it, and also Hussein's guarantor. But Nasser's death and the emergence of Anwar Sadat as his successor, who expelled all Soviet advisers in July 1972, soon increased America's options. From this point onward, relations with Egypt improved dramatically. Yet until this trend reached its culmination, the White House relied entirely on Israel, whom they began to arm heavily after early 1972. And while neither the president nor Kissinger had ever thought much of Secretary of State William Rogers's December 1969 plan that recognized UN Resolution 242, calling for Israel's withdrawal from occupied territories, they ceased to press it altogether because of Israel's adamant opposition. Israel now exercised a de facto veto on U.S. diplomatic policy in the region as the reward for its obedience in other domains, even though the Administration thought Israel often unreasonable. Washington did not consider the peace process crucial, however, because it persisted in regarding all regional issues as basically aspects of Soviet-American rivalry with few purely local roots, and Kissinger's main goal was to reduce Soviet influence. This was soon to prove a major error, for, as Kissinger was later to confess, the Soviet advisers in Egypt were probably a major constraint preventing Sadat from using his now formidable military power. When on October 6, 1973, the Egyptians struck the completely surprised Israeli army in Sinai, inflicting huge losses on its tanks and aircraft over the next weeks, they also irreversibly changed the entire military, economic, and political situation in the Middle East.

Israel's allegedly invincible army was now shown to be highly vulnerable, and while the White House warned Moscow not to intervene, it also did nothing to stop the Soviets from resupplying the Egyptians when the battle turned against them. Politically the United States was unwilling to range itself against the entire Arab world, including its Saudi and Persian Gulf allies who supported with both words and funds Egypt's surprise attack and who on October 17 increased the price of oil 17 percent as the initial step in their profound transformation of the world oil structure and its relation to the global economy. As the first reverberations of the October War were felt and a massive oil boycott was set in train, the United States and the USSR united in the UN to try to terminate the fighting.

The radical changes that were to occur in the Middle East after 1973 revealed that the United States' two-decade effort to assume primary control over the area had been a chimera based on illusions and false assumptions from the inception. The British had been completely supplanted, and the Arab world had exploited Soviet willingness to provide enormous quantities of arms even though not a single Marxist state had been established. It was perfectly obvious that nationalism was far more potent than radicalism and that the festering Arab-Israeli conflict guaranteed that this would remain the case, making anti-Americanism inevitable. "In retrospect," George McGhee, one of the key architects of Middle East policy, admitted in 1974, "this was always a greater danger in the Arab States than communism itself, which didn't find fertile ground among the Arabs." By 1974 the United States, despite Iran,

Saudi Arabia, and Israel by its side, was losing control over Middle Eastern oil—the main objective of its efforts there since 1945.

The quickening cycle of change and crisis meant that the region would never again be relegated to the sidelines, and it would increasingly become a central challenge to U.S. foreign policy. Indeed, by the 1970s the Middle East had become the area most likely to draw America into a major war that ultimately risked direct conflict with the Soviet Union itself. Given the vast responsibilities in the region the United States was prepared to assume and its need both to depend on and protect surrogate regimes of questionable stability, only unresolvable crises loomed before it.

The CIA in the World in the 1950s

Mary Ann Heiss, ed.

Iran, 1953: Making It Safe for the King of Kings

There has been little disagreement about whether the CIA was actually involved in the coup that overthrew Mossadegh. Instead, most debate concerns the need for the coup and its effects. The following excerpt, which views the coup in a negative manner, is from William Blum, Killing Hope: U.S. Military and CIA Interventions since World War II *(Monroe, Maine, 1995), 65–9.*

The original initiative to oust Mossadegh had come from the British, for the elderly Iranian leader had spearheaded the parliamentary movement to nationalize the British-owned Anglo-Iranian Oil Company (AIOC), the sole oil company operating in Iran. In March 1951, the bill for nationalization was passed, and at the end of April Mossadegh was elected prime minister by a large majority of Parliament. On 1 May, nationalization went into effect. The Iranian people, Mossadegh declared, "were opening a hidden treasure upon which lies a dragon."

As the prime minister had anticipated, the British did not take the nationalization gracefully, though it was supported unanimously by the Iranian parliament and by the overwhelming majority of the Iranian people for reasons of both economic justice and national pride. The Mossadegh government tried to do all the right things to placate the British: It offered to set aside 25 percent of the net profits of the oil operation as compensation; it guaranteed the safety and the jobs of the British employees; it was willing to sell its oil without disturbance to the tidy control system so dear to the hearts of the international oil giants. But the British would have none of it. What they wanted was their oil company back. And they wanted Mossadegh's head. A servant does not affront his lord with impunity . . .

. . .When the British were later expelled from Iran, . . . they had no alternative but to turn to the United States for assistance in toppling Mossadegh. In November 1952, the Churchill government approached [Kermit] Roosevelt, the *de facto* head of the CIA's Middle East division, who told the British that he felt that there was "no chance to win approval from the outgoing administration of Truman and Acheson. The new Republicans, however, might be quite different."

John Foster Dulles was certainly different. The apocalyptic anti-communist saw in Mossadegh the epitome of all that he detested in the Third World: unequivocal neutralism in the cold war, tolerance of Communists, and disrespect for free enterprise, as demonstrated by the oil nationalization. . . . To the likes of John Foster Dulles, the eccentric Dr. Mohammed Mossadegh was indeed a madman. And when the Secretary of State considered further that Iran was a nation exceedingly rich in the liquid gold, and that it shared a border with the Soviet Union more than 1,000 miles long, he was not unduly plagued by indecision as to whether the Iranian prime minister should finally retire from public life.

As matters turned out, the overthrow of Mossadegh in August 1953 was much more an American operation than a British one. Twenty-six years later, Kermit Roosevelt took the unusual step of writing a book about how he and the CIA carried out the operation. He called his book *Countercoup* to press home the idea that the CIA coup was staged only to prevent a takeover of power by the Iranian Communist Party (the Tudeh) closely backed by the Soviet Union. Roosevelt was thus arguing that Mossadegh had to be removed to prevent a Communist takeover. . . .

In actuality, although the Tudeh Party more or less faithfully followed the fluctuating Moscow line on Iran, the relation of the party to Mossadegh was much more complex than Roosevelt and other cold-war chroniclers have made it out to be. The Tudeh felt very ambiguous about the wealthy, eccentric, land-owning prime minister who, nonetheless, was standing up to imperialism. Dean Acheson, Truman's Secretary of State, described Mossadegh as "essentially a rich, reactionary, feudal-minded Persian," hardly your typical Communist Party fellow-traveler. . . .

. . . [T]he Shah was persuaded to issue royal decrees dismissing Mossadegh as prime minister and replacing him with one Fazlollah Zahedi, a general who had been imprisoned during the war by the British for collaboration with the Nazis. Late in the night of 14/15 August, the Shah's emissary delivered the royal decree to Mossadegh's home, which was guarded by troops. . . . [U]nsurprising[ly], Mossadegh did not abdicate. The prime minister, who maintained that only Parliament could dismiss him, delivered a radio broadcast the following morning in which he stated that the Shah, encouraged by "foreign elements," had attempted a *coup d'état*. Mossadegh then declared that he was, therefore, compelled to take full power unto himself. He denounced Zahedi as a traitor and sought to have him arrested, but the general had been hidden by Roosevelt's team.

The Shah, fearing all was lost, fled with his queen to Rome via Baghdad without so much as packing a suitcase. Undeterred, Roosevelt went ahead and directed the mimeographing of copies of the royal decrees for distribution to the public, and sent two of his Iranian agents to important military commanders to seek their support. . . .

Beginning on 16 August, a mass demonstration arranged by the National Front, supporting Mossadegh and attacking the Shah and the United States, took place in the capital city, Teheran. . . .

Among the demonstrators there were as well a number of individuals working for the CIA. According to Richard Cottam, an American academic and author reportedly in the employ of the Agency in Teheran at this time, these agents were sent "into the streets to act as if they were Tudeh. They were more than just provocateurs, they were shock troops, who acted as if they were Tudeh people throwing rocks at mosques and priests," the purpose of which was to stamp the Tudeh and, by implication, Mossadegh as being anti-religion.

. . . [O]n 18 August [Mossadegh] ordered the police and army to put an end to the Tudeh demonstrations which they did with considerable force. According to the accounts of Roosevelt and Ambassador [Loy] Henderson, Mossadegh took this step as a result of a meeting with Henderson in which the ambassador complained of the extreme harassment being suffered by US citizens at the hands of the Iranians. It is left unclear by both of the Americans how much of this harassment was real and how much manufactured by them for the occasion. . . .

The following day, 19 August, Roosevelt's Iranian agents staged a parade through Teheran. With a fund of some one million dollars having been established in a safe in the American embassy, the "extremely competent professional 'organizers,'" as Roosevelt called them, had no difficulty in buying themselves a mob, probably using but a small fraction of the fund. (The various accounts of the CIA role in Iran have the Agency spending from $10,000 to $19 million to overthrow Mossadegh. The larger amounts are based on reports that the CIA engaged in heavy bribery of members of Parliament and other influential Iranians to enlist their support against the prime minister.)

Soon a line of people could be seen coming out of the ancient bazaar, led by circus and athletic performers to attract the public. The marchers were waving banners, shouting "Long live the Shah!" Along the edges of the procession, men were passing out Iranian currency adorned with a portrait of the Shah. The demonstrators gathered followers as they went, people joining and picking up the chants, undoubtedly for a myriad of political and personal reasons. The balance of psychology had swung against Mossadegh.

Guatemala, 1953-1954: While the World Watched

The CIA used the lessons it had learned from the operation against Mossadegh in the coup that toppled Guatemalan President Jacabo Arbenz Guzman not quite a year later. Ostensibly, Arbenz was overthrown because he was leading Guatemala toward communism, although critics of the operation, such as the author of the selection here, question whether that was really the case. Excerpted from William Blum, Killing Hope: U.S. Military and CIA Interventions since World War II (Monroe, Maine, 1995), 73–78, 80.

Dwight Eisenhower, [Secretary of State] John Foster Dulles and [Director of Central Intelligence] Allen Dulles had decided that the legally-elected government of Jacabo Arbenz was "communist", therefore [it] must go; and go it did, in June 1954.

In the midst of the American preparation to overthrow the government, the Guatemalan Foreign Minister, Guillermo Toriello, lamented that the United States was categorizing "as 'communism' every manifestation of nationalism or economic independence, any desire for social progress, any intellectual curiosity, and any interest in progressive liberal reforms."

Toriello was close to the truth, but Washington officials retained enough contact with reality and world opinion to be aware of the inappropriateness of coming out against nationalism, independence or reform. Thus it was that Secretary of State Dulles asserted that Guatemalans were living under a "Communist type of terrorism" . . . President Eisenhower warned about "the Communist dictatorship" establishing "an outpost on this continent to the detriment of all the American nations" . . . the US Ambassador to Guatemala, John Peurifoy, declared that "We cannot permit a Soviet Republic to be established between Texas and the Panama Canal" . . . [and] others warned that Guatemala could become a base from which the Soviet Union might actually seize the Canal. . . .

The Soviet Union could be excused if it was somewhat bewildered by all the rhetoric, for the Russians had scant interest in Guatemala, did not provide the country with any kind of military assistance, did not even maintain diplomatic relations with it. . . .

With the exception of one occasion, the countries of Eastern Europe had as little to do with Guatemala as did the Soviet Union. A month before the coup, that is, long after Washington had begun preparation for it, Czechoslovakia made a single arms sale to Guatemala for cash, something the Czechs would no doubt have done for any other country willing to pay the price. . . .

The American propaganda mill made much of this arms transaction. Less publicized was the fact that Guatemala had to seek arms from Czechoslovakia because the United States had refused to sell it any since 1948 due to its reformist governments, and had pressured other countries to do the same despite Arbenz's repeated pleas to lift the embargo.

. . . The Guatemalan president, who took office in March 1951 after being elected by a wide margin, had no special contact or spiritual/ideological ties with the Soviet Union or the rest of the Communist bloc. . . .

The centerpiece of Arbenz's program was land reform. The need for it was clearly expressed in the all-too-familiar underdeveloped-country statistics: In a nation overwhelmingly rural, 2.2 percent of the landowners owned 70 percent of the arable land; the annual per capita income of agricultural workers was $87. . . .

The expropriation of large tracts of uncultivated acreage which was distributed to approximately 100,000 landless peasants, the improvement in union rights for the workers, and other social reforms, were the reasons Arbenz had won the support of Communists and other leftists, which was no more than to be expected. . . .

The party formed by the Communists, the Guatemalan Labor Party, held four seats in Congress, the smallest component of Arbenz's ruling coalition which commanded a total of 51 seats in the 1953-54 legislature. Communists held several important sub-cabinet posts but none was ever appointed to the cabinet. In addition, there were Communists employed in the bureaucracy, particularly in the administration of land reform. . . .

The first plan to topple Arbenz was a CIA operation approved by President Truman in 1952, but at the eleventh hour, Secretary of State Dean Acheson persuaded Truman to abort it. However, soon after Eisenhower became president in January 1953, the plan was resurrected.

Both administrations were pressured by executives of United Fruit Company, much of whose vast and uncultivated land in Guatemala had been expropriated by the Arbenz government as part of the land reform program. The company wanted nearly $16 million for the land, the government was offering $525,000, United Fruit's own declared valuation for tax purposes.

United Fruit functioned in Guatemala as a state within a state. It owned the country's telephone and telegraph facilities, administered its only important Atlantic harbor, and monopolized its banana exports. A subsidiary of the company owned nearly every mile of railroad track in the country. The fruit company's influence amongst Washington's power elite was equally impressive. On a business and/or personal level, it had close ties to . . . various State Department officials, congressmen, the American Ambassador to the United Nations, and others. Anne Whitman, the wife of the company's public relations director, was President Eisenhower's personal secretary. . . .

Under Arbenz, Guatemala constructed an Atlantic port and a highway to compete with United Fruit's holdings, and built a hydro-electric plant to offer cheaper energy than the US-controlled electricity monopoly. Arbenz's strategy was to limit the power of foreign companies through direct competition rather than through nationalization, a policy not feasible of course when it came to a fixed quantity like land. In his inaugural address, Arbenz stated that:

> *Foreign capital will always be welcome as long as it adjusts to local conditions, remains always subordinate to Guatemalan laws, cooperates with the economic development of the country, and strictly abstains from intervening in the nation's social and political life.*

This hardly described United Fruit's role in Guatemala. Amongst much else, the company had persistently endeavored to frustrate Arbenz's reform programs, discredit him and his government, and induce his downfall.

Arbenz was, accordingly, wary of multinationals and could not be said to welcome them into his country with open arms. This attitude, his expropriation of United Fruit's land, and his "tolerance of communists" were more than enough to make him a marked man in Washington. The United States saw these policies as being inter-related: that is, it was communist influence—not any economic or social exigency of Guatemalan life—which was responsible for the government's treatment of American firms.

In March 1953, the CIA approached disgruntled right-wing officers in the Guatemalan army and arranged to send them arms. United Fruit donated $64,000 in cash. The following month, uprisings broke out in several towns but were quickly put down by loyal troops. The rebels were put on trial and revealed the fruit company's role in the plot, but not the CIA's.

The Eisenhower administration resolved to do the job right the next time around. With cynical glee, almost an entire year was spent in painstaking, step-by-step preparation for the overthrow of Jacabo Arbenz Guzman. . . . With the release of many formerly classified government papers, the following story has emerged.

Headquarters for the operation were established in Opa Locka, Florida, on the outskirts of Miami. The Nicaraguan dictator Anastasio Somoza lent/leased his country out as a site for an airstrip and for hundreds of men—Guatemalan exiles and US and Central American mercenaries—to receive training in the use of weapons and radio broadcasting, as well as in the fine arts of sabotage and demolition. . . . The Canal Zone was set aside as a weapons depot from which arms were gradually distributed to the rebels who were to assemble in Honduras under the command of Colonel Carlos Castillo Armas before crossing into Guatemala. Soviet-marked weapons were also gathered for the purpose of planting them inside Guatemala before the invasion to reinforce U.S. charges of Russian intervention. And, as important as arms, it turned out, hidden radio transmitters were placed in and around the perimeter of Guatemala, including one in the US Embassy. . . .

Eventually, at Ambassador Peurifoy's urging, a group of high-ranking officers called on Arbenz to ask that he dismiss all communists who held posts in his administration. The president assured them that the communists did not represent a danger, that they did not run the government, and that it would be undemocratic to dismiss them. . . .

Arbenz himself was offered a bribe by the CIA, whether to abdicate his office or something less is not clear. A large sum of money was deposited in a Swiss bank for him, but he, or a subordinate, rejected the offer.

On the economic front, contingency plans were made for such things as cutting off Guatemalan credit abroad, disrupting its oil supplies, and causing a run on its foreign reserves. But it was on the propaganda front that American ingenuity shone at its brightest. Inasmuch as the Guatemalan government was being overthrown because it was communist, the fact of its communism would have to be impressed upon the rest of Latin America. Accordingly, the US Information Agency (USIA) began to place unattributed articles in foreign newspapers labeling particular Guatemalan officials as communist and referring to various actions by the Guatemalan government as "communist-inspired." In the few weeks prior to Arbenz's fall alone, more than 200 articles about Guatemala were written and placed in scores of Latin American newspapers. . . .

The USIA also distributed more than 100,000 copies of a pamphlet entitled "Chronology of Communism in Guatemala" throughout the hemisphere, as well as 27,000 copies of anti-communist cartoons and posters. The American propaganda agency, moreover, produced three films on Guatemala, with predictable content, and newsreels favorable to the United States for showing free in cinemas. . . .

In May, the CIA covertly sponsored a "Congress Against Soviet Intervention in Latin America" in Mexico City. The same month, Somoza called in the diplomatic corps in Nicaragua and told them, his voice shaking with anger, that his police had discovered a secret Soviet shipment of arms (which had been planted by the CIA) near the Pacific Coast, and suggested that the communists wanted to convert Nicaragua into "a new Korean situation." A few weeks later, an unmarked plane parachuted arms with Soviet markings onto Guatemala's coast. . . .

The offensive began in earnest on 18 June with planes dropping leaflets over Guatemala demanding that Arbenz resign immediately or else various sites would be bombed. CIA radio stations broadcast similar messages. That afternoon, the planes returned to machine-gun houses near military barracks, drop fragmentation bombs and strafe the National Palace.

Over the following week, the air attacks continued daily—strafing or bombing ports, fuel tanks, ammunition dumps, military barracks, the international airport, a school, and several cities; nine persons, including a three-year-old girl, were reported wounded; an unknown number of houses were set afire by incendiary explosives. During one night-time raid, a tape recording of a bomb attack was played over loudspeakers set up on the roof of the US Embassy to heighten the anxiety of the capital's residents. When Arbenz went on the air to try and calm the public's fear, the CIA radio team jammed the broadcast. . . .

Arbenz finally received an ultimatum from certain army officers: Resign or they would come to an agreement with the invaders. The CIA and Ambassador Peurifoy had been offering payments to officers to defect, and one army commander reportedly accepted $60,000 to surrender his troops. With his back to the wall, Arbenz made an attempt to arm civilian supporters to fight for the government, but army officers blocked the disbursement of weapons. The Guatemalan president knew that the end was near. . . .

The Castillo Armas forces could not have defeated the much larger Guatemalan army, but the air attacks, combined with the belief in the invincibility of the enemy, persuaded Guatemalan military officers to force Arbenz to resign. No Communists, domestic or foreign, came to his aid. He asked the head of the officers, Army Chief of Staff Col. Carlos Díaz, only that he give his word not to negotiate with Castillo Armas, and Díaz, who despised the rebel commander as much as Arbenz did, readily agreed. What Díaz did not realize was that the United States would not be satisfied merely to oust Arbenz. Castillo Armas had been groomed as the new head of government, and that was not negotiable.

Lauding the CIA's Work in Iran

Although recent scholarship has depicted the CIA's involvement in the coup against Mossadegh negatively, contemporary accounts applauded the Agency's efforts to stop the spread of communism in a nation vital to American security. This account, published shortly after the coup and sanctioned by the CIA, paints a positive picture of American involvement. Excerpted from Richard and Gladys Harkness, "The Mysterious Doings of CIA," Saturday Evening Post, *6 November 1954, 66, 68.*

[An early] CIA-influenced triumph was the successful overthrow, in Iran in the summer of 1953, of old, dictatorial Premier Mohammed Mossadegh and the return to power of this country's friend, Shah Mohammed Riza Pahlevi.

On May 28, 1953, President Eisenhower received a letter from Mossadegh amounting to a bare-faced attempt at international blackmail: The United States would fill his bankrupt treasury with American dollars—or else. The "or else," Mossadegh hinted darkly, would be an economic agreement and mutual-defense pact with Russia.

Mossadegh was conspiring with the communist Tudeh Party as it operated from the back alleyways of the ancient Iranian capital of Teheran. He had only one asset to pledge in return for financial assistance from Russia—the resources of the rich Iranian oil fields and the refinery at Abadan, which Mossadegh had seized from Britain's Anglo-Iranian Oil Company under the guise of nationalization. With that economic stroke accomplished, Moscow would be in a position to achieve what has been the prime objective of Russian foreign policy since the days of the Czars—access to a warm-water outlet on the Persian Gulf, the free world's life line to the Far East. A Russian score there would mean the crumbling of the democracies' position in the Middle East from Cairo to Baluchistan.

The White House stalled Mossadegh for one month; then turned down the crafty premier with a blunt no. This was a calculated risk at best. It was a daring gamble, in fact, that Mossadegh would not remain in power to carry out his threat. It was, as well, a situation which required a little doing. The doing began in short order. . . .

On Thursday, August thirteenth [1953], the shah suddenly issued a double-edged ukase: Mossadegh was ousted by royal decree and his successor as premier was to be General [Fazlollah] Zahedi. The shah ordered the colonel of the Imperial Guards to serve the notice on Mossadegh. Two days later, at midnight of Saturday, August fifteenth, the colonel went to Mossadegh's residence to find himself and his platoon surrounded by tanks and jeeps. The colonel was clapped in jail, and Mossadegh proclaimed that the revolt had been crushed. The shah and his queen, taking events at face value, fled to Rome by way of Iraq.

"America's Secret Agents: The Mysterious Doings of CIA," by Richard and Gladys Harkness, reprinted from *The Saturday Evening Post*, November 1954.

On Wednesday, August nineteenth, with the army standing close guard around the uneasy capital, a grotesque procession made its way along the street leading to the heart of Teheran. There were tumblers turning handsprings, weight lifters twirling iron bars and wrestlers flexing their biceps. As spectators grew in number, the bizarre assortment of performers began shouting pro-shah slogans in unison. The crowd took up the chant and there, after one precarious moment, the balance of public psychology swung against Mossadegh.

Upon signal, it seemed, army forces on the shah's side began an attack. The fighting lasted a bitter nine hours. By nightfall, following American-style military strategy and logistics, loyalist troops drove Mossadegh's elements into a tight cordon around the premier's palace. They surrendered, and Mossadegh was captured as he lay weeping in his bed, clad in striped silk pajamas. In Rome a bewildered young shah prepared to fly home and install Zahedi as premier, and to give Iran a pro-Western regime.

Thus it was that the strategic little nation of Iran was rescued from the closing clutch of Moscow. Equally important, the physical overthrow of Mossadegh was accomplished by the Iranians themselves. It is the guiding premise of the CIA's third force that we must develop and nurture indigenous freedom legions among captive or threatened people who stand ready to take personal risks for their own liberty.

Downplaying the CIA, Emphasizing Communism

As the following selection suggests, not all scholars credit the CIA with playing a decisive role in the overthrow of Arbenz. A minority position within the scholarly community downplays the importance of American involvement in the coup. Excerpted from Frederick W. Marks III, "The CIA and Castillo Armas in Guatemala, 1954: New Clues to an Old Puzzle," Diplomatic History 14 (Winter 1990), 67–68, 78–79, 82–83, 86. Note how this selection emphasizes the seriousness of the Communist threat to Guatemala.

Few episodes in the history of the Eisenhower administration have engendered more controversy or drawn heavier fire from academic chroniclers of the past than American intervention in Guatemala. Secretary of State John Foster Dulles said that "military force should not be used aggressively to achieve national goals." Yet during his tenure at Foggy Bottom [the State Department], American planes and American advisers helped secure the overthrow of a popularly elected president, Jacobo Arbenz Guzmán. Arbenz, for his part, claimed to view American policy as the cat's paw of corporate greed and attributed a large share of his nation's problems to the United Fruit Company (UFC), maintaining that communism posed no threat to his people and that American aid to rebel leader Carlos Castillo Armas constituted unwarranted interference in the domestic affairs of another country. Essentially, he held that the revolutionary movement which overthrew him was "Made in the U.S.A." by the Central Intelligence Agency (CIA) and that its base of support among the Guatemalan masses had been negligible. He also minimized the military strength of the opposition, making it appear as if the downfall of his government could be explained solely in terms of clever

"America's Secret Agents: The Mysterious Doings of CIA," by Richard and Gladys Harkness, reprinted from *The Saturday Evening Post*, November 1954.

propaganda beamed from clandestine radio stations in conjunction with a campaign of aerial bombing, all of it orchestrated by Washington. This has been the position taken by his friends ever since, just as it has been prominently featured in scholarly monographs. . . .

Although there were no Communists in the Arbenz cabinet, it was not a cabinet with real power such as belonged to the heads of key military and civilian groups and, above all, to Arbenz himself. The president, whose campaign was managed by José Manuel Fortuny, the founder of the Guatemalan Communist party, had at his side an energetic and politically active wife who had become ardently and openly pro-Communist after studying in the United States. Moreover, the Communist party itself, using popular-front techniques, had joined with the Labor party to fill fifty-one out of fifty-six seats in congress. By April 1954, four out of ten party delegates who advised Arbenz on national policy were Communists, and though there were only four outright Communists in the legislature, they chaired the crucial committees. . . .

Communists or Communist sympathizers soon took over the education ministry, the social security administration, and the agrarian reform program, not to mention the official press and radio, which echoed Moscow's voice on world events. By March 1954, the hammer and sickle had begun to appear in government offices, and newspaper correspondents representing Reuters and the *New York Times* had been expelled. Church leaders found death threats in their mail. Religious processions were banned. Scores of people simply disappeared. At the same time Soviet-bloc arms were beginning to pour into the country in quantities suggestive of an intent to supply guerrilla movements across the border, and documents were captured confirming Moscow's plans for a takeover of the entire Central American region. The link between Guatemala City and Moscow could hardly have been closer judging from the volume of traffic between the two capitals. . . .

The precise value of American aid in assuring the success of the revolution may never be known. On the positive side, Washington acted to neutralize the influence of the Communist bloc by obtaining the anti-Communist Caracas Declaration in March 1954. It also signed defense pacts with Nicaragua and Honduras, shipped small quantities of arms, and put a stop to the large influx of munitions and military equipment coming from Eastern Europe. When the *Alfhem*, a Swedish freighter, arrived in Guatemala on 15 May and unloaded two thousand tons of glassware and "optical goods" which turned out to be Czech arms worth 50 percent more than the annual military budget of Guatemala, this appeared well in excess of anything the country needed for its protection and Dulles denounced the connection with Moscow. . . .

It has been suggested that the CIA not only provided Castillo Armas with planes and pilots, financed a media blitz, and attempted unsuccessfully to bribe Arbenz and his army officers but also that it planted boxes of Russian-marked rifles in Nicaragua to be "found" by Nicaraguan police. There is no question that the United States Information Agency reproduced and distributed one hundred thousand copies of a "Chronology of Communism in Guatemala." Eisenhower replaced two fighter bomber planes lost in action by rebel forces, and aerial operations did figure significantly in Castillo Armas's victory. However, to conclude from this that the role of the United States dwarfed all other factors, that the Liberation movement lacked popular support, or that Castillo Armas did not defeat government forces on the ground in a brief but extensive series of engagements requires an extraordinary leap of the imagination. Robert Cutler, Ike's special assistant for national security affairs and director of the National Security Council, was closer to the truth when he termed American aid "indirect" and "very minor.". . .

There are several essentials to bear in mind, then, when recalling Castillo Armas and his Liberation movement: communism constituted a genuine threat and Arbenz had forfeited the confidence of most of the Guatemalan people by the summer of 1954. One can perhaps argue over the degree of danger to Guatemalan freedom and American security, but there can be no quarreling over the existence of a menace of some kind or about the seriousness with which it was viewed by policymakers in Washington. Neither can there be any denial of the tactical skill and military power represented by Castillo Armas.

This is not to deny that the CIA had a definite role and that it went about its business efficiently on one of the few occasions when it succeeded in eviscerating a leftist regime regarded in most quarters as ripe for a Communist takeover. But the current emphasis on CIA operations slights factors that were equally decisive and equally, if not more, important. As in the case of the straw that broke the camel's back, many straws were required to do the job and the importance of straw number ten does not preclude the importance of each of the others, some of which may have weighed a good deal more.

The Legacy of Vietnam

George Herring

For all concerned, "peace with honor" came at a very high price. Official American estimates place the number of South Vietnamese battle deaths for the years 1969–1973 at 107,504, and North Vietnamese and Vietcong at more than a half million. The tonnage of bombs dropped on Indochina during the Nixon era exceeded that of the Johnson years, wreaking untold devastation, causing permanent ecological damage to the countryside, and leaving millions of civilians homeless. The United States suffered much less than Vietnam, but the cost was nevertheless enormous. An additional 20,553 Americans were killed in the last four years of the war, bringing the total to more than 58,000. Continuation of the war fueled an inflation which neither Nixon nor his successors could control. The war polarized the American people and poisoned the political atmosphere as had no issue since slavery a century before. Although Nixon had held out for peace with honor in order to maintain America's position in the world, the United States emerged from the war with its image considerably tarnished abroad and its people weary of international involvement. For Nixon, too, the price was steep. By January 1973, he was exhausted and isolated, his administration reduced to a "small band of tired, dispirited, sometimes mean and petty men, bickering among themselves, wary and jealous of one another." More than any other single issue, Vietnam brought a premature end to the Nixon presidency. The extreme measures he took to defend his Vietnam policy against enemies real and imagined led directly to the Watergate scandals which would eventually force his resignation. Thus, when the final Vietnam crisis came in 1975, the architect of peace with honor was no longer in the White House and the nation was in no mood to defend the agreement he had constructed at such great cost.

The "peace" agreements of January 1973 merely established a framework for continuing the war without direct American participation. North Vietnam still sought unification of the country on its terms; South Vietnam struggled to survive as an independent nation, and some U.S. officials, including President Nixon, continued to support its aspirations.

Reprinted from *America's Longest War: The United States and Vietnam*, (1986), McGraw-Hill Companies.

Dependent on the United States from its birth, the Saigon government had great difficulty functioning on its own. Moreover, because of the Watergate scandals and American war-weariness, Nixon was not able to live up to the commitments he had made to Thieu, and indeed in August 1974 he was forced to resign. Congress drastically cut back aid to South Vietnam. When North Vietnam mounted a major offensive in the spring of 1975, South Vietnam collapsed with stunning rapidity, dramatically ending the thirty-year war and leaving the United States, on the eve of its third century, frustrated and bewildered.

The "postwar war" began the instant that peace was proclaimed. The United States had difficulty arranging with the North Vietnamese and Vietcong the return of its 587 prisoners of war, at one point threatening to delay further troop withdrawals in the absence of cooperation. By the end of March, the POWs had been released, returning home to receive the only heroes' welcome of the war, and all U.S. troops had been withdrawn. But these were the only tangible accomplishments of the teams assigned to implement the peace accords. From the start, efforts to effect a cease-fire were unavailing. None of the Vietnamese combatants had abandoned his goals.

Although the Paris agreements provided that the future of South Vietnam would be settled by the Vietnamese, the United States persisted in its commitment to Thieu. Deeply frustrated by the months of tortuous negotiations and anxious to get on to other things, Kissinger appears to have sought nothing more than a "decent interval" between the signing of the agreements and a final settlement in Vietnam. Nixon, on the other hand, was no more willing in 1973 than he had been in 1969 to be the first American President to lose a war.

Fully aware of the fragility of the agreements, Nixon and Kissinger used every available means to strengthen the Thieu government. To secure Saigon's acquiescence, Nixon had secretly promised to continue "full economic and military aid" and to "respond with full force" should North Vietnam violate the agreements. The military advisory group was replaced by a "civilian" team of some 9,000 men, many of them hastily discharged from military service and placed in the employ of the government of Vietnam.

The administration attempted to use the leverage available to it to prevent North Vietnam from upsetting the delicate equilibrium in the south. As part of the Paris package, the United States had agreed to provide Hanoi $4.75 billion in aid for reconstruction. On several occasions in the spring of 1973, Nixon threatened to withhold the funds unless North Vietnam adhered to the letter of the agreements, and he eventually suspended talks on postwar aid in protest against continued infiltration into South Vietnam and intensification of the fighting in Cambodia. The President and Kissinger also sought to keep alive the threat of American military intervention. The last American troops were withdrawn from Vietnam by the end of March, but the United States kept a formidable armada of naval and air power in the Gulf of Tonkin and in Thailand and Guam. The bombing of Cambodia was continued, in part to support Lon Nol against a determined Khmer Rouge offensive and in part to maintain Nixon's "reputation for fierceness."

The North Vietnamese ignored the American warnings, however, and by early summer Nixon's ability to threaten was severely curtailed by a rebellious Congress. The Congressional challenge of 1973 reflected a war-weariness and a widespread feeling among the American people that once American troops had been safely removed, the nation should extricate itself entirely from the conflict.

Perceiving the steady erosion of America's control over events in Indochina, Kissinger journeyed to Paris in May in a futile effort to persuade Le Duc Tho to observe the cease-fire. The diplomats could agree on nothing more than an innocuous communiqué reaffirming the January accords.

By the end of 1973, Nixon was virtually powerless. Watergate had reduced his popular approval ratings to an all-time low and left him fighting a desperate rearguard action to save his political life. In November, Congress passed over another veto the so-called War Powers Act, a direct response to the exercise of presidential authority in Vietnam. The legislation required the President to inform Congress within forty-eight hours of the deployment of American military forces abroad and obligated him to withdraw them in sixty days in the absence of explicit Congressional endorsement.

Apparently still confident of U.S. support despite Watergate, Thieu formally proclaimed the start of the "Third Indochina War," and in late 1973 stepped up ground and air attacks on enemy bases and launched a series of land-grabbing operations in PRG-held territories along the eastern seaboard, in the Iron Triangle, and in the delta. This time, the North Vietnamese and PRG counterattacked.

By the fall of 1974, the military balance had shifted in favor of North Vietnam. More than half of South Vietnam's million-man army was tied down in static defense positions and scattered throughout the northern provinces.

The American abandonment of South Vietnam was manifest by the end of 1974. Nixon was forced to resign in August, removing from power the individual who had promised Thieu continued support. Throughout the year, Kissinger pleaded with an increasingly defiant Congress to expand American military aid to $1.5 billion, insisting that the United States had a moral obligation to South Vietnam and warning that failure to uphold it would have a "corrosive effect on our interests beyond Indochina." The arguments that had been accepted without challenge for nearly a quarter of a century now fell flat. Inflation in the United States evoked insistent demands for reducing expenditures, and many members of Congress agreed with Senator William Proxmire that there was less need for continued military aid to South Vietnam than for "any other single item" in the budget. In September 1974, Congress approved an aid program of $700 million, half of which comprised shipping costs.

The aid cuts of 1974 had a tremendous impact in South Vietnam. Without the continued large infusion of American funds and equipment, the armed forces could not fight the way the Americans had trained them. Air force operations had to be curtailed by as much as 50 percent because of shortages of gasoline and spare parts. Ammunition and other supplies had to be severely rationed. The inescapable signs of waning American support had a devastating effect on morale in an army already reeling under North Vietnamese blows, and desertions reached an all-time high of 240,000 in 1974.

In early 1975, Hanoi concluded that the "opportune moment" was at hand. In December 1974, North Vietnamese main units and PRG regional forces attacked Phuoc Long, northeast of Saigon, and within three weeks had killed or captured 3,000 South Vietnamese troops, seized huge quantities of supplies, and "liberated" the entire province. The ease of the victory underscored the relative weakening of the ARVN during the past year and made clear, as North Vietnamese Chief of Staff Van Tien Dung later put it, that Thieu was now forced to fight a "poor-man's war."

The collapse came with a suddenness which appears to have surprised even the North Vietnamese. Massing vastly superior forces against the stretched-out ARVN defenders, Dung attacked Ban Me Thuot in the Central Highlands on March 10 and took it within two days. To secure control of the highlands before the end of the dry season, he quickly moved north against Pleiku and Kontum. A panicky Thieu unwisely ordered his forces to withdraw from the highlands, but no plans had been drawn for retreat and the North Vietnamese had cut the major roads. The withdrawal turned into a rout. Hundreds of thousands of refugees fled with the departing soldiers, clogging the avenues of escape. Much of the army was captured or destroyed, and thousands of civilians died from enemy or ARVN gunfire and from starvation in what journalists called the "Convoy of Tears." Pleiku and Kontum fell within a week. The disastrous abandonment of the highlands cost Thieu six provinces, at least two divisions of soldiers, and the confidence of his army and people. It opened the way for even greater catastrophe in the coastal cities of South Vietnam.

Hanoi now sensed for the first time that total victory could be attained in 1975 and immediately put into effect contingency plans for the conquest of all of South Vietnam. When North Vietnamese forces advanced on Hue and Danang, the defending army along with hundreds of thousands of civilians fled for Saigon, duplicating on an even larger and more tragic scale the debacle in the highlands. Soldiers looted and money-hungry citizens charged refugees up to two dollars for a glass of water.

The United States was stunned by the collapse of South Vietnam but was resigned to the outcome. American intelligence had correctly predicted that the major North Vietnamese thrust was not planned until 1976, but the capacity of the South Vietnamese to resist was again overestimated, and Washington was shocked by the sudden fall of the highlands.

Weary of the seemingly endless involvement in Vietnam and pinched by an economic recession at home, Americans were not in a generous mood. Why throw good money after bad, they asked. At a time when they themselves were in "desperate financial straits," they saw no reason to continue to sacrifice for a government that was "not only corrupt but grossly wasteful and inefficient." It was about time that the South Vietnamese were made to stand on their own feet, one "fed-up taxpayer" exclaimed. "My God, we're all tired of it, we're sick to death of it," an Oregonian wrote. "55,000 dead and $100 billion spent and for what?"

The certainty that the United States would not intervene ended whatever slim hope of survival South Vietnam may have had. North Vietnamese forces advanced from Danang to the outskirts of the capital in less than a month, meeting strong resistance only at Xuan Loc, where a small contingent of ARVN forces fought desperately against superior numbers and firepower. On May 1, 1975, Vietcong soldiers triumphantly ran up the flag over a renamed Ho Chi Minh City. Several days earlier, Gerald Ford formally proclaimed what had already become obvious: the Vietnam War is "finished as far as the United States is concerned."

The American withdrawal revealed in microcosm much of the delusion, the frustration, and the tragedy that had marked the American experience in Vietnam. U.S. officials persisted in the belief that South Vietnam would mount an effective defense until the North Vietnamese were at the gates of Saigon. Ambassador Graham Martin stubbornly supported Thieu long after it was evident the President had no backing within his own country: Martin headed off several coup attempts and encouraged Thieu's refusal to resign, resignation perhaps being the only chance of avoiding unconditional surrender. Fearful of spreading panic in Saigon, Martin delayed implementation of evacuation plans until the last minure. The United States managed to get its own people out, as well as 150,000 Vietnamese, but the operation was chaotic and fraught with human suffering. Corruption ran rampant, escape frequently going to the highest bidder, and the U.S. Embassy paid exorbitant fees to get exit visas for some of those seeking to flee. Because of the unavailability of adequate transport, many South Vietnamese who wished to leave could not. The spectacle of U.S. Marines using rifle butts to keep desperate Vietnamese from blocking escape routes and of angry ARVN soldiers firing on the departing Americans provided a tragic epitaph for twenty-five years of American involvement in Vietnam.

The United States shared with the South Vietnamese leadership responsibility for the debacle of April 1975. In the two years after the signing of the Paris agreements, the United States gave Thieu enough support to encourage his defiance but not enough to ensure his survival. Nixon's ill-advised promises tempted him to reject the admittedly risky choice of negotiations and to launch a war he could not win. The reduction of American involvement in the war and the cutbacks of American aid weakened South Vietnam's capacity and will to resist, and the refusal of the United States to intervene in the final crisis sealed its downfall. On the other hand, Thieu's intransigence, his gross tactical errors, and his desperate attempts to save himself while his nation was dying suggest that the outcome would probably have been the same regardless of what the United States had done. Without leadership from Thieu and the army's high command, the South Vietnamese people gave way to hysteria, each person doing only what he could to save his own skin. The nation simply collapsed.

The fall of South Vietnam just fifty-five days after the onset of the North Vietnamese offensive was symptomatic of the malaise which had afflicted the nation since its birth. Political fragmentation, the lack of able far-sighted leaders, and a tired and corrupt elite which could not adjust to the revolution that swept Vietnam after 1945 afforded a perilously weak basis for nationhood. Given these harsh realities, the American effort to create a bastion of anti-Communism south of the seventeenth parallel was probably doomed from the start. The United States could not effect the needed changes in South Vietnamese society without jeopardizing the order it sought, and there was no long-range hope of stability without revolutionary change. The Americans could provide money and weapons, but they could not furnish the ingredients necessary for political stability and military success. Despairing of the capacity of the South Vietnamese to save themselves, the United States had assumed the burden in 1965, only to toss it back in the laps of its clients when the American people tired of the war. The dependency of the early years persisted long after the United States had shifted to Vietnamization, however. To the very end and despite overwhelming evidence to the contrary, Thieu and his cohorts clung desperately to the belief that the United States would not abandon them.

With the North Vietnamese victory, the "dominoes" in Indochina quickly toppled. Cambodia in fact fell before South Vietnam, ending a peculiarly brutal war and initiating a period of unprecedented cruelty of totalitarianism and began the forced relocation of much of the population.

The end in Laos was less convulsive. The Laotian "settlement" of 1962 had been a dead letter from the start. A flimsy coalition government nominally upheld a precarious neutrality, while outsiders waged war up and down the land. The North Vietnamese used Laotian territory for their infiltration route into South Vietnam, and supported the insurgent Pathet Lao with supplies and as many as 20,000 "volunteers." While backing the "neutralist" government, the United States from 1962 to 1972 waged a "secret war" against North Vietnamese positions in Laos.

The U.S. withdrawal from South Vietnam left the government without any chance of survival. An agreement of February 1973 created a coalition government in which the Pathet Lao held the upper hand. With the fall of Cambodia and South Vietnam, the Pathet Lao took over, making no effort to hide its subservience to North Vietnam.

The impact on world politics of America's failure in Vietnam was considerably less than U.S. policymakers had predicted. From Thailand to the Philippines, there was obvious nervousness, even demands for the removal of U.S. bases. Outside of Indochina, however, the dominoes did not fall. On the contrary, in the ten years after the end of the war, the non-Communist nations of Southeast Asia prospered and attained an unprecedented level of stability.

In Vietnam itself, the principal legacy of the war has been continued human suffering. The ultimate losers, of course, were the South Vietnamese. For those who remain in Vietnam there have been poverty, oppression, forced labor, and "reeducation" camps.

Even for the ostensible winners, victory has been a bittersweet prize. The Hanoi regime has achieved what may have been its goal from the outset—hegemony in former French Indochina—but the cost has been enormous. An estimated 180,000 soldiers remain in Cambodia, facing stubborn resistance from a number of different guerrilla groups, a drain on an economy already strained to the breaking point. The task of maintaining hegemony in Laos and Cambodia and defending against a hostile China requires one of the world's twelve poorest countries to maintain the world's fourth largest army. Vietnam's postwar aggressiveness has cost it much of the international good will it earned in the war against the United States.

Moreover, Hanoi's long-standing objective of unifying Vietnam under its control appears still to have been achieved in name only. Historic differences between north and south were sharpened during the war, and even the brutal and heavy-handed methods employed by the Hanoi regime have not forced the south into a northern-made mold. Just as it resisted American influence in the 1960s, southern Vietnam continues to resist outside influence today, making the task of consolidation quite difficult.

For all Vietnamese, the most pressing legacy has been economic deprivation. Thirty years of war left the country in shambles, and the regime's ill-conceived postwar efforts to promote industry and collectivize agriculture made things worse. The economic growth rate has hovered around 2 percent instead of the 14 percent optimistically projected in the five-year plan of 1975.

A central goal of the thirty-year war was to rid Vietnam of foreign domination, and here again victory has been less than complete. Because of its poverty and its forced isolation from the United States and China, Hanoi has been forced into a dependence on the Soviet Union that causes growing uneasiness and resentment. To many Vietnamese, the Soviet presence is increasingly obnoxious, and some appear to regard their new ally as merely another in the long line of foreigners who have exploited their country. To a considerable degree, the legacy of victory for the Vietnamese has been one of disappointed dreams and continuing sacrifice and pain. The goals of the thirty-year war have been achieved only partially, if at all.

Ten years after the fall of Saigon, Vietnam appeared eager to break out of its diplomatic isolation from the West. Hanoi probably bungled an opportunity to establish relations with the United States in 1977 by demanding $3 billion in war reparations as a precondition. Relations between the two former enemies thereafter grew steadily worse. Vietnam's seeming indifference to the fate of some 2,500 U.S. servicemen still listed as missing in action in Southeast Asia deeply antagonized Americans. Its increasing closeness to the Soviet Union and its invasion of Cambodia widened an already large chasm. On the other side, Washington's reconciliation with China in 1979 reinforced Vietnam's already strong hostility toward the United States. The need for Western aid and technology and a wish to secure recognition of its position in Cambodia encouraged Hanoi in 1985 to seek an improvement of relations.

In the United States, the effects of the war have been more in the realm of the spirit than tangible. The fall of Saigon had a profound impact. Some Americans expressed hope that the nation could finally put aside a painful episode from its past and get on with the business of the future. Among a people accustomed to celebrating peace with ticker-tape parades, however, the end of the war left a deep residue of frustration, anger, and disillusionment. Americans generally agreed that the war had been a "senseless tragedy" and a "dark moment" in their nation's history. Some comforted themselves with the notion that the United States should never have become involved in Vietnam in the first place, but for others, particularly those who had lost loved ones, this was not enough. "Now it's all gone down the drain and it hurts. What did he die for?" asked a Pennsylvanian whose son had been killed in Vietnam. Many Americans expressed anger that the civilians did not permit the military to win the war. Others regarded the failure to win as a betrayal of American ideals and a sign of national weakness which boded poorly for the future. "It was the saddest day of my life when it sank in that we had lost the war," a Virginian lamented. The fall of Vietnam came at the very time the nation was preparing to celebrate the bicentennial of its birth, and the irony was painfully obvious. "The high hopes and wishful idealism with which the American nation had been born had not been destroyed," *Newsweek* observed, "but they had been chastened by the failure of America to work its will in Indochina."

In the immediate aftermath of the war, the nation experienced a self-conscious, collective amnesia. The angry debate over who lost Vietnam, so feared by Kennedy, Johnson, and Nixon, consisted of nothing more than a few sharp exchanges between the White House and Capitol Hill over responsibility for the April 1975 debacle. Perhaps because both parties were so deeply implicated in the war, Vietnam did not become a partisan political issue; because the memories were so painful, no one cared to dredge them up. On the contrary, many public figures called for restraint. "There is no profit at this time in hashing over the might-have-beens of the past," Mike Mansfield stated. "Nor is there any value in fingerpoint." Vietnam was all but ignored by the media. It was scarcely mentioned in the presidential campaign of 1976. "Today it is almost as though the war had never happened," the columnist Joseph C. Harsch noted in late 1975. "Americans have somehow blocked it out of their consciousness. They don't talk about it. They don't talk about its consequences."

Resentment and disillusionment nevertheless smoldered beneath the surface, provoking a sharp reaction against nearly three decades of crisis diplomacy and global intervention.

Even before the war had ended, the traumatic experience of Vietnam, combined with the apparent improvement of relations with the Soviet Union and China and a growing preoccupation with domestic problems, produced a drastic reordering of national priorities. From the late 1940s to the 1960s, foreign policy had consistently headed the list of national concerns, but by the mid-1970s, it ranked well down the list. The Vietnam experience also provoked strong opposition to military intervention abroad, even in defense of America's oldest and staunchest allies. A majority of Americans endorsed military intervention only in defense of Canada. "Vietnam has left a rancid aftertaste that clings to almost every mention of direct military intervention," the columnist David Broder observed. Having passed through a stormy period of global involvement, the United States appeared to be reverting to its more traditional role of abstention.

Those Americans who fought in the war were the primary victims of the nation's desire to forget. Younger on the average by seven years than their World War II counterparts, having endured a war far more complex and confusing, Vietnam veterans by the miracles of the jet age were whisked home virtually overnight to a nation that was hostile to the war or indifferent to their plight. Some were made to feel the guilt for the nation's moral transgressions; others, responsibility for its failure. Most simply met silence. Forced to turn inward, many veterans grew profoundly distrustful of the government that had sent them to war and deeply resentful of the nation's seeming ingratitude for their sacrifices. The great majority adjusted, although often with difficulty, but many veterans experienced problems with drugs and alcohol, joblessness, and broken homes. Many also suffered from post-traumatic stress disorder, the modern term for what had earlier been called shell shock or battle fatigue. The popular image of the Vietnam veteran in the immediate postwar years was that of a drug-crazed, guntoting, and violence-prone individual unable to adjust to civilized society. When America in 1981 gave a lavish welcome home to a group of hostages returned from a long and much-publicized captivity in Iran, Vietnam veterans poured out the rage that had been bottled up for more than half a decade. They themselves constructed a memorial in Washington to honor the memory of the more than 58,000 comrades who did not return.

Within a short time after the end of the war, Vietnam's place in the national consciousness changed dramatically. By the mid-1980s the war was being discussed to a degree and in ways that would have once seemed impossible. Vietnam produced a large and in some cases distinguished literature, much of it the work of veterans. Hollywood had all but ignored the war while it was going on, but in its aftermath filmmakers took up the subject in a large way, producing works ranging from the haunting *Deer Hunter*, to the surreal and spectacular *Apocalypse Now*, to a series of trashy films in which American superheroes returned to Vietnam to take care of unfinished business. No television leading man was worth his salt unless he had served in Vietnam. The Vietnam veteran, sometimes branded a war criminal in the 1960s, became a popular culture hero in the 1980s, the sturdy and self-sufficient warrior who had prevailed despite being let down by his government and nation. Two million Americans a year visited the stark but moving V-shaped memorial on Washington's mall, making it the second leading tourist attraction in the nation's capital.

If they were more willing to talk about Vietnam, Americans remained confused and divided about its meaning, particularly its implications for U.S. foreign policy. The indifference and tendency toward withdrawal so manifest in 1975 declined sharply over the next ten years. Bitter memories of Vietnam combined with the frustration of the Iranian hostage crisis to produce a growing assertiveness, a highly nationalistic impulse to defend perceived interests, even a yearning to restore the United States to its old position in the world. The breakdown of détente, the steady growth of Soviet military power, and the use of that power in Afghanistan produced a heightened concern for American security. The defense budget soared to record proportions in the early 1980s, and support for military intervention in defense of traditional allies increased significantly.

The new nationalism was tempered by lingering memories of Vietnam, however. Many Americans remained deeply skeptical of 1960s-style globalism and dubious of such internationalist mechanisms as foreign aid or even the United Nations. Ten years after the end of the war, a whopping majority still believed that intervention in Vietnam had been a mistake. Recollection of Vietnam produced strong opposition to intervention in third-world crises in Lebanon and Central America. Thus, in the aftermath of Vietnam, the public mood consisted of a strange amalgam of nostalgia and realism, assertiveness and caution.

Vietnam was a "landmark event" that left "deep and profound" divisions. Americans agree that to construct a viable foreign policy they must learn from Vietnam. But they disagree sharply over what they should learn.

The basic issue remains the morality and wisdom of intervention in Vietnam. In the light of Hanoi's postwar actions, Americans are less likely to openly condemn their nation's intervention as immoral, an important sign of change in itself. Those who continue to feel that intervention was wrong argue that it was unnecessary or impractical or both, and most liberals still contend that at best it represented overcommitment in an area of peripheral national interest, at worst an act of questionable morality.

The conservative point of view has been more vocal in recent years and it takes two forms. Some, including President Ronald Reagan, have found in postwar events in Indochina reason to speak out anew on what they always felt was a fundamental reality—that, as Reagan has repeatedly stated, Vietnam was "in truth a noble war," a selfless attempt on the part of the United States to save a free nation from outside aggression. Others concede that the United States might have erred in getting involved in Vietnam in the first place, but they go on to insist that over time an important interest was established that had to be defended for the sake of U.S. credibility throughout the world.

The second great issue, on which Americans also sharply disagree, concerns the reasons for U.S. failure in Vietnam. Many of the leading participants in the war have concluded that America's failure was essentially instrumental, a result of the improper use of available tools. General Westmoreland and others blame the "ill-considered" policy of "graduated response" imposed on the military by civilian leaders, arguing that had the United States employed its military power quickly, decisively, and without limit, the war could have been won. Other critics view the fundamental mistake as the choice of tools rather than how they were used, and they blame an unimaginative military as much as civilians. Instead of trying to fight World War II and Korea over in Vietnam, these critics argue, the military should have adapted to the unconventional war in which it found itself and shaped an appropriate counterinsurgency strategy to meet it. Still other commentators, including some military theorists, agree that military leaders were as responsible for the strategic failure as civilians. Critics such as Colonel Harry G. Summers, Jr., argue that instead of mounting costly and-counterproductive search-and-destroy operations against guerrillas in South Vietnam, the United States should have used its own forces against North Vietnamese regulars along the seventeenth parallel to isolate the north from the south. Military leaders should also have insisted on a declaration of war to ensure that the war was not fought in "cold blood" and that popular support could be sustained.

The lessons drawn are as divergent as the arguments advanced. Those who feel that the United States lost because it did not act decisively conclude that if the nation becomes involved in war again, it must employ its military power with a view to winning quickly before public support erodes. Those who feel that the basic problem was the formulation rather than the execution of strategy insist that military and civilian leaders must think strategically, that they must examine more carefully the nature of the war and formulate more precisely the ways in which American power can best be used to attain clearly defined objectives.

Such lessons depend on the values and belief systems of those who pronounce them, of course, and those who opposed the war have reached quite different conclusions. To some former doves, the fundamental lesson is never to get involved in a land war in Asia; to others, it is to avoid intervention in international trouble spots unless the nation's vital interests are clearly at stake.

The ghost of Vietnam hovered over an increasingly divisive debate on the proper American response to revolutions in Central America. Shortly after taking office in 1981, President Reagan committed U.S. prestige to defending the government of El Salvador against a leftist-led insurgency, in part in the expectation that success there might exorcise the so-called Vietnam syndrome—the perceived reluctance of the American public in the wake of Vietnam to take on responsibilities in third-world countries. When the quick victory did not materialize, the administration expanded U.S. military aid to El Salvador, created a huge military base in Honduras, and launched a not-so-covert war to overthrow the Sandinista government of Nicaragua. The administration insisted that the United States must support non-Communist forces to avert in Central America the bloodshed and misery that followed the end of the war in Vietnam. At the same time, the military and the Defense Department have made clear that they will not go to war under the conditions that prevailed in Vietnam. On the other side, dovish critics ominously warn that U.S. intervention in Central America will lead straight into a quagmire like Vietnam.

Vietnam made clear the inherent unworkability of a policy of global containment. In the 1940s the world seemed dangerous but manageable. The United States enjoyed a position of unprecedented power and influence, and achieved some notable early successes in Europe. Much of America's power derived from the weakness of other nations rather than from its own intrinsic strength, however, and Vietnam demonstrated conclusively that its power, however great, had limits. The development of significant military capabilities by the Soviet Union and China made it extremely risky for the United States to use its military power in Vietnam on a scale necessary to achieve the desired results. Conditions in Vietnam itself and the constraints imposed by domestic opinion made it impossible to reach these goals with limited means. Vietnam makes clear that the United States cannot uphold its own concept of world order in the face of a stubborn and resolute, although much weaker, foe. The war did not bring about the decline of American power, as some have suggested, but was rather symptomatic of the limits of national power in an age of international diversity and nuclear power.

To adapt to the new era, the United States must recognize its vulnerability, accept the limits of its power, and accomodate itself to many situations it does not like. Americans must understand that they will not be able to dictate solutions to world problems or achieve all their goals. Like it or not, Vietnam marked the end of an era in world history and American foreign policy, an era marked by constructive achievements but blemished by ultimate, although not irreparable, failure.

The GI Bill of Rights

Michael J. Bennett

An enormous price had been paid for peace, but, for the survivors, there were great rewards. Never before had so many people been so free economically, educationally, and socially. Astonishing numbers of people were entering and leaving the workforce. Military enrollment plunged from 11.4 million in 1945 to 3.4 million in 1946. Another nearly 2 million were discharged between 1946 and 1947, bringing military strength down to 1.5 million in 1947. At the same time, civilian employment climbed from 53.8 million in 1945 to 57.5 million in 1946, and to 60.8 million in 1947. In other words, while 10 million were discharged from military service, civilian employment increased by 7 million. In the jargon of statisticians, the labor market was "churning." Amid all those zigzagging figures, in theory as many as 7 million to 8 million were out of work at all times during those two years. Indeed, almost 9 million veterans drew 52-20 benefits between 1944 and 1949, but presumably because they were counted as part of the civilian labor force, the unemployment rate was unaffected. On the other hand, they did so for an average of only seventeen weeks—less than a third of the fifty-two weeks they were entitled to.

Where were those people who were out of work but not apparently looking for jobs? A great many were in school. About 7.8 million World War II veterans, in all, enrolled in some sort of educational or training program under the GI Bill. Total college and university enrollment leaped from 1,676,856 in 1945, with 88,000 veterans attending, to 2,078,095 in 1946 with veterans accounting for 1,013,000, or 48.7 percent of the total. In 1947, veteran enrollment peaked at 2,338,226 with 1,150,000 veterans, or 49.2 percent.

Reality is conveyed better in individual terms, in stories about a few of the many millions whose lives were transformed during those years. One such story was that of Les Faulk of Turtle Creek, Pennsylvania. Faulk graduated from high school in May 1944 and celebrated the death of Hitler and the overthrow of the Nazi regime a year later as a Seventh Army infantryman in Germany. When Faulk had left Turtle Creek, he had a pretty clear notion of

Reprinted from *When Dreams Come True: The GI Bill of Rights and the Making of Modern America*, (1996), Brassey's, Inc.

what his life would be like after the war—assuming he survived. He'd come back to the small town wrapped in industrial haze and get his old jobs back—if he was lucky—caddying at the local golf course and racking balls at Kindler's poolroom. In time, he could expect to get a "good" job stoking an open-hearth steel mill or winding copper armatures in the Westinghouse generator plant.

Faulk was one of twelve Turtle Creek High School graduates that Edwin Keister, Jr., interviewed for an article in *Smithsonian Magazine* in 1994, a class that was a microcosm of hundreds of thousands of others. The young man who left high school in 1944 expecting to become no more than a steel mill stoker or an armature winder instead spent thirty-eight years as a teacher and an elementary school principal. Les Faulk had not only gone to college he also had acquired both a bachelor's and a master's degree and several credits toward his doctorate, even though the name on his high school diploma was "Falcocchio." That name—and his decision to change it—was significant. In those days, being the son of an Italian immigrant family with a "foreign" name could be almost as much a barrier to getting into college as a black skin. "College," as Faulk recalled fifty years later, "was for teachers' kids, and the preacher's kids. For the rest of us, with names like Tarantini and Trkula it was a distant dream."

Faulk and his classmates in Mrs. Whittum's American history class had been urged to believe that that dream, no matter how distant, could come true for them. But the hopes held out in school didn't stand up very well to the living and working conditions Faulk and his classmates grew up in. Turtle Creek was a factory town where half the male students dropped out of high school. Only five percent went on to any kind of postsecondary education, even barber or secretarial school, the latter being one of the few avenues to white-collar work then pursued by men as well as women. The war and the GI Bill changed everything. Faulk, like millions of other young Americans sent off to war, grew up fast in a foxhole. That alone might have made it difficult to accept what Turtle Creek had to offer when he came back home, even with a job awaiting him as an apprentice bricklayer, a job arranged by his father. That wasn't the reason he quit after one day, though, throwing away an opportunity for a skilled, well-paid, and prestigious job at the time. He had heard of the GI Bill, and he had made a decision. "I went to the poolroom and told my old boss, 'I'm going to college.' He said, 'I read that only one vet in 20 who enters college will finish.' I said, 'I'm going to be that one.'" The government had turned him into a soldier who had helped beat the best the German army had to offer; now the same government thought he had the makings of a college graduate. Who was he to argue?

Faulk wasn't alone. Among the eleven other graduates of Turtle Creek High School who joined him at the fiftieth reunion of the Class of '44 were an aerospace engineer, a federal judge, a microchip engineer, a professor of law who is also a research scientist, and an engineer specializing in military survival techniques. . . .

Chesterfield Smith signed up for pre-law at the University of Florida back in 1935, but as his wife, Vivian Parker, recalled years later, "He was just a pokerplaying, crap-shooting boy who couldn't settle down." By his own account, Smith "chose the easy life in college. I'd go to school a semester and then drop out for a semester to earn enough money to return"—in style. "I'd rather drop out and work than skimp in school." He worked as a clerk in the Florida legislature, a soda jerk, a debt collector, and a candy and tobacco vendor. By the time he was drafted in 1940, though, he had managed to complete three and a half years of college. Commissioned in the National Guard, he was assigned to a field artillery unit in France beginning about D day plus 45" and served through the Battle of the Bulge before returning to the University of Florida in 1946.

By the standards of the day, Smith had done well financially, saving $5,000 from his pay and winning another $3,000 in craps on the long voyage home. But the man who had married Vivian in 1944 before shipping out for Europe had changed when he came back in 1945. She recalled, "He was a serious man when he returned." Smith didn't give up the good life entirely; he found time to golf five days a week through law school. Financially, his carefully budgeted savings and a teaching job obtained in his second year at law school meant the couple "had more than most." But he also budgeted his time as carefully as his money. "I didn't go drink coffee or sit out on the bench and bull it all the time. I never missed a day of class. I kept a work schedule just like I had a job. If I had a paper due in three weeks, I started it right away and finished a week early. Hell, here I was, almost thirty years of age—I wanted to get that law license and get into practice and make myself some money. The idea of playing around a university for unnecessary months or years had no appeal to me whatsoever."

Twenty years later, Smith was the president of the American Bar Association and the principal partner in a Tampa-Orlando law firm. "The way I was going before the war," Smith said, "I don't think I would ever have made it through law school. But after the war, I felt I had something invested in my country—five years of my life. I said to myself, 'Boy, you've got to settle down and make something of yourself, otherwise you ain't going to 'mount to nothing.' My classmates in the '40s, after the war, we wanted to get on with our lives. We were men, not kids, and we had the maturity to recognize that we had to go get what we wanted, and not just wait for things to happen to us.". . .

. . . social change on a seismic scale was happening and nowhere more so than at Harvard. Harvard was the oldest elite institution traditionally preparing the sons of America's WASP families to take their places as the economic and social leaders of the country. Yet it helped pioneer the new meritocratic society that . . . the GI Bill made possible. Harvard had taken the lead a generation before under President A. Lawrence Lowell in restricting the percentage of Jewish students. But under President Conant after the war, the university began vigorously recruiting students from every ethnic and religious background and section of the country, often to the discomfort of alumni who assumed admission of their sons into Harvard Yard was part of the family patrimony. For the veterans who were unexpectedly within the walls of the Yard, it was both a disconcerting and liberating experience.

Frank O'Hara, for example, who was to become a leading literary and art figure of New York in the 1950s and 1960s, wasn't even sure the GI Bill of Rights was a good idea. He had been an enlisted man working as a sonar operator in San Pedro, California, in 1946 when a conversation with a bunkmate, Douglas "Diddy" Starr, turned to the GI Bill. O'Hara, unlike most of his fellow sailors who were singularly pleased with the windfall, was wary, according to his biographer, Brad Gooch. O'Hara had read and been impressed with an article by President Hutchins of the University of Chicago in Collier's arguing the bill would turn the nation's colleges into "educational hobo jungles." He was also suspicious of a bandwagon mood that assumed education was the answer to all problems. Nonetheless, O'Hara, whose father graduated from the College of the Holy Cross in Worcester, Massachusetts, applied for and was accepted at Harvard—and so far as living arrangements were concerned, might as well have been back in the Navy. "In 1946, you might as well have been living in an American Legion post as in one of the Houses," a graduating senior reminisced in the 1950 *Harvard Yearbook*. Four thousand veterans were among the record 5,435 students enrolled at Harvard in 1946, filing through registration points in Memorial Hall at the rate of three a minute. The spectacle of seventeen-year-old beardless youths in white buck shoes, unloading Vuitton bags from their convertibles outside the "Gold Coast" houses along the Charles River was overshadowed by the sea of older faces surging into the red brick dormitories reserved for veterans on the north side of the Yard. Double-deck bunk beds had to be moved into some dorms, and cots were set up in the Indoor Athletic Building's basketball court to accommodate latecomers.

The words "invasion" and "siege" were predictably and incessantly used by *The Harvard Crimson* as lines formed everywhere—to register, eat, get books, cash checks. The more popular lecturers spoke in classrooms where students arrived early to claim seats on windowsills. The old rules still applied. Jackets and ties were required in the Union, the dining hall, but manufacturers had stopped making blazers and white shirts during the war, and veterans couldn't afford them even if they were available at the Coop, the university's cooperative store. So military coats were cut to hip length, service-issue trousers given a quick press, and insignia cut off old khaki shirts.

O'Hara found it amazing that he was at Harvard at all, Gooch wrote. A mere three months before he had been an enlisted man on the U.S.S. *Nicholas* who, without the GI Bill, would never have been able to afford Harvard's stiff fees. Yet not all of the nuances of Harvard pleased him. He couldn't help feeling the pressure of elitism, and he wasn't sure if being at Harvard meant anything to anybody except snobs. He also felt pigeonholed by being Irish even though Irish-Catholics had been the first minority admitted to Harvard back in the 1870s. There had always been a subtle rivalry between Protestants and Catholics, Gooch wrote, although it usually didn't take any more serious form than drinking contests. O'Hara was also unlike relatively sophisticated big-city and wealthy Irish-Catholics like the Kennedys. He was from a small Massachusetts farm town, Grafton near Athol, and a graduate of a parochial high school. Almost another twenty years would pass before graduates of public and parochial high schools outnumbered the products of select private schools among the undergraduates of Harvard. One acquaintance described O'Hara at the time as looking "potato Irish, lower class, with pasty skin." He was often kidded as coming from "Asshole" and told a boyhood friend from Grafton, Phil Charron, "I'm going to Harvard; they say it's the death knell of all Catholics." O'Hara reacted to the social fencing, Gooch wrote, as did many others, by developing a personal style of speech using "arch Angloisms" to both blend in and subtly mock the accents and manners of WASP culture.

Arch Angloisms weren't any part of the style of another member of the class of 1950, although his potato face did go well with the Germanic accent he has retained. Henry Kissinger [later to become Secretary of State], before being drafted into the army, had enrolled as a college student in what was often called the Jewish Harvard, CCNY. The German-Jewish immigrant had planned on becoming an accountant, like his father. "My horizons were never that great when I was in City College," Kissinger said, according to his biographer, Walter Isaacson.

Kissinger, who had fled Nazi persecution in Germany with his parents, became an American citizen in the army. The naturalization ceremony at dusty Camp Croft in South Carolina had been just another event in the daily process of, as Kissinger wrote to his brother, "being pushed around and inoculated, counted and stood to attention." The erstwhile accountant returned to Germany, Isaacson wrote,

> *as part of a vast democratizing force, one that transformed how Americans lived. Soldiers from small towns in South Carolina and Louisiana for the first time saw places like Paris and Berlin, turning all-American boys with hardscrabble heritages into cosmopolitan conquerors. And, on a smaller scale, the army took young refugees from Nuremberg and Furth, put them into places such as Camp Croft and Camp Claiborne, then marched them off to war in melting pot platoons, thus turning cosmopolitan allies into acculturated American citizens. For immigrant boys, such as Kissinger, serving in the war made citizenship more than a gift merely bestowed; it was an honor they had earned. Having defended the United States, they now had as much claim as any Winthrop or Lowell to feel it was their nation, their country, their home. They were outsiders no more.*

Lowells and Cabots mingled quite freely with O'Haras and Kissingers and the other provincial young men tossed up on the banks of the Charles River by the GI Bill. The war, after all, had given all of them the same veneer. Kissinger himself liked to say later that his experience with "the real middle American boys" in his regiment from Wisconsin, Illinois, and Indiana "made me feel like an American." He quoted Helmet Sonnenfeld, a national security adviser, as observing, "The Army, made the melting pot melt faster." Indeed, the melting pot experience young men had undergone in the military was much more readily replicated on college campuses than in established multigenerational and ethnically dominated cities such as Boston, where veterans were sometimes suspected of getting above themselves. That was particularly true of Harvard in comparison to the Boston-Cambridge community where racial, ethnic, and religious tensions would plague the community long after they had subsided on the Harvard campus. Boston, in the late '40s, wasn't quite the city made famous by the doggerel toast of an Irish-Catholic alumnus of Boston College at the turn of the century: "Here's to Boston, the home of the bean and the cod, where the Lowells speak only to the Cabots and the Cabots speak only to God." Nevertheless, it was still a community in which the Yankees spoke rarely to the Irish; the Irish avoided conversation with their fellow Catholics, the Italians; and Jews talked with the Yankees, Irish, and Italians only on business. At the time, in fact, the Cabots were, according to a widely circulated story, suing a Jewish family named Cabotsky. The Cabotskys had changed their name so they could advertise their pharmacy as "Cabot's Drugs." Presumably the old toast had been changed to: "Here's to the home of the bean and the cod, where the Lowells speak to no one, for the Cabots, speak Yiddish, by God!"

Kissinger's Germanic accent no doubt stood him in good stead on the Harvard campus and unquestionably helped him in his determination to avoid assimilation into democratic anonymity. His Teutonic tonalities served the same purpose as O'Hara's arch Angloisms. The difference was intriguing and enticing for insiders who not only accepted, but thought more highly of them for being outsiders. Kissinger had listened carefully to his first mentor, Fritz

Gustave Anton Kraemer, a German refugee of Prussian background, who was his boss in the American military government of Germany. Kraemer advised him: "Go to a fine college. A gentleman does not go to the College of the City of New York." Kissinger was admitted to Harvard, however, only because the college was willing to take students whose papers were filed late, unlike Princeton and Columbia where he also applied. Isaacson attributed that to the fact that Conant, whom he incorrectly described as a driving force behind the GI Bill, had appointed an outreach counselor to make sure veterans had access to his university.

Once the bill was passed, Conant added his own support to the bill's influence in breaking down the ethnic, religious, and especially anti-Semitic prejudices on campus, although Jews entering Harvard in 1947 were usually assigned other Jews as roommates. The college administration did caution residential housemasters not to take more Jews "than the traffic will allow," for several years after the war, but the practice was discontinued by the end of the decade. So, too, was the custom of designating the names of Jews on college records with asterisks. Actual enrollment of Jews in the late '40s was about 17 percent, slightly lower than the level in the 1920s when President Lowell imposed quotas. The difference wasn't in the numbers so much as the degree of acceptance. "Harvard welcomed us with open arms," remembered Henry Rosovsky, who served with Kissinger in Germany and later became an economics professor, dean of the faculty, and the first Jewish member of the Harvard Corporation. Discrimination was a reality in some departments of the university, Isaacson observed, but it was least evident in government where Louis Hartz, a Jew was professor of political theory and one-time chairman. . . .

Blacks especially came back from the war walking—and feeling—like free men. They took advantage of the GI Bill in the same way whites did, as individuals, not as members of a group except insofar as membership in the American Legion, the VFW, or the DAV might be helpful in negotiating red tape. Of course, blacks weren't free in the same way whites were, and it seems probable they didn't take advantage of the education benefits in the same percentages as whites. No authoritative numerical estimates of black beneficiaries are available other than an assertion, without documentation, in the Encyclopedia of the Second World War that 250,000 blacks were given the opportunity to go college for the first time under the GI Bill. The percentage of those who wouldn't otherwise have gone to college was certainly much higher than whites, according to Reginald Wilson, senior scholar at the American Council on Education, citing a study that "approximately 20 percent of veterans could not have gone to college without the GI Bill. I would conjecture the figure was much higher for African-American veterans. Besides, having come from families that were disproportionately poorer, most had been subjected to underfunded, segregated schools. However, when special accommodations were made and relatively open admissions' policies were put in place, black veterans flocked to the colleges and universities and did well academically." At his own alma mater, Wayne State University in Detroit, Wilson recalled, "it is estimated that nearly a third of the veterans enrolled between 1946 and 1950 were African-Americans, and during those years, veterans were almost a majority of the school's students."

The northern and western colleges many blacks attended didn't keep racial census figures, at least not in any systematic fashion. Statistics for black colleges are the best indices for determining the numbers of Negroes who took advantage of the bill. In 1940, enrollment in black colleges was 1.08 percent of the U.S. college enrollment. By 1950, in a greatly expanded student population, it had almost tripled, to 3.6 percent. Overall enrollment in the Negro Land-Grant colleges after the war was 50 percent higher than before. More significantly, the number of veterans in the black colleges was double the entire 1937–38 enrollment. Partially because black colleges had been traditionally shortchanged in funding for building purposes, another federal bill, the Lanham Act of 1946, actually made proportionately more money available for construction and repair at black institutions. Acting under the law, the officers of the Commission of Education recognized the relatively large need of the Negro institutions, according to Wilson. Consequently, funds were distributed to institutions on the assumption that 33.4 square feet of construction was needed for veterans in black colleges as compared with 17.4 square feet in white schools. Nevertheless, despite the additional money for construction, black colleges had to turn away twenty thousand veterans for lack of space.

The shortage of seats was more than made up by colleges and universities in the North and West. "Black veterans with vouchers in hand, paid for by the federal government, were an attractive commodity to many institutions in the North that would not have welcomed them in vast numbers (nor could many have afforded to go before the war)," Wilson wrote. "The white colleges welcomed them and made special provisions to accommodate all of the veterans; they were given additional points on admission tests; in some instances, admission requirements were waived; they were given credit for special training received in the military; tutors were provided in recognition of the veterans being three to five years out of school; and, despite sometimes mediocre high school records, they were welcomed."

The special provisions, it should be noted, applied to many white veterans, not just blacks. As early as February 9, 1942, for example, the University of Wisconsin approved granting ten elective college credits to former enlisted men and fifteen to ex-officers. Wisconsin made other concessions, too. In March 1944, a veteran could even apply four special war credits to the sixteen high school credits needed for admission. If that wasn't enough to meet the admission requirements, a veteran could take an oral or written examination proving he was capable of college work. Credit was also given for college-level work completed in service schools and military training schools, and veterans were exempted from taking the physical education courses compulsory for other students. Wisconsin's medical school lowered admission requirements from three to two years of premed training. Refresher courses were offered in mathematics and English; a full-semester summer school was created; the engineering college operated on a trimester schedule with classes starting in March, July, and November.

The innovations and accommodations pleased some veteran students and didn't appeal to others. A navy officer, responding to a survey sent to former students by Columbia University, had mixed feelings about accelerated courses. "Education is too important to me to be rushed through," he wrote. "I want to have the feeling of leisure to do an honest job with the most valuable time of my life." A year-round trimester program would turn college into a factory, he thought. But a P-51 fighter pilot had a different attitude: "I remember how we used to think that a full year would be a tough grind, but it was probably laziness that prompted that feeling."

Robert A. Eubanks was a black veteran who wasn't the least bothered about going to college full time; he thrived on it. He was bright enough to have graduated in 1942 from high school at the age of fifteen. But he couldn't get a job because he was black and couldn't take advantage of a tuition-only scholarship to Howard University in Washington, D.C., because he didn't have enough money to live on. So he joined the army, and he heard about the GI Bill through word-of-mouth—as most veterans did—when he mustered out in 1946. Eubanks got into a year-round program at the Illinois Institute of Technology (IIT) and earned a degree in theoretical and applied mechanical engineering in 1950. Once again, his job-hunting forays ran up against whites-only hiring policies, so he stayed on at IIT, earning a master's and then a doctoral degree in 1953, all on the GI Bill. With the changing social climate after the Brown decision, he was able to get high-paying work in industry. Later, he was lured back to academia, first as a visiting professor at the University of Illinois. After six months, he was offered a tenured full professorship and stayed on until retirement in 1986, teaching and conducting research. "It's very hard to explain how things were during the 1940s," Eubanks said in reflecting on this life. "The restrictions on blacks then were rough. The GI Bill gave me my start on being a professional instead of a stock clerk." . . .

As a matter of reality, with the great exception of the GI Bill of Rights, government programs to help people haven't directly given people the resources to help themselves. That was the GI Bill's greatest characteristic and accomplishment. It didn't have to appeal to shared human values and social goals by persuading people that institutions knew what was best for them. It gave the individuals the power to decide for themselves what was best for themselves and, at the same time, freed educational institutions to do what they did best, teach. It caused a silent revolution, not by the force of the state, but by using the resources of the state to encourage what George Mason spelled out in the Virginia Declaration much more explicitly than Thomas Jefferson did in the Declaration of Independence: the means of acquiring and possessing prosperity for pursuing and obtaining happiness and safety. The GI Bill gave people the economic resources to train their minds, their most important property, and they went out and used it to pursue happiness and safety.

Holding the Line in Little Rock

Mary Dudziak

Little Rock has unfortunately become a symbol of Negro-White relations in the United States.

American Consulate,
Lourenço, Marquesz, Mozambique
to Department of State,
September 30, 1957

The school year would not begin easily in Little Rock, Arkansas, in 1957. On September 4 of that year, nine African American students tried to enroll at Little Rock's Central High School. Their admission had been ordered by a federal district court. However, just two days earlier, Arkansas Governor Orval Faubus declared that the students' enrollment threatened "imminent danger of tumult, riot and breach of the peace and the doing of violence to persons and property." He proclaimed a state of emergency and ordered the Arkansas National Guard into service. These troops surrounded Central High School on September 4 and turned the students away as they tried to enter the school.

What transpired that day would capture the attention of the international media and of President Dwight D. Eisenhower. School desegregation in Little Rock was no longer a local or state issue, but a critical national problem.

As the *Arkansas Gazette* reported it,

The first Negro applicant to try to enroll at Little Rock Central High School . . . , Elizabeth Eckford, 15, was twice blocked from entering the grounds, walked calmly down two blocks then sat out 35 minutes of vocal abuse while waiting for a bus to go home. . . . When she approached Guardsmen at the corner they drew together and blocked her entrance to the sidewalk.

Eckford was harassed in front of television cameras as "a crowd of 200 saw her and rushed to the scene." A white woman, Grace Lorch, ultimately came to her defense and boarded a bus with Eckford, taking her away from the scene. Seven of the nine students arrived together and, on orders of the governor, were also turned away.

Governor Faubus was something of a latecomer to resistance. Little Rock had a reputation as a progressive southern community, and Faubus had been thought of as a moderate. In contrast to Georgia Governor Herman Talmadge, Faubus had given no speeches of defiance after *Brown* was decided. Instead, he gave African Americans a role in the state Democratic leadership during the 1954 gubernatorial campaign. In addition, there was progress, albeit with mixed success, toward desegregation in other communities in Arkansas after 1954. Faubus's most direct statements on school desegregation prior to Little Rock were to declare the issue a local one, to be handled by local school boards.

As school prepared to open in 1957, however, Faubus announced his "prayerful" decision to call in the troops. "They will act not as segregationists or integrationists," he pledged, "but as soldiers called to active duty to carry out their assigned tasks." Their duty was to maintain order, but, Faubus continued, it would not be possible to maintain order "if forcible integration is carried out tomorrow in the schools of this community."

A school desegregation plan had been developed by the Little Rock school board. As did many other communities, Little Rock set about exploring how it might implement *Brown v. Board of Education* immediately after that decision was handed down. Community support for compliance with *Brown* was evident when the school board was reelected after the desegregation plan was announced. With desegregation set to begin with the opening of the 1957–58 school year, however, the opposition became more active and vocal. Mrs. Clyde D. Thomason, a member of a Little Rock mothers' committee opposed to desegregation, filed suit in state court in August 1957, seeking an injunction against the plan. Based on unsubstantiated testimony by Governor Faubus of an increase in gun sales in the Little Rock area, the state court issued an injunction on August 29. The school board then turned to the federal district court. As fate would have it, the case came before a nonsouthern judge. Judge Ronald N. Davies from South Dakota was sitting by designation in federal district court in Arkansas. Judge Davies ordered desegregation to go forward. When Faubus called out the National Guard on September 2, the school board returned to the district court. Judge Davies noted that "[t]he chief executive of Little Rock has stated that the Little Rock police have not had a single case of inter-racial violence reported to them and that there has been no indication from sources available to him that there would be violence in regard to this situation" and denied the school board's petition to delay desegregation.

As the crisis deepened, the federal government was drawn in. Judge Davies called upon U.S. Attorney General Herbert Brownell to investigate allegations that African American students had been denied admission to Central High. President Eisenhower ultimately found himself involved in the crisis as well. While Faubus telegraphed the president complaining of federal interference and concerns that his phone lines were being tapped by federal agents, Little Rock Mayor Woodrow Wilson Mann urged Eisenhower to become more involved. Eisenhower's response to Faubus was to emphasize that "when I became President, I took an oath to support and defend the Constitution of the United States. The only assurance I can give you is that the Federal Constitution will be upheld by me by every legal means at my command."

For the next three weeks, desegregation in Little Rock was at an impasse. As school went on at Central High, the "Little Rock Nine" stayed home, unable to pass through the national guardsmen still surrounding the school. The Little Rock crisis was to become a defining moment. It was not the first civil rights event in Eisenhower's presidency to capture widespread international attention. Following the 1954 *Brown* decision, Emmet Till's brutal murder in 1955 had outraged the world, the 1955–56 Montgomery bus boycott had focused international media attention on civil rights protest, and Autherine Lucy's attempt to cross the color line at the University of Alabama in 1956 had become a civil rights crisis with international impact. Little Rock, however, was a crisis of such magnitude for worldwide perceptions of race and American democracy that it would become the reference point for the future. Later presidents, facing crises of their own, would try their best to avoid "another Little Rock." Foreign commentators would judge American progress by how far the nation had come from Little Rock. If slavery had been the benchmark against which American racial progress had been measured in the past, Little Rock provided a new measure, as the Cold War required more of the leader of the free world.

When school first opened in September 1957, the *Arkansas Gazette* had expressed its confidence that "the world will see that we are lawabiding people." The world would, unfortunately, draw a different lesson from Little Rock.

On September 11, the people of Little Rock learned that even Secretary of State John Foster Dulles was concerned about the difficulties in their city. The *Arkansas Gazette* quoted Dulles as saying that the Little Rock crisis, along with school desegregation battles elsewhere in the South, "are not helpful to the influence of the United States abroad." The *Gazette* reported that "Radio Moscow has been chirping happily about the troubles of integration," and the Little Rock crisis was a particular subject of its attention. President Eisenhower later described the situation in his memoirs. He wrote that Faubus's "outrageous action" in Little Rock

> called to my mind the first act of the Rodgers and Hammerstein musical *South Pacific* in which the hero, a Frenchman, mistakenly calls the heroine's American hometown *"Small Rock."* Before September 1957, that line was meaningless to foreign audiences. Thereafter, no one anywhere would miss the point: the name of Little Rock, Arkansas, would become known around the world.

According to Eisenhower, "Overseas, the mouthpieces of Soviet propaganda in Russia and Europe were blaring out that 'anti-Negro violence' in Little Rock was being 'committed with the clear connivance of the United States government.'"

Coverage of the Little Rock crisis had blanketed the international media beginning with the incidents of September 4. Elizabeth Eckford's trials appeared on front pages around the world. The London *Times*, the *Times of India*, the *Tanganyika Standard*, the *South China Morning Post*, and many other papers carried stories virtually every day for the entire month of September. According to the U.S. embassy in Brussels, Little Rock "has been followed in the Belgian press with far greater interest than any other American domestic issue in recent years. The more dramatic aspects of the case, including photographs of beatings and other violence, have usually been given greater prominence in the press than leading local or foreign news articles." International coverage of the crisis was so noteworthy to U.S. newswriters that there was widespread coverage in U.S. papers of the coverage abroad.

On September 6, for example, the *Times of India* carried a story on its front page under the title "Armed Men Cordon Off White School: Racial Desegregation in Arkansas Prevented." That same day the front page of the *Tanganyika Standard* declared, "Troops Stop Negroes Going to School." "Little Rock Troubled" proclaimed a page-one headline in the *East African Standard*, followed by a front-page story the next day: "Eisenhower Intervenes as School Bars Negroes." The *Egyptian Gazette* repeatedly placed Little Rock in the context of school desegregation struggles elsewhere in the American South. The paper's September 5 front-page story outlining the facts of the exclusion of the Little Rock Nine from school was tempered with news of successful school desegregation efforts in Van Buren and Ozark, Arkansas, and Louisville, Kentucky.

The September 4, 1957, edition of the London *Times* described Eisenhower's reaction to the Little Rock crisis with some skepticism:

> *Questions about the action taken by the state government in Arkansas brought forth from the President only a restatement of the axioms on which he has based his own "gradualist" approach to the problem. "You cannot change people's hearts merely by laws," he observed, and the Supreme Court's ruling in 1954 therefore had caused "emotional difficulties" for both sides. Southerners, he implied, were genuinely frightened by what they thought would lead to "a mongrelization of the races."*
>
> *Difficult though the problem might be, he added, "We are going to whip it in the long run by Americans being true to themselves, and not by law"—a comment that seems to be as wide of the real issue as was Polonius's advice. Who is to say that the southerners—who see in attempts to integrate their schools a threat to the whole social fabric of their communities, and who try to prevent it by every means—are not being true to themselves?*

International papers often commented on the international attention itself. According to the *Montreal Star*, "The world watches Negroes in the United States going to Southland schools under the muzzles of loaded rifles, just ninety-four years after the Emancipation Proclamation was signed by another Republican, Abraham Lincoln." In London, the *Times* spoke of "the lonely, isolated negro children whose pictures have touched and shamed millions, in the United States and abroad." Student organizations and other groups around the world also registered their support for the Little Rock Nine and their opposition to Faubus's actions.

Dutch papers noted that Little Rock harmed American prestige. In Stockholm, Sweden, *Svenska Dagbladet* wrote that the events in Arkansas "will be watched with concern throughout [the] Western world." If the federal government did not take a strong stand, it would pose a serious threat "not only to President Eisenhower's personal prestige but also to [the] position of [the] U.S. in [the] eyes [of the] free world." According to the *Irish Times*, the crisis had "given Communist propagandists the text for innumerable sermons to coloured peoples everywhere." The Swiss press expressed dismay over the "incalculable harm done" by Little Rock to the "Occidental position throughout [the] non-European world."

At home, the impact of the Little Rock crisis on world opinion was widely understood. Harry S. Ashmore wrote in 1958 that Little Rock "has become a symbol that arouses strong emotions among people everywhere in the world." The crisis "was about as handy a package as the Russians have had handed them since they set out to woo the colored peoples of the earth." William Ross of Brooklyn, New York, wrote to Governor Faubus that he was "furnishing the Communists with priceless propaganda material and hurting our standing with Asian and African countries."

It was a short step, in the consciousness of 1950s Americans, from international criticism to Cold War implications. U.S. editorial writers and political figures regularly noted the negative impact Little Rock was thought to have on the nation's standing in the Cold War. The Soviet Union's extensive use of Little Rock in anti-American propaganda—often simply republishing facts disseminated by U.S. news sources—reinforced the concern that Little Rock redounded to the benefit of America's opponents in the battle for the hearts and minds of peoples around the world.

For example, *Komosomolskaya Pravda* carried a Little Rock story under a banner headline declaring "Troops Advance Against Children!" According to the *Current Digest of the Soviet Press*, related articles were accompanied by photographs including "[a] photo of the national guard unit in Little Rock directing a Negro girl away from the high school." The Soviet paper *Izvestia* suggested that "[r]ight now, behind the facade of the so-called 'American democracy,' a tragedy is unfolding which cannot but arouse ire and indignation in the heart of every honest man." The tragedy was that in the southern states of the United States

> *fascist thugs of the Ku Klux Klan are organizing a savage hunt for Negro children because the latter plan to sit in the same classrooms with white boys and girls. National guard soldiers and policemen armed to the teeth bar Negro children from entering the schools, threaten them with bayonets and tear-gas bombs and encourage hooligans to engage in violence with impunity.*

In Little Rock, "troops in full battle dress, armed with rifles with unsheathed bayonets and with tear-gas bombs, surrounded the high school to 'defend' it against nine Negro children who wished to study there." These circumstances raised questions about the American form of government.

> *The patrons of Governor Faubus . . . who dream of nooses and dynamite for persons with different-colored skins, advocates of hooliganism who throw rocks at defenseless Negro children—these gentlemen have the audacity to talk about "democracy" and speak as supporters of "freedom." In fact it is impossible to imagine a greater insult to democracy and freedom than an American diplomat's speech from the tribunal of the U.S. General Assembly, a speech in which Washington was pictured as the "champion" of the rights of the Hungarian people.*

Izvestia believed that "the events in the U.S. South cannot remain a matter of indifference. The tale of the American racists, who abuse human dignity and stoop to the level of animals, must be told." Since the United States promoted democracy abroad, it was "even more impossible to remain silent when these gentlemen attempt to act as the world's mentors."

Americans were well aware of the existence of such coverage. Drawing upon this widespread understanding, a political cartoon in the September 7 *Minneapolis Star* suggested that the "Three 'R's" in Arkansas were "Race Hate," "Rights Denial," and "Red Propaganda Boost."

Governor Faubus's actions were seen to be such a strong aid to the Soviet propaganda machine that *Confidential* magazine suggested that the governor's role might actually be part of a communist plot and the governor a communist agent. "The Commies Trained Gov. Faubus of Arkansas," declared a full-page headline framing a photo of the governor. According to the article,

> *When Governor Orval Faubus of Arkansas openly defied the government of the United States on the school integration issue, he handed to the Communists the handsomest gift they could possibly have received from any American. Four-fifths of the people of the world are colored. All over the world—in Asia and Europe, in Africa and the Middle East— the Communists have invoked the name of Little Rock to tell colored people that the United States is a land of lynching and repression. . . . [T]hanks to Faubus' actions and the Red propaganda that plays upon them, no American can travel abroad without being asked by every foreigner about Little Rock.*

For *Confidential*, these circumstances naturally led to the question, Was Faubus "unwittingly playing a pro-Communist game? Or is he deliberately aiding the Soviet propaganda machine?"

The state of Arkansas had its own suspicions of communist influence, which culminated in a hearing held before the Special Education Committee of the Arkansas Legislative Council in December 1958. State Attorney General Bruce Bennett told the committee that the hearings would prove that Little Rock was one of the "predetermined trouble areas . . . designated officially by the Communist Party many years ago to be developed for trouble purposes." He argued that "from 1928 to 1958 an intensive communist conspiracy climaxed in Little Rock, and . . . the purpose of these incidents is to attract and use the Negro—not to help the Negro." The NAACP had been heavily involved in promoting school desegregation in the city, and Bennett believed that "[m]any of the officials of this organization both local and national, have an almost incredible tie-in with Communist and Communist front organizations." Local organizer Daisy Bates and legal director Thurgood Marshall were among the NAACP leaders singled out for their allegedly subversive connections.

U.S. embassies around the globe sent dispatches to the State Department detailing the international impact of events in Little Rock. In Copenhagen, the U.S. embassy telegraphed the State Department that the mission was "embarrassed over heavy local press play and general Danish reaction [to the] Little Rock race problems." In Lourenço Marques, Mozambique, the American consul warned that the crisis had "unfortunately become a symbol of Negro-White relations in the United States." He believed that "[o]ur moral standing has been very considerably damaged and . . . any pretension of an American to advise any European Government on African affairs . . . would be hypocrisy." In the Netherlands, the Dutch reportedly reacted to Little Rock with "quiet indignation," while some saw in Little Rock "the well-worn analogy between Hitlerian methods and the activities of American racists." The fact that many thought there was "very little difference between the two" was "what hurts America in the eyes of the world." In São Paulo, Brazil, a legislator took the United States to task in the legislative assembly.

The so-called American democracy has been able by means of the world press to hold itself out as a standard for other peoples but we, the Brazilians, will always reject racial fights and never will agree that any restriction may be imposed on a Brazilian whatever his origin simply because he was born with a black skin.

According to the U.S. embassy in Paramaribo, Surinam, press reports had led to "an open reinforcement of suspicions about some of the moral emphasis which the United States places on world affairs problems." As a result of Little Rock "[t]he reporting officer has heard more volunteered negative criticism in the last week about race matters in the United States than he has in the year he has been here." According to the officer, this was "not helpful to our national standing in Surinam."

Not all nations were critical. The U.S. embassy in Bonn reported that Germans did not feel it was their place to cast aspersions on the United States, and press coverage, with the exception of "tabloids and east zone press" was not sensationalized. "Persecution and extermination of millions of Jews do not permit us [to] blame Americans or report with indignation events [in] Arkansas." The U.S. embassy in South Africa reported that "[t]he effect of Little Rock, of course was to confirm to South African 'Apartheid' supporters—most white South Africans—that the forces against integration were gaining in the United States." In South Africa, a nation "caught up in their own apartheid policy," whites "appear to derive some inner consolation and a feeling of greater support for their own ideas out of incidents such as Little Rock."

As the world looked on, governor Faubus dug in. On September 10, the Governor received a summons ordering him to appear in federal court and "show cause why he should not be charged with contempt." Faubus then let President Eisenhower's staff know that he was looking for a way out. Eisenhower and Faubus met at Eisenhower's vacation retreat in Newport, Rhode Island, on September 14. In private, Eisenhower stressed the importance of a peaceful resolution of the crisis and told Faubus that he wished to avoid embarrassing him publicly. When the meeting ended, the president believed that he had received an assurance from Governor Faubus not to violate the orders of the court.

As Faubus returned to Arkansas, the foreign and domestic press published smiling photos of the governor and the president. Eisenhower believed, and the nation hoped, that the men had come to an agreement that would end the impasse. Yet within a couple of hours, plans for a joint statement started to unravel. Faubus later insisted that "he would remove the guardsmen only on condition that the Justice Department recommend a delay in desegregation pending a Supreme Court test of the state's interposition law." In spite of this clear defiance, Eisenhower remained reluctant to intervene.

As the Arkansas National Guard continued to encircle Central High, the London *Times* reported the president's "deep disappointment that voluntary means had not been found to comply with the court's orders" yet noted that "many people feel that a greater exertion of authority by the President might have avoided a head-on collision in the courts." The *Times* blamed Faubus's personal ambition and desire for reelection to a third term for the crisis in Little Rock. Yet the paper commented that moderates in Arkansas were angry about "the part President Eisenhower is playing in this bitter controversy—or rather not playing." There was "a feeling of helplessness—of betrayal almost—among moderates, who feel that there is no one but the President who can speak clearly and strongly for them. The sour joke is current: 'If President Eisenhower were alive all this wouldn't have happened.'"

The pressure on Faubus from the president was followed by a federal court order. On September 20, Judge Davies enjoined Governor Faubus from interfering with desegregation. If Faubus wanted to call in the troops, "the proper use of that power in this instance was to maintain the Federal Court in the exercise of its jurisdiction . . . and not to nullify it."

Faubus responded to the court order by withdrawing the National Guard, then promptly leaving town. At the Southern Governors' Conference at Sea Island, Georgia, Faubus told a reporter that he expected violence if integration were attempted. Back in Little Rock, Mayor Mann urged residents to be calm.

The morning of September 23, 1957, came to be known as "Black Monday" in Little Rock. *Sacramento Bee* reporter Relman Morin described a "frightening sight." Eight African American students had walked calmly into school that morning as the city police held back the crowds surrounding Central High. Momentarily distracted by a diversion, the crowd soon realized that the students had entered the school, and mayhem broke loose. The crowd had already beaten three "Yankee" reporters for *Life* magazine and four African American reporters whom they believed had intentionally created a diversion to enable the students to enter the school. Now the crowd battled the police.

Concerned that growing crowds would be even more threatening to the safety of the students by the end of the school day, the mayor, the school superintendent, and the assistant police chief decided to remove them in the middle of the day. As one of the African American students, Melba Pattillo Beals, remembered it, the students were hurried down a dark passageway to the basement of the school. There they got into two cars driven by frightened white men. "Listen to your driver's instructions," the assistant police chief warned the students. "Your lives depend on it." The students were ordered to put their heads down, and the cars sped past the crowds and beyond the reach of rocks and sticks hurled in their direction. The students made it safely home.

From his Newport retreat, President Eisenhower decided that the time had come for action. He issued a proclamation finding a "wilful obstruction of justice" in Little Rock and commanding those engaged in obstruction of justice to cease and desist. The president thought that "every right-thinking citizen will hope that the American sense of justice and fair play will prevail in this case. It will be a sad day for this country—both at home and abroad—if school children can safely attend their classes only under the protection of armed guards."

The following day, crowds surrounded the school, and the Little Rock Nine waited at home. Mayor Mann sent the president a telegram saying that "[t]he immediate need for federal troops is urgent." He warned that the "[s]ituation is out of control and police cannot disperse the mob." Mann urged, "I am pleading to you as President of the United States in the interest of humanity law and order and because of democracy world wide to provide the necessary federal troops within several hours." By this time, for Eisenhower, "the question had become not whether to act, but what force I should use to insure execution of the court's order." Eisenhower decided to rely on federal troops, and by that afternoon, five hundred paratroopers from the 101st Airborne Division were stationed in the city. Another five hundred arrived later in the day. Armed with bayonets, the troops ringed Central High School on the morning of September 25. From the perspective of Governor Faubus and his supporters, the "occupation" of Little Rock had begun.

Only two months before, in July 1957, Eisenhower had told reporters, "I can't imagine any set of circumstances that would ever induce me to send Federal troops . . . into any area to enforce the orders of a federal court." What had caused the president to change his mind so dramatically?

Eisenhower's decision to act was not based on support for desegregation. He was not a supporter of court-ordered desegregation or of the *Brown* decision itself. Eisenhower communicated his feelings about the desegregation cases to Chief Justice Earl Warren while the cases were pending. He invited Warren to a dinner at the White House. Following the meal, Warren later wrote, Eisenhower took him by the arm, and "as we walked along, speaking of the Southern states in the segregation cases, he said, 'These are not bad people. All they are concerned about is to see that their sweet little girls are not required to sit alongside some big overgrown Negroes.'" Justice Warren felt that President Eisenhower's lack of support for *Brown* contributed to the resistance to the decision. He believed that "much of our racial strife could have been avoided" if the president had stood up for the principal of equality. The nation seemed to agree with Justice Warren's assessment. According to a 1955 Gallup Poll, one of the main criticisms of Eisenhower's leadership was that he "encourages segregation." When *Brown* was decided, Eisenhower was asked whether he had "any advice to give the South as to just how to react to the recent Supreme Court decision banning segregation." The president responded, "Not in the slightest." He thought that South Carolina Governor James Byrnes "made a very fine statement when he said let us be calm, and let us be reasonable, and let us look this thing in the face." As for his own role, Eisenhower said, "The Supreme Court has spoken, and I am sworn to uphold the Constitutional process in this country. And I am trying—I will obey it."

Notwithstanding his lack of enthusiasm for *Brown*, Eisenhower became deeply involved in managing the Little Rock crisis. He was concerned, in part, with the threat the crisis posed for the rule of law. As Eisenhower described it in his memoirs, "[t]hat situation, if a successful defiance of federal court orders continued, could lead to a breakdown of law and order in a widening area." Eisenhower was also angry with Governor Faubus, who he felt had defied him. But the breakdown of law and order and the management of an insubordinate governor were not all that was at stake. In addition, Eisenhower wrote, "around the world it could continue to feed the mill of Soviet propagandists who by word and picture were telling the world of the 'racial terror' in the United States." It was a mix of factors, domestic and international, that led to Eisenhower's extraordinary action in Little Rock.

The president's top aides emphasized the international impact of the Little Rock crisis. The U.S. ambassador to the United Nations, Henry Cabot Lodge, wrote President Eisenhower that:

> *Here at the United Nations I can see clearly the harm that the riots in Little Rock are doing to our foreign relations. More than two-thirds of the world is non-white and the reactions of the representatives of these people is easy to see. I suspect that we lost several votes on the Chinese communist item because of Little Rock.*

Secretary of State John Foster Dulles was "sick at heart" over the Little Rock crisis. On September 24, 1957, as President Eisenhower was returning to Washington to deliver his public address on Little Rock, Dulles put in a call to Attorney General Herbert Brownell. As the two exchanged concerns about Little Rock, Dulles told Brownell that "this situation was ruining our foreign policy. The effect of this in Asia and Africa will be worse for us than Hungary was for the Russians." Dulles thought that "there should be an awareness of the effect of all this." Brownell indicated that he had taken Eisenhower "the USIA report which mentioned the use Nasser and Khrushchev were making of it." He believed that President Eisenhower "was very alert to this aspect." In addition "[t]here has been considerable in the papers since then." Brownell believed that Secretary Dulles's "part of the problem would not be solved" by Eisenhower's decision to send in the troops, "although firm action would certainly help a lot." According to records of the phone call, the men "discussed the seriousness of the situation at some length." Brownell asked Dulles to look over a draft of the president's speech, which Dulles agreed to do.

Later in the day, Dulles called Eisenhower with suggestions to "put in a few more sentences in this draft speech emphasizing the harm done abroad." Dulles dictated the following statement to the president's secretary:

> *It would be difficult to exaggerate the harm that is being done to the prestige and influence, and indeed to the safety, of our nation in the world. Our enemies are gloating over this incident and using it everywhere to misprepresent [sic] our nation. We are portrayed as a violator of the standard of conduct which the peoples of the world united to proclaim in the Charter of the United Nations whereby the peoples reaffirmed "faith in fundamental human rights and in the dignity and worth of the human person" and did so "without distinction as to race, sex, language, or religion."*

According to the draft language, Eisenhower would "beg the people of Arkansas to erase the blot upon the fair name and high honor of our nation." This was a time when the nation "faces the gravest of peril" from enemies abroad, and "patriotism cannot be reconciled with conduct which injures grievously our nation."

The president returned to Washington to take his case to the nation. He hoped that speaking "from the house of Lincoln, of Jackson and of Wilson" would best convey his sadness and "the firmness with which I intend to pursue this course." Eisenhower's televised address drew heavily upon Dulles's suggestions. He reminded the nation of the Supreme Court's ruling in *Brown*. "Our personal opinions about the decision have no bearing on the matter of enforcement," he suggested. "[T]he responsibility and authority of the Supreme Court to interpret the Constitution are very clear." Many southern communities had begun the process of desegregation and in doing so had "demonstrated to the world that we are a nation in which laws, not men, are supreme." The president regretted that "this truth—the cornerstone of our liberties—was not observed" in Little Rock. Because of resistance to court-ordered desegregation in that city, "both the law and the national interest demanded that the President take action."

According to the president,

A foundation of our American way of life is our national respect for law. In the South, as elsewhere, citizens are keenly aware of the tremendous disservice that has been done to the people of Arkansas in the eyes of the nation, and that has been done to the nation in the eyes of the world.

This situation had perilous implications.

At a time when we face grave situations abroad because of the hatred that Communism bears toward a system of government based on human rights, it would be difficult to exaggerate the harm that is being done to the prestige and influence, and indeed to the safety, of our nation and the world.

Our enemies are gloating over this incident and using it everywhere to misrepresent our whole nation. We are portrayed as a violator of those standards of conduct which the peoples of the world united to proclaim in the Charter of the United Nations.

The president called upon the citizens of Arkansas to put an end to obstruction of the law in their state.

If resistance to the Federal Court orders ceases at once, the further presence of Federal troops will be unnecessary and the City of Little Rock will return to its normal habits of peace and order and a blot upon the fair name and high honor of our nation in the world will be removed.

Thus will be restored the image of America and of all its parts as one nation, indivisible, with liberty and justice for all.

Ending with the exact language of the last words of the Pledge of Allegiance, Eisenhower appealed to patriotism. Little Rock was not simply an internal dispute: the nation, the national image, and national security were at stake. Patriotism required that the needs of the nation be placed ahead of sectional loyalties.

Secretary Dulles was pleased with the president's speech. But as Attorney General Brownell had suggested, Dulles's "part of the problem" was not yet solved, and Little Rock's impact on U.S. foreign affairs continued to be felt.

The president's address to the nation was also an address to the world, and it was widely covered in the international press. Eisenhower's actions were widely and favorably viewed as safeguarding the image of democracy. In the Netherlands, the independent newspaper *Algemeen Dagblad* announced that "Eisenhower's airborn troops again are bearers of democracy's banner on which [is] inscribed [the] words 'human rights,'" just as they had been during World War II. The largest newspaper in Wales praised Eisenhower for demonstrating "the ultimate political courage." In Brazil, the Bahia state legislature passed a motion approving of the president's action. In Hong Kong, the *South China Morning Post* found Eisenhower's action to be "firm and decisive." It was "an answer both to legal quibblers and to the lawless few whose conduct unjustly exposed Americans as a whole to new propaganda blasts from the Kremlin." On September 30, the *Egyptian Gazette* ran a story devoted to a commentary in the British

Observer. That paper called Eisenhower's actions "belated but strong" and claimed that although a crisis like Little Rock could not happen in Britain, "it could happen in Kenya or Central Africa where the British Government has certain rights and duties comparable" to the U.S. government's relationship to the State of Arkansas.

According to a front-page editorial in the Luxembourg paper *Tageblatt*, Eisenhower had "save[d] not only a principle but the soul of a country which, if it had permitted the situation in Little Rock to continue, could no longer have laid claim to being the leader of the free bloc." Although Little Rock had made a "deep impression" on the Portuguese in Mozambique, the one "ray of light" was Eisenhower's stand, demonstrating "a determination to see to it that American democracy is no farce." Eisenhower's action was seen as upholding the rule of law and maintaining the principles laid down by the Supreme Court. According to an editorial in the Brazilian *Diario de Noticias*, "the drastic step of the American President will not surprise those who know the respect for law in that country and the part which the Supreme Federal Tribunal plays in the structure of American political life."

Political parties of all kinds came out in support of Eisenhower. In Uganda, the secretary general of the United Congress Party asked the American consul to "convey to the President and the people of the United States the sincere appreciation of the United Congress Party of Uganda for the President's sustained efforts and firm stand on the question of enforcing the Ruling of the Supreme Court against segregation in American schools." Even communist leaders could find favor with Eisenhower's action. Costa Rican Communist Party leader Manuel Mora Valverde suggested that "[n]ot every man . . . would have dared to take the step taken by Eisenhower. . . . I am of the personal opinion that Mr. Eisenhower is worthy of admiration as a man, even though he continues to be the President of an imperialist power." There were, of course, dissenters. In China, the *People's Daily* thought that the "U.S. government did not really intend to protect black people's rights, but to hoodwink the public domestically and abroad." . . .

U.S. officials tried to put the best face possible on the nation's handling of the Little Rock crisis. AFL-CIO President George Meany, U.S. delegate to the United Nations General Assembly's Social and Humanitarian Committee, told that committee that the Little Rock crisis was "only one episode in a peaceful revolution which had been going on for several years." In response to wide-spread criticism in France, Secretary Dulles sent a telegram to the U.S. embassy in Paris on September 30 with the text of a statement that embassy personnel could use in reporting on Little Rock. The statement stressed that

> *there is one essential point to be drawn from the events at Little Rock: that is, that the full force of the United Government [sic], both moral and physical, has been directed to enforcing the law and order and to ensure the carrying out of the decision of the Supreme Court. Although we deplore the events themselves and make no RPT no effort to excuse those who have caused them, it nevertheless has appeared to me worthy of note here that our national authority is being used to ensure the education of children, in dramatic contrast to the uses to which Soviet armed might was put last year in Hungary.*

Although many saw a foreign affairs boost from Eisenhower's actions, Georgia Senator Herman Talmadge drew upon international affairs in quite a different way. "We still mourn the destruction of the sovereignty of Hungary by Russian tanks and troops in the streets of

Budapest," he said. "We are now threatened with the spectacle of the President of the United States using tanks and troops in the streets of Little Rock to destroy the sovereignty of the state of Arkansas." Senator Richard Russell of Georgia called the action "totalitarian." "Our founding fathers . . . would turn over in their graves" upon hearing of it, he insisted. Similarly, Senator James O. Eastland of Mississippi considered the action an attempt to "destroy the social order of the South" and thought that "[n]othing like this was ever attempted in Russia."

As Orval Faubus would have it, his own vision of democracy was implicated by the Little Rock crisis. In an address that was nationally broadcast while federal troops ringed Central High, the governor asked, "In the name of God whom we all revere, in the name of liberty we hold so dear, in the name of decency which we all cherish, what is happening in America?" Faubus claimed that federal intervention in Little Rock had resulted in a denial of constitutional rights to the people of Arkansas.

The dispute between Eisenhower and Faubus about the meaning of democracy paralleled a debate about the nature of the U.S. system of government in the international press. What was the nation's true nature? Was the face of democracy represented by Orval Faubus and the white women and men who screamed and struggled with authorities upon hearing the horrifying news that African American students had entered Central High School? Or was the face of democracy that of President Eisenhower, the general who had helped lead the Allies through World War II and who now seemed poised to lead his nation through another important test?

The intensity of the international media coverage of Little Rock finally declined in October 1957, and observers drew lessons from the crisis. In the Netherlands, *De Maasbode* believed that the Little Rock crisis "must be seen as one of last violent convulsions of [a] system and mentality that is [a] thing of past."

According to *Hindustan Times* reporter Michael Owen, the furor over Little Rock

> *has had repercussion all over the world, causing a further denigration of American democratic stock in Asia and once again posing the old question that if this is how America feels towards those whose pigmentation of skin is not the shade of their own, that if the Governor of a comparatively unimportant state can defy the Supreme Court of the nation, then what exactly are the real feelings of Americans towards Asians, brown, black or yellow?*

In Indonesia, Owen wrote, one newspaper asked "whether Governor Faubus should not be hauled before the Un-American Activities Committee for alienating half of the world from the U.S." In Japan, Owen reported, "a conservative citizen of some prominence raised the question: 'If Americans can regard Negroes as inferior, how do they really regard Asians?'"

Owen believed that Eisenhower's actions did not "appreciably mitigate the international effects of the affair." The president's statements had not "[r]esulted in reassuring Asia that their ingrained suspicion that the shape of American democracy is in reality only 'skin-deep,' is unfounded." He felt that "[t]he periodical occurrence of episodes like that at Little Rock are not only subversive to international concord and understanding but also serve to drive more and more Asians to the conclusion that there cannot be, at least not in this sorry generation, any real meeting ground between Occident and Orient."

Meanwhile, President Eisenhower had difficulty deflecting attention from Little Rock. The *South China Morning Post* reported that on October 3, "Reporters attempting to question the President on Foreign Affairs had a difficult time at to-day's 28-minute press conference because of the intense pre-occupation of most correspondents over the situation in Little Rock. . . . Out of 17 questions asked at the press conference, 13 concerned the Little Rock situation."

As Central High settled into an extraordinary school year under military guard, Arthur Larson, director of the USIA, suggested to the president that he send an open letter to the Central High School students. In Larson's view, "the students themselves are the best source of hope in this situation." Larson thought that Eisenhower should encourage students to act in a "democratic manner that does justice to our proud heritage." Such efforts would mean that "the good name of Arkansas . . . could be held up for all to admire. At the same time you would help to show the world that freedom and equality not only are enshrined in our laws but also dwell in the hearts of our people." In this and other instances, Eisenhower declined to follow his staff's advice to appeal personally to members of the Little Rock community.

As a semblance of order, if not tranquillity, descended at last on Little Rock, the military presence declined. The 101st Airborne would leave the city by early November, and the Arkansas National Guard deployment was decreased by four-fifths. The remaining troops would patrol Central High School for the rest of the school year. Then, during the summer of 1958, the future of integration in Little Rock was placed, again, in the hands of the courts. On June 20, 1958, District Judge Harry J. Lemley, who had replaced Judge Davies, ordered that desegregation be postponed for two-and-a-half years. Judge Lemley agreed with the school board, which had sought the postponement, that the students' education suffered under the difficult conditions Central High had endured that school year. According to Judge Lemley, the difficulties in Little Rock

> *did not stem from mere lawlessness. . . . Rather, the source of the trouble was the deep seated popular opposition in Little Rock to the principle of integration, which, as is known, runs counter to the pattern of southern life which has existed for over three hundred years. The evidence also shows that to this opposition was added the conviction of many of the people of Little Rock, that the Brown decisions do not truly represent the law.*

Providing a "breathing spell" in Little Rock was, in Lemley's view, an appropriate exercise of the court's discretion and consistent with the Supreme Court's requirement in *Brown v. Board of Education II* of desegregation "with all deliberate speed."

Many reacted with outrage and disappointment to the district court's ruling. Maurice H. Goodenough of Clichy-sous-Bois, France, expressed his views directly to Judge Lemley. "Those who welcome that kind of publicity can thank you for having put Little Rock back on the front pages of the world's newspapers," he wrote the judge.

> *Last fall, here in France, the population was literally "lapping up" their daily portion of Little Rock. They were following it with the same interest they give to their national sports,*

and I assume that other peoples around the globe were doing the same. Little Rock had become America's entry in an international exhibit.

You must be very ignorant of where America is in relationship to time and space; if not, you must be willfully seeking the loss of America's prestige and position, with its ultimate disasterous [sic] consequences.

Civil rights leaders A. Philip Randolph, Lester B. Granger, Reverend Martin Luther King Jr., and Roy Wilkins sent a joint statement to President Eisenhower claiming that Judge Lemley's decision had "shocked and outraged Negro citizens and millions of their fellow Americans. This opinion is being construed, rightly or wrongly, as a green light to lawless elements in their defiance of Federal authority." They felt that "[t]he process of peaceful advancement toward equality of citizenship for all Americans" had "reached a critical turn." Resistance to civil rights reform had "assumed a significance beyond the question of racial justice, important as that is. The welfare of the whole country is involved." The nation faced important internal and external concerns. Among the people, there was "a pattern of cal-loused disrespect for law. Moral values have been corrupted. Mob violence has emerged as an instrument to maintain the status quo." Basic constitutional liberties were threatened, and politicians at all levels had disobeyed the law. Externally,

It is no secret that the foreign relations program of our nation has been hampered and damaged by the discriminatory treatment accorded citizens within the United States, solely on the basis of their race and color. In our world-wide struggle to strengthen the free world against the spread of totalitarianism, we are sabotaged by the totalitarian practices forced upon millions of our Negro citizens.

The statement called for "a clear national policy and a program of implementation" to eradicate racial segregation. They urged the president to direct the Justice Department to file a brief supporting desegregation in an appeal from the Lemley decision and to take other steps to ensure that, throughout the nation, "the law will be vigorously upheld with the total resources at [the president's] command."

While the NAACP prepared an appeal of the district court order, Orval Faubus avowed his opposition to "integration by force" and was overwhelmingly reelected to an unprecedented third term as governor of Arkansas. Faubus explained his July 29 victory in the Democratic primary, which assured his November reelection, as "a condemnation by the people of illegal Federal intervention in the affairs of the state and the horrifying use of Federal bayonets in the streets of an American city and in the halls of a public school." Just over two weeks later, noting the governor's involvement in encouraging opposition to the court ordered integration plan, the court of appeals reversed Judge Lemley's postpone-ment. According to the court,

The issue plainly comes down to the question of whether overt public resistance, including mob protest, constitutes sufficient cause to nullify an order of the Federal court directing the board to proceed with its integration plan. We say the time has not yet come in these United States when an order of a federal court must be whittled away, watered down, or shamefully withdrawn in the face of violent and unlawful acts of individual citizens in opposition thereto.

As the opening of the school year neared and the Supreme Court took up the Little Rock case, one reporter found that "[t]he situation at Little Rock looks infinitely more dangerous today than it did a year ago." Relman Morin wrote that "[s]entiment has crystallized. Resistance to desegregating Central High School . . . has become truly massive." It was "a tense moment in the history of the South and the whole nation."

* * *

In spite of the alarm over Little Rock's impact on international opinion, when foreign opinion was surveyed it appeared at first glance that in Western Europe the survey results were not much worse than before. A November 1957 report found that "opinions of race relations in the U.S. are highly unfavorable, but apparently have not become materially more so as a result of Little Rock." Compared to April 1956, there were no great changes when survey respondents were asked, "From impressions you have received from any sources, would you tell me your opinion of the treatment of Negroes in the U.S.[?]" According to the report, "[t]hat the Little Rock happenings have apparently had no major effect in worsening opinion of the treatment of Negroes in the U.S. . . . may be owing to the fact that America's standing in the area of race relations was already in a very depressed state prior to the Arkansas desegregation incidents, and hence not readily susceptible to further decrease." Discrimination against Autherine Lucy at the University of Alabama "was an international *cause célèbre* in early 1956 and . . . in all probability did much to lower U.S. standing in the race area to the very unfavorable levels" found in April 1956. In other words, European opinion could not go down because it was already so low. The figures were quite discouraging. In Norway, 82 percent of respondents had a bad opinion or a very bad opinion of the way the United States treated African Americans. In Great Britain, France, and West Germany, the percentages were 66 percent, 65 percent, and 53 percent, respectively. In Italy, only 34 percent had a bad or very bad opinion of U.S. race relations, but only 12 percent had a good or very good opinion.

According to the report, the lack of significant change in these numbers did not mean that Little Rock had not had an effect. "The absence of any general decline . . . does not preclude the possibility, of course, that the Little Rock happenings have had considerable effect in confirming and solidifying already held unfavorable attitudes." Such an occurrence was "rather strongly suggested" by the survey results.

A favorable overall opinion of the United States persisted despite these highly negative views about race. The report suggested that this may have been due in part to the respondents' belief that, over the previous decade, "on balance Negroes in the U.S. have been drawing closer to equality with whites." There were policy implications from these survey results. The more favorable views about the improvement of racial conditions over time "underscore the value of making every effort to place recent racial developments in a broader perspective" in the projection of America abroad. This broader perspective, reflected in documents such as *The Negro in American Life*, could present racial change as a gradual, democratic process and America as being on a trajectory toward ever greater equality.

The USIA took on the task of developing a strategy for responding to international criticism. The director of planning for the agency described its approach in a September 24, 1957, memorandum for a staff report for the president:

As the Soviet propagandists step up their attacks on "racial terror" in the United States following recent developments in Little Rock, USIA media are attempting to minimize the damage by summarizing anti-integration events on a factual basis, supplying facts whenever possible to balance adverse sensational items, quoting editorials and official statements which indicate steady determined progress toward integration, and informally suggesting to friendly editors possible constructive treatment.

The report noted that "USIS posts in all areas reported heavy but reasoned coverage of the Little Rock episode" through the previous week. "News photos were particularly damaging to U.S. prestige." The foreign relations crisis was continuing. "Agency officials are apprehensive that this week's violence in Little Rock will have serious adverse public reaction abroad."

For its response, the State Department prepared "Talking Points to Overcome Adverse Reaction to Little Rock Incident." The document was "intended for guidance on a world-wide basis." The first strategy recommended was to place the Little Rock crisis "in perspective." To do that, U.S. officials could suggest that "[t]he events at Little Rock are widely misunderstood and misinterpreted. Distressing as they are, they arise from the force and strength of the American people's insistence upon complete equality. They measure, in a sense, the sweeping and basic character of one of the most important reforms in our history." The talking points stressed that "marked progress toward integration" had been achieved "in most parts of the country; it will inevitably spread throughout our entire nation." Unrest was perpetrated by a "small minority." It was the "basic nature of the American people" to be law abiding. Finally, "[t]he President's intervention has demonstrated the determination of the American people and the effectiveness of the American system in preserving the rights of the individual under law." Overall, "tremendous strides have been made in removing racial barriers in the US."

Another way to put Little Rock in perspective was to talk about the difficulties other nations faced. "The problems we are experiencing are not unique to the US," the talking points emphasized. "These situations result from the effort of free societies to maintain and expand the freedom and equality of the individual," and were "not be confused with those tragic disturbances that arise through the efforts of certain other nations to repress human liberty." Ultimately, Little Rock provided an opportunity to compare Cold War adversaries.

In the US, national authority is being used not to suppress individual equality and freedom but to uphold them. In the Little Rock incident national authority has been invoked to maintain equal rights of a minority. In the Soviet Union national authority has been repeatedly invoked to suppress the rights of minorities.

A USIA pamphlet on school desegregation, *The Louisville Story*, was distributed before Little Rock news broke, and it provided a useful counter to Little Rock. The American consulate in Port Elizabeth, South Africa, found these materials "most welcome." After distributing copies of the pamphlet, the *Port Elizabeth Evening Post* published a story comparing Little Rock with Louisville in just the way the consulate had hoped. According to the paper, "There is trouble in Arkansas," but "let us keep eruptions like this . . . affair in perspective. Let us not be misled by news of such transitory happenings into believing that the vast programme for the removal of the schools colour bar in the United States is not progressing very well." The *Post* believed that "[t]he truth about the 'desegregation' programme in the United States is that it is making surprisingly smooth progress and already is far advanced." To put Little Rock in perspective, the paper described desegregation in Louisville. The Louisville story was "told in a happy, illustrated brochure recently published by the United States Information Service." It highlighted "the great change achieved in only three years in the United States, since the Supreme Court ruled that to keep the children apart in tax-supported schools was a denial of equal opportunity and, therefore, unconstitutional." In spite of this "balanced" coverage, the American consulate reported that South African blacks remained "somewhat shocked" over Little Rock but "realized that the events at Little Rock were counter . . . to U.S. national policy."

USIS staff in different countries supplied news media with materials on race in the United States that could result in coverage American officials were more comfortable with. As one American consulate put it, "Through friendly contacts with the local editors and others, we can, through judicious selection of materials, bring our point of view to bear in different situations." American efforts at spin control had their successes. In Rio de Janeiro, the U.S. embassy reported that "[s]everal papers frontpaged USIS photos showing peaceful integration elsewhere." According to a report concerning U.S. efforts in Africa, Nigerians "were willing to accept our explanation that Little Rock was not all of the US, nor was it typical of America." USIS material was also distributed in Australia to good effect. It was used by prominent radio and television commentators. "The effort was particularly effective in Sydney where a commentator who had previously been critical reversed his stand."

The USIA described its efforts to provide "perspective" on Little Rock in a semiannual report to Congress. The agency's strategy was to present the crisis "in the context of the significant advances of our Negro population as well as the general development of integration in the public schools." The agency "supplied facts and photographs on typical integrated schools" for use in Voice of America broadcasts and newsreels. Overseas officers organized discussions with "distinguished American Negro personalities." For example, singer Marian Anderson discussed American race relations during a concert tour in Asia. As might be expected, the agency reported to Congress, the source of its appropriations, that its efforts had been successful. "Reports from posts abroad indicate that this consistent, factual handling of the racial question contributed substantially to the generally restrained and well-balanced reaction to the Little Rock story overseas." While there had been communist-inspired sensationalism, "the main body of responsible foreign newsmen and officials described the general situation accurately and referred to Little Rock as an episode in a period of social change."

A reprieve from Little Rock coverage would come, but not quite the way American officials would have hoped. On October 4, 1957, the Soviet Union launched the Sputnik satellite, rushing dramatically ahead of the United States in the space race. For Americans, the idea of a Soviet spaceship circling overhead led to a crisis in national confidence and, ultimately, a renewed commitment to improving education as well as accelerating the space race itself. Internationally, Sputnik, following Little Rock, was a second blow to U.S. prestige. In Genoa, Italy, news of Sputnik "crowded out Little Rock coverage." The American embassy reported that Sputnik had had a "greater and more adverse impact upon local attitudes and United States prestige." Sputnik and a subsequent Soviet spacecraft "for the time being overshadowed Little Rock and other U.S. racial news items" in South Africa as well.

When the initial shock of Sputnik had subsided, the task of rehabilitating America's image remained. The double blow to U.S. prestige in Arkansas and in the heavens made the task all that much more compelling. As had been the case with *Brown*, strong federal government action would always provide the greatest benefit. Rather than spending their efforts placing negative news "in context" and attempting to divert the world's attention from racial incidents, meaningful government action gave the USIA and other government officials something worth reporting. In the Little Rock crisis, helpful action came first in Eisenhower's order to send in the troops. It came again in the form of a definitive Supreme Court ruling in *Cooper v. Aaron*.

* * *

When the school year ended at Central High in June 1958, Melba Pattillo took her schoolbooks into the backyard of her home, placed them in a pile, and set them on fire. The flames consuming her schoolwork could not take away the searing memories of her difficult year, and the sixteen-year-old girl stared into the flames, wondering if she could go back the next fall. Eight of the nine African American students had made it through the school year. Minnijean Brown was expelled when, fed up with constant harassment by white students, she retaliated. "One Nigger Down, Eight to Go" read cards distributed by white high school students who supported segregation. At the end of the year, a measure of victory could be felt as Ernest Green, the lone senior in the group, became the first African American student ever to graduate from Central High School.

While the summer provided a respite for the students, the political and legal conflict over integration at Central High continued. Governor Faubus called the state legislature into a special session on August 26, just two days before the U.S. Supreme Court was to hear the Little Rock case. The legislature passed a series of bills that gave the governor broad latitude to oppose desegregation. As historian Tony Freyer has put it, "the central purpose of most of the measures was to establish a legal basis for closing any public schools under court order to desegregate and to transfer public funds to private, segregated institutions."

Because the opening of the school year in Little Rock was set for the following Monday, the Supreme Court acted without delay. On Friday, September 12, the day after oral arguments, the Court issued a per curiam order unanimously affirming the judgment of the court of appeals, thereby reinstating the original district court order to enforce desegregation in Little Rock. A full opinion would follow on September 29.

In Arkansas, the Court's order prompted Governor Faubus to put his signature to the legislation passed during the summer's special session. One statute granted him authority to close public schools "whenever the Governor shall determine that such action is necessary in order to maintain the peace against actual or impending domestic violence . . . because of integration of the races in any school of the district." Faubus called for a local referendum in Little Rock, as provided for under the new law, and on September 27 the vote was 19,470 to 7,561 in favor of closing the schools rather than desegregating. High school would not open in Little Rock that fall.

On September 29, two days after the Little Rock referendum rejecting its judgment, the Supreme Court issued its opinion in *Cooper v. Aaron*. The opinion was written by Justice William Brennan, but it was signed by all nine members of the Court. Having all members of the Court sign the opinion together reinforced the strength of their unanimity behind the principles articulated in the case.

The Court saw the case as raising "questions of the highest importance to the maintenance of our federal system of government." According to the Court, "[t]he constitutional rights of respondents are not to be sacrificed or yielded to the violence and disorder which have followed upon the actions of the Governor and Legislature. . . . [L]aw and order are not here to be preserved by depriving the Negro children of their constitutional rights." The Court unanimously reaffirmed its holding in *Brown* that segregated schools violated the Fourteenth Amendment's equal protection clause.

> *The principles announced in [Brown] and the obedience of the States to them, according to the command of the Constitution, are indispensable for the protection of the freedoms guaranteed by our fundamental charter for all of us. Our constitutional ideal of equal justice under law is thus made a living truth.*

The Court's strong statement in *Cooper* helped reinforce the point the USIA and U.S. embassy staffs had been emphasizing for so long. *Cooper* illustrated the working of American constitutionalism, and it preserved the argument that racial equality was an American ideal. While *Brown* had proclaimed that the tenets of American democracy embodied in the Constitution were fundamentally inconsistent with racial segregation, *Cooper* rescued that principle from the threat of extinction posed by massive resistance.

The Supreme Court ruling in *Cooper v. Aaron* was widely covered in the international press. The London *Times* described it in detail, noting that the Court had "virtually exploded the Little Rock school case in a shining opinion which indirectly disposed of all attempts in the south to evade the desegregation law." The paper also covered the continuing difficulties in Little Rock in detail but blamed the problems on Governor Faubus, who "needed an issue if he were not to be out of office at the end of his second term." The paper carried stories about Little Rock on a daily basis for much of September 1958, but the articles appeared on the interior pages. The impression left by the *Times*'s coverage was that continuing racial tensions in the South were attributable more to individual actors, such as Faubus, than to the sanctioning of racism by the American government.

As the start of the school year approached in the fall of 1958, the *South China Morning Post* in Hong Kong had expressed skepticism about President Eisenhower's commitment to desegregation, criticizing the president's lack of support for *Brown*. In the aftermath of *Cooper*, however, Eisenhower was no longer the focus of concern. The paper instead highlighted a speech in Hong Kong by Dickinson College political science professor Donald Flaherty, who argued that continuing difficulties were the product of American federalism. Speaking at a Rotary Club luncheon, Flaherty told his audience that the Little Rock crisis was "related to the U.S. system of government," and "there was always the possibility of strife between the national government and one or more of the state governments under the federal system." Flaherty believed that "complete integration would be accomplished gradually. If this could be done peacefully . . . then the federal system of government would have achieved something of major importance." The *Times of India* carried a lengthy analysis of federalism and desegregation by American journalist Anthony Lewis, who also argued that conflict over desegregation was a product of American federalism.

In many other countries, the press highlighted *Cooper*, then covered continuing difficulties sporadically and off the front page. Little Rock schools were closed. Massive resistance had taken hold in the community, but these circumstances did not precipitate a foreign affairs crisis.

Social change in the Little Rock crisis was both dramatic and dramatically limited. President Eisenhower's strong stand in sending in federal troops was a clear statement that the federal government stood behind federal law. It showed, as well, that regardless of his personal views, the president was committed to upholding the Supreme Court's judgments. Yet when school reopened in Little Rock in the fall of 1959, Jefferson Thomas was the lone African American student in attendance at Central High. At Little Rock's Hall High School, three African American students were enrolled and 730 whites. By the spring of 1960, five African Americans could be counted among Central's student body of 1,515. The following year, eight more African American students were assigned to these schools. In spite of these tiny numbers, Central and Hall were now regarded as desegregated schools.

The small numbers of African American students at Little Rock high schools did not reflect a reluctance of African American parents to send their children to these schools. Rather, Little Rock had adopted a student-assignment process benignly called a "Pupil Placement Law." Compared with the resistance measures of 1958, the Arkansas pupil placement law was quite dispassionate. The purpose of the act appeared on its face to have nothing to do with desegregation, but rather with the need for flexibility and selectivity in student assignments. The legislature determined that "any general or arbitrary reallocation of pupils heretofore entered in the public school system according to any rigid rule of proximity of residence or in accordance solely with request on behalf of the pupil would be disruptive to orderly administration." When a student wished to be reassigned, a parent or guardian was required to file a petition with the school board on behalf of the individual child. A hearing would then be held to determine the appropriateness of the transfer. The statute identified a long list of criteria relevant to pupil placement decisions, including "[a]vailable room and teaching capacity . . . ; the suitability of established curricula for particular pupils; the adequacy of the pupil's academic preparation . . . ; the scholastic aptitude and relative intelligence or mental energy or ability of the pupil; the psychological qualification of the pupil . . . ; the psychological effect upon the pupil of attendance at a particular school; . . . the home environment of the pupil," and on and on. The one factor that spoke directly to the context of desegregation in Little Rock was the fact that in deciding whether a transfer was appropriate the school board could take into consideration "the possibility of breaches of the peace or ill will or economic retaliation within the community."

Bureaucratizing the process meant that racial integration was minimized. School boards now had a cumbersome process that by itself would delay integration. They could use a long list of facially neutral criteria as a basis for refusing individual requests by African American students to attend white schools. As NAACP Legal Defense Fund lawyer Jack Greenberg put it, "violence and physical obstruction having failed, bureaucracy in the form of pupil assignment laws became the principal means of fighting integration." The Supreme Court nevertheless allowed such plans to stand. There would be no drama attending the Court's handling of this important issue. The lack of fanfare would not cause this issue to go unnoticed. To white southerners, the path was clear: bureaucratization could accomplish most of what overt resistance had not.

This lesson took hold in the South, yet the lesson was lost in Africa and Asia. The international press did not notice the pupil placement cases, perhaps because these cases did not undermine the formal and abstract principle of racial equality articulated in *Brown* and reaffirmed in *Cooper*. As a result, the bureaucratization of segregation did not pose a threat to America's democratic image. There is no indication that the federal government was concerned with the impact of pupil placement plans on foreign affairs, even though it was clear that these plans would undermine efforts to integrate public schools. National policy projected overseas continued to be framed in the broad outlines of *Cooper* and *Brown*.

In spite of its minimal impact on actual school desegregation, the Supreme Court ruling in *Cooper* remained of tremendous significance in another arena. *Cooper* safeguarded the basic principle of *Brown* in the face of massive resistance. *Cooper* emphasized the supremacy of federal law and the role of the Court in defining federal constitutional principles. In so doing, the Court protected the idea of a rule of law. Individual rights could not be taken away by mob violence. By upholding the basic principles of U.S. constitutionalism, the Court protected the image of democracy. *Cooper* upheld the principle that American democracy functioned to protect individual rights and that racial equality was a value the courts would defend. Because of *Cooper*, the narrative of race and democracy in *The Negro in American Life* would still have salience.

Measured, at least, by the degree and pace of integration, it may be that *Cooper* succeeded more in maintaining democracy's image than in actually desegregating the schools. From the perspective of President Eisenhower, the core interests at stake in Little Rock had more to do with federal authority and foreign affairs than with racial equality. Having established those broad principles, the president and his administration withdrew their presence from the continuing struggle. To the extent that safeguarding the image of America was behind Eisenhower's involvement, he got what he needed with *Cooper v. Aaron*. At this juncture, the Cold War imperative could be addressed largely through formal pronouncements about the law. More substantive social change would await another day.

Suburban Segregation

Rosalyn Baxandall and Elizabeth Ewen

African Americans who sought to live out the postwar suburban dream on Long Island had limited options. Segregated housing patterns had been the rule long before the war and continued long after. Most African Americans in Freeport, for instance, lived in Bennington Park, which *Newsday* considered "the worst slum in New York State," despite the fact that it was a stone's throw from the new and prosperous Levittown. Bennington Park had been built in the first decade of the century to house southern blacks who came to work as domestics in the wealthy South Shore estates.

By the 1940s many who worked as domestics and artisans had accumulated enough to buy their own houses and plots of land. World War II brought greater employment opportunities through the burgeoning defense industries. Even though the opportunities were not equal and most blacks were employed in the service and maintenance area, a few managed to work in the industrial sector despite ongoing discrimination.

Charles and Meta Meredy, for instance, came from South Carolina to Long Island in 1927. He worked as an artisan: blacksmith, mechanic, and all around handyman. She worked briefly as a domestic servant. For years they lived with various relatives in Hempstead, looking on and off for property they could afford. In 1940 they finally discovered a piece of land in an undeveloped area of Roosevelt and slowly built a house. Although he was a skilled mechanic, Charles got a job at Grumman as a porter and supplemented his income by driving a truck. When war broke out he was finally given a temporary job as Grumman's first black mechanic.

> *I worked at Grumman for three and a half years and never got a raise or was promoted. I took every course which was supposed to qualify me for a raise but I never got one. I even invented a special pliers and several other tools but Grumman took all the credit. All they ever gave me was a $25 prize.*

Although a few residents, like the Meredys, managed to build or purchase homes, most rented substandard housing, often in the same dilapidated buildings that had housed residents since the 1920s. After the war Bennington Park had become an "eyesore." By 1948 the Bennington Park slum contained 250 black families, "people crowded six and eight and ten to a room without sanitation, without electricity, some without even adequate ventilation." Shacks that were worn out a quarter of a century earlier straddled the area that could have provided high taxes as business property. Bennington Park in fact resembled the shanty towns and tobacco roads of the South, from which many of its residents had migrated in search of a better life. As *Newsday* editorialized, "A Negro who escapes the bonds of his life in the South expects to find in the North all the equality the damn Yankees boast so loudly about. Instead, he feels that at every hand the darting cat's paw of discrimination that won't admit it exists."

The Village of Freeport was promoted by the real estate industry in advertising tacitly understood to be for white families only. "You've got a garden and a place to keep a boat . . . people around here take pride in their homes. It's cool in summer, too, with all the bay. All the fishing and swimming you want, complete with schools and a busy, friendly shopping area, new residents, and you don't have to go into New York for a thing." Yet despite enthusiastic promotion, real estate agents knew they couldn't sell Freeport as an idyllic garden locality if potential residents saw a slum in the city center when they came to visit.

Not that others hadn't tried to eradicate the "vicious man-made jungle," as *Newsday* called Freeport's ghetto. In 1941 an interdenominational group of clergymen formed the Freeport Housing Authority to petition the state for funds to rebuild the area. The New York State Housing Commission studied the situation. When it completed the investigation in 1946 it declared the area the worst in the state, in need of immediate rehabilitation, and offered the village a $741,000 loan to build 100 units of new housing to replace the old. The procedure should have been simple; the loan was to be paid back by rents collected on the new buildings.

But things got complicated very fast. The Freeport Village Board, composed solely of conservative property owners committed to segregation, refused to guarantee the loan and turned to other village property owners for a referendum—the first of its kind to be held in the country. Only property owners were allowed to vote in the referendum. "None of the people most closely affected by the vote—the residents of Bennington Park—could vote. . . . Of the village's 25,000 population, only 2,676 voted on the question. They turned the loan down, 1,682 to 994." Not only then did Freeport make the reactionary and racially loaded move of disenfranchising nonproperty owners, it also took the unprecedented step of refusing public housing loan monies.

The residents of Bennington Park did not give up. In 1951, the Nassau County Women's Forum and the American Veterans Committee asked the Freeport Board of Trustees to use the new provisions of the National Housing Act of 1949 "to provide decent homes for our citizens, who are now living in conditions not fit for human beings." They also requested a new referendum. This time the new liberal Freeport mayor and the Village Board both decided to support public housing and a new referendum that read, "Shall the Village of Freeport take advantage of available federal and state funds to eliminate slums and for that purpose establish an authority to erect housing for eligible families in the Village of Freeport?"

Despite broader support for it, public housing remained intensely controversial. Armed with propaganda and over 200 active ground forces, the Northeast Civic Association, located in Freeport's most prosperous neighborhood, led a campaign against the referendum. Employing the hallmark rhetoric that always had been effective for the anti-public housing lobby, the association argued that the referendum represented the threat of "socialistic principles and unlimited power given to an appointed committee, not answerable to the voters of Freeport." They also insisted—unconvincingly—that the slum could be renovated under existing laws.

The mayor called it like it was. Village Board members, he said, were "conservative businessmen who have no use for socialism or any other ism. . . . We are however realistic enough to know that we are faced with a problem which we cannot solve alone. . . . Public housing and the elimination of slums is the best answer to communism since by it you remove one of the conditions in which communism breeds." The mayor also argued that the existing laws had proven useless: "Enforcing local ordinances to eliminate slums has resulted only in removing families and aggravating already crowded conditions."

Newsday supported the eradication of the slums as it had in 1946, this time with daily articles, editorials and arguments calling for the community to approve the referendum. So much press undoubtedly made a difference. There was a good turnout for the referendum. It passed in sixteen out of seventeen election districts. Perhaps the dramatic change also was due to a recent influx of property owners who were more liberal and cosmopolitan than older residents, many of whom were actively involved with the Ku Klux Klan.

Although the referendum passed, changing federal housing policy caused delays and setbacks. In 1953 Congress refused to pass a housing bill that would have made funds available for Freeport's housing project. In 1955 President Eisenhower finally signed legislation extending the Federal Housing Program, clearing the way for low-rent housing contruction in Freeport. The Moxey A. Rigby housing project, named after the first black judge in Nassau County, was completed in 1959. Although this was a small-scale skirmish in the battle for suburban public housing, it is significant that even to this day little public housing has been built in suburbia.

After World War II many African Americans believed that the war for democracy abroad would change segregated practices at home. In the postwar period, however, older, preexisting segregated suburban communities relied on "interlocking friendships, mutual loyalties and existing social pressure . . . as an adequate barrier against Negroes." In suburban boom communities financed largely through Federal Housing Authority (FHA) mortgages, covenants to maintain segregation became a matter of policy, as these communities were new and custom could not be relied on. A 1947 FHA guidebook for suburban development, *Planning Profitable Neighborhoods*, stated, "Protective covenants are essential to the sound development of proposed residential areas, since they regulate the use of land and provide a basis for the development of harmonious, attractive neighborhoods." In 1946 the NAACP charged that the FHA was supporting racist housing practices, and in 1948 the U.S. Supreme Court outlawed protective covenants. Yet the FHA waited two years after the Court's decision to announce that it would no longer officially issue mortgages in restricted housing developments. Unofficially the FHA accepted unwritten agreements and traditions of segregation as late as 1968, long after the boom was over.

By the 1950s suburban development was open to white, ethnically diverse middle- and working-class families, but racial diversity continued to be purposely avoided by policy makers and real estate interests. Urban ghettos were reserved for African Americans and other minorities; suburbs were to remain lily white. As early as 1949 Thurgood Marshall articulated the problems inherent in this bifurcation:

> *Housing in our society today is more than a shelter. It includes the whole environment in which the home is maintained. A well-built house in a poorly planned, impoverished, slum area, without adequate schools, community facilities, etc., does not provide good housing. Nor does a well-built house in a ghetto provide good housing in a democratic society.*

Ignoring the courts and the sound social advice Marshall offered, Levitt, who had moved mountains to shift age-old housing practices, chose to carry on age-old patterns of racism. As he explains, Levitt originally moved to suburbia in the first place to escape the black residents of Brooklyn:

> *In the 17th century, in 1624 exactly, a man by the name of Captain Hawkins, an Englishman, bought the first boat load of slaves to Virginia. Up until then there were no black people on this continent. But now the black people were here, they multiplied geometrically until finally a couple of centuries later as they moved into the north, they moved onto the same street we lived on in Brooklyn. Next to us a black assistant DA moved in. Fearing a diminution of values if too many came in, we picked up and moved out. We then got into the suburbs, into building.*

Levitt thus was a pioneer of white flight with both a personal and business stake in keeping Levittown all white. Some Levittown residents wanted to live in an integrated community and organized to change Levitt's policies. In 1947 they formed the Committee to End Discrimination. This organization was an especially irksome thorn in Levitt's side. It brought out all his racism, arrogance, and talent for revenge. In 1949 he refused the committee permission to meet in the Levittown Community Hall, which he could do because all applications for the hall's use had to be cleared by his Manhassett headquarters. He publicly branded committee members as troublemakers and Communists.

Newsday, the major Long Island newspaper whose fortunes were tied to building circulation in communities like Levittown, agreed with Levitt's assessment:

> *It is lamentable that the Levitts have been currently under attack by local troublemakers. Organizations which appear to be either communist dominated or communist inspired have been attempting to raise a racial issue at Levittown. The issue did not exist until it was fostered by people not immediately affected by it. Their only real motive seems to be to set race against race, and, if possible, to bog down the Levitt building program which means homes for thousands of people.*

Echoing the common suspicion that organizations fighting for racial justice were probably Communists, the same editorial condemned the Levittown integrationists, claiming that

> *their sneaky tactics are demonstrated by mimeographed hand bills which they slip under doors at night in Levittown. Addressed to Levittown veterans, one of these rants, 'Remember*

how we were told that we were fighting for the four freedoms which were supposed to be for ALL? We believed in it then and we believe in it now. BUT IT'S TIME WE SAW IT IN REAL LIFE!"

Levitt cracked down on the group in other ways, too. In 1950 he evicted two white families because they had invited black children to spend some summer afternoons playing with their children; they also happened to be committee members. Even after the Fair Housing Act banning segregation in housing was upheld by the U.S. Supreme Court, Levitt continued to justify segregation on the basis of private enterprise. Opening his community to blacks and other minorities, Levitt argued, would be economic suicide: "Most whites prefer not to live in mixed communities. . . . The responsibility [for this] is society's. . . . It is not reasonable to expect that any one builder could or should undertake to absorb the entire risk and burden of conducting such a vast social experiment." Most realtors agreed. White suburbia made them more money.

Although liberals continued to challenge the "caucasian only" clause in Levittown, throughout the 1950s and 1960s racism remained the dominant ideology and outsiders were ostracized. The Arroyo family, for example, is one of two Puerto Rican families who moved to Levittown in the late fifties from the Puerto Rican countryside. They were different in many respects from their neighbors. Both parents worked full time, they had five children, and they spoke Spanish. They were subjected to continual harassment and racism by the community and the schools. Nancy Arroyo, the eldest daughter, recalled the situation:

Since I was so big, I knew there was prejudice. Not a day went by when we weren't called "spics." The people next door even taught their three- and four-year-old grandchildren to say racial slurs. The neighbors on the other side did incredible things. They would throw dirt onto my mother's kitchen when she left the kitchen door open for fresh air. It took ten years for things to calm down somewhat. Still after thirty-six years we are not yet fully accepted.

This harassment extended to the schools.

When I went to school I had problems everyday. I had a cousin who was darker and always in fights. My younger sister had a problem with a teacher and every morning my sister would scream. She was terrified to go to school. My mother, suspecting racism, took off work and in her broken English went to confront the teacher. My mother asked, "What is the problem that my daughter is so terrified? Is it prejudice?" After that the teacher was nicer. On another occasion the school even came to our house and told my mother not to speak to us in Spanish. What else could she speak to us in?

In response to this situation the Arroyos relied on each other. Their extended family became their community. As Nancy states, "We kept to ourselves. We had a strong family structure. We maintained each other, we partied together, we were always together, we defended each other." The two African-American families who slipped through the cracks and moved to Levittown left after a short stay rather than endure the daily provocation that the Arroyos lived through. Levitt's racist policy reigned. Today Levittown remains primarily a white community.

A few builders, however, began to see minorities as an untapped market. They constructed Cape Cod bungalows, six-room ranch houses, and "custom-built specials" in communities already designated for racial minorities—which on Long Island usually meant African Americans. Builder Thomas Romana, hoping to mine this marginalized market, decided to develop Ronek Park, Long Island, without "regard for race, creed or color." The story of Ronek Park is a sobering story of parallels and divergences between the histories of white and black suburbia.

Romano built 1,000 houses in Ronek Park to be sold for $6,999 a piece. In 1950, when Ronek's Park's first model house was shown, most of the 3,000 people who rushed to see it were African Americans. Some had tried to buy in Levittown. Ann Gilmore and her husband, for instance, recall looking for a house there in 1948: "It was a Sunday, and when we got there . . . well, it was strange because we finally approached a salesman to ask for an application. Well, he didn't say anything, but just walked away from us. It was as if we were invisible." The Gilmores' dream home thus demolished in Levittown was restored by the purchase of a modest ranch house in Ronek Park. The Gilmores were not alone in this experience. James Merrick was living in Harlem when he saw an advertisement for the Ronek Park homes and explained his excitement over buying his first house: "We all had new homes. . . . We had never owned a home, most of us."

By the 1960s integration was the major goal of the growing civil rights movement. Although the South is usually remembered as the focus of the struggle, integration battles were fought in the North, too—even in suburbia itself. A new housing crisis was brewing. This time the question was whether government would use its power to enforce residential integration. Gains had been made in integrating public accommodations, education, and transportation. The riots of that decade made clear that inadequate housing was still a major component of poverty and segregation.

In 1971 George Romney, head of Housing and Urban Development, decided that one solution to urban poverty was to build low-income public housing in the suburbs. The government, however, unwilling to finance public housing, ignored Romney. As in the post—World War II period, the federal government turned to private enterprise, subsidizing the real estate industry and guaranteeing banks low-income mortgages for individual home owners, this time for minorities. President Nixon, in a speech about housing, explained the government's policy, maintained that "we will not seek to impose economic integration upon an existing local jurisdiction; at the same time, we will not countenance any use of economic measures as a subterfuge for racial discrimination." In other words, the federal government would not mandate integration or underwrite new integrated housing developments in suburbia. Nevertheless, African Americans and Hispanics challenged these policies by insisting on their rights to join the great suburban migration.

Between 1940 and 1960 three million African Americans left the still mostly rural South for the cities of the North hoping to find industrial jobs that would let them share in postwar prosperity as well as relief from oppressive and often lethal southern racism. These hopes were kindled by civil rights activism from the late 1950s to the 1970s. At the same time, white people left the cities for the suburbs. Cities became more segregated, crime-ridden, and impoverished. The suburban migration absorbed enormous amounts of federal aid for housing and highways, draining the cities of resources. Meanwhile, however, the civil rights movement inspired new local and federal policies in education, health, social welfare, housing, and law enforcement. These government programs, together with the vast expansion of the civil service sector, helped foster the growth of a new black middle class. From 1960 to 1976 the black middle class tripled in size.

Middle-class black families who sought better housing, schools, and integrated neighborhoods were drawn to the suburbs. Hazel Dukes, a longtime Democratic Party and NAACP activist, explains:

> *They didn't think they were escaping, they were looking for something better for their children. They wanted backyards and frontyards, they wanted a garage for themselves, they wanted comfortable spaces. They didn't want apartments, they wanted houses. People then were getting a salary that wasn't being eaten up in taxes. They could afford a car and could drive back and forth to the city, if they worked there. They wanted good schools for their children, they wanted a better life for their children.*

Long Island's South Shore, particularly the Roosevelt, Freeport, and Hempstead areas, had special allure for black suburbanites. Located close to New York City, convenient to jobs in both the city and the suburbs, the South Shore offered less costly houses and an attractive place to live. Like white suburbanites, some African Americans traded a familiar community for a suburban home. Jean Wyatt, who worked for the motor vehicles bureau, and her husband, who worked for the post office, lived in a deteriorating housing project in Brooklyn. They thought of moving to the suburbs when their son reached the first grade. Jean explains:

> *We thought our son would have a better life in suburbia. We began looking in the newspapers and found a place in Freeport. I transferred my job to Long Island. We were both city kids, but we thought we'd give the suburbs a try. We'd live the suburban dream. We tried it and it was a bit of a dream and a bit of a nightmare. I loved my house, not having to come into an elevator. But I was lonelier here than in the city. The projects were an automatic community, here it was more difficult to make friends and generally people didn't need to be as supportive here.*

Helena White, a schoolteacher, and her husband, an accountant, also lived in the city but felt their children needed more space. They moved into a modern house in Freeport. Her husband wanted to move there because

> *he wanted a house with push buttons and a garage you drive into. . . . He considers himself a successful black professional. Along with that image and a successful self-esteem, there has to be this life style that justifies a reason for going to work every day. It has to have a certain look. That look is a green manicured lawn and a modern house with push-button facilities. My image is different, living in an old house in a more ritzy community like Garden*

City [an exclusive, segregated North Shore community]. But it's his lifestyle ideas that were important when we moved.

Turner Bond moved to New York City from North Carolina. First a share-cropper's son, he moved from the cotton fields of Carolina to the opportunities of the city in the early 1960s. After many years he earned a degree from City College. After several years doing odd jobs, Turner got a job at Con Edison. One dream lingered—his desire to own a house on Long Island. Long Island was portrayed as "the place to be. It was a place where you could raise a good prosperous family, just like on television. The home, the picket fence, Long Island was the epitome of the American dream." After living for years in a housing project in Queens, in 1985 he finally bought a house in Freeport.

Such dreams could be realized only in those suburban communities that had a sizeable black presence. Levittown was closed to African Americans, but the older communities of Roosevelt and Freeport drew African-American families and single people through word of mouth, family ties, and job opportunities. In 1967 the *New York Times* reported that Roosevelt was becoming a racially mixed community where "houses sell anywhere from $15,000 to $50,000. Many of the Negroes who have moved in are college graduates who are teachers, personnel managers and other professionals. Another group is made up of such workers as truck drivers and gardeners."

* * *

The new black middle class originally regarded Roosevelt as a place where integration was possible. John Rice, Jr., a Harvard graduate in 1950 and an Air Force major in the Strategic Air Command in the 1960s, moved into a split-level house in Roosevelt in 1968 with his wife and three children. At the time, all his neighbors were white. He felt he had arrived. Yet within ten years all his white neighbors had moved and his block was inhabited solely by African American families. Parts of Roosevelt, once well-off, became impoverished. One would not know this by looking at his house, his two Jaguars, or his extensive gardens. All his life he sought a place among the American elite, yet in many ways this prospect still eludes him.

John Scott grew up in Roosevelt. He remembers that when he was a boy, "the town was mainly white and most of his friends were white," although he recalls an incident when a white mother refused to let her five-year-old son come out to play with him. "At first I was confused, but came to realize it was due to my race. I was extremely upset because before this incident I was absolutely color-blind." By the time he was in high school, "more and more black people started to come to Roosevelt, there were almost as many blacks as there were whites." After Martin Luther King, Jr., was murdered, "the whites began to notice the many blacks coming to town. Then whites started to leave in great numbers." Scott left too, married, and had four children. Since the couple both had college degrees, they obtained work in the city at the Department of Social Services in 1967. John and his wife wanted to move to Long Island, but in an integrated community. They were turned down for a house in Baldwin and shown a place in a poorer part of town. Ironically, the Scotts now own a house in Roosevelt, where in his own lifetime he experienced the community change from white to integrated to segregated.

In part the transformation of Roosevelt had to do with whites' fears about integration—in the town in general, and the schools in particular. As African-American families moved to Roosevelt, they were steered to the southeast section of town, where a small number of black people already lived. These families enrolled their children in the Theodore Roosevelt elementary school. As black children began attending the school, white parents withdrew their children and enrolled them in the Centennial school on the largely white northeast side of town. By 1965 this led to de facto school segregation. As a result, the Education Department of New York State ordered the integration of the Roosevelt school system by March 1966.

While some white parents accepted integrated schools, others enrolled their children in private or parochial schools, as had been done in the South. By 1967 For Sale signs began to appear in larger numbers. The school integration plan, while somewhat successful, in the end backfired. Even parents satisfied with integration were moving out of Roosevelt. In 1967 Dr. Daniel Terry, superintendent of the Roosevelt school system for eighteen years, told a *New York Times* reporter that while integration had gone very smoothly, "We have no feuds in school, no gangs against the Negroes. It hasn't reached the parents. Many parents have said to me that their child is getting along just fine, but 'we' are going to move anyway. Negro and white children play together on the sidewalks and the community had had no racial disturbances. Still, there will be quite an exodus again at the end of this year."

At the same time, journalists were busy writing sensationalistic stories about Roosevelt that focused on the threat of school busing, the "dumping" of welfare families, and the fear of lowered property values. The media added fuel to white flight. Stories with headlines such as "The Making of a Black Ghetto," "Harlem Comes to Long Island," and "Negroes Invade Roosevelt" played on racial stereotypes and created constant fear on the part of white home owners. To this day local Roosevelt residents blame the media for what happened to their town, particularly what they call "the yellow journalism" of *Newsday*.

To a large degree white flight was helped by a hidden hand. Recognizing that quick money was to be made from these residents and available federal mortages, real estate brokers, agents, and speculators also moved in, employing two strategies that deeply affected black suburban migration: blockbusting and racial steering.

By the early 1960s the South Shore of Long Island was a prime target. Roosevelt is an excellent example of a successfully blockbusted South Shore Long Island community. It is a small, unincorporated village in Nassau County without a local government, train station, or sizeable commercial center. From 1920 to 1960 Roosevelt was a predominantly white middle- and working-class town with a small black community. Then suddenly, overnight, it fell prey to blockbusting and racial steering.

Blockbusting is a tactic real estate agents use to create an unstable housing market through fear and intimidation. Their strategy is to create a climate in which long-term residents sell their houses at lower prices, and agents then can resell homes at higher prices. Blockbusting was used far and wide: the suburbs of Boston, Philadelphia, and Cleveland, for example, all were targets of these campaigns. Through the use of telephones, leaflets, and word of mouth, families were told that the influx of racial and ethnic minorities would make property values plummet, or worse, the real estate agent would say, "You have a twelve-year-old daughter.

What if she were raped? You'd have a mulatto grandchild." Fearful families then would make deals with agents to sell their houses for less than their value. One blockbuster, twenty years later, described what he was told to do:

> We were told you get the listings any way you can. It's pretty easy to do; I just scare the hell out of them. And that's what we did. We were not only making money, we were having fun doing what we were doing. We all liked selling real estate—if you want to call what we were doing selling real estate. And it got to a point that in order to have fun while we were working, we would try to outdo each other with the most outlandish threats that people would believe and chuckle at the end of the day. . . . I had fun at it. I'd go down the street with a [black] buyer and ask, Which house do you want? He'd pick one, and I'd ring the door bell and say, these people want to buy your house. If the lady said no, I'd say the reason they're so interested is that their cousins, aunts, mother, whatever, it's a family of twelve, are moving in across the street, and they want to be near them. Most of the time, that worked. If that didn't work, you'd say their kid just got out of jail for housebreaking, or rape or something that would work.

Blockbusting employs the neighborhood version of the domino theory. Neighbors start to hear that families down the street moved in the middle of the night and before you know it, large numbers of white families become susceptible to the offers of real estate brokers. In some cases blockbusters resorted to extreme measures. "There were instances of housebreaks that were arranged only to scare people out. That was the worst. . . . I don't think anybody to this day is aware that anybody arranged this. Nobody was ever arrested for it, convicted of it, or anything else.

Before 1968 brokers and speculators benefited by a game called multiple mortgages. As New York Secretary of State John Lomenzo testified before the Senate Judiciary Committee, "Let's say the market value of the house was $15,000. The speculator would offer to buy it for $10,000, all cash with the homeowners readily accepting as they became panicked." The next step is to offer it at double the price or more to a minority family with the incentive of an automatic mortgage qualification with no money down. The plan is backed by a complex scheme of buying triple money mortgages on the purchased house and selling them to banks and insurance agencies at discounts. The broker then could make a profit of nearly 90 percent. The major flaw is that the high mortgages carried by the minority family are usually far in excess of the worth of the property, making default of payment a constant worry.

Yvonne Simmons, one of the few black real estate agents on Long Island, explained how this happened in Roosevelt:

> The houses were less out here. Real estate agents would steer black people to certain areas and the white people got nervous as they do sometimes. The real estate agents wanted to make money and this was the way to do it; to steer people to certain areas and create fear in white home owners. It's all about money. For people that were prejudiced, this was like pushing their buttons. This was great for the people doing the steering. There are myths that when blacks move into an area, the property values go downhill.

These prejudices are precisely what blockbusters count on. Simmons went on:

> *Frightened people would sell cheap, they would try to get the most they could, but their overriding desire is to leave. On the other hand, blacks wanted better living conditions than they had in the city. They wanted their kids to go to better schools. So the brokers would sell to blacks at inflated prices, really upping the price. After a while some families who couldn't really afford it would get into financial trouble and lose their houses. But the brokers were long gone.*

Another profitable blockbusting tactic real estate agents use is moving welfare families to a neighborhood. These families, residents are told, have no stake in the preservation and upkeep of their homes or community, and property values will plunge. Fast money is made this way. In Roosevelt, for instance, most of the houses originally were one-family dwellings. Landlords and real estate speculators illegally subdivided single-family houses. Then each subdivision was offered to the county's welfare department which ignored the law and tripled the rent. Willie Pyatt, father of eight, told a *New York Times* reporter that he had had difficulties finding an apartment for his family in communities other than Roosevelt. Mr. Pyatt said that the welfare department had put him in a subdivided house, paying $200 for five bottom rooms. In all, the welfare department was paying $3,600 a month to an absentee landlord on behalf of the house's eighteen occupants. Pyatt said that "The Welfare Department is spreading the cancer by putting four or five families in a one family house and paying exorbitant rents for them."

Yvonne Simmons confirms Pyatt's observation and blames the Nassau County welfare department for placing large numbers of welfare families in Roosevelt.

> *It's the fault of people in power. The county is in charge of the welfare system. If you have welfare families it would seem that you could divide them equitably, so that there wouldn't be a whole influx of them in one area. So many landed in Roosevelt. Of course when people don't own their own homes they tend not to take care of them as well as someone who can afford to take care of them. If you get your welfare check and you have a certain amount of money for A, B, C, and D, when it comes to getting some grass seed for the lawn, they're not going to think about that; they just think about survival.*

In addition to blockbusting, racial steering helped ensure ongoing segregation. Real estate brokers and agents designated certain communities as either white or black. No matter what community a family desired to live in, they would be taken to communities brokers and agents deemed racially appropriate. To attract particular constituencies, real estate agents advertised in papers such as the *Amsterdam News* in New York City and in southern papers read by blacks. Billboards on major roads leading out of southern cities showed black families living in attractive suburban houses in Roosevelt. Similarly, whites were shown houses in white communities, even if they asked about other towns. Ads in newspapers and magazines read mainly by whites displayed images of white suburban home ownersp.

Alvin Dorfman, a lawyer with a long history of civil rights work in Freeport, and his wife, Shelly, a community activist, moved to Freeport from Brooklyn in 1963. They wanted to buy a house in an integrated neighborhood, but "the real estate agent wouldn't show us houses in black areas. When we pressed them, they showed us poor houses in Roosevelt and a few that were much too expensive. Then they showed us good houses in Freeport, near the Baldwin school district, an all-white neighborhood."

In contrast, Ivan and Cynthia Ashby, who moved to Brooklyn from Barbados, wanted to move to Long Island when they had a child. The decision was tough for Cynthia; she didn't want to leave her family and friends. In 1977 the Ashbys went to a real estate agent because they were interested in buying a house in Baldwin on Long Island. "The real estate agent showed little interest in us and what we wanted because we were black. The neighborhood was all white and the house was expensive, but we had good credit to get a mortgage. We did show a great deal of interest in the house, but the agent sold that house to someone else. We still pass by the house every once in a while and see what could have been." Eventually the Ashbys bought a house in Freeport, which Cynthia was excited about, but Ivan "was so deeply concerned about the mortgage payments that he lost a great deal of weight."

Louise Simpson, who worked at the Federal Reserve Board, and her husband, who worked for the post office, had to move from their Brooklyn project because they were earning too much according to housing authority guidelines. She recalls:

> We had to move. I really wanted to live near the city but since there were no fair housing ordinances in 1960, we didn't find any houses close to the city. We were steered to northeastern Freeport, really a part of Roosevelt. We were going to move to Lakeview, which was also being developed, but I felt the realtor pulled a deal and we ended up here. I'm sure I could not have purchased a house except in northeast Freeport.

Ramona Crooks, who was head of the Freeport antiblockbusting real estate agency, explains,

> There were brokers in Massapequa, brokers in Seaford, brokers in Merrick [nearby non-integrated towns], and when a black person went to them, they weren't going to show them a house in Seaford or Merrick. Most black people I interviewed wanted to live in an integrated neighborhood, but if you and your wife were black, if you went to a broker in Massapequa, you'd end up buying a house in Roosevelt or Freeport.

Racial steering was so successful that it exists as a real estate tactic to this day.

Racial steering and blockbusting shattered Roosevelt. Local residents almost uniformly describe the transformation of their town as an instant event, quick as a prairie fire. Blockbusting in fact takes considerable time. In Roosevelt it took at least fifteen years. In 1957 the population of Roosevelt was 80 percent white and 20 percent black. In 1967 it was 60 percent white and 40 percent black. By 1980 it was 80 percent black.

Blockbusting, however, did not occur without a struggle. The Roosevelt Community Relations Council, organized by Catholic, Jewish, Protestant, and other community leaders, worked hard to counteract fear and intimidation. Initiatives came from religious leaders, as Roosevelt was an unincorporated village in the town of Hempstead and had no political structure of its own. In Hempstead, political life was dominated by a Republican machine, unresponsive to integration and essentially racist. The council sent out the following call to Roosevelt residents in 1963:

> *For some time, a group of community leaders, both white and Negro, and the clergymen representing the churches of our community, have been meeting to discuss the real estate situation in Roosevelt. We are aware that certain real estate dealers have been using Roosevelt to effect the "fast sell" of homes. They have been doing this by cards left under doors, by phone calls, and by other more dramatic means of pressure, commonly referred to as blockbusting.*
>
> *The "Block Buster" is a dealer in real estate who gets people scared about property values by promoting rumors of invasion by minority groups such as Negroes. He buys their property for a song and resells for a large profit. He tries to panic a great number of families into listing their homes. His tools are ignorance, fear, falsehoods and rumors.*

The council advised residents to stand firm, resist the real estate brokers' high pressure and bring them to the attention of the council. If selling is necessary, residents were told, be sure to be represented by someone who knows your interests. If family homes are used by more than one family in your area, bring it to the attention of your clergyman. The council reiterated that "both the white and Negro populace are interested in keeping our town inhabited by God-fearing, law-abiding and loyal Americans."

By 1967 another group, the United Civic Organization (UCO), composed of twenty civic, fraternal, and church groups, also was working to discourage blockbusting and maintain the 60 percent to 40 percent race ratio. One UCO member, Arthur Choice, who ran a successful local fuel oil business, summed up the feelings of many black residents: "There's one thing I don't understand. The view that just because Negroes are moving in, the town will turn into a ghetto. This is insulting to the Negro." UCO's program called for federal intervention in the form of money to maintain racial balance and an end to blockbusting in all its forms—including the collusion between the Nassau County Department of Welfare and greedy absentee landlords who were placing welfare families in houses recently abandoned by whites. But Morton Decker, UCO's president, was doubtful about his organization's power to stop white flight. "How do you get through to white people who have stereotyped images and have never really known a Negro socially?"

In spite of these community actions, by 1980 Roosevelt was 80 percent black, economically depressed, educationally deprived, and widely regarded as a ghetto—though not all Roosevelt home owners agree. Community organizations and churches have active memberships. Ruth Grefe, one of the remaining white residents, finds Roosevelt to be a hospitable community. With her husband, Grefe built her own house in Roosevelt in the 1940s. The Grefes raised a family and were pillars of their church and community. In the 1960s the Grefes did not succumb to the blockbusting scare; they stayed in Roosevelt, as they had permanent roots there—Ruth's family was one of the founders. Even after her husband died Roosevelt remained her town. Her neighbors look in on her and help her out, and she has many friends. She is still active in her church, where she is one of three white members. She describes Roosevelt not as a ghetto but as "a big family where everyone cares for everyone else."

America's foremost community organizer, Saul Alinsky, once caustically observed that "integration is the time between when the first black family moves in and the last white family moves out." This still rings true in many cases, and suburban segregation confirms the pattern. Only the tactics change, and most of Long Island—as well as the nation's suburbs—remain segregated, regardless of attempts to reverse the course. Sometimes, however, communities learn from the failures of others and successfully beat back the blockbusters, creating integrated communities. Freeport is one such town.

Black Power

Allen J. Matusow

The history of black protest in the 1960s bore striking resemblance to the history of the new left, moving as it did from liberal hope to radical disillusionment. But there was a difference. Unlike white leftists, black protesters never doubted that they were true outcasts in America. It mattered not that progress in alleviating racial discrimination was occurring. Progress was part of the problem. As liberal accomplishment in racial reform fell short of expectations, an embittered minority of black Americans commenced the journey from civil rights to black nationalism. The quickening impulse toward racial separatism found expression at mid-decade both in the slogan "black power" and, more ambiguously, in the great ghetto riots then convulsing the cities of the nation. The task confronting nationalist spokesmen was obvious—to convert black power from slogan to ideology and thereby to harness the furies of the ghetto for a sustained social movement. How black power evolved out of the civil rights movement and then failed the ideological challenge was one of the decade's more melancholy stories.

I

It was the story, in large measure, of the Student Nonviolent Coordinating Committee, which remained through the decade on the cutting edge of the black revolution. SNCC was born in the spring of 1960 when the leaders of the sit-in movement formed a body to coordinate their scattered efforts. Mostly students from southern black colleges, the original members were thoroughly imbued with liberal values and beliefs, including racial integration, nonviolence, the beneficence of the federal government, and the blessings of making it in middle-class America. Integrate the lunch counters, they said, and first-class citizenship would follow. At SNCC's founding meeting in Raleigh, May 1960, Miss Ella Baker of the Southern Christian Leadership Conference tried to warn the students that it would take "more than a hamburger," that they would have to expand their social vision. "Aw," they retorted, "ain't nothing more to it than a hamburger. If we can eat this hamburger, everything will be straight." In fact, in the course of the coming years, they would put to the test each of their liberal premises and find good reasons for rejecting them all.

SNCC remained only briefly an instrument to achieve the aspirations of the black bourgeoisie. In 1961, with strong encouragement from the Kennedy administration, the organization headed into the Deep South to register black voters. No longer the extracurricular activity of college students, SNCC became an organization of sixty to eighty paid full-time staff members, working for $20 a week, mainly in southwest Georgia and Mississippi. Its purpose was to achieve political power for the black masses rather than to desegregate public facilities. Participatory democracy was SNCC's implicit goal, anarchism its intuitive philosophy. The hardships its members suffered, the unremitting terrors they endured, knit them into a close fraternity—"a band of brothers, a circle of trust." Respectful of their illiterate constituents, arrogant toward outsiders, dressed in the denim overalls of the poor, SNCC learned to see the world from the bottom up, and as it did, scornfully rejected middle-class aspirations. Gradually the radical conviction took hold that a nation which tolerated Mississippi's poverty and racism was fundamentally flawed.

Among the goals that SNCC came to repudiate was racial integration. The problem was not so much the southern racists who frankly declared their hatred, but the northern whites who risked their lives to join the struggle. There had been whites in the organization from the start, but SNCC's great interracial experiment really began in the fall of 1963, when one hundred Yale and Stanford students worked for two weeks in a mock gubernatorial election that turned out eighty thousand disfranchised Mississippi blacks. SNCC leaders were sufficiently impressed by the students' contribution to propose inviting hundreds more into the state in 1964 for a Freedom Summer—envisioned as a massive biracial assault on the segregation system. But, when the idea came up for debate in SNCC, a substantial number of black members expressed resentment against the growing proportion of whites in the organization (20 percent of 150 members in 1964) and the tendency of whites to take over positions of leadership. Only the personal intervention of Robert Moses, the director of the voting project in Mississippi, rescued the proposal from defeat.

A black Harlemite with a master's degree in philosophy from Harvard, Moses commanded unusual respect by virtue of his courage, intelligence, and selflessness. "There was something about him, the manner in which he carried himself, that seemed to draw all of us to him . . ." SNCC's Cleveland Sellers wrote. "He had emerged as the kind of person we wanted to be." Moses settled the argument over Freedom Summer by announcing, "I will not be part of a racist organization." David Dennis of CORE, who worked closely with Moses on the summer project, admitted later that more than idealism lay behind Moses's desire to import whites into the state. "We knew that if we had brought in a thousand blacks, the country would have watched them slaughtered without doing anything about it. . . . If there were gonna take some deaths to do it, the death of a white college student would bring on more attention to what was going on than for a black college student getting it. . . . You see . . . we were in a war."

Freedom Summer began on June 8, 1964, when seven hundred selected students judged by a staff psychiatrist from MIT to be an "extraordinarily healthy bunch of kids" came to Oxford, Ohio, for two weeklong training sessions. From the start racial relations were uneasy. The students, most of whom were white, expected gratitude for having enlisted their bodies in the cause. The staff, most of whom were black, barely masked their antagonism. Tension seethed under the surface for some days, until one evening white students watching a racist voting registrar on the TV news broke into derisive laughter. Six SNCC people, infuriated by what they regarded as an insensitive response, stalked out of the room. In the discussion that followed, the students complained that the staff were distant and uncommunicative and "looked down on us for not having been through what they had." A staff member replied,

> *If you get mad at us for walking out, just wait until they break your head in, and see if you don't have something to get mad about. Ask Jimmy Travis over there what he thinks about the project. What does he think about Mississippi. He has six slugs in him, man, and the last one went through the back of his neck when he was driving a car outside Greenwood. Ask Jesse here—he has been beaten so that we wouldn't recognize him time and time and time and time again. If you don't get scared, pack up and get the hell out of here because we don't need any favors of people who don't know what they are doing here in the first place.*

Bitter words these, but they had a cathartic effect, and the meeting culminated in emotional singing. Said one volunteer, "The crisis is past, I think."

Hardly. On June 22 Moses quietly informed the volunteers at Oxford that three project workers who had entered Neshoba County, Mississippi, the day before had not been heard from since. One was Michael Schwerner, a white social worker who operated the CORE office in Meridian; the second was James Chaney, a twenty-one-year-old black Mississippian and CORE worker; and the third was Andrew Goodman, a white college student from New York, who had just completed his orientation in Ohio. Responding to widespread public outrage, President Johnson at last took federal action in Mississippi, dispatching FBI agents, military helicopters, and two hundred sailors to hunt for the missing. What kind of a nation was it—embittered SNCC workers asked—that mourned only when a white boy died?

Despite a racist reign of terror that accounted for more than one thousand arrests, eighty beatings, and thirty-seven burned churches, white volunteers and black staff stuck it out for the rest of the summer. But relations between them did not improve. A woman student wrote that the staff "were automatically suspicious of us, the white volunteers; throughout the summer they put us to the test, and few, if any, could pass. . . . It humbled, if not humiliated, me to realize that *finally they will never accept me.*" Meanwhile, the project sponsored Freedom Schools for 3,000 children, registered 1,600 black voters, and above all signed up 80,000 disfranchised blacks as members of the newly created Mississippi Freedom Democratic party.

The Freedom Democrats bet their chips on SNCC's alliance with white liberals, particularly politicians in the Democratic party. That alliance was already under terrific strain because of the administration's steadfast refusal to furnish civil rights workers with physical protection. The Freedom Democratic party offered white liberals their last chance to prove good faith. Since the regular Mississippi Democrats excluded blacks, Moses conceived the Freedom Democrats as an extralegal alternative capable of challenging the white monopoly of political power in the state. Built by the book from the precinct up, the party held a convention early in August and selected sixty-eight delegates, four of them white, to attend the Democratic Convention in Atlantic City, there to challenge the credentials of the regulars and win recognition as the only legitimate Democratic party in the state. On the eve of the national convention SNCC had enough liberals lined up at least to get the issue out of the credentials committee and onto the convention floor. But, once Lyndon Johnson made known his opposition to the Freedom party's claims, SNCC's liberal support melted away. Angry SNCC people, refusing to compromise, got on the buses to go home, convinced that white liberals had cynically sold them out. After Atlantic City, Cleveland Sellers wrote, SNCC's goal was no longer civil rights but "liberation."

Along with racial integration and the alliance with liberals, SNCC also abandoned non-violence. SNCC's commitment to nonviolence had always been more tactical than philosophical, and some members had long packed guns in defiance of policy. Even among believers the willingness to remain passive in the face of unrelenting terror eventually wore thin. In August 1964 the shallow graves of Schwerner, Chaney, and Goodman were discovered in Neshoba County. At their funeral in Jackson, CORE's David Dennis, who had been traveling through the state urging blacks to "Put your gun down," broke down in anger. "I'm sick and tired of going to the funerals of black men who have been murdered by white men . . ." he said, weeping. "I've got vengeance in my heart tonight. . . . If you go back home and sit down and take what these white men in Mississippi are doing to us . . . if you take it and don't do something about it . . . then God damn your souls."

In the fall of 1964 SNCC underwent something akin to a collective nervous breakdown, not only because it had lost direction and was suffering battle fatigue, but because the years of nonviolence had begun to exact a high psychological toll. Alvin Poussaint, a black psychiatrist close to SNCC, listened to black civil rights workers who had been beaten by whites insist that they loved those who beat them. "Now, what do they really do with their rage?" he wondered. In time, Poussaint reported, many of those who had been "talking about being nonviolent and 'loving the sheriff' that had just hit them over the head," began rampaging "around the project houses beating up each other. I frequently had to calm Negro civil-rights workers with large doses of tranquilizers for what I can describe clinically only as acute attacks of rage." By 1965 the days of nonviolence in SNCC were clearly numbered, and when at last they would be gone, the long accumulated rage would find its inevitable target in the entire white race.

One symptom of the growing malaise in SNCC was the emergence after Freedom Summer, for the first time, of factional conflicts. James Forman, the organization's executive secretary and the glue that kept it together, hoped to transform SNCC into a disciplined cadre devoted to building a mass-based political party. Bob Moses, truer to the original anarchist impulse, believed that SNCC should remain an informal group of community organizers who "go where the spirit say go, do what the spirit say do." At a staff meeting in Atlanta in February 1965, Forman's "hardliners" took control and began to impose a modicum of order, prompting many of "the floaters" gathered around Moses subsequently to drift away from the organization. One night during the Atlanta meeting, after passing around some cheese and an empty wine bottle, Moses announced that, to relieve the pressures on him, he was changing his name to Robert Parris (his middle name). In the course of the next year, no longer speaking to whites, he gradually cut his ties with SNCC and then disappeared into Africa.

Though SNCC initiated some new projects after the Atlanta meeting, Mississippi remained the major theater of struggle. In 1965, uncertain of what else to do, the organization made the curious decision to invite northern students back into the state. That summer the arrival of three hundred whites reduced SNCC's Mississippi projects to a shambles. Racial tensions caused some projects to break up and prevented serious work in others. Problems only dimly perceived a year before now assumed stark clarity. At staff meetings blacks would silence whites with such remarks as "How long have you been here?" and "How do you know what it's like being black?" and "If you don't like the way we do it, get the hell out of the state." Not all the blame for the breakdown belonged to the staff, however. The questionable motivation of some white students led Alvin Poussaint to add a new neurosis to medical terminology—the white African Queen or Tarzan complex. The victim of this neurosis harbored repressed delusions of himself as an "intelligent, brave, and handsome white man or woman, leading the poor down-trodden and oppressed black men to freedom and salvation."

The worst problem, not surprisingly, turned out to be sex. White women, Poussaint reported, found themselves "at the center of an emotionally shattering crossfire of racial tensions that have been nurtured for centuries." A veteran worker tried to explain what happened when a Mississippi black man encountered a white woman in a civil rights project. "What you have here is a man who had no possible way of being a man in the society in which he lives, save one. And that's the problem. . . . He's just trying to find his manhood and he goes especially to the places that have robbed him of it. . . . And so in a sense, what passes itself as desire is probably a combination of hostility and resentment—because he resents what the society has done to him and he wants to take it out on somebody who symbolizes the establishment of society." A white woman reported at the end of summer, "Well, I think that the white female should be very well prepared before she comes down here to be bombarded, and she also has to be well prepared to tell them to go to hell and be prepared to have them not give up. . . . I've never met such forward men as I have in Mississippi." The problem was complicated by the jealousy of black women toward their white rivals and by neurotic whites who sought to ease their guilt by permitting blacks to exploit them sexually and financially. On leaving the state, a few white women told Poussaint, "I hate Negroes." By the end of the summer of 1965 there was no doubt that many SNCC people reciprocated the feeling.

As its commitment to the goals of the civil rights movement dimmed, SNCC became attracted to its opposite—black nationalism—gradually placed in an anti-imperialist framework. As early as the spring of 1964 SNCC chairman John Lewis, a theology student closer to Martin Luther King's views than was any other person in the organization, noted approvingly that blacks were now identifying with people of color throughout the world. "There's been a radical change in our people since 1960," Lewis said; "the way they dress, the music they listen to, their natural hairdos—all of them want to go to Africa." In September 1964, as guest of singer Harry Belafonte, several SNCC leaders including Lewis, Moses, Forman, Julian Bond, and Fannie Lou Hamer took a trip to Guinea in "Mother Africa," as Forman called it, and rejoiced to see competent black people running their own affairs. "There were no sheriffs to dread," Forman remarked, "no Klan breathing down your neck, no climate of constant repression." In February 1965 Lewis declared that whether in Angola or Harlem, Mozambique or Mississippi, "the struggle is . . . the same. . . . It is a struggle against a vicious and evil system that is controlled and kept in order for and by a few white men throughout the world." That spring at an antiwar teach-in at Berkeley, Moses declared himself to be "a member of the Third World," linked the struggle of Vietnamese peasants to that of black Mississippians, and proposed the study of racial oppression in the South as the best way to learn how this country "plans and executes murders elsewhere in the world." In January 1966 SNCC became the first civil rights group to speak out against the war, issuing a statement in support of draft resistance and denouncing the government for its efforts to squash "liberation movements."

The man who would articulate most forcefully the emerging tendencies in SNCC and assure their dominance was Stokely Carmichael. A native of the black Caribbean island of Trinidad, who immigrated to Harlem at age eleven, Carmichael had been a self-described radical ever since his days as a student at the Bronx High School of Science, where he had read Marx and consorted with white leftists. In September 1960 he entered Howard University and immediately plunged into the civil rights movement. As a freshman he spent Christmas vacation helping evicted sharecroppers in Fayette County, Tennessee, served forty-nine days in jail for freedom riding, and spent his summer vacation working in McComb, Mississippi, registering black voters with Bob Moses. Throughout his college years Carmichael devoted nearly every weekend to demonstrating and every summer to organizing in Mississippi. Much of the time he was in jail. During a 1964 confrontation with the National Guard in Cambridge, Maryland, he swallowed so much gas he almost died.

Handsome, volatile, eloquent and fearless, Carmichael became a magnet in SNCC for the militants and proto-nationalists. He was one of the first in the organization to challenge the philosophy of nonviolence, triumphantly reminding a minister during one argument, "Jesus said, 'I come to bring the sword, not the shield, and no remission of sin without the shedding of blood.'" When Moses proposed bringing whites into Mississippi for Freedom Summer in 1964, Carmichael opposed him. When Carmichael lost that argument, he announced that no white volunteers would be welcome in the 2nd Congressional District, where he was project leader. After he failed to recruit enough black students to do the work, Carmichael agreed to accept whites, but only on condition that they train blacks, not replace them. When SNCC decided to press the case of the Mississippi Freedom Democratic party in Atlantic City, Carmichael objected because once again blacks would be petitioning whites for redress of grievances. Blacks needed a political party that would go it alone, he insisted. After the Democrats dashed SNCC's hopes, as Carmichael knew they would, he moved to Lowndes County, Alabama, where blacks constituted 80 percent of the residents but none of the registered voters. There he founded an all-black political party—the Lowndes County Freedom Organization—which took as its symbol the black panther and had as its object control of the county government. Ironically he got nowhere until federal examiners, acting under the 1965 Voting Rights Act, entered the county and began enrolling black voters. The issue for the new voters in Lowndes was whether to join Carmichael's Panthers or the Democrats. Among those refusing to support the Panthers was SNCC's own chairman, John Lewis, an opponent of separatist tendencies, who spoke statewide over the radio during the 1966 Alabama primary election for the Democratic party. "After that," Carmichael recalled, "I wanted his blood." Enough blacks voted for the Panthers in the primary to assure the party a place on the November ballot.

In May 1966, only days after his recent triumph in Lowndes, Carmichael joined 130 others in Kingston Springs, Tennessee, for SNCC's annual staff meeting. His purpose was to replace John Lewis as chairman. In truth, Lewis was little more than a figurehead who played virtually no role in administering the organization, serving mostly as a spokesman and fund-raiser. But, because Lewis was out of touch with the rising nationalist sentiment in SNCC, Carmichael felt he had to go. In the end Carmichael's faction succeeded in overturning one vote in favor of Lewis and winning the chairmanship for Carmichael himself on the next ballot. SNCC then issued a statement calling among other things for "black Americans to begin building independent political, economic, and cultural institutions that they will control and use as instruments of social change in this country."

A few weeks later the full import of Carmichael's election became clear to the whole nation. The occasion was the famous Meredith March through Mississippi in June 1966. James Meredith, the man who integrated the University of Mississippi in 1962 with the help of the United States Army, embarked on a 220-mile walk from Memphis to Jackson to show the black people of Mississippi that they could walk to the voting booths without fear. On June 6, twenty-eight miles out of Memphis, a white man felled Meredith with buckshot. Erroneously believing that Meredith had been killed, civil rights leaders immediately flew to Mississippi to continue his walk against fear. So it was that arm in arm Martin Luther King of SCLC, Floyd McKissick of CORE, and Stokely Carmichael of SNCC marched down U.S. Highway 51.

Early efforts of the three leaders to maintain surface unity rapidly disintegrated. Significantly, the first issue that divided them was the role of white people in the Meredith march. King's workers publicly thanked northern whites for joining the procession. McKissick also thanked the northerners but announced that blacks must now lead the civil rights movement. And Carmichael mused aloud that maybe the whites should go home. As the column moved onto the back roads and southern white hostility increased, the leadership of the march failed to agree on how to respond to violence. At the Neshoba County courthouse, Dr. King, conducting a memorial service for Goodman, Chaney, and Schwerner amid three hundred jeering whites, said he believed in his heart that the murderers were "somewhere around me at this moment." Declaring that "I am not afraid of any man," he then delivered a Christian sermon. But, after the service was over and local whites got rough, the marchers returned punch for punch.

The real spokesman for the march turned out to be Carmichael. In Greenwood, after spending a few hours in jail, Carmichael told the crowd, "This is the 27th time I have been arrested—I ain't going to jail no more. I ain't going to jail no more. Every courthouse in Mississippi ought to be burned down to get rid of the dirt." Carmichael then issued the cry that made him famous. Five times he shouted, "We want black power!" and, the *New York Times* reported, "each time the younger members of the audience shouted back, 'Black power.'" Informed of this new slogan, Dr. King expressed disapproval, and SCLC workers exhorted crowds to call not for black power but for "freedom now." By the end of the march the new cry had drowned out the old.

Instantly the black power slogan—uttered in a sleepy Mississippi town by a virtual unknown—caused a national furor, mainly because fearful whites sensed the racial animosity it implied. Few who denounced it understood the concrete historical circumstances that both produced the slogan and made it explicable. SNCC had believed in integration and tried it within its own organization, but black and whites together had not worked. "Integration," said Carmichael, "is a subterfuge for the maintenance of white supremacy" and "reinforces, among both black and white, the idea that 'white' is automatically better and 'black' is by definition inferior." SNCC had allied with white liberals, only to discover that whenever it suited their convenience they would betray powerless blacks. In dealing with blacks, Carmichael said, white liberals "perpetuate a paternalistic, colonial relationship." SNCC had tried nonviolence and found it not only ineffective but psychologically destructive. The "days of the free head-whipping are over," Carmichael wrote. "Black people should and must fight back." And SNCC had shed its blood for legal equality only to conclude that the main problem for blacks was not the unfair application of the laws but economic and social inequalities embedded in society itself. But what did black power imply beyond rejection of a failed liberalism? What blueprint for the salvation of the black masses, if any, did it offer? Having proclaimed the notorious slogan, Carmichael was soon besieged by critics and constituents alike demanding elaboration of its meaning.

II

This was no easy task. Though black nationalism had been an intermittent force among American blacks for a century, none of its spokesmen had ever explained how the goal of racial separation could be accomplished practically. Nationalism in general implied a historic connection between a people with a distinct culture and a nation, a homeland. But black nationalists claimed a historic link with Africa, which was a continent, not a nation, and possessed not one culture but a melange of cultures. African cultural connections, moreover, would largely have to be fabricated, since generations in America had turned Africans into Americans. The desire of the nationalists to separate was no doubt genuine, but what could separation logically mean except returning to Africa, which, for a population of millions, was wholly impractical? As Carmichael and a host of other nationalist intellectuals wrestled with these riddles, they looked for inspiration above all to the thought and lives of two men—Malcolm X and Frantz Fanon.

Malcolm Little was a Harlem hustler who was convicted of burglary in 1946 at the age of twenty-one and then redeemed in prison by the Nation of Islam, popularly known as the Black Muslims. Paroled in 1952, he became Malcolm X, a Muslim minister and protégé of the Muslim leader, Elijah Muhammad. By 1960, operating from his temple in Harlem, Malcolm had emerged as America's favorite bad nigger, a fiercely proud black man who used his oratorical gifts and razor-sharp wit to articulate ghetto rage. Malcolm's popularity among poor blacks owed little to his Muslim theology, which consisted of a fantastic description of how an evil scientist thousands of years ago used genetics to create white devils out of black people; nor was his appeal owing to his strict Muslim moral code, which condemned such pleasures as pork, alcohol, gambling, and fornication. He had no political program, radical or otherwise, and his economics were a black variant of the Protestant ethic.

Malcolm was a hero because, with no hint of fear and before almost anyone else, he dared confront the blue-eyed devils and accuse them of their crimes. To black men filled with shame, Malcolm preached race pride; for those without hope in racist America he called unequivocally for separation from the white man, either by returning to Africa or by exclusive occupation of territory within the United States. No man, white or black, was more scornful than he of the civil rights movement and its goal of racial integration. While Martin Luther King was inspiring America at the 1963 March on Washington with his dream, Malcolm X was saying,

> *Whoever heard of angry revolutionists all harmonizing "We Shall Overcome . . . . Suum Day . . . while tripping and swaying along arm-in-arm with the very people they were supposed to be angrily revolting against? Who ever heard of angry revolutionists swinging their bare feet together with their oppressor in lily-pad park pools, with gospels and guitars and "I Have a Dream" speeches?*

While police were clubbing SNCC workers in Mississippi, Malcolm was saying, "If someone puts a hand on you send him to the cemetery." While SNCC was pondering the meaning of Atlantic City, Malcolm was saying, "We *need* a Mau Mau. If they don't want to deal with the Mississippi Freedom Democratic Party, then we'll give them something else to deal with."

Unfortunately for Malcolm, his growing prominence aroused jealousy among Muslim leaders, including apparently Elijah Muhammad, who silenced him late in 1963 and eased him out of the organization in the spring of 1964. Freed by necessity from Muslim dogma, Malcolm spent the last year of his life groping for a new position, exploring new ideas, even making the remarkable discovery on a pilgrimage to Mecca that not all white men were devils. But he remained an uncompromising nationalist, convinced that most white Americans were irredeemably racist and that Africa was the true homeland of his people. When an interviewer asked him in December 1964 where he was heading, Malcolm replied, "I have no idea. I can capsulize how I feel—I'm for the freedom of the 22 million Afro-Americans by any means necessary. By any means necessary." Two months later he was gunned down in Harlem by his Muslim enemies. Every angry nationalist who came afterward acknowledged Malcolm as a model and honored him for the honest expression of his hatred.

Malcolm was not a revolutionary, though he might have become one. Frantz Fanon was. A black native of the French colonial island of Martinique, then a psychiatric student in Paris, Fanon knew European racism and colonialism firsthand, which was why, when he went to Algeria to practice his profession, he eventually joined the rebels in the Algerian war for independence. In 1961 as he lay dying of leukemia in a Washington hospital, Fanon's most famous book, *The Wretched of the Earth*, was published in Paris. This was his attempt to distill the lessons of the Algerian war for anticolonial movements everywhere. In 1965 an English translation appeared in the United States, just in time to influence emergent black nationalism.

Though Fanon explicitly disavowed "negritude" as the basis for a revolutionary nationalism, black militants in America nonetheless hailed him as a prophet because *The Wretched of the Earth* offered a passionate defense of the violence to which they were increasingly drawn. The violence of colonial rule made counterviolence inevitable, Fanon argued, violence the native could turn either self-destructively inward or outward against the oppressor. Violence alone could purge the native's land of the colonial presence, even as it could transform those whom colonialism had rendered infantile into men. "At the level of individuals, violence is a cleansing force," he wrote. "It frees the native from his inferiority complex and from his despair and inaction; it makes him fearless and restores his self-respect." It was a simple, if misleading, step for American nationalists to argue that ghettos were analogous to colonies and could be liberated in the same way. Thus did *The Wretched of the Earth* provide militants with an apologia for the ghetto riots. "You'd better get this book," Dan Watts of the black magazine *Liberator* told journalists during the hot summer of 1967. "Every brother on a rooftop can quote Fanon."

Drawing on history, experience, and thinkers as diverse as Malcolm and Fanon, leading nationalists now attempted to develop an ideology relevant to the situation of contemporary Afro-Americans. Carmichael himself had possessed nothing approaching a real ideology when he first proclaimed black power, and during the year of his SNCC chairmanship he literally had to think out loud to manufacture one. The results of his ruminations were less than intellectually impressive, but had at least this merit: at one time or another, Carmichael advanced the three main nationalist positions—the pluralist, the cultural, and the revolutionary—despite the fact that each was incompatible with the others.

Stung by the nationwide denunciation of black power, Carmichael's initial reaction was to seek safe refuge behind the pluralist interpretation of his slogan. Just as European ethnic groups had done, he argued, blacks should turn inward and develop cohesive community institutions of their own—for example, schools, interest groups, businesses—so that when they turned outward to participate in America's pluralist society, they could do so from a position of strength. Politically, this meant avoiding unequal coalitions with whites inside the two major parties and creating instead independent freedom parties whenever possible. Once organized as a separate political force, blacks might consider allying with whites for mutually beneficial purposes. But, Carmichael emphasized, "let any ghetto group contemplating coalition be so tightly organized, so strong that . . . it is an 'indigestible body' which cannot be absorbed or swallowed up." The rhetoric all sounded reassuringly American, except that Carmichael envisioned an unlikely coalition of poor whites and poor blacks to achieve a radical reconstruction of the nation's economic and social life.

At the same time that he posed as a traditional pluralist, Carmichael was also defining black power as essentially a matter of culture. It did not bother him that, while the pluralist vision assumed some ultimate common interest with whites, cultural nationalism emphasized fundamental differences in values and ways of living. Whites had maintained their dominance over blacks, Carmichael argued, by brainwashing them into accepting their own inferiority—by inculcating in them shame of race. The first task of black people, therefore, was to undertake psychological reconstruction by uncovering their cultural roots, rediscovering their African heritage, and learning from history that they were a "vibrant, valiant people." Hence the vogue among blacks during the sixties of afros, Swahili, dashikis, and black-studies programs in the universities. Some cultural nationalists stressed the cultural differences between white Americans and Afro-Americans: blacks had "soul," whites did not. Carmichael's cultural nationalism, on the other hand, transcended America and emphasized the common African heritage of blacks everywhere. By the end of the decade he would become a passionate Pan-Africanist who believed blacks should return to Africa and who would even go to live there himself.

But, before he embraced Pan-Africanism, Carmichael enjoyed a brief fling as a revolutionary nationalist. This was an especially odd variant of black nationalism, much influenced by Fanon and stressing not negritude but the common struggle of all Third World peoples—yellow, brown, and black—against Western capitalist imperialism. Carmichael's anti-imperialist phase emerged in the radical summer of 1967 against the backdrop of cities on fire. It was then that he affirmed the solidarity of Afro-Americans with other oppressed people and declared willingness to join the global struggle against Yankee imperialism. Though he soon moved in a different direction, his successor as SNCC chairman, H. Rap Brown, seriously advocated an anti-imperialist guerrilla war in the ghetto to free the Afro-American colony. Revolutionary nationalists dismissed cultural nationalism as "pork-chop" nationalism and its emphasis on African culture as reactionary. What counted was guns. The main source of nourishment for the revolutionary hope was, of course, the ghetto riots. Were not these evidence, after all, that guerrilla warfare for liberation was not only possible in America but had already begun?

III

The archetypical ghetto riot of the 1960s was Watts, which so closely resembled most of the others that to understand its character was to understand theirs also. Most of the 300,000 residents in the ghetto of southeast Los Angeles lived in neat homes along spacious streets. But, underneath the pleasant surface, the usual depressing conditions prevailed—segregated schools, an unemployment rate twice that of the national average, inadequate transportation to decent jobs. In Watts, the neighborhood at the core of the sprawling ghetto, the social order was in the process of disintegrating—four persons in ten were poor, 38 percent of the families were headed by women, 47 percent of the children under eighteen lived in broken homes. The site of the worst fury, Watts gave its name to the great riot that began on August 11, 1965, in an ordinary encounter between white policemen and the blacks who hated them. Officer Lee Minikus of the California Highway Patrol stopped a car driven by Marquette Frye, a twenty-one-year-old unemployed black man, on a main thoroughfare near the Watts neighborhood. When Frye, who had been drinking, resisted arrest, a crowd gathered, forcing police to summon reinforcements. Within an hour a thousand blacks were on the street hurling rocks and bottles at the cops and shouting "Burn, Baby, Burn!" the hip slogan of a local disc jockey, the Magnificent Montague. Thus did Officer Minikus and Marquette Frye become historical personages by virtue of having caused, in the phrase of the sociologists, "the precipitating event." In 1949 the black poet Langston Hughes knew that someday Watts would come:

Negroes,
Sweet and docile,
Meek, humble, and kind:
Beware the day
They change their minds!

Wind
In the cotton fields
Gentle breeze
Beware the hour
It uproots trees.

That first night along Avalon Boulevard youths attacked cars driven by whites, beat up white newsmen, and battled the police. On the next night the looting and burning began. Calmly and without shame, people smashed the windows of liquor, grocery, and department stores and helped themselves to whatever they could carry. By the third day, as rioting spread throughout southeast Los Angeles, a dull orange haze from a thousand fires hung over the city. On the streets of Watts crowds milled about amid a carnival atmosphere, exhilarated by their collective act of defiance and proud that at last they were forcing attention to be paid. With the arrival of the National Guard early in the morning of the fourth day, the authorities began to gain the upper hand, and the fire and the fury slowly burned themselves out. "Now we're on the top, and they're on the bottom," declared Police Chief William H. Parker. The toll: 34 killed, 1,072 injured, 977 buildings damaged or destroyed, 4,000 persons arrested.

The McCone Commission, appointed by the governor of California to study the riot and named after its chairman, former CIA director John McCone, explained Watts as most conservatives would explain all the other riots—as a "senseless" explosion by a handful of alienated blacks. This was a thesis no knowledgeable observer endorsed. Surveys of the riot area revealed that at one time or another at least 30,000 blacks had participated in the looting, burning, and sniping, while approximately 60,000 more had been in the streets as supportive spectators. Rioters and spectators together formed a majority of the riot-age population (14–65 years old). Moreover, the typical rioter was not socially on the margin—i.e., "riff-raff"—but a young man somewhat better educated than the typical non-rioter and holding a job. Sociologists called the character type of which the rioter was representative "the New Ghetto Man."

Bred on the asphalt pavements of the northern cities, this new man bore scant resemblance to the stereotypical black—docile and submissive—of plantation days. Proud of his race, politically hip, savvy to discrimination, tolerant of violence, the New Ghetto Man reached maturity in the 1960s, which explained why centuries of repressed black anger erupted when it did. The riots were the new man's contribution to the black protest movement, his announcement that he would not passively submit to a life of discrimination and poverty. The announcement contained clear nationalist overtones. Whites were the target of the rioters' wrath, especially whites in the ghetto who had humiliated, cheated, or exploited them. Thus rioters chased white passersby, fought white police, and meted out their version of justice to thieving white merchants. The most arresting fact about Watts—and most of the other riots—was this: Looters and arsonists moved along the streets destroying white-owned stores but ordinarily sparing stores with signs reading "Negro-owned" or "Blood." Scornful of the black middle class and the traditional black leadership, the rioters heeded no counsel except their own violent impulses. Martin Luther King was on the streets during the riot, preaching nonviolence. The rioters ignored him. Mervyn Dymally, who represented Watts in the state legislature, urged his constituents to stay cool. One New Ghetto Man handed him a bottle, saying, "If you're with the people, throw it."

Black riots became such a regular feature of the decade that their annual appearance soon ceased to occasion surprise. By official count 43 racial disorders occurred in 1966 and 164 during the first nine months of 1967, the year when the insurrectionary fever peaked. Thirty-three of the 1967 disorders were serious enough to require the intervention of the state police; eight required the National Guard. Two of them—Newark and Detroit—were cataclysms on the scale of Watts.

The rioters of Newark manifested remarkable discipline, looting white-owned businesses but not black, smashing windows but avoiding arson since black families usually lived above the wooden stores. Newark also featured a counterriot by "peace-keeping" forces, a form of violence all too common in the decade. National Guardsmen—white, ill-trained, and terrified of snipers—proved a trigger-happy lot. "Down in the Springfield Avenue area it was so bad," reported Police Director Dominick Spina, "that, in my opinion, Guardsmen were firing upon police and police were firing back at them. . . . I really don't believe there was as much sniping as we thought." Spina watched two columns of unprovoked Guardsmen riddle a housing project with bullets. By the time they finished, three women were dead. Meanwhile, police and soldiers charged down streets, shooting up black-owned stores that had been spared by the looters. Early in the morning of the fourth day, uncertain what to do, New Jersey governor Richard J. Hughes privately summoned Tom Hayden to ask his advice. Hayden, who had spent three years organizing the Newark ghetto and the past few days "looking at the streets of violence," recalled warning the governor that if he did not pull back the Guard, "the troops are gonna massacre more people, and you're going to go down in history as one of the biggest killers of all time." A few hours later, Hughes withdrew the Guard, and calm returned to Newark.

Less than a week later, on July 23, 1967, the worst American riot in a century erupted in Detroit. Beginning the usual way, with a police incident, it rapidly spread through fourteen square miles of black slums. But Detroit was different from the major riots that preceded it, for here disciplined violence gave way to the sheerest nihilism. Rioters looted black stores and white stores, burned down businesses and burned down homes. Middle-class Negroes in big cars joined with the poor in hauling off merchandise. Carefree kids, excited by the fires, sacked and burned for the pleasure of it, appearing to one observer to be "dancing amidst the flames." Police and National Guardsmen were helpless in the face of this massive breakdown of public order—or else fed the furies of the people by their own excesses. George Romney had no choice except to become the first governor of the decade to request the intervention of federal troops. Shortly after midnight on July 25, Lieutenant General John L. Throckmorton, who had served General Westmoreland as an aide in Vietnam, began to deploy 4,700 paratroopers from Fort Bragg and Fort Campbell to pacify Detroit. The carnage of the riot, when it ended, was stunning in magnitude—43 dead, 7,000 arrested, 1,300 buildings destroyed, and 2,700 businesses looted. Surveying his city, Mayor Jerome Cavanagh grimly remarked, "It looks like Berlin in 1945."

Intoxicated by the blood and fire, militant nationalists concluded in 1967 that rioters were urban guerrillas engaged in a nationalist revolution to free the black colony. Theirs was a perverse interpretation. Spontaneous uprisings against deeply felt grievances, the riots were neither revolutionary nor even consistently nationalist. Rioters harassed the white man, but even snipers did not try to kill him. Wrath was directed less against whites in general than against those whites whose presence in the ghetto had aroused local antagonism—i.e., white cops and shopkeepers. Rioters were less hostile to the National Guard than to the local police and downright friendly to the federal troops. They attacked retail stores but left untouched public institutions like schools, hospitals, banks, and government buildings. They looted not in the name of socialism but because looting was one way to acquire the material possessions that they believed, in typical American fashion, would make them happy. They did not invade nearby white neighborhoods, engage in terrorism, or manifest the slightest interest in mounting a sustained struggle against the government. Torn between a desire to assert control over their own turf and the hope for full participation in America, they wanted above all to deliver a message to their white fellow citizens: progress halting, patience gone. Gabriel Pope (the name was a pseudonym), one of the new ghetto men figuring prominently in Robert Conot's fine book on Watts, *Rivers of Blood, Years of Darkness*, expressed the ambivalence of the rioters and summed up their purpose:

> *We'll give this country a chance. We'll give 'em a chance to make up for what they've done in the past, we'll give 'em a chance to say "We know we've done you wrong, and we're gonna do our best to change it!" But I'm not gonna have nobody tell me what to do . . . I'm gonna be the master of my life, and if they try to run over me, I'm gonna demolish them! And next time, baby, let me tell you, it's not gonna be a gentle war like it was, it's not gonna be the soul people doing all the bleeding. . . . If we get pushed again, it's gonna be goodbye, baby."*

In perceiving the riots as nationalist revolutions, the militants were creating an inapt metaphor—a wish projection—that served to titillate the radical sensibility but otherwise did only harm. The guerrilla fantasy fed the raging ghetto fires but proved so wildly at odds with reality that in time it would discredit the nationalist impulse itself. The two leading advocates of revolutionary nationalism were Carmichael and the man who succeeded him as chairman of SNCC, Hubert Geroid Brown, known as "Rap." Born and educated in Baton Rouge, Brown had been on the fringes of SNCC for years until 1965 when he joined Carmichael fulltime in Lowndes County, Alabama. He was called Rap because of his ability to communicate with the brothers on the street—hardly a remarkable achievement, despite a few years of college, because in all essential respects Brown was one of them. Lean, cool, menacing, peering impassively at the world from behind his dark glasses, H. Rap Brown was white America's dreaded image of the New Ghetto Man. Curiously, the SNCC staff elected him in 1967 to replace Carmichael, who stepped down voluntarily, because it thought Brown would maintain a low profile and keep out of trouble. Carmichael knew better. Introducing Brown to the press, he said, "You'll be happy to have me back when you hear from him— he's a bad man."

Every step of the incendiary journey of these two across America in 1967 took them closer to the revolutionary mirage. The journey began for Carmichael in Nashville, Tennessee, in April when he exhorted the students at all-black Fisk University to "take over" the administration. One day later some of those who heard him attacked police with rocks and pellet guns. "The pellets . . . pinged off the metal helmets of the officers as cries of 'black power' rang through the area," reported the *New York Times*. When Carmichael was arrested in Prattville, Alabama, early in June 1967, after shouting "black power" at a passing police car, angry snipers engaged police in a three-hour gun battle. A few days later youth in Atlanta emerged from a church where Carmichael had urged resistance to the "honky" and went on a rampage at a local shopping center. ("Honky" was an ethnic epithet once reserved for Hungarian immigrants but expanded by Carmichael to include all whites.)

On July 19 as Newark was cooling down, Rap Brown was nearby in racially tense Jersey City urging blacks to "wage guerrilla war on the honkie white man." A few days later, while Detroit was burning, Brown delivered a memorable summation of his credo in Cambridge, Maryland, to a night rally of three hundred blacks. "If America don't come around, we going to burn it down," he said. "The white man talks about black people looting. Hell, he the biggest looter in the world. He looted us from Africa. He looted America from the Indians . . . you can't steal from a thief." The brothers in Plainfield, New Jersey, got hold of guns and when "the peckerwood" went down there, "they stomp one of them to death. They stomp the cop to death. Good. He's dead!" The honkies own all the stores around this town, he said: "You got to own some of them stores. I don't care if you have to burn him down and run him out . . . The streets are yours. Take 'em." Police ambushed Brown a few moments later, grazing his head with a shotgun pellet. The next day ashes from the Cambridge ghetto covered the city.

On August 11, the second anniversary of the Watts riot, Carmichael was in Havana, making a speech. He said,

> *Comrades of the third world of Asia, Africa, and Latin America, I want you to know that Afro-North Americans within the United States are fighting for their liberation. It is a struggle of total revolution in which we propose to change the imperialist, capitalist and racialist structure of the United States which oppresses your outside and us within. We have no alternative but to take up arms and struggle for our total liberation and total revolution.*

And in Detroit, to commemorate the greatest riot of them all one month after it happened, Brown declared, "We live in the belly of the monster. So it's up to us to destroy its brain. When we do this not only will Africa be free but all people oppressed by 'the man.'" By the time he made that statement, it is likely that H. Rap Brown was the most feared and hated man in America.

Carmichael's status as a celebrity antagonized many on the staff who felt the controversy he aroused undercut field work and invited official repression. Stalwarts of the early years like John Lewis, Julian Bond, and Charles Sherrod became ideologically alienated and departed. Bitter quarrels over the continued presence of whites on the staff persisted until the last of them was expelled in December 1966. Field work in the South virtually ceased, and new projects in the North floundered. Widespread pot smoking and pill popping became symptoms of lax discipline and declining morale. Funds dried up as liberals recoiled from SNCC's honky baiting and its decision in 1967 to support the Arab struggle against Zionism. Local police harassed the organization, and J. Edgar Hoover made it a high-priority target for FBI counter-intelligence operations. Of the remaining seventy-six staff members in mid-1967, sixteen faced legal action for draft resistance. In July Chairman Brown added to the internal turmoil by getting himself indicted for inciting a riot in Cambridge, Maryland, and in August by getting arrested for carrying a semiautomatic carbine across state lines. SNCC obviously needed an infusion of fresh energy, which was why, early in 1968, it took under consideration an offer to merge with its most likely successor, the Black Panther Party for Self-Defense—the purest expression of the revolutionary impulse and its ultimate corruption.

250

IV

The sole characteristic distinguishing Huey P. Newton from a thousand other angry "brothers on the block" was audacity. It was audacious, indeed, for a twenty-four-year-old college dropout living off petty crime to believe he could found a new party for the liberation of blacks. And it was audacious, too, to think that he and his lone disciple, Bobby Seale, could spend one evening at an Oakland, California, antipoverty office in October 1966 and draw up a nationalist program that could say anything new. Most of their platform—composed in twenty minutes—was a routine rehearsal of the prevailing nationalist line: blacks needed self-determination; whites robbed the ghetto; salvation lay in "land, bread, housing, education, clothing, justice, and peace." But point seven was in fact something different. It said, "We believe we can end police brutality in our black community by organizing black self-defense groups that are dedicated to defending our black community from racist police oppression and brutality." What Newton had in mind was guns. Calling his party the Black Panthers, he recruited a handful of street brothers in the fall of 1966, dressed them in black pants, black leather jackets, and black berets and sent them into the Oakland ghetto to keep tabs on the hated police. Since California law forbade carrying concealed weapons but not weapons borne openly, the Panthers ostentatiously carried guns on patrol, an act so audacious that it intimidated the police and made Newton a neighborhood hero.

Newton attained true celebrity status in the Bay Area on February 21, 1967, when he undertook to provide an armed escort for the widow of Malcolm X on the occasion of her visit to San Francisco. While the Panthers stood guard at the office of *Ramparts* magazine, waiting for Sister Betty to conclude an appointment, the police arrived in force, obviously itching for a showdown. As one group of Panthers whisked Sister Betty away to safety, five others including Newton confronted the enemy. A beefy cop stepped forward and undid the strap holding his pistol in its holster. "O.K.," Newton shouted as he pumped a bullet into the chamber of his shotgun. "You big fat racist pig, draw your gun!" The cop backed off and Newton walked away, laughing. Newton topped himself on May 2, 1967, by sending a delegation to the state capitol in Sacramento for the purpose of protesting a proposed change in the gun laws. When 30 armed Panthers brushed past guards and walked onto the very floor of the state assembly, the new party instantly became a hot national news item.

Meanwhile, Newton was revealing a useful capacity for ideological flexibility. A devoted student of Frantz Fanon, he moved easily with the times in the radical summer of 1967 by adopting the imperialist hypothesis and the emerging guerrilla fantasy. Black people constituted a colony in the mother country of the American empire, he said, and like all victims of oppression, could legitimately resort to revolution—meaning guns. "Only with the power of the gun can the Black masses halt the terror and brutality perpetuated against them by the armed racist power structure," he wrote; "and in one sense only by the power of the gun can the whole world be transformed into the earthly paradise dreamed of by the people since time immemorial." The task of the Black Panther party was to show the people the way.

When the Vanguard group destroys the machinery of the oppressor by dealing with him in small groups of three and four, and then escapes the might of the oppressor, the masses will be overjoyed and will adhere to this correct strategy. When the masses hear that a gestapo

*policeman has been executed while sipping coffee at a counter, and the revolutionary
executioners fled without being traced, the masses will see the validity of this type of approach
to resistance.*

"The heirs of Malcolm X," Newton rejoiced, "have picked up the gun. . . ."

On October 28, 1967, Newton demonstrated the limitations of his teachings by getting shot in the stomach during a gun battle with police. The facts of this encounter remain
in dispute. Newton claimed that two policemen stopped his car at five o'clock in the morning, ordered him unarmed into the street, and then opened fire, not only wounding him but
accidentally shooting each other. One officer was killed, the other wounded. Alameda County,
on the other hand, charged Newton with initiating the exchange and indicted him for murder. Jailed without bond, Newton would be out of circulation for the next three years. The
Panthers appeared to be doomed in any case. The active membership was down to fifteen,
the base of party operations remained limited to Oakland, and the state of California had
passed a law in July designed to take the guns out of Panther hands, thus effectively halting
the police patrols that were the only Panther program.

Enter Eldridge Cleaver, by far the brightest and most charismatic member of the
small Panther circle, and the man who took control of the party after Newton's incarceration.
A convict for nearly seventeen of his thirty-one years, Cleaver had found redemption in the
black Muslim religion, only to abandon it upon the excommunication of his hero, Malcolm X.
Cleaver had so deeply hated whites that during his criminal phase he raped white women as
an "insurrectionary act" and once, while in prison, ranted against white people with such violence that he wound up in a padded cell. Yet, when Malcolm returned from Mecca in 1964 to
proclaim that not all white men were devils, Cleaver felt "glad to be liberated from a doctrine
of hate and racial supremacy." A writer of genuine talent, he joined the staff of *Ramparts* in
December 1966, after having served nine years in Soledad prison for attempted murder. Cleaver
was on the steps of *Ramparts* in February 1967 when Huey Newton—"the baddest mother-
fucker ever to step foot inside of history," Cleaver called him—faced down the San Francisco
police force. Committing himself to the Panthers on the spot, Cleaver became Panther minister of education, and after Newton's removal, the savior of the party.

Cleaver's accomplishment was truly remarkable, for after cessation of the police patrols
in the summer of 1967, the Panthers never did much more to liberate the black colony than
talk about it. Cleaver made the Panthers the most prominent black militant group in the country in the late 1960s by advertising Newton as a revolutionary martyr, by practicing ideological opportunism, and by seeking alliances with other radical organizations. Cleaver, for
example, dreamed up the idea in late 1967 of a merger between the Panthers and SNCC,
whose famous leaders he wished to enlist in a "Free Huey" crusade and whose organizational talents he desperately needed. Approaching Carmichael first, Cleaver offered not only
to merge the two organizations but to make Carmichael the Panther prime minister.
Carmichael, who was already well acquainted with the Panther leaders and had previously
accepted a draft as an honorary Panther field marshal, appeared receptive. Unfortunately, he
was the wrong man to contact, since he was currently engaged in a losing struggle with James
Forman and Rap Brown for control of SNCC—or what was left of SNCC. Forman had disapproved of Carmichael's 1967 foreign tour, resented his refusal to accept censure after his

return and, most important, objected to his latest ideological direction, which was as unacceptable to Forman as it would be to the Panthers, once they understood it. When Cleaver got wind of the split in SNCC, he hedged his bets by adding both Forman and Rap Brown to the Panther cabinet, making one minister of foreign affairs and the other minister of justice.

Cleaver's efforts to arrange the merger reached a climax at a big rally on the occasion of Huey's birthday, February 17, 1968. Five thousand people gathered at the Oakland Auditorium to hear Cleaver, Carmichael, Forman, Rap Brown, and Bobby Seale. Cleaver kicked things off with the stunning announcement that the two most famous black nationalist organizations had indeed agreed to merge. Among those stunned was James Forman, who privately feared that SNCC would be swallowed alive by these Panther upstarts and took pains in his own remarks diplomatically to explain that the arrangement was more an alliance than a merger. As usual, Carmichael overshadowed all other performers with a fiery speech that incidentally revealed his latest—and final—position on the question of black liberation. Only a few months before, he had been in Havana, preaching the anti-imperialist revolution against American capitalism. But after Havana he had gone first to Hanoi, where Ho Chi Minh—of all people—asked him why black people did not return to their home in Africa; and then on to Guinea, where he fell under the spell of the exiled Ghanaian leader Kwame Nkrumah and his Pan-African ideology. Now in Oakland, making his first public statement since his return, he declared, "Communism is not an ideology suited for black people, period, period. Socialism is not an ideology fitted for black people, period, period." Black people must be provided with "an African ideology which speaks to our blackness—nothing else. It's not a question of right or left, it's a question of black." For the Panthers, who were becoming increasingly anti-capitalist and more friendly to white leftists, Carmichael's speech was an inauspicious beginning to the new alliance.

Indeed, the two groups took few steps during the following months to implement their alliance, finally falling out in July 1968 when a SNCC-Panther press conference at the United Nations to promote Newton's case fell through amidst mutual recriminations. In August SNCC officially severed formal ties with the Panthers and at the same time expelled Carmichael. The Panthers for their part ceased to regard SNCC as anything but the enemy and eventually denounced Carmichael as an agent of the CIA. The collapse of the alliance made little practical difference, since each group could perform the revolutionary charade just as well separately as together.

More successful was the Panther's opening to the white left, a *démarche* made possible because Cleaver was one nationalist who was not a racist as well. In December 1967 he opened negotiations with the California Peace and Freedom party, a predominantly white group that hoped to provide a radical alternative to the two major parties in the next presidential election. Cleaver wanted access to white money and administrative skills for his "Free Huey" campaign. The Peace and Freedom party needed signatures in a hurry to qualify for a place on the state ballot, signatures Panthers could collect for them in the ghetto. Cleaver took pains to make sure that the terms of the alliance did not compromise his nationalist convictions. The Panthers would have exclusive responsibility for defining the Peace and Freedom program for the black community. Whites could define the party program for whites.

By venturing to become the only nationalist group in America to ally with whites, the Panthers emerged as the darlings of the new left. It did not matter that they consisted of a handful of blacks with a mimeograph machine. White radicals were so grateful to the Panthers for taking them seriously that many hailed the party as the vanguard of the revolution, wore its "Free Huey" buttons, and took up the unconscionable Panther cry "Off the Pig!" (i.e., kill cops). The Peace and Freedom party ran Newton for state assembly while he was in jail and nominated Cleaver for president at its national convention in August 1968. Meanwhile the growing fame of the Panthers extended into ghettos beyond Oakland. By the end of the year, the party had attained a membership of 1,500 to 2,000 in 25 cities.

Cleaver was in no position to enjoy his triumphs, including publication in March 1968 of his celebrated book, *Soul on Ice*. On April 6, on the way home after a day spent preventing a riot, a group of Panthers, including Cleaver, got in a shootout with police. Who ambushed whom was never established. Though the police quickly captured most of the others, Cleaver and seventeen-year-old Little Bobby Hutton, the party's treasurer and its first recruit, took refuge in a basement, where gunfire pinned them down for ninety minutes. Enveloped by flames and tear gas, Cleaver finally threw Hutton's rifle out the window and staggered on a wounded foot into the street. Little Bobby, who began to run, became the first dead Panther. After spending the next two months in jail, Cleaver was released by a county judge on grounds that he was a political prisoner. But in September a higher court ordered his return to prison within two months. Rather than comply, Cleaver jumped bail, becoming an exile first in Cuba and then in Algeria, where he resumed his duties as Panther Minister of Education and lost himself in ever more violent fantasies of the imminent American revolution.

During the next two years the Panthers remained highly visible. In 1969, abandoning black nationalism entirely, they declared themselves to be a Marxist-Leninist party committed to joining exploited people of all colors in a war against capitalism and imperialism. The entire white left—itself now enamored of revolution—hailed this shift as a historic departure. But the Panthers quickly became embroiled in the left's intramural quarrels, siding with Weatherman against the Progressive Labor party and then turning against Weatherman on the issue of community control of the police. By fall the Panthers had alienated virtually every organization on the white left, which nonetheless continued to use the Panthers as proof that fascist repression had come to America. Indeed, law-enforcement agencies illegally raided various local Panther headquarters, infiltrated the organization with spies and agents provocateurs, used forged letters and rumors eventually to help split Newton and Cleaver, and tried its leaders in the courts at every opportunity. In Chicago, on December 4, 1969, the police conducted a predawn raid on Panther headquarters, killing the leader of the state party, Fred Hampton, in his bed.

The Panthers were hardly innocent victims. Between 1967 and 1970 the Panthers killed more police (eleven) than the police killed Panthers (five). And, despite the party's effort to improve its image by sponsoring free breakfasts for the poor, many Panthers seemed more interested in crime than in social justice. Testimony by high-ranking Panthers alleged that David Hilliard, the Panther chief of staff and head man after Cleaver's exile, used the Oakland chapter to operate a burglary ring. Most of the 348 Panther arrests in 1969 stemmed not from politics but from charges of rape, robbery, and burglary. Meanwhile, the organization was undergoing periodic purges, its local chapters withered, and internal dissension thrived. In August 1970 an appeals court overturned Newton's conviction for murder and ordered a new trial. Back on the streets, the mythic Panther hero found little left of the organization he had served better in prison than he could ever do outside. Within a year Panthermania was no longer chic, and the Panthers themselves fell into obscurity, somehow maintaining a sleazy half-life in Oakland throughout the next decade. Few lamented their decline. They had, after all, existed mainly in the demented imaginations of white leftists who insisted on mistaking their poses as the stuff of real revolution. To such an inglorious pass had the nationalist impulse come.

V

Like civil rights, the nationalist phase of the black protest movement had a run of only a few years. The last great spasm of ghetto violence occurred in Chicago, Baltimore, and Washington in the wake of Martin Luther King's assassination, April 1968. Though hundreds of other racial disorders marred the civil peace during the following three summers, there were no more Wattses and no more Detroits. As the embers of the ghetto cooled, so did the oratory of nationalist militants, whose various efforts to fashion an ideology for the black masses had so badly misfired.

The pluralist version of black nationalism actually had much to recommend it. Given the shared racial identity that bound black Americans together, it made sense to develop institutions for their collective advancement in a pluralist context. But few of those who urged this course ever bothered to think through its implications or to undertake its implementation. SNCC had acquired considerable experience helping poor blacks build institutions in the South. But on moving north it made only feeble efforts to employ its community-organizing skills. Succumbing to the lure of the media, Stokely "Starmichael," as his critics in SNCC called him, chose the lecture platform over the store front and so left behind no enduring black institution.

Cultural nationalism was also not without its merits. If it was true that black people had been brainwashed into believing that black was bad, then one remedy was to insist that black was beautiful—to emphasize the positive features of black culture and black history. Black power probably hastened the process by which the new generation of northern-bred blacks—New Ghetto Men—forged an identity based on racial self-respect. Future historians may well conclude that, for blacks, the most important event of the decade was the conquest of the conk by the afro. But racial chauvinism, however psychologically beneficial in the shortrun, could provide only the beginning of a solution of the ghetto tragedy; it could never be the solution itself. A precondition for political and economic action, perhaps; a program for political and economic reconstruction, hardly.

Nothing did more to abort the nationalist impulse than the conversion of its leading exponents to revolution. If their exhortations had been taken seriously, the black masses would have undertaken a guerrilla struggle against the greatest military machine in the history of the world. That was a prescription for suicide, which in fact emerged as a leitmotif running through nationalist rhetoric as the decade wound down. Carmichael, for example, held a press conference after King's assassination predicting a race war in which blacks would "stand up on our feet and die like men. If that's our only act of manhood, then Goddammit, we're going to die." From a jail cell in New Orleans, where he had begun a hunger strike, H. Rap Brown proclaimed, "America, if it takes my death to organize my people to revolt against you . . . then, here is my Life!" James Forman announced with gloomy regularity his expectation of early assassination at the hands of authorities. And Huey Newton developed the doctrine of "revolutionary suicide" which held that blacks in America faced two choices—to acquiesce in oppression and die a spiritual death or to "oppose the forces that would drive me to self-murder" and die for humanity. Newton was no doubt prepared for death; the brothers on the block were not. As a result, the main casualty of the guerrilla fantasy turned out to be the nationalist impulse itself.

But the foremost cause of the rapid decline of black nationalism was its moral weakness. However understandable its emergence, black nationalism, like all nationalisms, emphasized what divided men rather than their common humanity. Remarkably, most black Americans resisted the temptation to counter white chauvinism with black, to answer rejection with rejection. All the polls showed that blacks continued overwhelmingly to favor civil rights, racial integration, and nonviolence. In 1966 King received the approval of 88 percent of the black rank and file, Carmichael only 19 percent. Among the black masses the classic liberal ideal, more important than any particular liberal failing of policy, never lost its appeal. That ideal envisioned a multi-ethnic, multiracial democracy characterized by equal justice and equal opportunity, and affording to each citizen reward according to merit. That ideal remained imperfectly realized in the late 1960s, and many blacks felt deep frustration at the slow rate of progress toward its achievement. Nevertheless, few of them ever doubted its ethical superiority over the bloody rantings of H. Rap Brown.

Three Voices from the Civil Rights Era

Martin Luther King, Jr., Malcolm X, and Cesar Chavez

Martin Luther King, Jr.

Letter from Birmingham Jail
April 16, 1963

My Dear Fellow Clergymen:

While confined here in the Birmingham city jail, I came across your recent statement calling my present activities "unwise and untimely." Seldom do I pause to answer criticism of my work and ideas. If I sought to answer all the criticisms that cross my desk, my secretaries would have little time for anything other than such correspondence in the course of the day, and I would have no time for constructive work. But since I feel that you are men of genuine good will and that your criticisms are sincerely set forth, I want to try to answer your statements in what I hope will be patient and reasonable terms.

I think I should indicate why I am here In Birmingham, since you have been influenced by the view which argues against "outsiders coming in." I have the honor of serving as president of the Southern Christian Leadership Conference, an organization operating in every southern state, with headquarters in Atlanta, Georgia. We have some eighty-five affiliated organizations across the South, and one of them is the Alabama Christian Movement for Human Rights. Frequently we share staff, educational and financial resources with our affiliates. Several months ago the affiliate here in Birmingham asked us to be on call to engage in a nonviolent direct-action program if such were deemed necessary. We readily consented, and when the hour came we lived up to our promise. So I, along with several members of my staff, am here because I was invited here I am here because I have organizational ties here.

But more basically, I am in Birmingham because injustice is here. Just as the prophets of the eighth century B.C. left their villages and carried their "thus saith the Lord" far beyond the boundaries of their home towns, and just as the Apostle Paul left his village of Tarsus and carried the gospel of Jesus Christ to the far corners of the Greco-Roman world, so am I compelled to carry the gospel of freedom beyond my own home town. Like Paul, I must constantly respond to the Macedonian call for aid.

Moreover, I am cognizant of the interrelatedness of all communities and states. I cannot sit idly by in Atlanta and not be concerned about what happens in Birmingham. Injustice anywhere is a threat to justice everywhere. We are caught in an inescapable network of mutuality, tied in a single garment of destiny. Whatever affects one directly, affects all indirectly. Never again can we afford to live with the narrow, provincial "outside agitator" idea. Anyone who lives inside the United States can never be considered an outsider anywhere within its bounds.

You deplore the demonstrations taking place In Birmingham. But your statement, I am sorry to say, fails to express a similar concern for the conditions that brought about the demonstrations. I am sure that none of you would want to rest content with the superficial kind of social analysis that deals merely with effects and does not grapple with underlying causes. It is unfortunate that demonstrations are taking place in Birmingham, but it is even more unfortunate that the city's white power structure left the Negro community with no alternative.

In any nonviolent campaign there are four basic steps: collection of the facts to determine whether injustices exist; negotiation; self- purification; and direct action. We have gone through an these steps in Birmingham. There can be no gainsaying the fact that racial injustice engulfs this community. Birmingham is probably the most thoroughly segregated city in the United States. Its ugly record of brutality is widely known. Negroes have experienced grossly unjust treatment in the courts. There have been more unsolved bombings of Negro homes and churches in Birmingham than in any other city in the nation. These are the hard, brutal facts of the case. On the basis of these conditions, Negro leaders sought to negotiate with the city fathers. But the latter consistently refused to engage in good-faith negotiation.

Then, last September, came the opportunity to talk with leaders of Birmingham's economic community. In the course of the negotiations, certain promises were made by the merchants—for example, to remove the stores humiliating racial signs. On the basis of these promises, the Reverend Fred Shuttles worth and the leaders of the Alabama Christian Movement for Human Rights agreed to a moratorium on all demonstrations. As the weeks and months went by, we realized that we were the victims of a broken promise. A few signs, briefly removed, returned; the others remained.

As in so many past experiences, our hopes had been blasted, and the shadow of deep disappointment settled upon us. We had no alternative except to prepare for direct action, whereby we would present our very bodies as a means of laying our case before the conscience of the local and the national community. Mindful of the difficulties involved, we decided to undertake a process of self-purification. We began a series of workshops on nonviolence, and we repeatedly asked ourselves: "Are you able to accept blows without retaliating?" "Are you able to endure the ordeal of jail?" We decided to schedule our direct-action program for the Easter season, realizing that except for Christmas, this is the main shopping period of the year. Knowing that a strong economic with with-drawl program would be the by-product of direct action, we felt that this would be the best time to bring pressure to bear on the merchants for the needed change.

Then it occurred to us that Birmingham's mayoralty election was coming up in March, and we speedily decided to postpone action until after election day. When we discovered that the Commissioner of Public Safety, Eugene "Bull" Connor, had piled up enough votes to be in the run-off we decided again to postpone action until the day after the run-off so that the demonstrations could not be used to cloud the issues. Like many others, we waited to see Mr. Connor defeated, and to this end we endured postponement after postponement. Having aided in this community need, we felt that our direct-action program could be delayed no longer.

You may well ask: "Why direct action? Why sit-ins, marches and so forth? Isn't negotiation a better path?" You are quite right in calling, for negotiation. Indeed, this is the very purpose of direct action. Nonviolent direct action seeks to create such a crisis and foster such a tension that a community which has constantly refused to negotiate is forced to confront the issue. It seeks so to dramatize the issue that it can no longer be ignored. My citing the creation of tension as part of the work of the nonviolent-resister may sound rather shocking. But I must confess that I am not afraid of the word "tension." I have earnestly opposed violent tension, but there is a type of constructive, nonviolent tension which is necessary for growth. Just as Socrates felt that it was necessary to create a tension in the mind so that individuals could rise from the bondage of myths and half-truths to the unfettered realm of creative analysis and objective appraisal, we must we see the need for nonviolent gadflies to create the kind of tension in society that will help men rise from the dark depths of prejudice and racism to the majestic heights of understanding and brotherhood.

The purpose of our direct-action program is to create a situation so crisis-packed that it will inevitably open the door to negotiation. I therefore concur with you in your call for negotiation. Too long has our beloved South land been bogged down in a tragic effort to live in monologue rather than dialogue.

One of the basic points in your statement is that the action that I and my associates have taken in Birmingham is untimely. Some have asked: "Why didn't you give the new city administration time to act?" The only answer that I can give to this query is that the new Birmingham administration must be prodded about as much as the outgoing one, before it will act. We are sadly mistaken if we feel that the election of Albert Boutwell as mayor will bring the millennium to Birmingham. While Mr. Boutwell is a much more gentle person than Mr. Connor, they are both segregationists, dedicated to maintenance of the status quo. I have hope that Mr. Boutwell will be reasonable enough to see the futility of massive resistance to desegregation. But he will not see this without pressure from devotees of civil rights. My friends, I must say to you that we have not made a single gain civil rights without determined legal and nonviolent pressure. Lamentably, it is an historical fact that privileged groups seldom give up their privileges voluntarily. Individuals may see the moral light and voluntarily give up their unjust posture; but, as Reinhold Niebuhr has reminded us, groups tend to be more immoral than individuals.

We know through painful experience that freedom is never voluntarily given by the oppressor; it must be demanded by the oppressed. Frankly, I have yet to engage in a direct-action campaign that was "well timed" in the view of those who have not suffered unduly from the disease of segregation. For years now I have heard the word "Wait!" It rings in the ear of every Negro with piercing familiarity. This "Wait" has almost always meant 'Never." We must come to see, with one of our distinguished jurists, that "justice too long delayed is justice denied."

We have waited for more than 340 years for our constitutional and God- given rights. The nations of Asia and Africa are moving with jetlike speed toward gaining political independence, but we still creep at horse-and-buggy pace toward gaining a cup of coffee at a lunch counter. Perhaps it is easy for those who have never felt the stinging dark of segregation to say, "Wait." But when you have seen vicious mobs lynch your mothers and fathers at will and drown your sisters and brothers at whim; when you have seen hate-filled policemen curse, kick and even kill your black brothers and sisters; when you see the vast majority of your twenty million Negro brothers smothering in an airtight cage of poverty in the midst of an affluent society; when you suddenly find your tongue twisted and your speech stammering as you seek to explain to your six- year-old daughter why she can't go to the public amusement park that has just been advertised on television, and see tears welling up in her eyes when she is told that Funtown is closed to colored children, and see ominous clouds of inferiority beginning to form in her little mental sky, and see her beginning to distort her personality by developing an unconscious bitterness toward white people; when you have to concoct an answer for a five-year-old son who is asking: "Daddy, why do white people treat colored people so mean?"; when you take a cross-county drive and find it necessary to sleep night after night in the uncomfortable corners of your automobile because no motel will accept you; when you are humiliated day in and day out by nagging signs reading "white" and "colored"; when your first name becomes "nigger," your middle name becomes "boy" (however old you are) and your last name becomes "John," and your wife and mother are never given the respected title "Mrs."; when you are harried by day and haunted by night by the fact that you are a Negro, living constantly at tiptoe stance, never quite knowing what to expect next, and are plagued with inner fears and outer resentments; when you no forever fighting a degenerating sense of "nobodiness" then you will understand why we find it difficult to wait. There comes a time when the cup of endurance runs over, and men are no longer willing to be plunged into the abyss of despair. I hope, sirs, you can understand our legitimate and unavoidable impatience.

You express a great deal of anxiety over our willingness to break laws. This is certainly a legitimate concern. Since we so diligently urge people to obey the Supreme Court's decision of 1954 outlawing segregation in the public schools, at first glance it may seem rather paradoxical for us consciously to break laws. One may won ask: "How can you advocate breaking some laws and obeying others?" The answer lies in the fact that there fire two types of laws: just and unjust. I would be the Brat to advocate obeying just laws. One has not only a legal but a moral responsibility to obey just laws. Conversely, one has a moral responsibility to disobey unjust laws. I would agree with St. Augustine that "an unjust law is no law at all"

Now, what is the difference between the two? How does one determine whether a law is just or unjust? A just law is a man-made code that squares with the moral law or the law of God. An unjust law is a code that is out of harmony with the moral law. To put it in the terms of St. Thomas Aquinas: An unjust law is a human law that is not rooted in eternal law and natural law. Any law that uplifts human personality is just. Any law that degrades human personality is unjust. All segregation statutes are unjust because segregation distort the soul and damages the personality. It gives the segregator a false sense of superiority and the segregated a false sense of inferiority. Segregation, to use the terminology of the Jewish philosopher Martin Buber, substitutes an "I-it" relationship for an "I-thou" relationship and ends up relegating persons to the status of things. Hence segregation is not only politically, economically and sociologically unsound, it is morally wrong and awful. Paul Tillich said that sin is separation. Is not segregation an existential expression 'of man's tragic separation, his awful estrangement, his terrible sinfulness? Thus it is that I can urge men to obey the 1954 decision of the Supreme Court, for it is morally right; and I can urge them to disobey segregation ordinances, for they are morally wrong.

Let us consider a more concrete example of just and unjust laws. An unjust law is a code that a numerical or power majority group compels a minority group to obey but does not make binding on itself. This is difference made legal. By the same token, a just law is a code that a majority compels a minority to follow and that it is willing to follow itself. This is sameness made legal.

Let me give another explanation. A law is unjust if it is inflicted on a minority that, as a result of being denied the right to vote, had no part in enacting or devising the law. Who can say that the legislature of Alabama which set up that state's segregation laws was democratically elected? Throughout Alabama all sorts of devious methods are used to prevent Negroes from becoming registered voters, and there are some counties in which, even though Negroes constitute a majority of the population, not a single Negro is registered. Can any law enacted under such circumstances be considered democratically structured?

Sometimes a law is just on its face and unjust in its application. For instance, I have been arrested on a charge of parading without a permit. Now, there is nothing wrong in having an ordinance which requires a permit for a parade. But such an ordinance becomes unjust when it is used to maintain segregation and to deny citizens the First Amendment privilege of peaceful assembly and protest.

I hope you are able to ace the distinction I am trying to point out. In no sense do I advocate evading or defying the law, as would the rabid segregationist. That would lead to anarchy. One who breaks an unjust law must do so openly, lovingly, and with a willingness to accept the penalty. I submit that an individual who breaks a law that conscience tells him is unjust and who willingly accepts the penalty of imprisonment in order to arouse the conscience of the community over its injustice, is in reality expressing the highest respect for law.

Of course, there is nothing new about this kind of civil disobedience. It was evidenced sublimely in the refusal of Shadrach, Meshach and Abednego to obey the laws of Nebuchadnezzar, on the ground that a higher moral law was at stake. It was practiced superbly by the early Christians, who were willing to face hungry lions and the excruciating pain of chopping blocks rather than submit to certain unjust laws of the Roman Empire. To a degree, academic freedom is a reality today because Socrates practiced civil disobedience. In our own nation, the Boston Tea Party represented a massive act of civil disobedience.

We should never forget that everything Adolf Hitler did in Germany was "legal" and everything the Hungarian freedom fighters did in Hungary was "illegal." It was "illegal" to aid and comfort a Jew in Hitler's Germany. Even so, I am sure that, had I lived in Germany at the time, I would have aided and comforted my Jewish brothers. If today I lived in a Communist country where certain principles dear to the Christian faith are suppressed, I would openly advocate disobeying that country's anti religious laws.

I must make two honest confessions to you, my Christian and Jewish brothers. First, I must confess that over the past few years I have been gravely disappointed with the white moderate. I have almost reached the regrettable conclusion that the Negro's great stumbling block in his stride toward freedom is not the White Citizen's Councilor or the Ku Klux Klanner, but the white moderate, who is more devoted to "order" than to justice; who prefers a negative peace which is the absence of tension to a positive peace which is the presence of justice; who constantly says: "I agree with you in the goal you seek, but I cannot agree with your methods of direct action"; who paternalistically believes he can set the timetable for another man's freedom; who lives by a mythical concept of time and who constantly advises the Negro to wait for a "more convenient season." Shallow understanding from people of good will is more frustrating than absolute misunderstanding from people of ill will. Lukewarm acceptance is much more bewildering than outright rejection.

I had hoped that the white moderate would understand that law and order exist for the purpose of establishing justice and that when they fan in this purpose they become the dangerously structured dams that block the flow of social progress. I had hoped that the white moderate would understand that the present tension in the South is a necessary phase of the transition from an obnoxious negative peace, in which the Negro passively accepted his unjust plight, to a substantive and positive peace, in which all men will respect the dignity and worth of human personality. Actually, we who engage in nonviolent direct action are not the creators of tension. We merely bring to the surface the hidden tension that is already alive. We bring it out in the open, where it can be seen and dealt with. Like a boil that can never be cured so long as it is covered up but must be opened with an its ugliness to the natural medicines of air and light, injustice must be exposed, with all the tension its exposure creates, to the light of human conscience and the air of national opinion before it can be cured.

In your statement you assert that our actions, even though peaceful, must be condemned because they precipitate violence. But is this a logical assertion? Isn't this like condemning a robbed man because his possession of money precipitated the evil act of robbery? Isn't this like condemning Socrates because his unswerving commitment to truth and his philosophical inquiries precipitated the act by the misguided populace in which they made him drink hemlock? Isn't this like condemning Jesus because his unique God-consciousness and neverceasing devotion to God's will precipitated the evil act of crucifixion? We must come to see that, as the federal courts have consistently affirmed, it is wrong to urge an individual to cease his efforts to gain his basic constitutional rights because the quest may precipitate violence. Society must protect the robbed and punish the robber.

I had also hoped that the white moderate would reject the myth concerning time in relation to the struggle for freedom. I have just received a letter from a white brother in Texas. He writes: "An Christians know that the colored people will receive equal rights eventually, but it is possible that you are in too great a religious hurry. It has taken Christianity almost two thousand years to accomplish what it has. The teachings of Christ take time to come to earth." Such an attitude stems from a tragic misconception of time, from the strangely rational notion that there is something in the very flow of time that will inevitably cure all ills. Actually, time itself is neutral; it can be used either destructively or constructively. More and more I feel that the people of ill will have used time much more effectively than have the people of good will. We will have to repent in this generation not merely for the hateful words and actions of the bad people but for the appalling silence of the good people. Human progress never rolls in on wheels of inevitability; it comes through the tireless efforts of men willing to be co-workers with God, and without this 'hard work, time itself becomes an ally of the forces of social stagnation. We must use time creatively, in the knowledge that the time is always ripe to do right. Now is the time to make real the promise of democracy and transform our pending national elegy into a creative psalm of brotherhood. Now is the time to lift our national policy from the quicksand of racial injustice to be solid rock of human dignity.

You speak of our activity in Birmingham as extreme. At first I was rather disappointed that fellow clergymen would see my nonviolent efforts as those of an extremist. I began thinking about the fact that stand in the middle of two opposing forces in the Negro community. One is a force of complacency, made up in part of Negroes who, as a result of long years of oppression, are so drained of self-respect and a sense of "somebodiness" that they have adjusted to segregation; and in part of a few middle class Negroes who, because of a degree of academic and economic security and because in some ways they profit by segregation, have become insensitive to the problems of the masses. The other force is one of bitterness and hatred, and it comes perilously close to advocating violence. It is expressed in the various black nationalist groups that are springing up across the nation, the largest and best-known being Elijah Muhammad's Muslim movement. Nourished by the Negro's frustration over the continued existence of racial discrimination, this movement is made up of people who have lost faith in America, who have absolutely repudiated Christianity, and who have concluded that the white man is an incorrigible "devil."

I have tried to stand between these two forces, saying that we need emulate neither the "do-nothingism" of the complacent nor the hatred and despair of the black nationalist. For there is the more excellent way of love and nonviolent protest. I am grateful to God that, through the influence of the Negro church, the way of nonviolence became an integral part of our struggle.

If this philosophy had not emerged, by now many streets of the South would, I am convinced, be flowing with blood. And I am further convinced that if our white brothers dismiss as "rabble-rousers" and "outside agitators" those of us who employ nonviolent direct action, and if they refuse to support our nonviolent efforts, millions of Negroes will, out of frustration and despair, seek solace and security in black- nationalist ideologies a development that would inevitably lead to a frightening racial nightmare.

Oppressed people cannot remain oppressed forever. The yearning for freedom eventually manifests itself, and that is what has happened to the American Negro. Something within has reminded him of his birthright of freedom, and something without has reminded him that it can be gained. Consciously or unconsciously, he has been caught up by the Zeitgeist, and with his black brothers of Africa and his brown and yellow brothers of Asia, South America and the Caribbean, the United States Negro is moving with a sense of great urgency toward the promised land of racial justice. If one recognizes this vital urge that has engulfed the Negro community, one should readily understand why public demonstrations are taking place. The Negro has many pent-up resentments and latent frustrations, and he must release them. So let him march; let him make prayer pilgrimages to the city hall; let him go on freedom rides-and try to understand why he must do so. If his repressed emotions are not released in nonviolent ways, they will seek expression through violence; this is not a threat but a fact of history. So I have not said to my people: "Get rid of your discontent." Rather, I have tried to say that this normal and healthy discontent can be channeled into the creative outlet of nonviolent direct action. And now this approach is being termed extremist.

But though I was initially disappointed at being categorized as an extremist, as I continued to think about the matter I gradually gained a measure of satisfaction from the label. Was not Jesus an extremist for love: "Love your enemies, bless them that curse you, do good to them that hate you, and pray for them which despitefully use you, and persecute you."

Was not Amos an extremist for justice: "Let justice roll down like waters and righteousness like an ever-flowing stream." Was not Paul an extremist for the Christian gospel: "I bear in my body the marks of the Lord Jesus." Was not Martin Luther an extremist: "Here I stand; I cannot do otherwise, so help me God." And John Bunyan: "I will stay in jail to the end of my days before I make a butchery of my conscience." And Abraham Lincoln: "This nation cannot survive half slave and half free." And Thomas Jefferson: "We hold these truths to be self-evident, that all men are created equal . . ." So the question is not whether we will be extremists, but what kind of extremists we will be. We be extremists for hate or for love? Will we be extremist for the preservation of injustice or for the extension of justice? In that dramatic scene on Calvary's hill three men were crucified. We must never forget that all three were crucified for the same crime—the crime of extremism. Two were extremists for immorality, and thus fell below their environment. The other, Jeans Christ, was an extremist for love, truth and goodness, and thereby rose above his environment. Perhaps the South, the nation and the world are in dire need of creative extremists.

I had hoped that the white moderate would see this need. Perhaps I was too optimistic; perhaps I expected too much. I suppose I should have realized that few members of the oppressor race can understand the deep groans and passionate yearnings of the oppressed race, and still fewer have the vision to see that injustice must be rooted out by strong, persistent and determined action. I am thankful, however, that some of our white brothers in the South have grasped the meaning of this social revolution and committed themselves to it. They are still too few in quantity, but they are big in quality. Some-such as Ralph McGill, Lillian Smith, Harry Golden, James McBride Dabbs, Ann Braden and Sarah Patton Boyle—have written about our struggle in eloquent and prophetic terms. Others have marched with us down nameless streets of the South. They have languished in filthy, roach-infested jails, suffering the abuse and brutality of policemen who view them as "dirty nigger lovers." Unlike so many of their moderate brothers and sisters, they have recognized the urgency of the moment and sensed the need for powerful "action" antidotes to combat the disease of segregation.

Let me take note of my other major disappointment. I have been so greatly disappointed with the white church and its leadership. Of course, there are some notable exceptions. I am not unmindful of the fact that each of you has taken some significant stands on this issue. I commend you, Reverend Stallings, for your Christian stand on this past Sunday, in welcoming Negroes to your worship service on a non segregated basis. I commend the Catholic leaders of this state for integrating Spring Hill College several years ago.

But despite these notable exceptions, I must honestly reiterate that I have been disappointed with the church. I do not say this as one of those negative critics who can always find something wrong with the church. I say this as a minister of the gospel, who loves the church; who was nurtured in its bosom; who has been sustained by its spiritual blessings and who will remain true to it as long as the cord of Rio shall lengthen.

When I was suddenly catapulted into the leadership of the bus protest in Montgomery, Alabama, a few years ago, I felt we would be supported by the white church felt that the white ministers, priests and rabbis of the South would be among our strongest allies. Instead, some have been outright opponents, refusing to understand the freedom movement and misrepresenting its leader era; an too many others have been more cautious than courageous and have remained silent behind the anesthetizing security of stained-glass windows.

In spite of my shattered dreams, I came to Birmingham with the hope that the white religious leadership of this community would see the justice of our cause and, with deep moral concern, would serve as the channel through which our just grievances could reach the power structure. I had hoped that each of you would understand. But again I have been disappointed.

I have heard numerous southern religious leaders admonish their worshipers to comply with a desegregation decision because it is the law, but I have longed to hear white ministers declare: "Follow this decree because integration is morally right and because the Negro is your brother." In the midst of blatant injustices inflicted upon the Negro, I have watched white churchmen stand on the sideline and mouth pious irrelevancies and sanctimonious trivialities. In the midst of a mighty struggle to rid our nation of racial and economic injustice, I have heard many ministers say: "Those are social issues, with which the gospel has no real concern." And I have watched many churches commit themselves to a completely other worldly religion which makes a strange, on Biblical distinction between body and soul, between the sacred and the secular.

I have traveled the length and breadth of Alabama, Mississippi and all the other southern states. On sweltering summer days and crisp autumn mornings I have looked at the South's beautiful churches with their lofty spires pointing heavenward. I have beheld the impressive outlines of her massive religious-education buildings. Over and over I have found myself asking: "What kind of people worship here? Who is their God? Where were their voices when the lips of Governor Barnett dripped with words of interposition and nullification? Where were they when Governor Walleye gave a clarion call for defiance and hatred? Where were their voices of support when bruised and weary Negro men and women decided to rise from the dark dungeons of complacency to the bright hills of creative protest?"

Yes, these questions are still in my mind. In deep disappointment I have wept over the laxity of the church. But be assured that my tears have been tears of love. There can be no deep disappointment where there is not deep love. Yes, I love the church. How could I do otherwise? I am in the rather unique position of being the son, the grandson and the great-grandson of preachers. Yes, I see the church as the body of Christ. But, oh! How we have blemished and scarred that body through social neglect and through fear of being nonconformists.

There was a time when the church was very powerful in the time when the early Christians rejoiced at being deemed worthy to suffer for what they believed. In those days the church was not merely a thermometer that recorded the ideas and principles of popular opinion; it was a thermostat that transformed the mores of society. Whenever the early Christians entered a town, the people in power became disturbed and immediately sought to convict the Christians for being "disturbers of the peace" and "outside agitators'" But the Christians pressed on, in the conviction that they were "a colony of heaven," called to obey God rather than man. Small in number, they were big in commitment. They were too God intoxicated to be "astronomically intimidated." By their effort and example they brought an end to such ancient evils as infanticide. and gladiatorial contests.

Things are different now. So often the contemporary church is a weak, ineffectual voice with an uncertain sound. So often it is an archdefender of the status quo. Par from being disturbed by the presence of the church, the power structure of the average community is consoled by the church's silent and often even vocal sanction of things as they are.

But the judgment of God is upon the church as never before. If today's church does not recapture the sacrificial spirit of the early church, it will lose its authenticity, forfeit the loyalty of millions, and be dismissed as an irrelevant social club with no meaning for the twentieth century. Every day I meet young people whose disappointment with the church has turned into outright disgust.

Perhaps I have once again been too optimistic. Is organized religion too inextricably bound to the status quo to save our nation and the world? Perhaps I must turn my faith to the inner spiritual church, the church within the church, as the true ekklesia and the hope of the world. But again I am thankful to God that some noble souls from the ranks of organized religion have broken loose from the paralyzing chains of conformity and joined us as active partners in the struggle for freedom, They have left their secure congregations and walked the streets of Albany, Georgia, with us. They have gone down the highways of the South on tortuous rides for freedom. Yes, they have gone to jail with us. Some have been dismissed from their churches, have lost the support of their bishops and fellow ministers. But they have acted in the faith that right defeated is stronger than evil triumphant. Their witness has been the spiritual salt that has preserved the true meaning of the gospel in these troubled times. They have carved a tunnel of hope through the dark mountain of disappointment.

I hope the church as a whole will meet the challenge of this decisive hour. But even if the church does not come to the aid of justice, I have no despair about the future. I have no fear about the outcome of our struggle in Birmingham, even if our motives are at present misunderstood. We will reach the goal of freedom in Birmingham, and all over the nation, because the goal of America is freedom. Abused and scorned though we may be, our destiny is tied up with America's destiny. Before the pilgrims landed at Plymouth, we were here. Before the pen of Jefferson etched the majestic words of the Declaration of Independence across the pages of history, we were here. For more than two centuries our forebears labored in this country without wages; they made cotton king; they built the homes of their masters while suffering gross injustice and shameful humiliation-and yet out of a bottomless vitality they continued to thrive and develop. If the inexpressible cruelties of slavery could not stop us, the opposition we now face will surely fail. We will win our freedom because the sacred heritage of our nation and the eternal will of God are embodied in our echoing demands.

Before closing I feel impelled to mention one other point in your statement that has troubled me profoundly. You warmly commended the Birmingham police force for keeping "order" and "preventing violence." I doubt that you would have so warmly commended the police force if you had seen its dogs sinking their teeth into unarmed, nonviolent Negroes. I doubt that you would so quickly commend the policemen if you were to observe their ugly and inhumane treatment of Negroes here in the city jail; if you were to watch them push and curse old Negro women and young Negro girls; if you were to see them slap and kick old Negro men and young boys; if you were to observe them, as they did on two occasions, refuse to give us food because we wanted to sing our grace together. I cannot join you in your praise of the Birmingham police department.

It is true that the police have exercised a degree of discipline in handing the demonstrators. In this sense they have conducted themselves rather "nonviolently" in public. But for what purpose? To preserve the evil system of segregation. Over the past few years I have consistently preached that nonviolence demands that the means we use must be as pure as the ends we seek. I have tried to make clear that it is wrong to use immoral means to attain moral ends. But now I must affirm that it is just as wrong, or perhaps even more so, to use moral means to preserve immoral ends. Perhaps Mr. Connor and his policemen have been rather nonviolent in public, as was Chief Pritchett in Albany, Georgia but they have used the moral means of nonviolence to maintain the immoral end of racial injustice. As T. S. Eliot has said: "The last temptation is the greatest treason: To do the right deed for the wrong reason."

I wish you had commended the Negro sit-inners and demonstrators of Birmingham for their sublime courage, their willingness to suffer and their amazing discipline in the midst of great provocation. One day the South will recognize its real heroes. They will be the James Merediths, with the noble sense of purpose that enables them to face Jeering, and hostile mobs, and with the agonizing loneliness that characterizes the life of the pioneer. They will be old, oppressed, battered Negro women, symbolized in a seventy-two-year-old woman in Montgomery, Alabama, who rose up with a sense of dignity and with her people decided not to ride segregated buses, and who responded with ungrammatical profundity to one who inquired about her weariness: "My fleets is tired, but my soul is at rest." They will be the young high school and college students, the young ministers of the gospel and a host of their elders, courageously and nonviolently sitting in at lunch counters and willingly going to jail for conscience' sake. One day the South will know that when these disinherited children of God sat down at lunch counters, they were in reality standing up for what is best in the American dream and for the most sacred values in our Judaeo-Christian heritage, thereby bringing our nation back to those great wells of democracy which were dug deep by the founding fathers in their formulation of the Constitution and the Declaration of Independence.

Never before have I written so long a letter. I'm afraid it is much too long to take your precious time. I can assure you that it would have been much shorter if I had been writing from a comfortable desk, but what else can one do when he is alone in a narrow jail cell, other than write long letters, think long thoughts and pray long prayers?

If I have said anything in this letter that overstates the truth and indicates an unreasonable impatience, I beg you to forgive me. If I have said anything that understates the truth and indicates my having a patience that allows me to settle for anything less than brotherhood, I beg God to forgive me.

I hope this letter finds you strong in the faith. I also hope that circumstances will soon make it possible for me to meet each of you, not as an integrationist or a civil rights leader but as a fellow clergyman and a Christian brother. Let us all hope that the dark clouds of racial prejudice will soon pass away and the deep fog of misunderstanding will be lifted from our fear-drenched communities, and in some not too distant tomorrow the radiant stars of love and brotherhood will shine over our great nation with all their scintillating beauty.

Yours for the cause of Peace and Brotherhood, Martin Luther King, Jr.

Malcolm X

Speech at Cory Methodist Church

April 3, 1964
Cory Methodist Church in Cleveland, Ohio

Mr. Moderator, Brother Lomax, brothers and sisters, friends and enemies: I just can't believe everyone in here is a friend and I don't want to leave anybody out. The question tonight, as I understand it, is "The Negro Revolt, and Where Do We Go From Here?" or "What Next?" In my little humble way of understanding it, it points toward either the ballot or the bullet.

Before we try and explain what is meant by the ballot or the bullet, I would like to clarify something concerning myself. I'm still a Muslim, my religion is still Islam. That's my personal belief. Just as Adam Clayton Powell is a Christian minister who heads the Abyssinian Baptist Church in New York, but at the same time takes part in the political struggles to try and bring about rights to the black people in this country; and Dr. Martin Luther King is a Christian minister down in Atlanta, Georgia, who heads another organization fighting for the civil rights of black people in this country; and Rev. Galamison, I guess you've heard of him, is another Christian minister in New York who has been deeply involved in the school boycotts to eliminate segregated education; well, I myself am a minister, not a Christian minister, but a Muslim minister; and I believe in action on all fronts by whatever means necessary.

Although I'm still a Muslim, I'm not here tonight to discuss my religion. I'm not here to try and change your religion. I'm not here to argue or discuss anything that we differ about, because it's time for us to submerge our differences and realize that it is best for us to first see that we have the same problem, a common problem, a problem that will make you catch hell whether you're a Baptist, or a Methodist, or a Muslim, or a nationalist. Whether you're educated or illiterate, whether you live on the boulevard or in the alley, you're going to catch hell just like I am. We're all in the same boat and we all are going to catch the same hell from the same man. He just happens to be a white man. All of us have suffered here, in this country, political oppression at the hands of the white man, economic exploitation at the hands of the white man, and social degradation at the hands of the white man.

Now in speaking like this, it doesn't mean that we're anti-white, but it does mean we're anti-exploitation, we're anti-degradation, we're anti-oppression. And if the white man doesn't want us to be anti-him, let him stop oppressing and exploiting and degrading us. Whether we are Christians or Muslims or nationalists or agnostics or atheists, we must first learn to forget our differences. If we have differences, let us differ in the closet; when we come out in front, let us not have anything to argue about until we get finished arguing with the man. If the late President Kennedy could get together with Khrushchev and exchange some wheat, we certainly have more in common with each other than Kennedy and Khrushchev had with each other.

If we don't do something real soon, I think you'll have to agree that we're going to be forced either to use the ballot or the bullet. It's one or the other in 1964. It isn't that time is running out—time has run out! 1964 threatens to be the most explosive year America has ever witnessed. The most explosive year. Why? It's also a political year. It's the year when all of the white politicians will be back in the so-called Negro community jiving you and me for some votes. The year when all of the white political crooks will be right back in your and my community with their false promises, building up our hopes for a letdown, with their trickery and their treachery, with their false promises which they don't intend to keep. As they nourish these dissatisfactions, it can only lead to one thing, an explosion; and now we have the type of black man on the scene in America today— I'm sorry, Brother Lomax—who just doesn't intend to turn the other cheek any longer.

Don't let anybody tell you anything about the odds are against you. If they draft you, they send you to Korea and make you face 800 million Chinese. If you can be brave over there, you can be brave right here. These odds aren't as great as those odds. And if you fight here, you will at least know what you're fighting for.

I'm not a politician, not even a student of politics; in fact, I'm not a student of much of anything. I'm not a Democrat, I'm not a Republican, and I don't even consider myself an American. If you and I were Americans, there'd be no problem. Those Hunkies that just got off the boat, they're already Americans; Polacks are already Americans; the Italian refugees are already Americans. Everything that came out of Europe, every blue-eyed thing, is already an American. And as long as you and I have been over here, we aren't Americans yet.

Well, I am one who doesn't believe in deluding myself. I'm not going to sit at your table and watch you eat, with nothing on my plate, and call myself a diner. Sitting at the table doesn't make you a diner, unless you eat some of what's on that plate. Being here in America doesn't make you an American. Being born here in America doesn't make you an American. Why, if birth made you American, you wouldn't need any legislation, you wouldn't need any amendments to the Constitution, you wouldn't be faced with civil-rights filibustering in Washington, D.C., right now. They don't have to pass civil-rights legislation to make a Polack an American.

No, I'm not an American. I'm one of the 22 million black people who are the victims of Americanism. One of the 22 million black people who are the victims of democracy, nothing but disguised hypocrisy. So, I'm not standing here speaking to you as an American, or a patriot, or a flag-saluter, or a flag-waver—no, not I. I'm speaking as a victim of this American system. And I see America through the eyes of the victim. I don't see any American dream; I see an American nightmare.

These 22 million victims are waking up. Their eyes are coming open. They're beginning to see what they used to only look at. They're becoming politically mature. They are realizing that there are new political trends from coast to coast. As they see these new political trends, it's possible for them to see that every time there's an election the races are so close that they have to have a recount. They had to recount in Massachusetts to see who was going to be governor, it was so close. It was the same way in Rhode Island, in Minnesota, and in many other parts of the country. And the same with Kennedy and Nixon when they ran for president. It was so close they had to count all over again. Well, what does this mean? It means that when white people are evenly divided, and black people have a bloc of votes of their own, it is left up to them to determine who's going to sit in the White House and who's going to be in the dog house.

It was the black man's vote that put the present administration in Washington, D.C. Your vote, your dumb vote, your ignorant vote, your wasted vote put in an administration in Washington, D.C., that has seen fit to pass every kind of legislation imaginable, saving you until last, then filibustering on top of that. And your and my leaders have the audacity to run around clapping their hands and talk about how much progress we're making. And what a good president we have. If he wasn't good in Texas, he sure can't be good in Washington, D.C. Because Texas is a lynch state. It is in the same breath as Mississippi, no different; only they lynch you in Texas with a Texas accent and lynch you in Mississippi with a Mississippi accent. And these Negro leaders have the audacity to go and have some coffee in the White House with a Texan, a Southern cracker—that's all he is—and then come out and tell you and me that he's going to be better for us because, since he's from the South, he knows how to deal with the Southerners. What kind of logic is that? Let Eastland be president, he's from the South too. He should be better able to deal with them than Johnson.

In this present administration they have in the House of Representatives 257 Democrats to only 177 Republicans. They control two-thirds of the House vote. Why can't they pass something that will help you and me? In the Senate, there are 67 senators who are of the Democratic Party. Only 33 of them are Republicans. Why, the Democrats have got the government sewed up, and you're the one who sewed it up for them. And what have they given you for it? Four years in office, and just now getting around to some civil-rights legislation. Just now, after everything else is gone, out of the way, they're going to sit down now and play with you all summer long—the same old giant con game that they call filibuster. All those are in cahoots together. Don't you ever think they're not in cahoots together, for the man that is heading the civil-rights filibuster is a man from Georgia named Richard Russell. When Johnson became president, the first man he asked for when he got back to Washington, D.C., was "Dicky"—that's how tight they are. That's his boy, that's his pal, that's his buddy. But they're playing that old con game. One of them makes believe he's for you, and he's got it fixed where the other one is so tight against you, he never has to keep his promise.

So it's time in 1964 to wake up. And when you see them coming up with that kind of conspiracy, let them know your eyes are open. And let them know you got something else that's wide open too. It's got to be the ballot or the bullet. The ballot or the bullet. If you're afraid to use an expression like that, you should get on out of the country, you should get back in the cotton patch, you should get back in the alley. They get all the Negro vote, and after they get it, the Negro gets nothing in return. All they did when they got to Washington was give a few big Negroes big jobs. Those big Negroes didn't need big jobs, they already had jobs. That's camouflage, that's trickery, that's treachery, window-dressing. I'm not trying to knock out the Democrats for the Republicans, we'll get to them in a minute. But it is true—you put the Democrats first and the Democrats put you last.

Look at it the way it is. What alibis do they use, since they control Congress and the Senate? What alibi do they use when you and I ask, "Well, when are you going to keep your promise?" They blame the Dixiecrats. What is a Dixiecrat? A Democrat. A Dixiecrat is nothing but a Democrat in disguise. The titular head of the Democrats is also the head of the Dixiecrats, because the Dixiecrats are a part of the Democratic Party. The Democrats have never kicked the Dixiecrats out of the party. The Dixiecrats bolted themselves once, but the Democrats didn't put them out. Imagine, these lowdown Southern segregationists put the Northern Democrats down. But the Northern Democrats have never put the Dixiecrats down. No, look at that thing the way it is. They have got a con game going on, a political con game, and you and I are in the middle. It's time for you and me to wake up and start looking at it like it is, and trying to understand it like it is; and then we can deal with it like it is.

The Dixiecrats in Washington, D.C., control the key committees that run the government. The only reason the Dixiecrats control these committees is because they have seniority. The only reason they have seniority is because they come from states where Negroes can't vote. This is not even a government that's based on democracy. It is not a government that is made up of representatives of the people. Half of the people in the South can't even vote. Eastland is not even supposed to be in Washington. Half of the senators and congressmen who occupy these key positions in Washington, D.C., are there illegally, are there unconstitutionally.

I was in Washington, D.C., a week ago Thursday, when they were debating whether or not they should let the bill come onto the floor. And in the back of the room where the Senate meets, there's a huge map of the United States, and on that map it shows the location of Negroes throughout the country. And it shows that the Southern section of the country, the states that are most heavily concentrated with Negroes, are the ones that have senators and congressmen standing up filibustering and doing all other kinds of trickery to keep the Negro from being able to vote. This is pitiful. But it's not pitiful for us any longer; it's actually pitiful for the white man, because soon now, as the Negro awakens a little more and sees the vise that he's in, sees the bag that he's in, sees the real game that he's in, then the Negro's going to develop a new tactic.

These senators and congressmen actually violate the constitutional amendments that guarantee the people of that particular state or county the right to vote. And the Constitution itself has within it the machinery to expel any representative from a state where the voting rights of the people are violated. You don't even need new legislation. Any person in Congress right now, who is there from a state or a district where the voting rights of the people are violated, that particular person should be expelled from Congress. And when you expel him, you've removed one of the obstacles in the path of any real meaningful legislation in this country. In fact, when you expel them, you don't need new legislation, because they will be replaced by black representatives from counties and districts where the black man is in the majority, not in the minority.

If the black man in these Southern states had his full voting rights, the key Dixiecrats in Washington, D.C., which means the key Democrats in Washington, D.C., would lose their seats. The Democratic Party itself would lose its power. It would cease to be powerful as a party. When you see the amount of power that would be lost by the Democratic Party if it were to lose the Dixiecrat wing, or branch, or element, you can see where it's against the interests of the Democrats to give voting rights to Negroes in states where the Democrats have been in complete power and authority ever since the Civil War. You just can't belong to that Party without analyzing it.

I say again, I'm not anti-Democrat, I'm not anti Republican, I'm not anti-anything. I'm just questioning their sincerity, and some of the strategy that they've been using on our people by promising them promises that they don't intend to keep. When you keep the Democrats in power, you're keeping the Dixiecrats in power. I doubt that my good Brother Lomax will deny that. A vote for a Democrat is a vote for a Dixiecrat. That's why, in 1964, it's time now for you and me to become more politically mature and realize what the ballot is for; what we're supposed to get when we cast a ballot; and that if we don't cast a ballot, it's going to end up in a situation where we're going to have to cast a bullet. It's either a ballot or a bullet.

In the North, they do it a different way. They have a system that's known as gerrymandering, whatever that means. It means when Negroes become too heavily concentrated in a certain area, and begin to gain too much political power, the white man comes along and changes the district lines. You may say, "Why do you keep saying white man?" Because it's the white man who does it. I haven't ever seen any Negro changing any lines. They don't let him get near the line. It's the white man who does this. And usually, it's the white man who grins at you the most, and pats you on the back, and is supposed to be your friend. He may be friendly, but he's not your friend.

So, what I'm trying to impress upon you, in essence, is this: You and I in America are faced not with a segregationist conspiracy, we're faced with a government conspiracy. Everyone who's filibustering is a senator—that's the government. Everyone who's finagling in Washington, D.C., is a congressman—that's the government. You don't have anybody putting blocks in your path but people who are a part of the government. The same government that you go abroad to fight for and die for is the government that is in a conspiracy to deprive you of your voting rights, deprive you of your economic opportunities, deprive you of decent housing, deprive you of decent education. You don't need to go to the employer alone, it is the government itself, the government of America, that is responsible for the oppression and exploitation and degradation of black people in this country. And you should drop it in their lap. This government has failed the Negro. This so-called democracy has failed the Negro. And all these white liberals have definitely failed the Negro.

So, where do we go from here? First, we need some friends. We need some new allies. The entire civil-rights struggle needs a new interpretation, a broader interpretation. We need to look at this civil-rights thing from another angle—from the inside as well as from the outside. To those of us whose philosophy is black nationalism, the only way you can get involved in the civil-rights struggle is give it a new interpretation. That old interpretation excluded us. It kept us out. So, we're giving a new interpretation to the civil-rights struggle, an interpretation that will enable us to come into it, take part in it. And these handkerchiefheads who have been dillydallying and pussy footing and compromising—we don't intend to let them pussyfoot and dillydally and compromise any longer.

How can you thank a man for giving you what's already yours? How then can you thank him for giving you only part of what's already yours? You haven't even made progress, if what's being given to you, you should have had already. That's not progress. And I love my Brother Lomax, the way he pointed out we're right back where we were in 1954. We're not even as far up as we were in 1954. We're behind where we were in 1954. There's more segregation now than there was in 1954. There's more racial animosity, more racial hatred, more racial violence today in 1964, than there was in 1954. Where is the progress?

And now you're facing a situation where the young Negro's coming up. They don't want to hear that "turn the-other-cheek" stuff, no. In Jacksonville, those were teenagers, they were throwing Molotov cocktails. Negroes have never done that before. But it shows you there's a new deal coming in. There's new thinking coming in. There's new strategy coming in. It'll be Molotov cocktails this month, hand grenades next month, and something else next month. It'll be ballots, or it'll be bullets. It'll be liberty, or it will be death. The only difference about this kind of death—it'll be reciprocal. You know what is meant by "reciprocal"? That's one of Brother Lomax's words, I stole it from him. I don't usually deal with those big words because I don't usually deal with big people. I deal with small people. I find you can get a whole lot of small people and whip hell out of a whole lot of big people. They haven't got anything to lose, and they've got every thing to gain. And they'll let you know in a minute: "It takes two to tango; when I go, you go."

The black nationalists, those whose philosophy is black nationalism, in bringing about this new interpretation of the entire meaning of civil rights, look upon it as meaning, as Brother Lomax has pointed out, equality of opportunity. Well, we're justified in seeking civil rights, if it means equality of opportunity, because all we're doing there is trying to collect for our investment. Our mothers and fathers invested sweat and blood. Three hundred and ten years we worked in this country without a dime in return—I mean without a dime in return. You let the white man walk around here talking about how rich this country is, but you never stop to think how it got rich so quick. It got rich because you made it rich.

You take the people who are in this audience right now. They're poor, we're all poor as individuals. Our weekly salary individually amounts to hardly anything. But if you take the salary of everyone in here collectively it'll fill up a whole lot of baskets. It's a lot of wealth. If you can collect the wages of just these people right here for a year, you'll be rich—richer than rich. When you look at it like that, think how rich Uncle Sam had to become, not with this handful, but millions of black people. Your and my mother and father, who didn't work an eight-hour shift, but worked from "can't see" in the morning until "can't see" at night, and worked for nothing, making the white man rich, making Uncle Sam rich.

This is our investment. This is our contribution—our blood. Not only did we give of our free labor, we gave of our blood. Every time he had a call to arms, we were the first ones in uniform. We died on every battlefield the white man had. We have made a greater sacrifice than anybody who's standing up in America today. We have made a greater contribution and have collected less. Civil rights, for those of us whose philosophy is black nationalism, means: "Give it to us now. Don't wait for next year. Give it to us yesterday, and that's not fast enough."

I might stop right here to point out one thing. When ever you're going after something that belongs to you, anyone who's depriving you of the right to have it is a criminal. Understand that. Whenever you are going after something that is yours, you are within your legal rights to lay claim to it. And anyone who puts forth any effort to deprive you of that which is yours, is breaking the law, is a criminal. And this was pointed out by the Supreme Court decision. It outlawed segregation. Which means segregation is against the law. Which means a segregationist is breaking the law. A segregationist is a criminal. You can't label him as anything other than that. And when you demonstrate against segregation, the law is on your side. The Supreme Court is on your side.

Now, who is it that opposes you in carrying out the law? The police department itself. With police dogs and clubs. Whenever you demonstrate against segregation, whether it is segregated education, segregated housing, or anything else, the law is on your side, and anyone who stands in the way is not the law any longer. They are breaking the law, they are not representatives of the law. Any time you demonstrate against segregation and a man has the audacity to put a police dog on you, kill that dog, kill him, I'm telling you, kill that dog. I say it, if they put me in jail tomorrow, kill that dog. Then you'll put a stop to it. Now, if these white people in here don't want to see that kind of action, get down and tell the mayor to tell the police department to pull the dogs in. That's all you have to do. If you don't do it, someone else will.

If you don't take this kind of stand, your little children will grow up and look at you and think "shame." If you don't take an uncompromising stand—I don't mean go out and get violent; but at the same time you should never be nonviolent unless you run into some nonviolence. I'm nonviolent with those who are nonviolent with me. But when you drop that violence on me, then you've made me go insane, and I'm not responsible for what I do. And that's the way every Negro should get. Any time you know you're within the law, within your legal rights, within your moral rights, in accord with justice, then die for what you believe in. But don't die alone. Let your dying be reciprocal. This is what is meant by equality. What's good for the goose is good for the gander.

When we begin to get in this area, we need new fiends, we need new allies. We need to expand the civil-rights struggle to a higher level—to the level of human rights. Whenever you are in a civil-rights struggle, whether you know it or not, you are confining yourself to the jurisdiction of Uncle Sam. No one from the outside world can speak out in your behalf as long as your struggle is a civil-rights struggle. Civil rights comes within the domestic affairs of this country. All of our African brothers and our Asian brothers and our Latin-American brothers cannot open their mouths and interfere in the domestic affairs of the United States. And as long as it's civil rights, this comes under the jurisdiction of Uncle Sam.

But the United Nations has what's known as the charter of human rights, it has a committee that deals in human rights. You may wonder why all of the atrocities that have been committed in Africa and in Hungary and in Asia and in Latin America are brought before the UN, and the Negro problem is never brought before the UN. This is part of the conspiracy. This old, tricky, blue eyed liberal who is supposed to be your and my friend, supposed to be in our corner, supposed to be subsidizing our struggle, and supposed to be acting in the capacity of an adviser, never tells you anything about human rights. They keep you wrapped up in civil rights. And you spend so much time barking up the civil-rights tree, you don't even know there's a human-rights tree on the same floor.

When you expand the civil-rights struggle to the level of human rights, you can then take the case of the black man in this country before the nations in the UN. You can take it before the General Assembly. You can take Uncle Sam before a world court. But the only level you can do it on is the level of human rights. Civil rights keeps you under his restrictions, under his jurisdiction. Civil rights keeps you in his pocket. Civil rights means you're asking Uncle Sam to treat you right. Human rights are some thing you were born with. Human rights are your God given rights. Human rights are the rights that are recognized by all nations of this earth. And any time any one violates your human rights, you can take them to the world court. Uncle Sam's hands are dripping with blood, dripping with the blood of the black man in this country. He's the earth's number-one hypocrite. He has the audacity—yes, he has— imagine him posing as the leader of the free world. The free world! And you over here singing "We Shall Overcome." Expand the civil-rights struggle to the level of human rights, take it into the United Nations, where our African brothers can throw their weight on our side, where our Asian brothers can throw their weight on our side, where our Latin-American brothers can throw their weight on our side, and where 800 million Chinamen are sitting there waiting to throw their weight on our side.

Let the world know how bloody his hands are. Let the world know the hypocrisy that's practiced over here. Let it be the ballot or the bullet. Let him know that it must be the ballot or the bullet.

When you take your case to Washington, D.C., you're taking it to the criminal who's responsible; it's like running from the wolf to the fox. They're all in cahoots together. They all work political chicanery and make you look like a chump before the eyes of the world. Here you are walking around in America, getting ready to be drafted and sent abroad, like a tin soldier, and when you get over there, people ask you what are you fighting for, and you have to stick your tongue in your cheek. No, take Uncle Sam to court, take him before the world.

By ballot I only mean freedom. Don't you know—I disagree with Lomax on this issue— that the ballot is more important than the dollar? Can I prove it? Yes. Look in the UN. There are poor nations in the UN; yet those poor nations can get together with their voting power and keep the rich nations from making a move. They have one nation—one vote, everyone has an equal vote. And when those brothers from Asia, and Africa and the darker parts of this earth get together, their voting power is sufficient to hold Sam in check. Or Russia in check. Or some other section of the earth in check. So, the ballot is most important.

Right now, in this country, if you and I, 22 million African-Americans—that's what we are—Africans who are in America. You're nothing but Africans. In fact, you'd get farther calling yourself African instead of Negro. Africans don't catch hell. You're the only one catching hell. They don't have to pass civil-rights bills for Africans. An African can go anywhere he wants right now. All you've got to do is tie your head up. That's right, go anywhere you want. Just stop being a Negro. Change your name to Hoogagagooba. That'll show you how silly the white man is. You're dealing with a silly man. A friend of mine who's very dark put a turban on his head and went into a restaurant in Atlanta before they called themselves desegregated. He went into a white restaurant, he sat down, they served him, and he said, "What would happen if a Negro came in here? And there he's sitting, black as night, but because he had his head wrapped up the waitress looked back at him and says, "Why, there wouldn't no nigger dare come in here."

So, you're dealing with a man whose bias and prejudice are making him lose his mind, his intelligence, every day. He's frightened. He looks around and sees what's taking place on this earth, and he sees that the pendulum of time is swinging in your direction. The dark people are waking up. They're losing their fear of the white man. No place where he's fighting right now is he winning. Everywhere he's fighting, he's fighting someone your and my complexion. And they're beating him. He can't win any more. He's won his last battle. He failed to win the Korean War. He couldn't win it. He had to sign a truce. That's a loss. Any time Uncle Sam, with all his machinery for warfare, is held to a draw by some rice eaters, he's lost the battle. He had to sign a truce. America's not supposed to sign a truce. She's supposed to be bad. But she's not bad any more. She's bad as long as she can use her hydrogen bomb, but she can't use hers for fear Russia might use hers. Russia can't use hers, for fear that Sam might use his. So, both of them are weapon less. They can't use the weapon because each's weapon nullifies the other's. So the only place where action can take place is on the ground. And the white man can't win another war fighting on the ground. Those days are over The black man knows it, the brown man knows it, the red man knows it, and the yellow man knows it. So they engage him in guerrilla warfare. That's not his style. You've got to have heart to be a guerrilla warrior, and he hasn't got any heart. I'm telling you now.

I just want to give you a little briefing on guerrilla warfare because, before you know it, before you know it. . . . It takes heart to be a guerrilla warrior because you're on your own. In conventional warfare you have tanks and a whole lot of other people with you to back you up, planes over your head and all that kind of stuff. But a guerrilla is on his own. All you have is a rifle, some sneakers and a bowl of rice, and that's all you need—and a lot of heart. The Japanese on some of those islands in the Pacific, when the American soldiers landed, one Japanese sometimes could hold the whole army off. He'd just wait until the sun went down, and when the sun went down they were all equal. He would take his little blade and slip from bush to bush, and from American to American. The white soldiers couldn't cope with that. Whenever you see a white soldier that fought in the Pacific, he has the shakes, he has a nervous condition, because they scared him to death.

The same thing happened to the French up in French Indochina. People who just a few years previously were rice farmers got together and ran the heavily-mechanized French army out of Indochina. You don't need it—modern warfare today won't work. This is the day of the guerrilla. They did the same thing in Algeria. Algerians, who were nothing but Bedouins, took a knife and sneaked off to the hills, and de Gaulle and all of his highfalutin' war machinery couldn't defeat those guerrillas. Nowhere on this earth does the white man win in a guerrilla warfare. It's not his speed. Just as guerrilla warfare is prevailing in Asia and in parts of Africa and in parts of Latin America, you've got to be mighty naive, or you've got to play the black man cheap, if you don't think some day he's going to wake up and find that it's got to be the ballot or the bullet.

I would like to say, in closing, a few things concerning the Muslim Mosque, Inc., which we established recently in New York City. It's true we're Muslims and our religion is Islam, but we don't mix our religion with our politics and our economics and our social and civil activities—not any more. We keep our religion in our mosque. After our religious services are over, then as Muslims we become involved in political action, economic action and social and civic action. We become involved with anybody, any where, any time and in any manner that's designed to eliminate the evils, the political, economic and social evils that are afflicting the people of our community.

The political philosophy of black nationalism means that the black man should control the politics and the politicians in his own community; no more. The black man in the black community has to be re-educated into the science of politics so he will know what politics is supposed to bring him in return. Don't be throwing out any ballots. A ballot is like a bullet. You don't throw your ballots until you see a target, and if that target is not within your reach, keep your ballot in your pocket. The political philosophy of black nationalism is being taught in the Christian church. It's being taught in the NAACP. It's being taught in CORE meetings. It's being taught in SNCC Student Nonviolent Coordinating Committee meetings. It's being taught in Muslim meetings. It's being taught where nothing but atheists and agnostics come together. It's being taught everywhere. Black people are fed up with the dillydallying, pussyfooting, compromising approach that we've been using toward getting our freedom. We want freedom now, but we're not going to get it saying "We Shall Overcome." We've got to fight until we overcome.

The economic philosophy of black nationalism is pure and simple. It only means that we should control the economy of our community. Why should white people be running all the stores in our community? Why should white people be running the banks of our community? Why should the economy of our community be in the hands of the white man? Why? If a black man can't move his store into a white community, you tell me why a white man should move his store into a black community. The philosophy of black nationalism involves a re-education program in the black community in regards to economics. Our people have to be made to see that any time you take your dollar out of your community and spend it in a community where you don't live, the community where you live will get poorer and poorer, and the community where you spend your money will get richer and richer. Then you wonder why where you live is always a ghetto or a slum area. And where you and I are concerned, not only do we lose it when we spend it out of the community, but the white man has got all our stores in the community tied up; so that though we spend it in the community, at sundown the man who runs the store takes it over across town somewhere. He's got us in a vise.

So the economic philosophy of black nationalism means in every church, in every civic organization, in every fraternal order, it's time now for our people to be come conscious of the importance of controlling the economy of our community. If we own the stores, if we operate the businesses, if we try and establish some industry in our own community, then we're developing to the position where we are creating employment for our own kind. Once you gain control of the economy of your own community, then you don't have to picket and boycott and beg some cracker downtown for a job in his business.

The social philosophy of black nationalism only means that we have to get together and remove the evils, the vices, alcoholism, drug addiction, and other evils that are destroying the moral fiber of our community. We our selves have to lift the level of our community, the standard of our community to a higher level, make our own society beautiful so that we will be satisfied in our own social circles and won't be running around here trying to knock our way into a social circle where we're not wanted.

So I say, in spreading a gospel such as black nationalism, it is not designed to make the black man re-evaluate the white man— you know him already—but to make the black man re-evaluate himself. Don't change the white man's mind—you can't change his mind, and that whole thing about appealing to the moral conscience of America—America's conscience is bankrupt. She lost all conscience a long time ago. Uncle Sam has no conscience. They don't know what morals are. They don't try and eliminate an evil because it's evil, or because it's illegal, or because it's immoral; they eliminate it only when it threatens their existence. So you're wasting your time appealing to the moral conscience of a bankrupt man like Uncle Sam. If he had a conscience, he'd straighten this thing out with no more pressure being put upon him. So it is not necessary to change the white man's mind. We have to change our own mind. You can't change his mind about us. We've got to change our own minds about each other. We have to see each other with new eyes. We have to see each other as brothers and sisters. We have to come together with warmth so we can develop unity and harmony that's necessary to get this problem solved our selves. How can we do this? How can we avoid jealousy? How can we avoid the suspicion and the divisions that exist in the community? I'll tell you how.

I have watched how Billy Graham comes into a city, spreading what he calls the gospel of Christ, which is only white nationalism. That's what he is. Billy Graham is a white nationalist; I'm a black nationalist. But since it's the natural tendency for leaders to be jealous and look upon a powerful figure like Graham with suspicion and envy, how is it possible for him to come into a city and get all the cooperation of the church leaders? Don't think because they're church leaders that they don't have weaknesses that make them envious and jealous—no, everybody's got it. It's not an accident that when they want to choose a cardinal as Pope over there in Rome, they get in a closet so you can't hear them cussing and fighting and carrying on.

Billy Graham comes in preaching the gospel of Christ, he evangelizes the gospel, he stirs everybody up, but he never tries to start a church. If he came in trying to start a church, all the churches would be against him. So, he just comes in talking about Christ and tells everybody who gets Christ to go to any church where Christ is; and in this way the church cooperates with him. So we're going to take a page from his book. Our gospel is black nationalism. We're not trying to threaten the existence of any organization, but we're spreading the gospel of black nationalism. Anywhere there's a church that is also preaching and practicing the gospel of black nationalism, join that church. If the NAACP is preaching and practicing the gospel of black nationalism, join the NAACP. If CORE is spreading and practicing the gospel of black nationalism, join CORE. Join any organization that has a gospel that's for the uplift of the black man. And when you get into it and see them pussyfooting or compromising, pull out of it because that's not black nationalism. We'll find another one.

And in this manner, the organizations will increase in number and in quantity and in quality, and by August, it is then our intention to have a black nationalist convention which will consist of delegates from all over the country who are interested in the political, economic and social philosophy of black nationalism. After these delegates convene, we will hold a seminar, we will hold discussions, we will listen to everyone. We want to hear new ideas and new solutions and new answers. And at that time, if we see fit then to form a black nationalist party, we'll form a black nationalist party. If it's necessary to form a black nationalist army, we'll form a black nationalist army. It'll be the ballot or the bullet. It'll be liberty or it'll be death.

It's time for you and me to stop sitting in this country, letting some cracker senators, Northern crackers and Southern crackers, sit there in Washington, D.C., and come to a conclusion in their mind that you and I are supposed to have civil rights. There's no white man going to tell me anything about my rights. Brothers and sisters, always remember, if it doesn't take senators and congressmen and presidential proclamations to give freedom to the white man, it is not necessary for legislation or proclamation or Supreme Court decisions to give freedom to the black man. You let that white man know, if this is a country of freedom, let it be a country of freedom; and if it's not a country of freedom, change it.

We will work with anybody, anywhere, at any time, who is genuinely interested in tackling the problem head-on, nonviolently as long as the enemy is nonviolent, but violent when the enemy gets violent. We'll work with you on the voter-registration drive, we'll work with you on rent strikes, we'll work with you on school boycotts—I don't believe in any kind of integration; I'm not even worried about it because I know you're not going to get it anyway; you're not going to get it because you're afraid to die; you've got to be ready to die if you try and force yourself on the white man, because he'll get just as violent as those crackers in Mississippi, right here in Cleveland. But we will still work with you on the school boycotts be cause we're against a segregated school system. A segregated school system produces children who, when they graduate, graduate with crippled minds. But this does not mean that a school is segregated because it's all black. A segregated school means a school that is controlled by people who have no real interest in it whatsoever.

Let me explain what I mean. A segregated district or community is a community in which people live, but outsiders control the politics and the economy of that community. They never refer to the white section as a segregated community. It's the all-Negro section that's a segregated community. Why? The white man controls his own school, his own bank, his own economy, his own politics, his own everything, his own community—but he also controls yours. When you're under someone else's control, you're segregated. They'll always give you the lowest or the worst that there is to offer, but it doesn't mean you're segregated just because you have your own. You've got to control your own. Just like the white man has control of his, you need to control yours.

You know the best way to get rid of segregation? The white man is more afraid of separation than he is of integration. Segregation means that he puts you away from him, but not far enough for you to be out of his jurisdiction; separation means you're gone. And the white man will integrate faster than he'll let you separate. So we will work with you against the segregated school system because it's criminal, because it is absolutely destructive, in every way imaginable, to the minds of the children who have to be exposed to that type of crippling education. Last but not least, I must say this concerning the great controversy over rifles and shotguns. The only thing that I've ever said is that in areas where the government has proven itself either unwilling or unable to defend the lives and the property of Negroes, it's time for Negroes to defend themselves. Article number two of the constitutional amendments provides you and me the right to own a rifle or a shotgun. It is constitutionally legal to own a shotgun or a rifle. This doesn't mean you're going to get a rifle and form battalions and go out looking for white folks, although you'd be within your rights—I mean, you'd be justified; but that would be illegal and we don't do anything illegal. If the white man doesn't want the black man buying rifles and shotguns, then let the government do its job. That's all. And don't let the white man come to you and ask you what you think about what Malcolm says —why, you old Uncle Tom. He would never ask you if he thought you were going to say, "Amen!" No, he is making a Tom out of you." So, this doesn't mean forming rifle clubs and going out looking for people, but it is time, in 1964, if you are a man, to let that man know. If he's not going to do his job in running the government and providing you and me with the protection that our taxes are supposed to be for, since he spends all those billions for his defense budget, he certainly can't begrudge you and me spending $12 or $15 for a single-shot, or double-action. I hope you under stand.

Don't go out shooting people, but any time, brothers and sisters, and especially the men in this audience—some of you wearing Congressional Medals of Honor, with shoulders this wide, chests this big, muscles that big—any time you and I sit around and read where they bomb a church and murder in cold blood, not some grownups, but four little girls while they were praying to the same god the white man taught them to pray to, and you and I see the government go down and can't find who did it. Why, this man—he can find Eichmann hiding down in Argentina somewhere. Let two or three American soldiers, who are minding somebody else's business way over in South Vietnam, get killed, and he'll send battleships, sticking his nose in their business. He wanted to send troops down to Cuba and make them have what he calls free elections—this old cracker who doesn't have free elections in his own country. No, if you never see me another time in your life, if I die in the morning, I'll die saying one thing: the ballot or the bullet, the ballot or the bullet.

If a Negro in 1964 has to sit around and wait for some cracker senator to filibuster when it comes to the rights of black people, why, you and I should hang our heads in shame. You talk about a march on Washington in 1963, you haven't seen anything. There's some more going down in '64. And this time they're not going like they went last year. They're not going singing "We Shall Overcome." They're not going with white friends. They're not going with placards already painted for them. They're not going with round-trip tickets. They're going with one way tickets.

And if they don't want that non-nonviolent army going down there, tell them to bring the filibuster to a halt. The black nationalists aren't going to wait. Lyndon B. Johnson is the head of the Democratic Party. If he's for civil rights, let him go into the Senate next week and declare himself. Let him go in there right now and declare himself. Let him go in there and denounce the Southern branch of his party. Let him go in there right now and take a moral stand—right now, not later. Tell him, don't wait until election time. If he waits too long, brothers and sisters, he will be responsible for letting a condition develop in this country which will create a climate that will bring seeds up out of the ground with vegetation on the end of them looking like something these people never dreamed of. In 1964, it's the ballot or the bullet. Thank you.

An Open Letter to the Grape Industry

Cesar Chavez

E. L. Barr, Jr., President
California Grape & Tree Fruit League

Dear Mr. Barr,

I am sad to hear about your accusations in the press that our union movement and table grape boycott has been successful because we have used violence and terror tactics. If what you say is true, I have been a failure and should withdraw from the struggle. But you are left with the awesome moral responsibility, before God and man, to come forward with whatever information you have so that corrective action can begin at once.

If for any reason you fail to come forth to substantiate your charges then you must be held responsible for committing violence against us, albeit violence of the tongue. I am convinced that you as a human being did not mean what you said but rather acted hastily under pressure from the public relations firm that has been hired to try to counteract the tremendous moral force of our movement. How many times we ourselves have felt the need to lash out in anger and bitterness.

Today on Good Friday, 1969, we remember the life and sacrifice of Martin Luther King, Jr., who gave himself totally to the nonviolent struggle for peace and justice. In his letter from Birmingham Jail, Dr. King describes better than I could our hopes for the strike and boycott: "Injustice must be exposed, with all the tension its exposure creates, to the light of human conscience and the air of national opinion before it can be cured." For our part, I admit that we have seized upon every tactic and strategy consistent with the morality of our cause to expose that injustice and thus to heighten the sensitivity of the American conscience so that farmworkers will have without bloodshed their own union and the dignity of bargaining with their agribusiness employers.

By lying about the nature of our movement, Mr. Barr, you are working against nonviolent social change. Unwittingly perhaps, you may unleash that other force that our union by discipline and deed, censure and education has sought to avoid, that panacean short cut: that senseless violence that honors no color, class, or neighborhood.

YOU MUST understand, I must make you understand, that our membership—and the hopes and aspirations of hundreds of thousands of the poor and dispossessed that have been raised on our account—are, above all, human beings, no better no worse than any other cross section of human society; we are not saints because we are poor but by the same measure neither are we immoral. We are men and women who have suffered and endured much and not only because of our abject poverty but because we have been kept poor. The color of our skins, the languages of our cultural and native origins, the lack of formal education, the exclusion from the democratic process, the numbers of our slain in recent wars— all these burdens generation after generation have sought to demoralize us, to break our human spirit. But God knows we are not beasts of burden, we are not agricultural implements or rented slaves, we are men. And mark this well, Mr. Barr, we are men locked in a death struggle against man's inhumanity to man in the industry that you represent. And this struggle itself gives meaning to our life and ennobles our dying.

As your industry has experienced, our strikers here in Delano and those who represent us throughout the world are well trained for this struggle. They have been under the gun, they have been kicked and beaten and herded by dogs, they have been cursed and ridiculed, they have been stripped and chained and jailed, they have been sprayed with the poisons used in the vineyards. They have been taught not to lie down and die or to flee in shame, but to resist with every ounce of human endurance and spirit. To resist not with retaliation in kind but to overcome with love and compassion, with ingenuity and creativity, with hard work and longer hours, with stamina and patient tenacity, with truth and public appeal, with friends and allies, with mobility and discipline, with politics and law, and with prayer and fasting. They were not trained in a month or even a year; after all, this new harvest season will mark our fourth full year of strike and even now we continue to plan and prepare for the years to come. Time accomplishes for the poor what money does for the rich.

This is not to pretend that we have everywhere been successful enough or that we have not made mistakes. And while we do not belittle or underestimate our adversaries, for they are the rich and powerful and possess the land, we are not afraid nor do we cringe from the confrontation. We welcome it! we have planned for it. We know that our cause is just, that history is a story of social revolution, and that the poor shall inherit the land.

Once again, I appeal to you as the representative of your industry and as a man. I ask you to recognize and bargain with our union before the economic pressure of the boycott and strike take an irrevocable toll; but if not, I ask you to at least sit down with us to discuss the safeguards necessary to keep our historical struggle free of violence. I make this appeal because as one of the leaders of our nonviolent movement, I know and accept my responsibility for preventing, if possible, the destruction of human life and property.

For these reasons and knowing of Gandhi's admonition that fasting is the last resort in place of the sword, during a most critical time in our movement last February, 1968, I undertook a 25-day fast. I repeat to you the principle enunciated to the membership at the start of the fast: if to build our union required the deliberate taking of life, either the life of a grower or his child, or the life of a farmworker or his child, then I choose not to see the union built.

MR. BARR, let me be painfully honest with you. You must understand these things. We advocate militant nonviolence as our means for social revolution and to achieve justice for our people, but we are not blind or deaf to the desperate and moody winds of human frustration, impatience, and rage that blow among us. Gandhi himself admitted that if his only choices were cowardice or violence, he would choose violence. Men are not angels and the time and tides wait for no man. Precisely because of these powerful human emotions, we have tried to involve masses of people in their own struggle. Participation and self-determination remain the best experience of freedom; and free men instinctively prefer democratic change and even protect the rights guaranteed to seek it. Only the enslaved in despair have need of violent overthrow.

This letter does not express all that is in my heart, Mr. Barr. But if it says nothing else, it says that we do not hate you or rejoice to see your industry destroyed; we hate the agribusiness system that seeks to keep us enslaved and we shall overcome and change it not by retaliation or bloodshed but by a determined nonviolent struggle carried on by those masses of farmworkers who intend to be free and human.

Sincerely yours, CESAR E. CHAVEZ 1969

Religious Politics and America's Moral Dilemmas

Isaac Kramnick
R. Laurence Moore

Morality and virtue are not issues that belong exclusively to the religious right or, for that matter, to religion. They concern everyone interested in the future of democratic society. Some of the founders of this nation were Christian; others were not. Many of them were members of churches; many others were not. What they shared was a view that religion should not divide people, an opinion that provided them with sufficient reason to exclude God-based claims from most sorts of political debate. On the other hand, their desire for nondivisive religious climate stemmed directly from their belief that religion was an indispensable civic resource. If the American people could not maintain moral standards in their public and private dealings, they could not make democracy work. A people without compassion or mercy, a people without a sense that social injustices suffered by their neighbors were social wounds to the entire commonwealth, a people without honesty or integrity, a people without the capacity to forgive and to sacrifice, a people who refused to care about the effect of their self-interested actions upon others, above all, a people who could not safeguard the hopefulness and idealism of its youth—such a people would surely perish from the earth, having prepared no future generation to mourn them.

Despite, or rather because of, this passionate concern for morality, the founding fathers made no constitutional provisions for the national government to instruct its citizens in matters of moral and religious conscience. They did not want America to be godless, only its government. How, then, did they imagine that a democratic state could ensure that its citizens would incorporate moral codes into private conscience? The simple answer is that they did not. A democratic government was not created to produce moral citizens. It was the other way around: moral citizens constructed and preserved democracy. The founders left the business of teaching morality to private concerns, a principle that should carry some weight with present-day conservatives. It follows from this formulation that if the United States at the end of the twentieth century has lost its moral way, many of our voluntary institutions, including our megachurches and our television ministries, have badly let us down.

Indeed they may have. But responsibility for moral problems is never easy to assign. We may take some comfort in recognizing that there never was a golden age of moral behavior in the American past. Pick any point in the history of the Republic. Read the journals,

Source: Chapter Eight, "Religious Politics and America's Moral Dilemmas," by Isaac Kramnick and R. Laurence Moore, reprinted from *The Godless Constitution*, 1997, W.W. Norton & Company.

newspaper editorials, and public addresses of the time. The depressing news about moral decay was as sensational then as it is now. Anyone who wishes to ignore these diatribes from not so long ago and insist that things, morally speaking, *were* better in the nineteenth century ought to note, with respect to the question of why our ancestors were our moral superiors, that churches were not as well attended then as they are now. Neither were the public schools in those halcyon days when McGuffey's Readers purportedly took care of the moral and religious instruction of the nation's children. However, trying to excuse ourselves by making flattering comparisons with the past is as nonproductive as imagining that there was once a golden age. Any nation with our current levels of violent assaults, drug-related murders and suicides, teenage pregnancies, child abuse, AIDS, and white-collar crimes had best concentrate on the present realities.

But, whatever our plight, we must never forget the many good reasons why the founders did not look to politicians and the state to inculcate morality. Our first presidents and legislators looked upon politics, as we understand the activity today, as a corrupting activity. Although Jefferson, called an atheist by the religious right of his time, believed fervently in the social importance of religion as the foundation of morality, he did not confuse the work of government with the work of churches and private citizens. As leaders of the religious right now correctly state, Jefferson insisted that government do nothing to interfere with the moral work of private agencies. What those leaders have stated less correctly is that his caveat that government not discourage religious work also placed upon government an obligation not to encourage it—not, in any case, in a way that privileged it over the work of nongovernmental secular agencies.

For Jefferson the moral possibilities of democracy depended on keeping America an agricultural nation. That is, he did not think that democracy and the morality necessary to sustain democracy could flourish under social conditions that destroyed the economic independence of individuals. When the United States, after Jefferson's death, committed its future to the industrial revolution, when it encouraged the growth of large cities and of gigantic economic institutions that hardened class lines in America, public morality encountered problems that it had not known before. That fact was clearly recognized by people of all political persuasions. Too many of the rich did not need morality. Too many of the poor could not afford it. The burden of sustaining public morality fell heavily on the already overburdened middle classes, and disproportionately on middle-class women, who, curiously, were told to stay at home and not interest their pretty heads in the corrupting business of politics.

Simply put, we live in a world where we cannot assume that moral behavior has universal appeal, regardless of what we teach. In fact, we are constantly discouraged by the reality that the people who should be our solid citizens, the people who know the moral rules and who by dint of all manner of privileges are in the best position to live by them, fall regularly into corrupt practices involving money, power, and sex. There is plenty to worry about and only limited help to be gotten from the founding fathers, who were nagged by their own particular problems of public morality and who could not have foreseen the special problems that hover over society at the end of the twentieth century. Nonetheless, the attitudes of the Enlightenment that shaped the course of the American Revolution have not lost their relevance. As we have argued throughout this book, the founders of this nation would regard the mixing of religion and politics in the ways now being engineered by the religious right as part of the problem of failing public morality, rather than as an answer.

We have indicated along the way that Pat Robertson is an excellent example of how the religious right has misread the intentions that lay behind the Constitution and of the dangers contained in that misreading. His case merits extended attention. A religious leader turned politician, Robertson ran for president in 1988, hoping to turn his appeal as an avuncular talk show host who has built a media empire into charisma on the hustings. In 1988 that didn't work. However, through the Christian Coalition, which he created, Robertson has effectively raised money for conservative candidates, provided an army of volunteer workers for politicians who share his views, and emerged as a powerful figure in the Republican party.

What is the message? Robertson's books and speeches decry the country's moral decline and blame the decline on the enemies of religion. He has a long and a short view of when this moral rot set in. The long view rests on the loopy conspiracy theory involving Freemasons and Illuminati who wandered through the eighteenth century stirring people up against kings and clerics. The story has been around a long time, and in most history departments, including in all likelihood the one at Robertson's own Regent University, it has been thoroughly discredited.

In Robertson's short view, America's moral decline started with a cabal of New Deal liberals, a category of secular cosmopolitans whose number just happened to include a lot of Jews who ran banks but liked Karl Marx. These secularists hated the Christian religion and have since the New Deal wormed their way into positions of power with the explicit intention of wiping out religious faith. Two seconds of reflection ought to convince anyone that this bizarre scenario has no credible basis in fact. But Robertson knows, and herein lies one of the dangers, that when people are worried, imagined enemies can take on supernatural abilities. Once liberals can be turned into agents of Satan, then Robertson doesn't have to supply them with plausible motives or explain how they can so cleverly fool well-meaning people.

Robertson's comments about the New Deal never once let on that the country was in the midst of the worst depression in its history—that men and women with families could not find work, that people were standing in line for food, that individuals were having their religious faith severely tested because their children were sick and hungry and because churches had run out of resources. The Americans who voted for the New Deal were not dupes. They formed, in fact, a political constituency that was heavily churched. Robertson's unfounded charges against liberals who hate God and moral decency is an inexcusably careless reading of the American past. As a misuse of religion to advance a political agenda, it constitutes exactly the sort of corruption that the founders feared when ambitious men rose up and announced that God had chosen them to found a political movement. It is the sort of thing that gives populism a bad name.

The people with the best reason to attack Pat Robertson are devout Christians who care about the credibility of their faith. They object to the partisan uses he has sought to make of the passion of Christ. There are many versions of Christianity. But not one of them worthy of respect, and especially not the Pentecostal faith where Robertson began, would trivialize the agony and suffering of its redemptive God into campaign slogans for politicians. Faith, to be blunt, is irrelevant to many of the political causes that Robertson has forcefully championed. Not to all of them, and we shall come to those issues. What needs emphasis now is the fact that Robertson's self-declared war to save the soul of America is not with secular humanists, as he says. It is with other Christians.

In truth, it is sometimes hard to make out just who counts as a Christian in Robertson's view of the world. On the one hand, Robertson is quite certain that America is a Christian nation and that its Christianity explains its greatness. For example, he contends that the United States has succeeded because "those men and women who founded the land made a solemn covenant that they would be the people of God and that this would be a Christian nation." Shoring up this argument, Robertson variously estimates that 90 percent of the American people are Christian and that almost 50 percent of them regularly attend church. Although there is room to quarrel with those figures, the general point that Robertson means to make is fair enough. Compared with most European nations, America boasts a high proportion of citizens who state that they believe in God, that religion is important in their lives, and that they identify in general terms with a Christian faith as opposed to any of its rivals, including atheism.

Yet Robertson fails to follow up the implications of what he has written about moral decline. If Americans are Christian—in fact, if they are by dint of church membership more Christian than they were a hundred years ago, and vastly more Christian than they were in the eighteenth century—then how do we explain the decline of religiously based morality? Can it really be that a cabal of God-hating liberals has succeeded, despite the overwhelming numbers confronting them, in driving religion from the public square? And without anyone's suspecting, before Robertson and other leaders of the religious right came along, what they were up to? An alternative theory might suggest that too many religious leaders have stopped doing what they do well and started doing what they do badly, in alliance with men who don't care much about religion at all except when it returns votes.

We thus have an anomaly. If moral decline is evidenced by the rate of divorce, the amount of extramarital sex, and the increase of abortions, all part of the record cited by Robertson, then clearly the 90 percent of Americans whom Robertson cites to prove that the United States is a Christian nation are deeply implicated in the decline. Why, then, does Robertson, as a religious leader, not turn his gaze on the Christian churches of America, and the kind of gospel message they preach, and look for problems that might exist there? For the most part, Robertson is uninterested in the strengths or the failures of organized religion, or the possibility that religion may be its own worst enemy. The villain for spiritual decline is the state, which never in this country carried the burden for maintaining the spiritual health of the people or for teaching them how to pray. Roger Williams would have smelled a rat. If religion isn't making people who profess to believe in it good, neither can the Republican nor the Democratic party.

Nonetheless, many religious Americans have been touched by claims made by the religious right that government is not neutral in religious and moral matters. They have been mobilized by calls to take some sort of cooperative political action to reverse what they perceive as liberal-led measures that abrogate a long-standing moral consensus about values, especially ones that touch on sexual behavior. The consequences in the political arena have been impressive. A number of smart pundits have suggested that in the midterm elections of 1994 that swept conservative Republicans into control of both houses of Congress, the Christian Coalition established itself as the single most powerful voting bloc in the nation.

If that is so, it is in no small measure due to the skills of Ralph Reed, a man with a Ph.D. in American history and an innocent youthful appearance that masks what is probably the shrewdest political mind in the religious right movement. Pat Robertson tapped Reed to give the Christian Coalition a less contentious aura. Most especially, Reed has labored, without deleting the word "Christian" from the name of the organization and its journal, to free the organization of its deserved reputation for anti-Semitism, bathroom humor directed at women in public office, and purveyance of sleazy political gossip.

The Christian Coalition, under Reed, ostentatiously welcomes Jewish members who share its value concerns. It publicly rejects the view of one Southern Baptist minister tied to conservative politics that God does not hear the prayers of Jews. In his own bailiwick Jerry Falwell seems to have gotten at least this point and has insisted that the Moral Majority imposes no religious test. He has stated, "I would feel comfortable voting for a Jew or a Catholic or an atheist as long as he or she agrees with us on the vital issues." After the United States, the greatest nation in the world, says Falwell, is Israel. That pronouncement rests on a quirky base, that is, the conversion of Israel to Christianity prior to the battle of Armageddon. Nonetheless, it explains why the Moral Majority and the Christian Coalition have been defended by the editors of the Jewish New York journal *Commentary*. In addition, many Catholics who were the primary victims of Protestant political movements in the nineteenth century have endorsed the Christian Coalition.

Since Falwell and others have repeatedly insisted that America was founded on the Christian faith, one must wonder about the consistency of the message that the Christian Coalition promulgates. But Reed seems determined, if not to take Christ out of the Christian Coalition, at least to move him to one side. It might be possible to do that. The authors note with gratitude that many of the people who use the facilities of the Young Men's Christian Association in Ithaca, New York, where they regularly play racquetball, are neither Christian nor male. The name of the YMCA is historic, meaningful to some, less meaningful to others. The important thing is that it does not get in the way of anyone who wishes to use and to support a resource that does, after all, make an important contribution to the moral life of the community. The strength of great religious traditions in the United States, we can all agree, should be a source of pride in American life, not a cause for embarrassment. However, a great religious tradition is not always served well by those who speak for it.

Reed is a born-again fundamentalist Christian, but he is a born political junkie with a specific but a flexible political agenda. What he has announced as the Christian Coalition's legislative proposals for a "Contract with the American Family" is an endorsement of the broad economic goals of conservative Republicans. Wrapping the secular and the moral up together, Reed uses the label "family values" to accomplish two things of practical political importance. It implies that those who oppose the package aren't loyal to their spouses and don't love their children. It also allows the Christian Coalition plenty of room to be pragmatic. If restrictions on abortion rights won't fly, then attack welfare spending. If prayer in the school doesn't appeal to enough conservative voters, then argue that increased spending for the military is Christian. If you sense that no one will vote for legislation to make divorce more difficult, and certainly not leading Republican men, then link high taxes to moral decline.

Religious fundamentalists are not necessarily happy with this sort of politics. Many of them suspect that Ralph Reed's leadership of the Christian Coalition has let the organization become the tool of the conservative wing of a Republican party that has no burning interest in its moral agenda. They are also suspicious of Reed's "stealth" tactics, in which Christian candidates are encouraged to play down a moral agenda while running for office. A moral purpose that has to disguise itself appears to them to be a poor way to change people's hearts and minds. Our view is that the fundamentalists are right in holding these suspicions. If so, it won't be the first time in American history that religious leaders with a moral political agenda will learn that big-league politicians who covet the Oval Office want power first and treat everything after that as negotiable, depending on prevailing political winds.

Reed does not intend to be anyone's patsy. He means to turn the Christian Coalition into something more formidable than the Sabbatarian organizations of the nineteenth century, the groups that up to this point the Christian right has most closely resembled. Sabbatarians imagined their enemy to be a party of secularists who wanted to destroy churches, tear down Sunday schools, and abolish the "Lord's Day" by delivering the mail on Sundays. Their political efforts fizzled because they were finally interested only in a single moral point. Reed is determined to avoid that weakness. His fundamental ambition, which he states candidly, is to take over the Republican party and, in effect, to create something that has always existed in many European nations but never in the United States—a religious or confessional political party.

Religious parties do not mark the end of freedom, as experience in many European states has indicated. That is because the religious aims quickly get submerged by secular issues that any ruling party needs to address if it is to stay in power. Yet a religious party seems distinctly out of place in a country that made the elimination of an established church one of the first orders of national business. Reed has repeatedly denied a number of charges leveled against the Christian Coalition—that it seeks to make Christianity the official religion of the United States, that it seeks to cram its moral values down the throats of other unwilling Americans, that it has contempt for people who are secular. That has been difficult, not because he doesn't believe in the broad base he wants to build for his political movement, but because many members of the Christian Coalition don't.

One model of religious politics that Reed frequently invokes is the civil rights movement led by Martin Luther King. King's genius, Reed correctly notes, was to tailor a religious message that could reach a largely secular culture. In Reed's mind, the sort of religious politics that propelled the civil rights movement can be used to create an analogous sort of religious politics to drive a profamily movement. His analogy isn't persuasive. Reed certainly understands what made King effective. King's message called for healing and reconciliation: "Our aim must never be to defeat or humiliate the white man but to win his friendship and understanding. We must come to see that the end we seek is a society at peace with itself, a society that can live with its conscience, that will be a day not of the white man, not of the black man, that will be the day of man as man." King's dream of society cleansed of racial injustice was an inclusive vision that called upon all Americans to share in a mission of simple justice.

Inclusion. That is what defeats Reed. If ever he can come up with a way to write a profamily speech, one that will be acceptable to the Christian Coalition, that calls upon gays and straights, feminists and Christian fundamentalists, atheists and Roman Catholics, unmarried welfare mothers and Pat Robertson to join hands and sing the words of the great spiritual "Free at last, Free at last, Thank God almighty, we are free at last," he will have done something that might yet move this nation. But that isn't the message he is even remotely close to delivering. The Christian Coalition is a political movement with too many sour voices in it, whose use of religion has divided and stigmatized people.

To be sure, Reed makes a good point against many of his critics when he notes that religious leaders on the left have often in American history promoted a liberal agenda of government relief programs for the poor and powerless. The Social Gospel of the left has more than once drawn up specific policy recommendations concerning pending legislation on such matters as child labor, minimum wage, and fair labor practices. The temptation to become a political lobbying group runs along the spectrum of religious politics. So does the temptation to morally stigmatize your opponents. The classic example in American history is the case of religious abolitionists who made slavery an issue of sin. Surely slavery was a great moral evil. Yet when those on the religious right suggest that you can't condemn the Christian Coalition without condemning the abolitionists or the liberal-oriented political action committees of the National Council of Churches, they almost have a point.

It isn't a direct score, because it ignores an important difference between the Social Gospel of Christians who have used the ethical teachings of Jesus to warn against class and racial injustice and their own version of applied Christianity that too often seems to be merely an apology for wealth. The Social Gospel movement at the end of the nineteenth century and during the first part of the twentieth argued that the moral teachings of the Bible put the case for the weak against the powerful. Christ spoke for the poor and defenseless and cast moral blame not on those who suffered but on those who could not be moved by their suffering.

Most of us are not about to go out and sell our property and give it to the poor. Human beings aren't ready to be that good, at either end of the social scale. On the other hand, if people can't be touched by the call of compassion that is central to the New Testament, if the comforts of privilege are so great that the religious contribution to public debate becomes an invitation to ignore the poor and the homeless, then religion has nothing distinctive to say. It becomes just another sad sign of the times that the country may have lost a conscience to reach, that no one wants to hear a political message, whether religious or secular, that makes people uncomfortable. The difference between King's moral plea for racial justice and too much of the Christian pro-family program of everlasting patriarchy is the difference between the voice of the religious prophet who calls upon an unjust society, for all societies are unjust, to transcend itself and the voice of ecclesiastical judges who have a particular set of sins with which to charge heretics. Granted, it isn't always easy to tell the difference, but with respect to any important effect that religion can have in the American public sphere, the difference matters.

The (Really) Conservative Media

Eric Alterman

ONE REASON THAT MANY PEOPLE, including some liberals, believe the myth of the liberal media is that they do not know how extensive and influential the conservative media is. It is not simply that when you add up the circulation/penetration of the Fox News Channel, the *Wall Street Journal* editorial page, the *New York Post, Washington Times, Weekly Standard, National Review, American Spectator, Human Events,* www.andrewsullivan.com, the Drudge Report, Rush Limbaugh, the entire universe of talk radio, and most of the punditocracy, you've got a fair share of the media. The ability of these deeply biased and frequently untrustworthy outlets to shape the universe of the so-called "liberal media" gives them a degree of power and influence that exceeds their already considerable circulations.

As we have seen in earlier chapters, nefarious political operatives, masquerading as journalists, helped turn the Clintons' unprofitable $30,000 investment in a failed savings and loan into a politically paralyzing, $70 million constitutional crisis. But they could not have done it without the full cooperation of such mainstream media outlets as the *Washington Post* and ABC News, which have grown increasingly cowed by false complaints of liberal bias and, hence, progressively more sympathetic to the most outlandish conservative complaints.

When *Washington Post* White House reporter John Harris noted that he and his fellow White House correspondents were proving far more sympathetic to the conservative George W. Bush than they had ever been to the "liberal" Bill Clinton, he chose as his main culprit "conservative interest groups, commentators and congressional investigators" who, beginning in 1993, "waged a remorseless campaign that they hoped would make life miserable for Clinton and vault themselves to power." This movement had been in the works for decades and had helped turn the tide in Washington toward conservatism as early as 1978, when Jimmy Carter was forced to switch directions in mid-presidency and embrace a host of measures that he had previously found to be anathema. But during the previous decade and a half, conservative interest groups had grown both more powerful and more conservative, outpacing liberals at first and soon matching and eventually exceeding in many cases the resources of the old establishment. Liberals have no such movement, not a fraction of the money, and what troops they possess can boast much less organizational discipline than that enjoyed by the right. As Harris noted, the left lacks the ability (if not the inclination) to weave all "manner of presidential miscues, misjudgments or controversial decisions" into a fabric of alleged scandal. As a result of the context created by the conservative warriors, Harris argued, "stories like the travel office firings flamed for weeks instead of receding into yesterday's news. And they colored the prism through which many Americans, not just conservative ideologues, viewed Clinton." I quote Harris at length because, working within the belly of the so-called beast, he knows that of which he speaks:

> For the most part, Clinton's foes and their contemptuous views of him were within the bounds of fair debate. But Democrats are not likely to give as good as they got. They simply aren't as well organized. And they are not shouting as loudly.
>
> Few liberal commentators see themselves self-consciously representing an ideological movement the way many conservatives do. The Brookings Institution tilts liberal but is not an ideological arsenal in the way the Heritage Foundation is. Who is the liberal version of Rush Limbaugh, who so colorfully rallied opposition to Clinton? Nor is there an obvious Democratic version of Rep. Dan Burton (R-Ind.), eager to aim the investigative apparatus of Congress at the White House. Bush is also catching a break from his own side: Clinton's nomination of a gay man as ambassador to Luxembourg caused outrage on the right; Bush's naming a gay AIDS czar was met largely with silence on Capitol Hill.
>
> In Clinton's first term, Rep. Richard K. Armey (R-Tex.) turned to Democrats and said, "Your president is just not that important to us." This underscores the irony that Bush, whose ascension was clouded by questions over whether he really won, has been accorded more legitimacy by the opposition than Clinton was—or than Gore would have been had he become president while winning the popular vote.
>
> The discrepancy also illustrates how Bush and his aides miss the point with their constant boasting about how Bush has "changed the tone" in Washington after the coarsening Clinton years. Clinton disgraced himself through his personal behavior and by then taking flight from honor and accountability. But Washington's snarling public tone was caused more by his opponents; he was as ready to meet with Republicans as Bush is with Democrats. Little of his rhetoric ever matched the vitriol that congressional Republicans aimed at him.

Franklin Foer of the not-so-liberal *New Republic* shares Harris's basic analysis of an objectively pro-conservative Republican Washington media, but believes that reporters let themselves and their colleagues off the hook too easily by blaming outside pressure groups. The problem, as Foer diagnoses it, is that "after years of listening to conservatives complain about their bias, and years of living in fear of overzealous media critics, liberal reporters have been completely cowed." Of course the two hypotheses are not exactly contradictory. Conservatives have spent billions during the past three decades, both to pressure the mainstream media to move rightward and to create their own parallel media structure, which serves the same purpose as it provides an alternative viewpoint both to the faithful and the gullible. Unbeknownst to millions of Americans who continue to believe that the media are genuinely liberal—or that conservatives and liberals are engaged in a fair fight of relative equality—liberals are fighting a near-hopeless battle in which they are enormously outmatched by most measures. Just take a look, for example, at the power and influence exercised within the media by the self-described "wild men" of the *Wall Street Journal* editorial page.

For twenty-nine years before he stepped down in 2001 to become a columnist for the paper, Robert Bartley led his *Journal* editorial page staff in the practice of a kind of journalism alien to most newspapers and newsmagazines. It was not typical editorial page opinion-mongering. It was not the objective style of reporting to which all national newspapers, including the *Wall Street Journal*, aspire. It was something else entirely; a reported polemic, written in a style akin to a Sunday sermon on hellfire and damnation, or perhaps a politically inverted Alexander Cockburn column. Michael Kinsley, a former columnist for the page, calls the page's methods "Stalinist" and couched in "intellectual dishonesty." Alex Jones, head of the Shorenstein Center at Harvard, termed Bartley's pages "perhaps the most influential, most articulate, most ferocious opinion page in the country." Its power, *New Yorker* editor David Remnick noted, is "amplified by the audience it reaches every day—five and a half million of the nation's best educated and most influential citizens." In January 2002, the *Journal* added the viewers of CNBC to its Dow Jones–powered global reach, as that station inexplicably chose the editors to present a weekly version of the extremist opinion-mongering it offers in print on a daily basis, with no balance from a single moderate, much less an actual liberal. Given this influence, it seems likely that if you added up every genuinely liberal voice in the American political discourse—every single newspaper pundit, talk-show co-host, opinion magazine columnist or writer, and Internet scribbler—you would not have accumulated even one half of the power enjoyed on a daily basis by the *Journal*'s firebreathing staff.

Under the curiously soft-spoken Bartley's direction, the *Journal*'s editorial pages did more than make American journalistic history; they made political and economic history too. During the late 1970s and early 1980s, as the economic historian Wayne Parsons observed, "without [the *Journal*'s] support it is difficult to see how the supply-side argument could possibly have achieved such a leading position in the economic policy debates." The amazing story of the *Journal*'s near single-handed promotion of a theory from economic outer space—one that lacked a single well-known and respected proponent in the economic profession at the time of its adoption by candidate and then President Ronald Reagan, has been told many times. When, after twelve years in which supply-side-inspired deficits threatened to strangle future growth, Bill Clinton was forced to clean up the economic mess, Bartley had no doubt about what would happen. Clinton's proposals, he predicted, would "cripple" the economy. When the plan passed, the paper promised, "[W]e are seeing the early signs of the stagflation that we knew so well during the Carter presidency." "Hysteria" would not be too strong a term to describe the *Journal*'s reaction to the Clinton plan. The headline, "The Class Warfare Economy" was attended by a cartoon of a guillotine. The tiny rise in the nation's top marginal tax rates to a level where they remained the second lowest in the industrialized world did not turn out well for the editors. The Clinton years resulted in an unbroken expansion of the economy in which the vast majority of its benefits were tilted toward the very wealthy, the people on whom "class war" had allegedly been declared.

The *Journal* editors are so deeply committed to the far-right propaganda they espouse, they frequently contradict the reporting in their own newspaper. For instance, in 1980 a *Journal* reporter broke a story proving that an alleged $100 million administration cost offered up by a group of California oil firms protesting a new state tax, was, in fact, a wildly exaggerated estimate of the expense of administering the tax. Two days later, the editorial page noted, "according to one estimate, enforcement of the tax would cost taxpayers $100 million. . . ." Four years later, Washington bureau reporter David Rogers discovered that the CIA had been illegally mining Nicaragua's harbors. The story ran on page six and was picked up by the *Washington Post*. Six days afterwards, the editorial page, standing foursquare behind the contrawar, criticized members of Congress for leaking the information to the *Post*. More recently, the paper's reporters won a Pulitzer Prize for exposing the misleading statements of tobacco company officials, leading to massive jury awards in tobacco liability cases. Meanwhile, Bartley and company ridiculed tobacco regulations as "further government-imposed nuisances, whose chief direct effect will be to make millionaires of a few more lawyers."

In August 2002, Bartley wrote a column in favor of war with Iraq in which he insisted that because the Bush administration had succeeded "for the first time exerting American leadership to unify the factions opposing Saddam." In uniting the Iraqi opposition, "The pieces are now in place to liberate Iraq." A day later, the *Journal* ran a heavily reported page one story that popped Bartley's hot air balloon. "The tension among Iraq's opposition groups amounts to a significant impediment as the Bush administration speaks more publicly about ousting Mr. Hussein," the *Journal* reporters explained, offering the kind of evidence entirely absent from his op-ed. Readers of only the editorial page might have been surprised, a day later, to discover that the most powerful Kurdish chieftain in northern Iraq, Massoud Barzani, had refused the Bush administration's invitation to attend its meeting. But one suspects the paper's readership among America's titans of industry are well aware as to which portions of the paper to trust when real money is on the line.

When it comes to the editors' ideological opponents, all gloves come off and most journalistic rulebooks go out the window. During the 1984 election, for instance, the *WSJ* editorial pages ran a story rejected by the newspaper about alleged connections between Geraldine Ferraro and the Mafia, based on her husband's business dealings. In the following election, it published rumors about Democrat Michael Dukakis's psychological state that originated with known nut-case Lyndon LaRouche and dealt mainly with Dukakis's brother.

Journal editors like to paint the media as soft on Communism, though the only credible example to which they can easily point is Rupert Murdoch's defense of China. (See below.) And while, to its credit, the *Journal* has been tough on Murdoch, its contributors have also been genuinely soft on fascism. The brutal Chilean dictator, Augusto Pinochet, they argued, "saved his country," transforming it from "a Communist beachhead to an example of free-market reform." That the so-called "Communist beachhead" was actually a democratically elected government, the editors do not mention. Former editor Jude Wanniski termed the death-squad leader and priest killer, Roberto D'Aubuisson of El Salvador to be the victim of a "McCarthyist" media cabal and "one of the most successful propaganda hoaxes of the decade." (Wanniski has also developed a decidedly soft spot for another would-be fascist, Louis Farrakhan, and serves as perhaps his most high-profile champion in America.) It's not easy, in the eyes of the editors, for any right-winger to go too far. But when it happens, it usually turns out to be the fault of leftists. For instance, when, in 1993, a right-wing terrorist murdered an abortion doctor named David Gunn in Pensacola, Fla., the editors blamed . . . the Sixties' New Left: "We think it is possible to identify the date when the United States . . . began to tip off the emotional tracks," they explained. "The date is

August 1968, when the Democratic National Convention found itself sharing Chicago with the street fighters of the anti–Vietnam War movement." The protesters, they went on, were responsible for "lowering the barriers of acceptable political and personal conduct." In other words, Jerry Rubin made me do it. Again, if, for the sake of balance, the Dow Jones corporation and CNBC wished to balance their politics with the equivalently extreme views from the left, they would have a hard time finding anyone at all in the United States, save perhaps Alexander Cockburn, who by sheer coincidence, no doubt, is also a former *Wall Street Journal* editorial page columnist.

The *Journal* editors, moreover, play by journalistic rules of their own making. In a lengthy examination in the *Columbia Journalism Review*, Trudy Lieberman examined six dozen examples of disputed editorials and op-eds in the paper. She discovered that "on subjects ranging from lawyers, judges, and product liability suits to campus and social issues, a strong America, and of course, economics, we found a consistent pattern of incorrect facts, ignored or incomplete facts, missing facts, uncorroborated facts." In many of these cases, the editors refused to print a correction, preferring to allow the aggrieved party to write a letter to the editor, which would be printed much later, and then let the reader decide whose version appeared more credible. Almost never is the record corrected or do the editors admit their errors.

The page's cavalier attitude toward facts and corrections is matched by an impressive ferocity of language. Frequently, its content is closer to a Rush Limbaugh radio rant or an Ann Coulter outburst than the Olympian tone employed by editorial writers on Fifteenth Street or in Times Square. Citizens who support consumer and safety regulation are termed "no-growth specialists, the safety and health fascists who try to turn real and imagined hazards to some political end." One editorial even referred to "so-called acid rain." To *Journal* editorial writers, the rest of the media—including presumably the paper's own reporting staff—is not merely liberal, but, as Mark Helprin wrote in its pages, "slavish[ly] obedien[t]" to Democratic liberals. This has, he insisted, "quintupled the arrogance of the most arrogant people in America, a triumphalist coterie of graduate students who accord to the hard left the same uneasy respect that most people reserve for the clergy, and grow teary-eyed over bats, squirrels and caribou as with barely concealable pleasure they sacrifice whole regions of rednecks."

Aside from the Chicken Little-like role vis-à-vis the Clinton economic plan, the primary task the paper set for itself during the 1990s was the responsibility for publishing virtually every anti-Clinton rumor ever started, no matter how farfetched or lightly sourced. When White House aide Vincent Foster committed suicide in a park outside Washington in 1993, he left a note saying "the *WSJ* editors lie without consequence." (The *Journal* had been insinuating nefarious activity on Foster's part.)

Politically, having the imprimatur of the *Journal* and its first-rate reporting staff gives its editorial pages far greater credibility and significance than they could possibly have achieved by mere force of argument. Many of the arguments made on its pages would be permanently relegated to the extreme fringes of political debate were it not for their appearance in one of the world's greatest newspapers. Nevertheless it was the *Journal*'s embrace of these strange tales that helped keep conservative hopes alive long enough for Kenneth Starr's investigation to find something—or anything—with which to impeach Bill Clinton.

The strange pursuit of poor Vince Foster, in death as in life, is a case in point. While it is obviously a bit unfair to blame the *Journal* writers for Foster's suicide—though he may have—their journalistic values with regard to his case left a great deal to be desired. "Until the Foster death is seriously studied, a Banquo's ghost will stalk . . . the Clinton administration," one long editorial warned, paying particular attention to Mrs. Clinton's movement on the day of Foster's death, as if to cast her as a contemporary Lady MacBeth. The *Journal* also praised other media outlets' outlandish pursuits with regard to this paranoid endeavor. Its assistant features editor, Erich Eichman, later books editor, expressed "a debt of gratitude" for the *New York Post's* irresponsible speculation that Foster's gun had been put in his hand after his death and the body had been moved to the spot where it was found. Two days afterward, the editors imagined a vicious physical attack on a reporter whose notes were allegedly stolen, no doubt to prevent the disclosure of some other dastardly deed. This piece was entitled "Censored in Arkansas" and argued that *Harper's* reporter L. J. Davis had met with foul play while reporting a story on Whitewater in Little Rock. But the *Journal* editors turned out to have played fast and loose with the facts, once again, though the facts themselves are quite confusing. Davis lost some pages of his notes after waking up unconscious in his hotel room. He told a reporter he did not remember much beyond that and admitted to having downed at least four martinis on the night in question. But the hotel manager later explained, "We have records that he was down here [at the hotel bar] at 10:30 that night," which was supposed to be the end of when he said he had been unconscious. The hotel bartender confirmed the manager's version and put the number of martinis Davis consumed at six. Davis, meanwhile, quite understandably, never mentioned the incident in print, thinking it insignificant and not trusting his own memory. He says he asked the *Journal* to print a retraction of its wild allegations, but of course it refused.

The Foster "murder" may have disappointed, but two months later, the paper went back to the paranoid well, this time on behalf of the infamous Jerry Falwell videotape, "The Clinton Chronicles," in which Clinton was blamed for Foster's murder, Davis's alleged assault, and even a mob-related killing during his Arkansas governorship. While the paper pretended to disassociate itself from the film's nuttiest charges—"finding no real evidence of a Clinton connection, and feeling the President of the United States is entitled to a presumption of innocence, we decline in the name of responsibility to print what we've heard"— it still felt compelled to print the 800 phone number so that its readers might obtain their own copy.

One of the prime movers of the *Journal's* anti-Clinton obsession was John Fund, who spent a great deal of time meeting with members of the Arkansas Project and some of the more notorious figures in the Paula Jones lawsuit and "Get-Clinton" conspiracy. Fund acted as kind of a father figure to many of them, helping to guide their strategy in secret while simultaneously writing editorials in the *Journal* accusing Clinton of all manner of unproven malfeasance. It was a complicated balancing act; it could not last. In a tale that appears almost too weird to write down, it seems that a woman named Melinda Pillsbury-Foster with whom Fund had had an affair more than twenty years ago, sent her young daughter, Morgan, to look up Fund when she went to New York. One thing led to another, and the results appear to have been a live-in relationship and an abortion.

Anyway, Fund's relationship with the daughter of his ex-girlfriend did not exactly work out, inspiring mother and daughter to take their revenge by uploading onto the Web a taped telephone call in which John attempts to reconcile his support for Morgan's abortion with his "family values" politics. Mrs. Foster then informed the media that John and Morgan had decided to wed after all. This turned out to be false, but the next thing you know, Fund was gone from the *Journal*'s editorial page and was apparently the victim of a series of bizarre but quite public campaigns designed to destroy his reputation—up to and including an arrest (with charges later dropped) for battery that included a restraining order. (Irony of ironies, the Rush Limbaugh ghost-writer is also cited in David Brock's book, among other places, as a likely source for Matt Drudge's false and malicious claim that Sidney Blumenthal was a wife-beater, though Fund denies this.) Fund denies the charges and, in the view of this writer, is almost certainly innocent. (I have always found him to be very much a gentleman in his personal dealings.) Still, the charges demonstrate the difficulties that so many conservatives face—the pot-smoking, draft-dodging, multiply adulterous, deadbeat dad named Newt Gingrich; Henry Hyde, who broke up another man's family at age 40 in his "youthful" adulterous fling; adulterers Robert Dole and Robert Livingston; to say nothing of men of the cloth such as Jim Bakker and Jimmy Swaggart—who seek to enforce their hypocritical moralistic standards on the rest of us as they ignore them. The fact that the media take these people seriously, while knowing of the hypocrisies that lie beneath their charges—is further evidence of the foolish fiction that promotes the SCLM myth.

When Robert Bartley turned over the keys to the editor's office, he did so to Paul Gigot, a former speechwriter for James Baker during the Reagan administration and the page's Washington columnist. Gigot achieved a kind of infamy when, in November 2000, he celebrated the violent Republican riot that shut down the vote counting in Miami-Dade County and helped pave the way for the Supreme Court's handing of the presidency to George. W. Bush. (See Chapter 9.) Still, he is not quite as nutty as Bartley and has even been known to do some reporting as a columnist in Washington, which tended to keep his analyses tethered, however tenuously, to earth. With Bartley gone and Fund removed from the page, the editorialists had to work hard to retain their reputation for loopiness. They did, however, have the advantage of enjoying the services of another former Reagan speechwriter, Peggy Noonan, who has set a standard that is hard to beat.

Noonan does not appear to research her columns. She just gets feelings about people and goes with them. ("Is it irresponsible to speculate? It is irresponsible not to," she wrote.) These feelings tend to match her political prejudices, particularly in the case of people of whom she happens to disapprove. "When I first met Hillary Clinton she was a plain, dumpy woman with glasses and a shawl. I thought she was sweet," she wrote. But "people have worked on her clothes and her image; she's gone through a lot and come out cold and ambitious. Neither she nor Bill loves America. They don't want the presidency to help the country but to use it as a platform to power." (*Journal* editorial writers have a thing about Hillary Clinton. Mark Helprin once used the pages to compare her to a "900-pound boyfriend of a voluptuous girl hitchhiker.")

Al Gore was no better, Noonan decided. He was, she wrote, "not fully stable" and "altogether as strange and disturbing as Bill Clinton." What's more, he was a liar. Once again, how did Noonan know? She just knew. Before the 2000 election, she wrote, with regard to partial birth abortion, the vice president "supports something he knows to be sick and wrong." The same was true regarding education. Gore, Noonan declared, somehow "knows [that] the most hopeful proposal of our time to make government schools better is the school liberation movement—including scholarship vouchers," but "Al Gore lies and says vouchers are bad." On Social Security, you guessed it: "Al Gore knows that it is responsible and constructive to allow greater freedom and choice in Social Security. . . . But he lies and says it's bad." Lucky for Gore and the Clintons that they are not Arabs. Noonan supports a war against, well, she is not quite clear against whom because "bad guys" tend to breed too quickly. "I tell you this," she explained to a reporter for the *Spectator* (UK). "It looks like the bad guys are breeding and proliferating pretty well already. You might say, quite literally, that at least an attack will keep a few of them from breeding at all."

Noonan likes to play the pundit game of attributing the things she "knows" to "everyone." For instance, when the Bush White House was actively seeking to deceive reporters and the nation with its phony "vandalism" scandal, she told readers, "Everyone I know is talking about the 'pranks' of the departing Clinton-Gore crew on the incoming White House staff—the W's pried off the keyboards, the garbage left in the vice president's offices. You just know when you read about it that it's worse than anyone is saying—the Bush people being discreet because they don't want to start out with complaints and finger pointing." The story, which turned out to have virtually no basis in fact, proved to Noonan that "The Clintons were at heart vandals."

Many observers thought Noonan outdid herself in late 2002 when she penned a mock–Paul Wellstone column from beyond the grave. Wellstone stood foursquare behind just about everything the *Journal* and Noonan opposed. But with the wisdom that comes with death—"You learn things here quickly. . . . You can literally see the big picture. You can see people's souls."—she informs Wellstone's supporters that the late senator disapproved of his memorial service. "You hurt a lot of people," Noonan has Wellstone's ghost telling those who loved him. "You offended and hurt and antagonized more than half the country. . . . Some of you need to get a good psychologist. . . ." It gets better. Noonan recruits a few other dead guys to make her case: "Jack Kennedy was here, and you're not going to like this, but he said what he said the day Nixon had his meltdown in '62. He looked at you and said, 'No class.' John Adams is here too. He turned away from you in disgust. 'Faction!' is what he said. It was no compliment." Her Wellstone admits to being sorry for what Peggy has him say, but like any good dead leftist populist Democrat being channeled by a right-wing corporatist Republican, he was only saying these harsh things "because I care about you."

The Wellstone-from-beyond-the-grave column might be considered Noonan's high point were it not for the masterpiece she crafted during the "Elian" episode of 2000, when she managed to set a standard for a combination of childlike hero worship and downright silliness that belongs in textbooks devoted to either quality. In that famous episode, in which a group of Miami Cubans did not wish to return a child whose mother had been killed at sea to his father in Cuba—with the support of the very same "family values" crowd among U.S. conservatives—Noonan complained that her hero, Reagan, would never have allowed his justice department to enforce the law and the court's decisions to return the child. Moreover, he "would not have dismissed the story of the dolphins [sent by God to rescue Elián, according to some of the young boy's protectors/kidnappers] as Christian kitsch, but seen it as possible evidence of the reasonable assumption that God's creatures had been commanded to protect one of God's children." She concludes, "But then he was a man." Indeed.

The *Wall Street Journal* editors enjoy the backing of the Dow Jones Corporation and CNBC, and even with their more than five million readers, a few hundred thousand viewers, and the uncounted numbers who read their opinions on the Internet, via www.opinionjournal.com, they have to be considered relative pikers compared to the empire amassed by the veritable Wizard of Oz, Rupert Murdoch. With a net worth hovering in the area of $5 billion, the Australian national's News Corporation has holdings that include:

- Fox Broadcasting Network;
- Fox Television Stations, including over twenty U.S. television stations, the largest U.S. station group, covering more than 40 percent of U.S. TV households;
- Fox News Channel;
- A major stake in several U.S. and global cable networks, including fx, fxM and Fox Sports Net, National Geographic Channel, Fox Kids Worldwide, and Fox Family Channel;
- Ownership or major interests in satellite services reaching Europe, the United States, Asia, and Latin America, often under the Sky Broadcasting brand;
- 20th Century Fox, with its library of over 2,000 films; 20th Century Fox International, 20th Century Fox Television, 20th Century Fox Home Entertainment, Fox Searchlight Pictures, Fox Television Studios;
- Over 130 English-language newspapers (including the *London Times* and the *New York Post*), making Murdoch's one of the three largest newspaper groups in the world;
- At least twenty-five magazines, including *TV Guide* and the *Weekly Standard*;
- HarperCollins, Regan Books, Zondervan Publishers;
- Fox Interactive, News Interactive, www.foxnews.com;
- Festival Records;
- The Los Angeles Dodgers.

While most of Murdoch's corporations are registered abroad to avoid taxes—News Corp. pays a paltry 7.8 percent effective tax rate in the United States—Murdoch gets more for his money as he is able to use the proceeds of one to support the other. Politically and commercially, he is determined to put "synergy" to work. Murdoch's magazines and newspapers support his television programs and movies and vice versa. His reporters make up news that other companies would have to pay public relations firms millions to try to place. No newspaper in America is less shy about slanting its coverage to serve its master's agenda—be it commercial or political—than the *New York Post*. Judging by the *Post*, almost every Fox program is either "jaw-dropping," "megasuccessful," "highly anticipated," or all three. Columnist Gersh Kuntzman once revealed that editors consider page two to be the "Pravda Page." "When there's a major [Murdoch] business deal going down, with no interest to readers," he explained, "it's on page two. Or when [then-conservative New York Senator Alfonse] D'Amato makes a pronouncement of no particular interest to readers, it's on page two." Oftentimes, this tendency turns the paper into kind of an extended inside joke in the media, where it is carefully read because of its obsessive media-oriented gossip. For instance, the *Post* declared the film *Titanic*, a Murdoch property, to have received "the first endorsement of any Hollywood movie by a Chinese official." The paper did not mention just who believed it or why this mattered. The entire article was based on a premise so farfetched—that the entire Chinese nation was agitating to see the sappy film a full month before it was scheduled to open—that the article read as a kind of satiric self-criticism session of the kind that Maoists used to undergo in the days when they plotted to overthrow the evil government of "Amerika."

Once famous for its loveably nutty "Headless Body in Topless Bar"–type headlines in the early 1980s, Murdoch's tabloid has lost him perhaps hundreds of millions of dollars over the years at a rate of $10 million to $30 million per annum. (Actual figures are a closely guarded secret.) But despite its down-market definition of news, the paper still provides Murdoch with an entree to the media elite because of its great gossip pages, and, hardly incidentally, its terrific sports section. Curiously, in a city that is so fierce about its cultural pride, in late 2002 the *New York Post* was run largely by Australian imports. The *Post's* current editor, hired in 2001, is Col Allan, a man who brags about peeing in the sink during editorial meetings and enjoys the nickname "Col Pot" back in Sydney. Allan took just six weeks to decide to fire the *Post's* only black editor, Lisa Baird, who was fighting a losing battle with breast cancer at the time. He also fired the paper's only liberal columnist, that feisty New York institution, Jack Newfield, preferring the columns of Victoria Gotti, the sexy daughter of a murderous mob boss. Allan also demonstrated his tin ear for New York politics quite early in his tenure when, upon Jim Jeffords's decision to switch sides in the Senate and vote with the Democrats—thereby giving that party a one-vote majority—he headlined the front page "Benedict Jeffords." New York, someone might have pointed out to him, has two Democratic senators and voted for both Al Gore and Bill Clinton by so large a margin that they barely needed to campaign there. Its denizens were not exactly angry about a switch in the Senate that gave their side more power.

Murdoch made no attempt to hide his paper's political agenda. Rudy Giuliani, who all but forced Time Warner to add Fox News Channel to its local roster of stations, was second only to Leonardo in the *Post's* pantheon of heroic Italians. Hillary Clinton, the "rejected wife," who proved the cause of "a veritable crime wave in the White House" and who, while running for senator, "couldn't find the Bronx unless she had a chauffeur, and couldn't find Yankee Stadium with a Seeing Eye dog," was, to say the least, treated rather less generously. To the degree that any racial problems existed anywhere in New York, they were always the fault of black people, who demand special treatment or merely raise a ruckus for its own sake—all of these views shared by many on the right. All Israelis were noble warriors; all Palestinians, vicious terrorists. These, however, were predictable prejudices for a right-wing ideologue. The most interesting bias exhibited by Murdoch media properties was that on behalf of Communist totalitarianism—at least of the variety practiced in Beijing.

Initially Murdoch held conventional views about murderous Communist dictatorships and praised the manner in which modern telecommunications "have proved an unambiguous threat to totalitarian regimes everywhere." But when Beijing shutdown his satellite broadcasts, Red Rupert switched sides, telling critics: "The truth is—and we Americans don't like to admit it—that authoritarian societies can work." When the Chinese complained about how the BBC portrayed them, Murdoch booted it off his Asian satellite network, Star TV. "The BBC was driving them nuts," he was quoted as saying. "It's not worth it." Sucking up to the killers soon became a family affair. Murdoch's son James even found some kind words to say about the Reds' enforcement of anti-religious repression.

Murdoch's publishing companies were put to work for the commies as well. Murdoch gave over a million bucks to Deng Xiaoping's daughter for an unreadable propagandistic tome that no sane person could ever have imagined would become a best-seller in the West. When Chris Patten's tough-minded memoir of his years as the governor of Hong Kong threatened to upset the Chinese, however, Murdoch canceled the contract and attacked its author. His explanation? "We're trying to get set up in China. Why should we upset them?"

Amazingly, Murdoch would not even take his own (adopted) nation's side in a conflict with the Chinese. During the hostage crisis of April 2001, while the Chinese were refusing to release U.S. soldiers, the paper seemed to undergo a personality transplant, all but ignoring the biggest story in the world. *Post* editorials, which usually declare war every time someone sneezes near the Stars and Stripes, were almost completely mum. John Podhoretz, who later advised George Bush to invade Iraq merely to get the corporate accounting scandals off the front page, was the perfect diplomat. Steve Dunleavy, who, as the *Post*'s almost insanely belligerent columnist, usually thinks of foreign policy as a subset of bar-fighting, proved to be remarkably patient and thoughtful in his discussion of the crisis. "Until happiness is restored to 24 American kids and their families, let's keep our sabers safely and silently sheathed," wrote the newly sissified tough guy. "Careless rhetoric can prove disastrous to freedom, as President Jimmy Carter harshly learned during the Iran hostage crisis."

In 1985 Murdoch acquired 20th Century Fox Studios, in much the same way he acquired the *New York Post*: with lots of cash and some crucial political interventions from the politicians he funded. He combined the company with the fledgling Metromedia television stations to launch America's first new broadcast network since the early days of television. Fox was given every break imaginable throughout the 1980s on the grounds that a new television network should be encouraged. Finally, in 1994, following nearly ten years of indifference, the Federal Communications Commission checked into the network's ownership to see if it was foreign-owned. It was; Murdoch's News Corporation was actually an Australian company, not an American one, as he had portrayed it. But rather than allow the commission to enforce the law, according to Reed Hundt, then the FCC chair, conservative Republicans "lambasted me for the audacity of having looked into the question."

While some of what the Fox network produced has been genuinely great—most notably *The Simpsons*—much of its programming appears devoted to answering the question "just how low can you go?" Conservatives like William Bennett and Pal Robertson enjoy condemning liberals for the promotion of casual sex and alternative lifestyles at the expense of society's bedrock social institutions like marriage and courtship, but Robertson has no more powerful and influential enemy in this regard than his business partner in the Fox Family Channel. In the spring of 2000, the network that had invented *Studs*, a dating show with stripping men, managed to amaze even its critics with *Who Wants to Marry a Millionaire?* Here, women were invited to prostitute themselves and debase the institution of marriage for the greater glory of Fox's ratings. (It almost didn't matter that the program's producers went about this task entirely incompetently, as the alleged "millionaire" was no such thing, but did have a few restraining orders in his past. The marriage was never consummated but the "bride" did get to pose naked in *Playboy*.) A year afterward, Fox managed to outdo itself in the cultural debasement sweepstakes with the debut of *Temptation Island*, in which four "committed" couples were dumped on an island and filmed "canoodling" in various combinations.

From the outset, the network's "news" programs demonstrated a similarly catholic interpretation of the term "family values" when it came to reeling in viewers (and hence profits). Its original flagship, *A Current Affair*, erased much of the journalistic rulebook. As Burt Kearns, one of its top producers, later recounted, in order to get a copy of a tape alleging to show the actor Rob Lowe having sex with some young women of "jailbait" age, at the 1988 Democratic convention in Atlanta, the producers lifted footage from an Atlanta station and claimed it as its own, paid a club owner for the sex tape even though he had no legal ownership, and physically destroyed the evidence in the face of a lawsuit. As Kearns put it. "The Rob Lowe tape was a milestone for the show and tabloid television. Sex, celebrity, politics, crime, morality and America's obsession with home video cameras were all rolled into one. . . . We were the fucking champions of the world." (In fact, the events caught on tape did not really take place in Atlanta but were filmed in France. There were no underage girls involved and hence, no story. But nobody ever reported that.) Details aside, Kearns was right. The conservative Roger Ailes, the former Reagan/Bush aide who then went on to head Fox News Channel, said he did not believe that such shows even require defense. "News is what people are interested in," Ailes insisted. "We're just getting the same girls to dance around shinier poles."

Despite this rather tricky track record, family-values wise, when Murdoch began Fox News Channel in 1996 with Ailes at the helm, conservatives fell all over themselves to praise it. "If it hadn't been for Fox, I don't know what I'd have done for the news," Trent Lott gushed during the Florida election recount. George W. Bush extolled Bush I-aide-turned-anchor Tony Snow for his "impressive transition to journalism" in a specially taped April 2000 tribute to Snow's Sunday-morning show. The eight-wing Heritage Foundation had to warn its staffers to stop watching so much Fox News on their computers, lest the entire system crash.

The conservative orientation of Fox is invaluable to the right, not merely because Fox offers the spin on reality conservatives prefer to have people see and hear, but also because it helps pull the rest of the not-terribly liberal media in its direction. In Chapter 10, I discussed the key role played by Fox and its election analyst, George W. Bush's loyal cousin, John Ellis, in helping create the media stampede to call the election for Bush. But the hiring of Ellis was no isolated incident; rather it was symbolic of business as usual. For instance, when, just before Election Day, the media discovered that George W. Bush had been hiding a DUI conviction, Fox seemed to spin the incident even more furiously than Karl Rove and Karen Hughes. Morton Kondracke of *Roll Call:* "A footnote." John Fund of the *Wall Street Journal:* "A blip." Mara Liasson of NPR: "Yes, I agree with that. I think it's a blip." The program in question—*Fox Special Report with Brit Hume*—did not even bother to devote much attention to the potentially election-altering news. Instead it focused, once again, on troubles Al Gore had in fighting off Ralph Nader.

When it did return to the story, the FNC spin focused on the Bush campaign's charge that the Gore team had somehow engineered the leak. FNC's Tony Snow went so far as to give credence to "rumors" that the Clinton administration had been involved and predicted that this might help the Bush campaign by creating sympathy for it—and therefore "backfire" on Gore. Snow never cited a shred of evidence for any of these claims, which was wise as none existed. Meanwhile, FNC's Paula Zahn mused aloud on the question of just how long Maine Democrats had "sat on the story." In fact, it was the local Maine newspaper, where the Bush family compound is located, that sat on the story, for whatever reason we cannot know. As Eric Boehlert noted, all this spin-oriented damage control is, indeed, a far cry from the days during the height of the Clinton scandals, when former FNC correspondent Jeb Duvall, according to his account in *New York Magazine*, was once met by a news producer who "came up to me, and, rubbing her hands like Uriah Heep, said, 'Let's have something on Whitewater today.'"

Such fare is, however, the norm for a station where a special about foreign policy is hosted by Fox commentator and former Republican House Speaker Newt Gingrich; *Heroes*, an irregular series, is hosted by Gingrich's ex-colleague in the Republican congressional leadership, John Kasich; and on *The Real Reagan*, a panel discussion on Ronald Reagan, hosted by Tony Snow, all six guests were Reagan friends and political aides, plus the ever-present Ollie North. Fox's coverage of the conflict in Afghanistan is similarly slanted but also kind of crazily flawed. Most famous, of course, was the incident in which Geraldo Rivera missed the spot of the "hallowed ground" from which he pretended to be reporting by a mere 200 miles.

But most news organizations have displayed a bias toward the American side in covering the events in Afghanistan. Indeed, how could they not? While none beside Rivera brag about "packing heat" and laughably threaten to take out bin Laden themselves, these reporters too are Americans, who saw the tapes of the horror of September 11. Most are not only deeply patriotic people themselves, personally sympathetic to the soldiers and their cause, but also quite understandably hostile and fearful of an enemy that has been targeting journalists with a gruesome (and occasionally bloodthirsty) effectiveness. These reporters are also, in many cases, extremely sensitive to the charge that the media is anti-American, and in the cases of both Fox and CNN have been warned against appearing so. It is a baseless charge, as any quick comparison between U.S. and British or European coverage of the fighting immediately demonstrates. To take just one "for instance," on December 30, 2001, U.S. airstrikes hit the village of Niazi Kala (also called Qalaye Niaze) in eastern Afghanistan, killing dozens of civilians. The attack was major news in several U.K. newspapers, with the *Guardian* and the *Independent* running front-page stories. The headlines were straightforward: "U.S. Accused of Killing Over 100 Villagers in Airstrike" (*Guardian*, January 1, 2002); "U.S. Accused of Killing 100 Civilians in Afghan Bombing Raid" (*Independent*, January 1, 2002); "'100 Villagers Killed' in U.S. Airstrike" (*London Times*, January 1, 2002). In contrast, the *New York Times* first reported the civilian deaths at Niazi Kala under the headline "Afghan Leader Warily Backs U.S. Bombing" (January 2, 2002). Keep in mind that the *New York Times* is usually considered Public Enemy Number One by conservatives. Note also that this antiwar/anti-American accusation, while useful to conservatives seeking to force news organizations to hew to their views, has always been false. In the most famous case, that of the Vietnam War, the media has been exonerated by none other than the official history of the U.S. Army. But as with the overall charge of bias, endless repetition, coupled with a multibillion-dollar propaganda offensive carried out over a period of decades, has had its intended effect. Much of the U.S. media is particularly wary of reporting any news that might be construed as "anti-American," regardless of the merit of the charge. For many, it is simply not worth the hassle.

Yet even in the deeply pro-American, patriotic context in which the U.S. media has been operating since September 11, 2001, Fox still manages to distinguish itself.

Osama bin Laden, its anchors, reporters, and guests explain, is "a dirtbag," "a monster" overseeing a "web of hate." His followers in Al Qaeda are "terror goons." Taliban fighters are "diabolical" and "henchmen." Fox is not interested in covering the civilian casualties of U.S. bombing missions. As Brit Hume explained, "We know we're at war. The fact that some people are dying, is that really news? And is it news to be treated in a semi-straight-faced way? I think not." To a considerable degree Fox's open bias in this case—and in many others—is refreshing. It is perhaps the only news station where news comes with a context, and is therefore made more understandable for consumers than the helter-skelter version to which most Americans have become accustomed. It's unfortunate, both for genuine liberals as well as for the cause of democratic discourse in the United States, that it is the only one available. And fortunately for the pro-war crowd in the United States, Rupert Murdoch has no significant investments in Iraq—nor any desire to convince Saddam Hussein to let his satellite network into that nation.

Because investments almost always appear to trump ideology in Murdoch's world—he supported Tony Blair in England against his conservative opponents and received some extremely curious favors from the government thereafter—the millions of dollars Murdoch pours into the low-circulation conservative opinion magazine, the *Weekly Standard*, is perhaps his most curious investment. Most of Murdoch's properties earn money. The *New York Post* may look like a money-loser, but it buys him a political voice in New York and with the media elite, which is extremely valuable when he needs a favor from one of the city or state's elected politicians. It also allows him to intervene directly in the copy of the newspaper, offering him the opportunity to punish enemies and reward allies. Fox News Channel, has, like its broadcast parent, turned out to be a surprisingly shrewd commercial proposition. Though its older, largely rural audience does not produce the revenues of CNN despite significantly higher ratings, it does give every indication of having become a profitable enterprise with remarkable rapidity.

But the *Weekly Standard*, unlike Fox, will never make a profit, as political opinion magazines never do. And unlike the *New York Post*, the *Standard*'s editors will not allow Murdoch to dictate its politics. When Murdoch's other publications were toadying up to the Chinese during the spy plane crisis of 2001, the *Standard* was denouncing the administration—and by extension, Rupert and James Murdoch, with fire and brimstone. When the kind of deal Murdoch was actively seeking was finally achieved by the Bush administration, William Kristol, together with Robert Kagan, thundered about "The profound national humiliation that President Bush has brought upon the United States." While writing a column on the topic, I made a few calls to the magazine to determine what their policies were with regard to criticizing their owner. Kristol, executive editor Fred Barnes, and senior writer Christopher Caldwell were all apparently too busy to get back to me. Opinion editor David Tell was helpful with critical pieces about China but also demurred on the question of Murdoch per se. Senior editor and best-selling swami David Brooks was all charm and no information: "I'm sorry. I'm having some computer problems. At first I thought you were asking me to comment on the son of my employer. Must be some garble." Murdoch could not have liked that.

Perhaps the owner was suckered in. In its original inception, the magazine, edited by Kristol, appeared to be exactly the same wavelength as its sugar daddy. Murdoch, recall, was trying to pay then-House Speaker Newt Gingrich more than $6 million for an unreadable book of speeches much in the fashion that he paid Deng's daughter. (The Murdoch "advance" was ruled out of order by the House ethics committee and was never paid. The book was an easily predicted flop.) The *Standard*, as it was originally conceived, appeared to be a kind of Newt Gingrich fanzine. The cover of its first issue, published in April 1995, portrayed Gingrich as Rambo, bravely swinging on a vine above a burning Capitol, and featured four pieces on Newt of the Jungle. Within two years, however, it was Gingrich and company who seemed bound for the nuthouse—or at least for disgrace and retirement. The *Standard* transferred its affection to Republican dissident and media darling John McCain, with Kristol and Kagan acting as a kind of unofficial brain trust during McCain's heady 2000 run. When Bush won, however, that was fine, too.

There is no question that the *Weekly Standard* has been home to many of the most talented political writers anywhere, conservative or no. Bill Kristol, David Brooks, Christopher Caldwell, and Tucker Carlson would have enjoyed considerable success no matter what politics they practiced. Even though the *Standard* had been a bastion of the McCain mutiny, the Bush administration swallowed its collective pride and raided it upon coming into office. Among the staffers who moved over to the administration were John DiIulio (to head up the president's faith-based initiative), Matt Reese (to work for U.S. Trade Representative Robert Zoellick), and David Frum and Ed Walsh (to join the White House speechwriting shop).

Of course things did not always work out perfectly. DiIulio quickly ran afoul of the Republican thought police when he seemed to take seriously his mandate to involve inner-city clergy to address real problems. Warned publicly for his apostasy by Grover Norquist, he was the first significant member of the administration to quit his job. David Frum lasted a bit longer, but also left under clouded circumstances. He was working as a supposedly anonymous White House speechwriter. But his wife, novelist Danielle Crittenden—who has a sideline in instructing women to use their husband's name professionally but used her own—could not bear to see hubby's genius go unrecognized. Following Bush's famous "Axis of Evil" State of the Union in 2002, Crittenden sent out a mass e-mail proudly proclaiming her husband's authorship of the phrase. Timothy Noah, Slate's gossip columnist, published the offending e-mail. ("It's not often a phrase one writes gains national notice . . . so I hope you'll indulge my wifely pride in seeing this one repeated in headlines everywhere!!") Noah also quoted Crittenden's stepfather's Canadian newspaper telling the same tale. And he cited other possible authors. Later Frum, thinking twice, decided it was Bush's idea after all. As speechwriters are not supposed to take credit for anything, even incoherent geopolitical formulations. Frum decided it would be a good time to, as the saying goes, "return to private life." Republican pooper-scooper Robert Novak blamed Crittenden's e-mail for the decision, but Frum said it wasn't so. Still, Frum did not improve his credibility with his announcement, in early 2002, that W. had already "proven himself to be one of the great presidents of American history."

Under the rhetorically challenged Bush, the *Standard*'s most important function was to become the primary public voice of America's war party, no matter who was the enemy. China, the Palestinians, the Iranians, the Syrians, the Cubans, and, of course, Al Qaeda and the Iraqis would all have qualified. When, for instance, some Republicans, including some of ex-President Bush's closest advisers, dissented from the policy of a U.S. war against Iraq in the summer of 2002, Kristol and company shot back—in the language of Joe McCarthy—that "an axis of appeasement–stretching from Riyadh to Brussels to Foggy Bottom, from Howell Raines to Chuck Hagel to Brent Scowcroft—has now mobilized in a desperate effort to deflect the president from implementing his policy." Those on the left who opposed an invasion of Iraq did so not out of pragmatic considerations about its effectiveness, lack of allied support, effect on the region and its inhabitants, or moral considerations about the launching of a pre-emptive war. Rather, they were "queasy about American principles." Others, "mostly foreign policy 'realists,'" opposed it because "they're appalled by the thought that the character of regimes is key to foreign policy." A few "cosmopolitan sophisticates of all stripes," Kristol noted, using the word that Stalin chose for Jews, were on the wrong side because they "hate talk of good and evil."

Kristol was hardly alone in this tactic. As John Judis noted in the *American Prospect*:

> *The Wall Street Journal identified Scowcroft's views with those of the "anti-war left." The New York Sun enumerated Scowcroft's current business ties and his founding of a "front group" that includes a "PLO apologist" on its board. As for Hagel, the Wall Street Journals editorial page accused him of trying to "grab a fast headline." And in an article titled "Sen. Skeptic (R., France)," the National Review insinuated that the Nebraskan was more European than American in his views. But the hawks didn't expend most of their ammunition on Scowcroft and Hagel. Instead, they took aim at the New York Times and its new executive editor, Howell Raines. The Wall Street Journal, The Weekly Standard, the Washington Times and columnists Charles Krauthammer and George Will charged that the New York Times was promoting opposition to the administration's Iraq plans by publishing false information about the dissenters in its news pages.*

The idea of honest, principled, and intelligent opposition to a war against Iraq was ruled out of order by most conservative pundits, no matter what the credentials of those giving voice to it. Note also that the very idea of reporting dissent—be it within the military, the Congressional Republican Party, or the Republican foreign policy establishment that had crafted George H. W. Bush's war with Iraq—was equated, once again, with the dreaded liberal bias, as if Brent Scowcroft, James Baker, Lawrence Eagleberger, Republican Chuck Hagel, and even House Republican Whip Dick Armey had somehow switched to the "liberal" side so that they might be charged with making common cause with the *New York Times*. Krauthammer even concluded, "Not since William Randolph Hearst famously cabled his correspondent in Cuba, 'You furnish the pictures and I'll furnish the war,' has a newspaper so blatantly devoted its front pages to editorializing about a coming American war as has Howell Raines' *New York Times*." Too bad for the pundit, Hearst never said this. It is a tale that ten minutes worth of research might have prevented his repeating, but never mind. (Curiously, Krauthammer, who is partially paralyzed, and Kristol—like most of the outspoken journalistic war hawks with regard to Iraq, including Bob Kagan, George Will, Rush Limbaugh, Marty Peretz, Andrew Sullivan, Jacob Heilbrunn, Christopher Hitchens, and Michael Kelly—share with George Bush, Dick Cheney, Republican Majority Whip Tom DeLay, the hawkish defense official Paul Wolfowitz, Senate Majority Leader Trent Lott, and the DOD adviser Richard Perle the quality of having managed to avoid military service of any kind during their entire lives. Hence, they are entirely innocent of any understanding of its character from the ground up. In the case of the vice president, who required four separate deferments to stay out of harm's way while the unlucky amongst his generation went off to fight and die to defend "freedom in South Vietnam," he has explained that he "had other priorities in the 60s than military service.")

It should surprise no one that when both the *Times* and the *Washington Post* egregiously underreported a massive antiwar demonstration in Washington in late October 2002 with a crowd estimated by local police to be well over 100,000 people not one of the above pundits bothered to complain. The *Times* was forced to run an embarrassing "make-up story" in which it admitted its earlier (buried) story on the demonstration, which claimed merely "hundreds" of demonstrators, had been profoundly misleading. The *Post* received a hard slap from its ombudsman, Michael Getler, who complained that the paper had "fumbled" the story of the biggest antiwar demonstration since the 1960s. Hypocrisy aside, the apparent lack of sympathy evinced by the editors of both papers would appear to put a crimp into the arguments of anyone accusing these media titans of an antiwar bias, which is perhaps why the hawkish pundits who focus obsessively on the coverage of Iraq in both papers, decided to ignore it entirely.

No one—not even *Times* superhawk William Safire—was more important in the media debate over Iraq than the *Weekly Standard's* William Kristol, McCarthyite language or no. When, in late August 2002, Vice President Cheney finally laid out a case for war, the *Washington Post's* Dana Milbank quoted Kristol and Kristol alone for analysis. "The debate in the administration is over," he declared in apparent triumph. "The time for action grows near." Of course it did not hurt that the pro-war side also had Howard Kurtz, asking this dumb question on its behalf: "By the way, do you think there were any Hill hearings on removing Adolf Hitler?" (Mr. Kurtz does not seem to be aware that it was Hitler who declared war on the United States, not the other way around.) As James Capozzola nicely put it on the Web log Rittenhouse Review, "That's the liberal media at work."

The notion of a conservative network capable of enforcing such a line on its members, drawing the mainstream media into its ideological corner, and mau-mauing even many liberals into parroting its line might be just a pipe dream today were it not for the generosity of one man. As of September 2002, sixty-nine-year-old Richard Mellon Scaife was, according to *Forbes*, the 209th richest person in America, with a personal fortune of just over a billion dollars. On a list of the strangest people in America, he might rank a bit higher. Had Scaife decided to commit his fortune to chasing orchids or beautifying his native corner of western Pennsylvania while writing the occasional six-figure check to the Republican Party, he would merely qualify as one more eccentric conservative billionaire. Instead Scaife put his fortune at the service of a group of visionary right-wing intellectuals and activists. His efforts proved so successful that it is not too much to say that the United States is a different country because of them.

A somewhat bulky, handsome man with hypnotic blue eyes, Scaife lives what a *Washington Post* writer once called "a life thickly insulated from the workaday tribulations of ordinary citizens." At that time, he had houses in Pittsburgh; Ligonier, Pennsylvania; Nantucket, Massachusetts; and Pebble Beach, California; and a private DC-9 jet with which to shuttle between them. He is apparently so shy and insecure that he never talks business unless surrounded by a bevy of assistants. Even then, underlings do most of the talking.

Scaife rarely if ever grants interviews, so most of his motivations must be intuited. When journalist Karen Rothmyer tried to interview him for a *Columbia Journalism Review* profile in the early 1980s, Scaife avoided her every inquiry. When she finally caught up with him on a Manhattan street as the billionaire departed a meeting of the First Boston Corporation, Rothmyer inquired as to why he chose to dedicate his fortune to the cause of conservative politics. Scaife replied in a booming voice, "You fucking Communist cunt, get out of here." He then volunteered his opinion that she was ugly and that her teeth were "terrible," before warning, "don't look behind you."

It's too bad that Scaife is so reluctant to speak to journalists because, politics aside, he is a fascinating guy. After William F. Buckley Jr., he is perhaps the single most important private citizen in the contemporary conservative movement. And yet to those who know him, he appears to be wholly uninterested in political ideas. When one journalist asked over a dozen conservative intellectuals receiving Scaife monies if they could recall a single book he ever mentioned, they all came up empty-handed. They did know he liked flowers and took an interest in geography. His penchant for conspiracy theories was also mentioned. As for newspapers, most of Scaife's reading according to those closest to him, focused on the gossip columns.

Scaife has certainly had ample opportunity to read about himself while scanning the gossip pages. Using his wealth and fame, he has scandalized polite society over and over during his career, carrying on an open affair while married and having at least two of his adversaries—including his brother-in-law—die under mysterious circumstances. This billionaire is also comically impecunious. He goes over the expenses submitted by his employees and has been known to strike out the cost of airport taxis and hotel shirt-laundering. He even wrote Richard Nixon 334 $3,000 checks to avoid the obligatory gift tax.

Scaife's great-grandfather Thomas Mellon founded the financial empire that bears his name. Mellon mused in 1885, "The normal condition of man is hard work, self-denial, acquisition and accumulation; as soon as his descendants are freed from the necessity of such exertion they begin to degenerate sooner or later in both body and mind." He would appear to be a prophet of sorts about his own family. Richard Mellon Scaife was raised by his mother, a "gutter drunk," according to her daughter Cordelia, and an ineffectual father in a family that excelled, in Scaife's sister's words only in "making each other totally miserable."

Richard grew up around Pittsburgh surrounded by buildings and institutions named either "Mellon" or "Scaife" or both. An important building at the University of Pittsburgh, where Scaife studied, is called Scaife Hall. Another university in town also has a Scaife Hall. Its name is Carnegie Mellon. Scaife's uncle, R. K. Mellon, proved adept at expanding the family fortune in the years after World War Two, but he thought little of his brother-in-law, Alan Scaife, and would not allow him near any important aspects of the business. As Richard Scaife would later put it, "My father was sucking hind tit." A failure in his own business ventures, Alan Scaife died a year after his son's graduation from college, and his son sold his corporation "for a dollar." In 1974, Scaife expressed some of his feelings about his family when he donated a new wing to the Carnegie Museum in Pittsburgh in honor of his mother. While she had always considered herself to be "Sarah Mellon Scaife," he insisted that the new structure be named the "Sarah Scaife" wing. Shortly thereafter, he also had the name "Mellon" removed from the foundation that bore his mother's name.

Like his father, Richard Scaife was refused any substantive responsibilities in the family business by his uncle. He had been thrown out of Yale University in an alcoholfueled incident in which he rolled a beer keg down a stairwell that broke both of a fellow student's legs and nearly left him crippled for life. Scaife managed to make it through the University of Pittsburgh, but one suspects this achievement was not unrelated to the presence of his father in the chairman's seat of the university's board of directors. Richard Scaife spent much of the years that followed as a mean drunk without any visible career or profession. According to Mellon family biographer, Burton Hersh, Scaife nearly drank himself to death, time and again.

Due to the U.S. tax law, Scaife was forced to become a philanthropist to protect his share of the family's wealth, lest large parts of it went to the IRS. In 1957, when *Fortune* magazine tried to rank the largest fortunes in America, four Mellons—including Richard's mother—were among the top eight. Sarah Scaife and, after her death in 1965, Richard Scaife, earned huge tax deductions from their trusts and foundations. Sarah Scaife's causes focused on family planning, the poor and disabled, hospitals, the environment, and various good works in and around Pittsburgh. Her most famous gift went to the University of Pittsburgh research laboratory during the late 1940s, when Jonas Salk happened to be there working on the formula for his successful polio vaccine. Richard Scaife would not help cure polio, but he would, eventually, help impeach a president.

Scaife's first donations to conservative groups began in 1962 with relatively meager grants to the American Bar Association's Fund for Public Education for "education against communism," and shortly thereafter, to the Hoover Institution, the Center for Strategic and International Studies, and the American Enterprise Institute. But 1964 proved to be a kind of rude political awakening for Scaife. An enthusiastic Goldwater supporter, that summer he ferried the candidate on his private plane to the annual Bohemian Grove retreat, where wealthy businessmen and male political leaders frolic together in the Northern Californian woods, happily peeing on plants. Scaife was extremely excited about the possibilities of a Goldwater presidency, and he may have let his hopes triumph over his ability to judge the likely course of events. Few people were surprised in November of that year when Johnson trounced the conservative Republican. Most pundits blamed the candidate's conservative views and connections to the conservative movement as the cause. The *New York Times's* James Reston wrote that Goldwater's conservatism "has wrecked his party for a long time to come." Also at the *Times,* Tom Wicker wrote that conservatives "cannot win in this era of American history." The *Los Angeles Times* interpreted the election outcome to mean that if Republicans continued to hew to the conservative line, "they will remain a minority party indefinitely." Political scientists Nelson Polsby and Aaron Wildavsky speculated that if the Republicans nominated a conservative again he would lose so badly "we can expect an end to a competitive two-party system."

According to one of Scaife's associates, the billionaire became convinced that politically, no genuinely conservative candidate could succeed in a nationwide election without first overcoming the advantage that liberalism appeared to have both in the media and in the war of political ideas that provided politicians their ideological foundation. By most measures, Scaife had precious little to show for his thirty-seven years by way of personal achievement. He lived, as he might put it, on his own family's "hind tit" as a drunk and a patsy for conservative fund-raisers. In 1969, however, he began to create his own independent power base by paying approximately $5 million to buy the *Tribune-Review* of Greensburg, Pennsylvania, a daily paper with just over 40,000 circulation in the country seat of Westmoreland County.

Scaife became the paper's publisher and soon established what would become his trademark management style. When the Associated Press ran a story in 1972 revealing Scaife's checks to Nixon, Scaife had every AP machine thrown out of the newsroom. He fired a young reporter who, in the aftermath of Vice President Agnew's resignation, had quipped, "one down and one to go." The firing inspired ten out of the paper's twenty-four editorial employees to resign in protest, charging that Scaife had interfered "continually in the opinion of the professional staff, interjected his political and personal bias into the handling of news stories." This was the first of a number of such incidents that became a regular feature of the newspaper, to the constant consternation of the professional reporters and editors who came to be employed there.

But of course if all Scaife was responsible for was publishing a silly Pennsylvania newspaper, he would hardly be of sufficient concern to merit discussion here. While many rumors have been attached to Scaife's alleged efforts to purchase either CBS or the *Washington Post* for the conservative movement, as of 2002, he had attempted only one other foray as a publisher. It proved both short and ignominious. In 1973, he bought Kern House Enterprises. While registered in the United States, the company ran a London-based news agency called Forum World Features, which offered stories to newspapers and magazines worldwide, including approximately thirty in the United States. But Scaife was forced to close the business down two years later, just before press reports revealed it to be a CIA front. According to ex-CIA director, the late Richard Helms, Forum World provided "a significant means to counter Communist propaganda."

Scaife's unhappy experiences with Nixon—with whom he broke just before the president's resignation in 1974—and the Kern House CIA debacle no doubt contributed to his subsequent decision to remain behind the scenes in national politics. It also taught him the folly of depending on any one politician to fulfill his vision. Though he continued to contribute to the Republican Party and to individual candidates, the bulk of his giving focused on conservative institution-building, and Scaife spread his money like manure. Of the more than 300 groups listed in the 2000 edition of the foundation guide to conservative research and pressure groups in Washington, 111 received grants from Scaife. These represent less than a third of the number of organizations to which his foundations have given grants during this period.

Scaife's contributions have been so varied and numerous that one searches in vain for a consistent theme beyond a shared commitment to conservative ideology. Some are media pressure groups, some legal pressure groups. Some are intellectual, some action-oriented. Some are devoted to scandal-stoking and are driven by fantastic notions of presidential-directed killings and drug-smuggling schemes. Others support educational PBS programming featuring Nobel laureates. Some have proven tremendously successful. Many have not.

Most histories associate the founding of the Heritage Foundation with the fortune of the conservative beer magnate, Joseph Coors. This is because Coors put up the original $250,000 in seed money in 1973. Inside of two years, however, Scaife's gifts had dwarfed those of Coors, totaling more than $35 million in inflation-adjusted dollars. At Heritage the joke went, "Coors gives six-packs; Scaife gives cases." In 1976, Heritage's third year of operation, Scaife ponied up over 40 percent of the foundation's total income of $1,008,557.

This proved "absolutely critical" to the organization's survival, according to its president, Edwin J. Feulner.

But Heritage represents just a small fraction of Scaife's giving during the past three decades. At least five additional organizations—the Hoover Institution on War, Revolution and Peace at Stanford University, the Center for Strategic and International Studies, Free Congress Research and Education Foundation, American Enterprise Institute for Public Policy Research—received in excess of ten million dollars from Scaife's foundations between 1974 and 1998. And even these together represent barely a quarter of the funds he disbursed to right-wing causes during this period.

Many of Scaife's most successful gifts have been directed towards shaping the long-term contours of intellectual and political thought, both within academia and outside of it. Since 1970, Scaife put up more than $8 million to fund scholars working on "law and economics" at places like the University of Chicago, the University of Miami, and George Mason University Law School. Legal scholars who identify intellectually with this movement have labored hard to redirect the emphasis in legal education and jurisprudence toward the efficiency of the market rather than the rights of the worker or consumer. Using Scaife money, these well-funded programs have invited hundreds of federal judges to attend seminars in luxurious vacation resorts in exchange for their participation in seminars on issues such as the efficacy of market solutions to problems such as the destruction of the environment or unsafe working conditions for workers. Law and economics scholarship has grown so mainstream that one of its founders, Richard Posner, was named as the mediator on the single largest antitrust case of the past two decades—the United States versus Microsoft—without a word of criticism in the media.

Scaife money was also instrumental in sustaining the Federalist Society, an organization that has developed into perhaps the most influential legal organization in America after the American Bar Association, and among the most conservative. Founded in 1982, the Federalists have received more than $1.3 million from Scaife's foundations since 1984. Today its membership exceeds 25,000. The society's proponents can frequently be found attacking liberal "judicial activism" while praising the allegedly "strict constructionist" judges who interpret the Constitution according to the founders' "orginal intent." But as Chris Mooney pointed out, the society's understanding of "original intent" is original indeed. While its name invokes the authors of the Federalist Papers, James Madison, Alexander Hamilton, and John Jay, its philosophy is more consistent with the view of these writers' opponents, the Anti-Federalists, who sought to defeat the Constitution. In other words, scholars have begun to interpret the Constitution based on the views of its opponents.

Within its ranks, the society includes some of the most influential judges in America, including an extremely high percentage of those selected by George W. Bush for promotion to the federal bench. This is no surprise, since the advisers selecting the judges and making the recommendation to President Bush are either members of, or closely tied to, the society as well. So, in late 2002, were four of nine members of the Supreme Court, though it is hard to be certain, as the society refuses to confirm or deny anyone's membership. During the Clinton impeachment hearings, virtually every member of Kenneth Starr's prosecutorial staff had some connection to the society. So did a number of the lawyers who worked on the Paula Jones lawsuit. At the 2002 twentieth-anniversary meeting of the society, the "Barbara K. Olson Memorial

Lecture"—in honor of the anti-Clinton radical activist and author who was married to Theodore Olson and died when her plane crashed on September 11—was delivered by none other than Kenneth Starr.

Since 1996, the society has published *ABA Watch*, documenting the American Bar Association's allegedly liberal stands on abortion, the death penalty, and gun control. President Bush was acting upon this legacy of criticism when he chose to eliminate the ABA's influence in the judicial selection process. As an only slightly tongue-in-cheek Grover Norquist told Thomas Edsall of the *Washington Post*, "If Hillary Clinton had wanted to put some meat on her charge of a 'vast right-wing conspiracy,' she should have had a list of Federalist Society members and she could have spun a more convincing story."

Scaife has also taken a considerable interest in the media on America's college campuses. According to the *Washington Post's* audit, Scaife's trusts and foundations have given at least $146 million to university programs, equal to more than $373 million in inflation-adjusted dollars. One of the chief beneficiaries has been the Intercollegiate Studies Institute, founded in 1953 with William F. Buckley Jr. as its first president. Through an organization called the Collegiate Network, ISI pays nearly all the costs of conservative publications on sixty campuses and offers graduate fellowships for the academically inclined. Former fellows include Antonin Scalia, Edwin J. Feulner Jr., Dinesh D'Souza, and William Kristol.

The conservative faculty organization the National Association of Scholars benefited from Scaife's generosity to the tune of over $2.6 million between 1988 and 1998. With an advisory board featuring Jeanne Kirkpatrick, Irving Kristol, and Chester Finn, the organization presents itself as a champion of "intellectual renewal" and "academic standards" in the face of their perceived decline at the hands of leftist academics and fashionable post-modern theories that blur the verities of our time behind a façade of impenetrable professional vernacular. The organization is more than willing, however, to play hardball politics at the campuses where it operates, particularly in the area of affirmative action, which it opposes most vehemently.

Of all of Scaife's political passions, however, the one that appears most inspirational to him is his view that the liberals who allegedly control the media are in league with the liberals who control the Democratic Party to commit all manner of malfeasance against law abiding Americans, including murder, extortion, kidnapping, drug-smuggling, and money-laundering. To this end Scaife has committed a sizable portion of his vast fortune to various organizations that profess to be able either to shed light on these forces, or even better, do battle with them. For years these gifts appeared to take a rather haphazard pattern. Scaife funded Gen. William C. Westmoreland's failed 1982 libel suit against CBS News. Beginning in 1977 he provided roughly $2 million to Reed Irvine's Accuracy in Media, a right-wing press critic, whose critiques of the alleged liberal bias in the media have led some to observe that "Accuracy in Media" bears the same relationship to accuracy in media that the Holy Roman Empire bore to holiness, Rome, and empires. (Back in 1978, Ben Bradlee famously termed Irvine "a miserable, carping, retromingent vigilante.") Like Brent Bozell's Media Research Center, David Horowitz's Center for the Study of Popular Culture, and other miserable, carping, retromingent vigilantes to whom Scaife has handed millions, Accuracy in Media's constant stream of propaganda, faithfully broadcast by the media it attacks, is a major reason that so many people inside and outside of the media share the misimpression of its "liberalism."

Scaife also supported the *Public Interest* and the *National Interest*, both of which are published under the aegis of neoconservative impresario Irving Kristol. The cranky neocon art critic, Hilton Kramer, got to edit the *New Criterion*, a cultural review. Scaife also provided necessary funds for *Reason*, the official publication of the libertarian Reason Foundation, and *Commentary*, the monthly magazine of the American Jewish Committee, edited for decades by the excitable neocon, Norman Podhoretz. Scaife also gave generously to *Encounter* magazine, before it folded, which had been the house organ of the CIA during the days of the intellectual battles over the Cold War in Europe in the 1950s and 1960s. Overall, these publications have enjoyed spending more than $10 million of Scaife's inheritance. Scaife money also helped fund television documentaries on the economics of Milton Friedman, the guru of the monetarist school of free-market economics, and on Cold War themes.

Suffice to say, none of these causes ever excited Scaife like the opportunity to "get" Bill Clinton, and nothing so loosened his purse strings. Scaife attributed his support for the project to his doubts that "the *Washington Post* and other major newspapers would fully investigate the disturbing scandals of the Clinton White House." He explained those doubts: "I am not alone in feeling that the press has a bias in favor of Democratic administrations." That is why, he continued, "I provided some money to independent journalists investigating these scandals."

Following Clinton's election in 1992, Scaife started handing out money to virtually every journalist who claimed to be able to prove Clinton a crook, however far-fetched the story. He termed Vincent Foster's suicide to be "the Rosetta stone to the Clinton administration," telling John F. Kennedy Jr., "Once you solve that one mystery, you'll know everything that's going on or went on—I think there's been a massive cover-up about what Bill Clinton's administration has been doing, and what he was doing when he was governor of Arkansas." Scaife had ominous specifics in mind: "Listen, [Clinton] can order people done away with at his will. He's got the entire federal government behind him." And: "God, there must be 60 people [associated with Bill Clinton]—who have died mysteriously." For a while, all any conservative had to do was to come to Scaife claiming to have solved the mystery—but for a few hundred thousand dollars in necessary investigative funds—and suddenly the money spigot was turned on. For instance, in 1995, Scaife donated $175,000 to Grover Norquist's Americans for Tax Reform, which hired "experts" to dispute the authenticity of Vince Foster's suicide note and produced a widely circulated video entitled *Unanswered: The Death of Vince Foster*. Accuracy in Media received $355,000 from Scaife in 1995 as well. It broadcast the theory that Vince Foster was lured into a "sex trap" from which he fled to where his body was found.

Among the most energetic pursuers of Scaife's "Rosetta Stone" was a hitherto unknown "journalist," Christopher Ruddy. Scaife hired Ruddy, after he had been fired by the *New York Post*, to continue his obsessive investigation of Foster's death in the hopes of trying to pin a murder rap on the president or those closest to him. Ruddy produced his theories on the basis of some imaginative writing, faulty logic, and vast leaps into the unknown and unknowable, both of which he claimed to know. Given that he was never able to prove any of his farfetched theories about the nature of Foster's death and was found to have made major errors when other journalists looked into them, his primary talent seems to have been to wring funds out of Scaife. He used the publicity he generated from these page-one stories to convince other relatively more reputable journalistic establishments, most notably Sun Myung Moon's *Washington Times*, Rupert Murdoch's *New York Post*, and Robert Bartley's *Wall Street Journal* editorial page, to give his tales undeserved publicity and marginally improved credibility.

Ruddy lived in a fully Scaife-contained world. He published on page one of Scaife's *Tribune Review*. His articles were picked up by the Western Journalism Center, based in suburban Sacramento, California, which billed itself in a biweekly newsletter as a "nonprofit tax-exempt corporation promoting independent investigative reporting" and "the only national news agency supporting a full-time probe of the mysterious death of White House deputy counsel Vincent W. Foster, Jr." What this means, it seems, is that the center mostly recycled stories written by Christopher Ruddy. When CBS's *60 Minutes* devoted a segment to exposing the hoariness of Ruddy's conspiracy theories—and the gullibility of those news organizations that treated them as legitimate news stories—Scaife helped fund the creation of a video called *The '60 Minutes' Deception*. He advertised this in the *Washington Times* (with discounted rates) but also through the Scaife-funded entities Free Congress Foundation and National Empowerment Television, along with the Western Journalism Center. In 1996, Ruddy was named the recipient of the Western Journalism Center's first "Courage in Journalism Award," replete with trophy and $2,000 cash prize.

Inspired by his obsession with Clinton, Scaife took seriously the advice Charles Foster Kane offered his underlings when they complained of a dearth of sensational news. He went out and made his own. Scaife's foundations provided funds to two public interest law firms staffed by rival litigators whose obsession with the misdeeds of the president and his administration were no less dogged than Ruddy's. Together, Judicial Watch and the Landmark Legal Foundation received more than $4 million of Scaife's foundations' funds. Founded in 1994 and run by the frequent cable television commentator, Larry Klayman, Judicial Watch pursued a strategy of repeatedly subpoenaing as many Clinton officials, friends of Clinton officials, and working journalists as the presiding judges in his various lawsuits against the Justice and Commerce Departments, among others, would allow. Klayman tried to unearth information about Vince Foster's death, Clinton's foreign policy, and a few other extremely unlikely conspiracies, but never managed to find any actual dirt. Meanwhile, the Landmark Legal Foundation took up the cause of Paula Jones's sexual harassment suit against the president, with its lawyers leaking information via pundit Ann Coulter's many media appearances. (She would do this frequently on MSNBC where I worked with her at the time.) In addition, an organization called the Fund for Living American Government (FLAG), a one-man philanthropy run by William Lehrfeld, a Washington tax lawyer who had represented Scaife, gave $59,000 to Paula Jones's sexual harassment suit against Clinton. FLAG received at least $160,000 in Scaife donations. Together with Landmark staffers and members of the Federalist Society, these firms helped provide low-cost legal advice to Paula Jones to keep her suit going long enough to hit proverbial paydirt with the discovery of Linda Tripp.

Undoubtedly, Scaife's most costly endeavor—judged purely in terms of the unwanted publicity and negative attention he received—was the so-called "Arkansas Project" based at the *American Spectator* magazine and its concurrent "Education Fund." Begun on a fishing trip on the Chesapeake Bay in the fall of 1993, the project managed to bilk the billionaire for millions, nearly destroy the magazine, and almost cost George W. Bush one of his most trusted advisers, his appointed solicitor general. The plot was originally hatched by Scaife's top aide, Richard M. Larry, right-wing entrepreneur and public relations man; David Henderson, a friend of Larry's; Washington lawyer Steven Boynton; *Spectator* editor R. Emmett Tyrell; and Theodore Olson, who later argued George W. Bush's election case before the Supreme Court and was rewarded with the job of solicitor general. Larry had already approached at least two other organizations seeking funding for a massive investigation into alleged Clinton wrongdoings back in Arkansas, but he was turned down cold. Eventually the *Spectator* would receive nearly $2.3 million for the project alone. According to the foundation's internal accounts, three-quarters of the Arkansas Project funding, or $1.8 million, was paid out in "legal expenses" with no further explanation provided.

The project was best known for the (now) admittedly dishonest reporting of the then-right-wing ideologue/hatchetman, David Brock. As he related in his booklength mea culpa, "I had stumbled onto something big, a symbiotic relationship that would help create a highly-profitable, right-wing Big Lie machine that flourished in book publishing, on talk-radio, and on the Internet in the 90s." Acting on the advice of one of his many mentors in the movement, Free Press publisher Erwin Glikes (now deceased), that "right-wing journalism had to be injected into the bloodstream of the liberal media for maximum effect," Brock leaked a copy of his fatally flawed Troopergate story to CNN—"astonished," he claimed, "to see how easy it was to suck [them] in"—where it led the evening newscast, and was further picked up from there. Scaife liked what he saw and continued to give more millions to further pollute the national discourse with baseless allegations and paranoid conspiracy theories.

Not even Brock believed his own reporting at the time. And neither did many of the people who helped publish him. Brock alleged that Olson pushed for the publication of the phony Vince Foster story because, Olson told him, the purpose was not to get at the truth but to throw mud at the Clintons and hope that something stuck. Brock wrote of Olson that "while he believed, as [independent counsel Kenneth] Starr apparently did, that Foster had committed suicide, raising questions was a way of turning up the heat on the administration until another scandal was shaken loose, which was the *Spectator*'s mission." The Paula Jones story, which Brock also published without believing it, was also a strategic advance by the right. George Conway, a $1-million-a-year partner at Wachtell, Lipton, Rosen, and Katz, who was secretly helping to promote Jones's suit, explained, according to Brock, "This is about proving Troopergate." The Conway team was, it turned out, planning to grill Clinton under oath about his consensual sex life and hopefully catch him lying about it. The aim, Jane Mayer noted, was to force Bill Clinton "to face open-ended questioning under oath about his sex life, a humiliation that, long before Monica Lewinsky ever bobbed up in the Rose Garden, promised to distract and embarrass the President, drain his political and financial resources, and lead to the tantalizing payoff of a charge of presidential perjury." To almost everyone's shock and amazement, it worked.

It rarely mattered to anyone that so much of Brock's story was made up or that his sources had been paid for their information and lacked even elemental credibility in the first place. Even in the rare moments when such concerns did matter to Brock, they did not matter to his editors. Brock recalled hearing an extremely complicated "Vince Foster murder scenario," at an airport hotel in Miami, along with tales of alleged drug-running out of a small airport in a town called Mena, Arkansas, that allegedly involved payoffs to Governor Clinton. The allegations had no basis in evidence, however, and he decided to ignore them. The magazine's editor in chief published them himself, managing the considerable feat of publishing lies that were beneath even David Brock.

A dearth of truth in reporting was not the only problem for Scaife's project. Its sloppy accounting methods and money-shuffling between the magazine and the foundation worried Ronald Burr, the magazine's longtime publisher and co-founder. When Burr decided to instigate an independent tax fraud audit by Arthur Andersen, Tyrell wrote back: "I do not want a 'fraud' audit of any project. I do not want any further audits until I have examined our accounting of the Arkansas Project. . . . This issue is now closed." He then informed the staff that Burr was suspected of having misallocated a million dollars of project money. Following an emergency session of the foundation's board held at Tyrrell's home, Burr was thrown overboard and replaced by Theodore Olson. Burr was allegedly paid $350,000 to sign a "mutual confidentiality" clause. The audit never took place.

No one, it appears, ever discovered what became of all of Scaife's contributions. But in the wake of Burr's firing, three of the magazine's board members quit: former United States Information Agency director Frank Shakespeare, the billionaire entrepreneur Theodore Forstmann, and Heritage Foundation vice president John von Kannon. Many of the magazine's highest profile writers also resigned in protest. The magazine soldiered on for a while, changing owners and editors, as its circulation fell from 300,000 during the height of the Clinton wars to fewer than 65,000 in 2002.

The Arkansas Project also came close to derailing Olson's nomination as solicitor general when Brock, following a crisis of conscience, testified under oath that Olson had been far more deeply involved in the Arkansas Project than his previous testimony had indicated. Olson had claimed, "It has been alleged that I was somehow involved in that so-called project; I was not involved in the project, in its origin or its management." He was also far from forthright about his role in ghost-writing anti-Clinton screeds in the magazine and his paid role representing David Hale, an anti-Clinton Whitewater witness. But Brock had the effect of jogging Olson's memory, and he later admitted to some involvement, though not nearly as much as Brock alleged. Despite the widening hole in his credibility, Olson was narrowly confirmed in the Senate. The Democrats, having just won control of the body vis-à-vis Jim Jeffords's decision to join them as an independent, did not think it tactically smart to pick a fight so quickly. The relative silence greeting Olson's confirmation to an office so influential that its holder is frequently termed the "tenth Supreme Court Justice" demonstrated the degree of double standard at work in the SCLM. Clinton did not dare even nominate anyone with analogous involvements, much less such radical views. Yet, in the Bush era, significant sections of the U.S. Justice Department were turned over to people who might fairly be termed radicals—working in league with a radical media whose practitioners knew few boundaries with regard to journalistic ethics or political morality. Again, the silence of the lamb-like "liberal media" turned out to be deafening.

Meanwhile Scaife himself also fell out of love with the project, though of course he never offered any explanation why. It might have had something to do with a November 1997 negative review of Christopher Ruddy's book, *The Strange Death of Vincent Foster: An Investigation*. Shortly after it was published, the Accuracy in Media newsletter reported that Scaife cut the *Spectator* off. It might be said that its work was done, however. While many people debased and degraded themselves on behalf of what appears to be a neurotic obsession with bringing down Bill Clinton, the mainstream media's bloodstream was successfully injected with the poison of Brock's and others' lies. The *American Spectator* provided the rumor. The mainstream did the rest.

The Arkansas Project may have ended unhappily for Scaife, but he had considerable reason to be proud of his contribution to American conservatism nevertheless. Not only did he help to create the necessary conditions to impeach Bill Clinton— and to convince the mainstream media to follow in the footsteps of the ideologues and adventurers whom he paid to blaze the trail—but he helped create an entire conservative infrastructure to carry on the fight against any president who sought to deviate from what his movement knew to be right and true. Just look at how they punish their apostates.

As he noted in his memoir, if young David Brock had come to Washington as an ambitious young liberal journalist to make his fortune in the early 1980s, he might well have been out of luck. There would have been no newspapers, magazines, think tanks, ready-made social life, mentors, and the like ready to embrace him, because of, rather than in spite of, his ideology. I am roughly Brock's age and came to Washington at about the same moment. Between 1982 and 1984, I think I earned a grand total of about $500 working as a liberal journalist, for articles in the *Nation, In These Times,* the *Washington Monthly,* the *Washington City Paper,* and *Arms Control Today.* Meanwhile the bars and softball fields of the capital were filled with young right-wingers living on generous salaries and fellowships provided by multi-million dollar institutions like the *Washington Times,* Heritage Foundation, and their various offshoots. At the advice of one the last great independent journalists, my friend I. F. Stone, who struggled for much of his life to feed his family before becoming a great success in the late 1960s, I returned to graduate school to earn my master's and eventually my doctorate. Brock, in contrast, was embraced by a wealthy and welcoming culture that not only showered money and riches on him but also provided a readymade social life; its only price was that he willingly lie about liberals in public and about his own homosexuality in private. Brock began by writing essays for the Scaife-funded Heritage Foundation's *Policy Review,* which then became op-eds on the Dow Jones-funded *Wall Street Journal* editorial page, which turned into a job offer from the loudly homophobic John Podhoretz, son of neocons Norman Podhoretz and Midge Decter, at the Moonie-funded *Washington Times* magazine *Insight,* and from there, to the Scaife-funded *American Spectator,* which led to a million dollar contract from Simon and Schuster to take down Hillary Clinton. The only question he was asked, according to Brock, by Jack Romanos, then the head of S&S—an alleged bastion of the liberal publishing world—was whether Hillary was really a lesbian. He didn't even have to bother with a book proposal.

The significance of the story of Brock's cozy rise to foundation-funded riches and infamy lies in the hundreds or perhaps thousands of other young conservative journalists whose stories are similar, if not quite so dramatic. (Many of the writers who worship at the shrine of the free market would be lost if any of them were ever forced to earn their living working in it.) For instance, look at the man who hired Brock at *Insight.* John Podhoretz, together with virtually his entire family, including father, Norman, mother, Midge Decter, and brother-in-law, Elliott Abrams, has lived most of his entire professional life sucking at the teat of conservative cash, be it Moon's, Murdoch's, or Scaife's. Currently a columnist for Murdoch's *New York Post,* after having been relieved of his duties as its editorial page editor, Podhoretz uses his perch to enforce what *Slate* editor Jacob Weisberg, invoking the old Communists, has termed "the Coninturn line." When Brock experienced his crisis of conscience, John called him a "disgrace" who was engaged in "almost boundless hypocrisy." The Scaifefunded polemicist and one-time Communist, David Horowitz, wrote, in *Salon*, "Brock, of course, cannot even present himself with any integrity that lasts for more than a sentence," adding that the author was "relentlessly squalid." Writing in *National Review*, Ramesh Ponnuru accused Brock of "narcissism and attitudinizing, constant revisionism, and false pieties masking low cunning." Earlier, his former friend and editor at the *Spectator*, Wlady Pleszczynski, had noted that in defending Hillary Clinton from the accusation of using an anti-Jewish slur, "Brock resorts to doing the only thing he's really interested in: talking about himself, reinventing himself, repositioning himself." Robert Bartley termed Brock "the John Walker Lindh of contemporary conservatism." Brock had long ago been excommunicated by the Coninturn. When he failed to get the goods on Hillary Clinton, Barbara Olson told him he better not come to any of its parties. Others spread rumors that he was having an affair with a male member of Mrs. Clinton's staff. Now he was being damned, like Lindh, to Hell as well.

Harkening to Richard Hofstadter's famous examination of the "paranoid style" of American conservative politics, Weisberg detected in the behavior of these conservatives the same kind of "imitation of the enemy" that Hofstadter saw in the extreme right-wing organizations of his day. Just as the KKK modeled itself after the Catholic Church, and the John Birch Society looked a lot like the CP front organizations it believed were hiding beneath virtually every bed, "Contemporary conservatives believe that the most powerful institutions in American society are part of a liberal conspiracy. They feel this gives them license to create conservative counterinstitutions, from magazines to think tanks. But these conservative institutions—the *Washington Times*, the Heritage Foundation—are part of an ideological mission in a way that 'liberal' ones—the *Washington Post*, the Brookings Institution—are not."

The *New Yorker*'s Hendrik Hertzberg noticed a similar, Communist-like dynamic at work in the world in which Brock swam when his gills tilted rightward:

Like the American and other Western Communist parties in their heyday, the American conservative movement has created a kind of alternative intellectual and political universe— a set of institutions parallel to and modeled on the institutions of mainstream society (many of which the movement sees, or imagines, as the organs of a disciplined Liberal Establishment) and dedicated to the single purpose of advancing a predetermined political agenda. There is a kind of Inner Movement, consisting of a few hundred funders, senior organization leaders, lawyers, and prominent media personalities (but only a handful of practicing politicians), and an Outer Movement, consisting of a few thousand staff people, grunt workers, and lower-level operatives of one kind or another. The movement has its own newspapers (the Washington Times, *the* New York Post, *the* Journal's *editorial page), its own magazines (*Weekly Standard, National Review, Policy Review, Commentary, *and many more), its own broadcasting operations (Fox News and an array of national and local talk-radio programs and right-wing Christian broadcast outlets), its own publishing houses (Regnery and the Free Press, among others), its own quasi-academic research institutions (the Heritage Foundation, the American Enterprise Institute), and even its* *own Popular Front—the Republican Party, important elements of which (the party's congressional and judicial leadership, for example) the movement has successfully commandeered. These closely linked organizations (the vanguard of the conservative revolution, you might say) compose an entire social world with its own rituals, celebrations, and anniversaries, within which it is possible to live one's entire life. It is a world with its own elaborate system of incentives and sanctions, through which—as Brock discovered—energetic conformity is rewarded with honors and promotions while deviations from the movement line, depending on their seriousness, are punished with anything from mild social disapproval to outright excommunication.*

The power of this conservative media world, of course, is not merely that it keeps conservatives in line who might be thinking deviationist thoughts. Rather, it skews the entire discourse toward the right because the Coninturn, unlike the Communists of yesteryear, is considered to be one of two—or perhaps two and a half—legitimate poles in the spectrum of American media discourse. Its power of gravity pulls the center rightward and leaves liberals off in outer space. Hence, its members dominate the punditocracy and receive highly favored treatment from media policemen like Howard Kurtz. And certainly no liberal can boast of such generous terms from any major television network as those enjoyed by the ideologically driven John Stossel, whose work is consistently questioned by his colleagues and yet whose diatribes are just as consistently broadcast by the network because of his strong following among right-wing viewers. Despite the sorry standards of his work, and the considerable grief and embarrassment they have caused the network, Stossel is able to spout his extremist views on ABC in the guise of genuine reporting in large measure because the conservatives have so powerfully succeeded in pushing discourse rightward, all the while whining "liberal bias."

Perhaps the best illustration of the power of the far right to draw the mainstream into its web of lies and unfounded insinuations is the treatment of Brock himself. When Brock was still a lying conservative hatchetman, for instance, his work was trumpeted and celebrated in such allegedly liberal bastions as the *New York Times*, the *LA Times*, and elsewhere. When he became a liberal, however, the attack on Brock was picked up by gossip columnist Timothy Noah in the allegedly liberal *Slate*, who first called the apostate conservative a liar on the basis of having read a CNN transcript. When it was later revealed that the person who typed the transcript had made a mistake, and Brock was not lying, Noah scored Brock instead for telling the truth not "very loudly." Here, Noah was joining in a misguided attack based on the mistaken transcript that had already been joined by the Media Research Center, Andrewsullivan.com, and William F. Buckley's *National Review*. Even though Brock had told the truth on the CNN program, as Noah admitted—the issue was whether he had ever been invited on Fox during "prime time"—Noah attacked him because had he been "less concerned about staying on message and more bent on conveying the truth," he would not have spoken in such a low voice. While the conservatives were unarguably incorrect when they attacked Brock for lying, Noah argued, "the conservatives were right to view Brock's remarks as misleading."

It is remarks like this one that demonstrate just how successful the Coninturn has been at intimidating allegedly liberal journalists apparently out of their wits. But Noah was hardly alone. The allegedly liberal *Washington Post* (accidentally, I assume) assigned Brock's book to be reviewed by a former writer for the *American Spectator* and published a malicious gossip item—originally reported by Matt Drudge—about his check-in to a mental health facility. (See chapter 3.) And it should surprise no one that Brock received none of that "brave contrarian who rooted for the wrong baseball team" treatment from *Post* media critic Howard Kurtz. In a 2,160 word profile, every single quote chosen by Kurtz came from right-wingers such as Wlady Pleszczynski or John Podhoretz, terming Brock to be either a liar or a psycho. Here, for instance, is the opening of Kurtz's profile. "David Brock is a liar. And a character assassin. And a turncoat. And a partisan hatchet man. And a lonely, tortured soul. And a practitioner of malicious journalism. And a bizarre guy. That, at least, is how he describes himself. . . ."

The reception of David Brock's memoir, while predictable, is a relatively minor matter. It is also complicated by the fact of Brock's past dishonesty which, to say the least, opens the door to the possibility that he might be lying again, though none of his conservative critics have been able to substantiate this accusation in any significant way. But the reaction is illustrative of far more significant ones. Don't forget that following the 2000 election, at least two liberal columnists, Richard Cohen and Al Hunt, suggested that it would be best if the guy who actually lost the election be allowed to be president because the threat to social peace presented by the right was too great to justify a genuinely democratic outcome. (Cohen suggested that Al Gore give up because "Bush would be better . . . at restraining GOP Dobermans." Al Hunt later wrote a column endorsing the Supreme Court's decision to hand Bush the election on exactly these grounds.) These liberals had their reasons, no doubt. They had seen and heard comments like those by Paul Gigot of the *Wall Street Journal* celebrating a Republican riot to stop the vote count. There was William Kristol promising that if a fair count were allowed, "We will not 'move on.' Indeed, some of us will work for the next four years to correct this affront to our constitutional order." There was John Podhoretz fulminating, a bit ominously, in the *New York Post*, "Let him have it. Let him attempt to govern the United States when untold tens of millions of Americans consider him an illegitimate president. Let him be the president who must preside over the economic slowdown with a program that will only accelerate that slowdown and a world in which terrorists and other provocateurs will delight in testing his dimpled presidency." Of course the media cannot by itself make the nation ungovernable for Democrats and liberals. But it can certainly legitimate behavior that does, no matter how unlawful or unconstitutional. This time it was America's first impeachment trial of an elected president and a close presidential election that eventually went to the wrong man. Next time, who knows? One thing is for certain, the longer we pretend that the media is actually controlled by "liberals," the easier it will be.

Out of Gas

David Goodstein

In the 1950s, the United States was the world's leading producer of oil. Much of the nation's industrial and military might derived from its giant oil industry. The country seemed to be floating on a rich, gooey ocean of "black gold." Nobody was willing to believe that the party would ever end. Well, almost nobody. There was a geophysicist named Marion King Hubbert who knew better.

Hubbert, the son of a central Texas farm family, was born in 1903. Somehow he wound up at the far-off University of Chicago, where he earned all his academic degrees right up to the Ph.D. Embittered with the academic world after an unhappy stint teaching geophysics at Columbia University, he spent the bulk of his professional career with the Shell Oil Company of Houston. That's where he was when, in 1956, very much against the will of his employer, he made public his calculation that American oil dominance would soon come to an end. To understand how he reached that conclusion and the relevance of his reasoning to world oil supplies today, we need to understand a bit about how oil came to be in the first place.

For hundreds of millions of years, animal, vegetable, and mineral matter drifted downward through the waters to settle on the floors of ancient seas. In a few privileged places on Earth, strata of porous rock formed that were particularly rich in organic inclusions. With time, these strata were buried deep beneath the seabed. The interior of Earth is hot, heated by the decay of natural radioactive elements. If the porous source rock sank just deep enough, it reached the proper temperature for the organic matter to be transformed into oil. Then the weight of the rock above it could squeeze the oil out of the source rock like water out of a sponge, into layers above and below, where it could be trapped. Over vast stretches of time, in various parts of the globe, the seas retreated, leaving some of those deposits beneath the surface of the land.

Oil consists of long-chain hydrocarbon molecules. If the source rock sank too deep, the excessive heat at greater depths—some three miles below the surface—broke these long molecules into the shorter hydrocarbon molecules we call natural gas. Meanwhile, in certain swampy places, the decay of dead plant matter created peat bogs. In the course of the eons, buried under sediments and heated by Earth's interior, the peat was transformed into coal, a substance that consists mostly of elemental carbon. Coal, oil, and natural gas are the primary fossil fuels. They are energy from the Sun, stored within the earth.

Until only two hundred years ago—the blink of an eye on the scale of our history—the human race was able to live almost entirely on light as it arrived from the Sun. The Sun nourished plants, which provided food and warmth for us and our animals. It illuminated the day and (in most places) left the night sky, sparkling with stars, to comfort us in our repose. Back then, a few people in the civilized world traveled widely, even sailing across the oceans, but most people probably never strayed very far from their birthplaces. For the rich, there were beautiful paintings, sophisticated orchestral music, elegant fabrics, and gleaming porcelain. For the common folk, there were more homespun versions of art, music, textiles, and pottery. Merchant sailing ships ventured to sea carrying exotic and expensive cargoes including spices, slaves, and, in summer, ice. At the end of the eighteenth century, no more than a few hundred million people populated the planet. A bit of coal was burned, especially since trees had started becoming scarce in Europe (they soon would begin to disappear in the New World), and small amounts of oil that seeped to the surface found some application, but by and large Earth's legacy of fossil fuels was left untouched.

Today we who live in the developed world expect illumination at night and air conditioning in summer. We may work every day up to a hundred miles from where we live, depending on multiton individual vehicles to transport us back and forth on demand, on roads paved with asphalt (another by-product of the age of oil). Thousands of airline flights per day can take us to virtually any destination on Earth in a matter of hours. When we get there, we can still chat with our friends and family back home, or conduct business as if we had never left the office. Amenities that were once reserved for the rich are available to most people, refrigeration rather than spices preserves food, and machines do much of our hard labor. Ships, planes, trains, and trucks transport goods of every description all around the world. Earth's population exceeds six billion people. We don't see the stars so clearly anymore, but on most counts few of us would choose to return to the eighteenth century.

This revolutionary change in our standard of living did not come about by design. If you asked an eighteenth-century sage like Benjamin Franklin what the world really needed, he would probably not have described those things we have wound up with—except perhaps for the dramatic improvement in public health that has also taken place since then. Instead of design or desire, our present standard of living has resulted from a series of inventions and discoveries that altered our expectations. What we got was not what we wanted or needed but rather what nature and human ingenuity made possible for us. One consequence of those inventions and changed expectations is that we no longer live on light as it arrives from the Sun. Instead we are using up the fuels made from sunlight that Earth stored up for us over those many hundreds of millions of years. Obviously we have unintentionally created a trap for ourselves. We will, so to speak, run out of gas. There is no question about that. There's only a finite amount left in the tank. When will it happen?

Throughout the twentieth century, the demand for and supply of oil grew rapidly. Those two are essentially equal. Oil is always used as fast as it's pumped out of the ground. Until the 1950s, oil geologists entertained the mathematically impossible expectation that the same rate of increase could continue forever. All warnings of finite supplies were hooted down, because new reserves were being discovered faster than consumption was rising. Then, in 1956, Hubbert predicted that the rate at which oil could be extracted from the lower forty-eight United States would peak around 1970 and decline rapidly after that. When his prediction was borne out, other oil geologists started paying serious attention.

Hubbert used a number of methods to do his calculations. The first was similar to ideas that had been used by population biologists for well over a century. When a new population—of humans or any other species—starts growing in an area that has abundant resources, the growth is initially exponential, which means that the rate of growth increases by the same fraction each year, like compound interest in a bank account. That is just how the geologists used to think oil discovery would grow. However, once the population is big enough so that the resources no longer seem unlimited, the rate of growth starts slowing down. The same happens with oil discovery, because the chances of finding new oil get smaller when there's less new oil to find. Hubbert showed that once the rate of increase of oil discovery starts to decline, it's possible to extrapolate the declining rate to find where growth will stop altogether. At that point, all the oil in the ground has been discovered, and the total amount there ever was is equal to the amount that's already been used plus the known reserves still in the ground. Hubbert noticed that the trend of declining annual rate of increase of oil discovery was established for the lower forty-eight states by the 1950s. Others have now pointed out that the rate of discovery worldwide has been declining for decades. The total quantity of conventional oil that Earth stored up for us is estimated by this method to be about two trillion barrels.

Hubbert's second method required assuming that in the long run, when the historical record of the rate at which oil was pumped out of the ground was plotted, it would be a bell-shaped curve. That is, it would first rise (as it has been), then reach a peak that would never be exceeded, and afterward decline forever. Now that it's far enough along, half a century after he made that assumption, it's clear that he was right in the case of the lower forty-eight. If the same assumption is correct for the rest of the world, and if you have the historical record of the rising part of the curve and a good estimate of the total amount of oil that ever was (two trillion barrels, see above), then it's not difficult to predict when the peak, Hubbert's peak, will occur. Hubbert had that information in the 1950s for the lower forty-eight. We have it now for the whole world. Different geologists using different data and methods get slightly different results, but some (not all) have concluded that the peak will happen at some point in this decade. The point can be seen without any fancy mathematics at all. Of the two trillion barrels of oil we started with, nearly half has already been consumed. The peak occurs when we reach the halfway point. That, they say, can't be more than a few years off.

Hubbert's third method applied the observation that the total amount of oil extracted to date paralleled oil discovery but lagged behind by a few decades. In other words, we pump oil out of the ground at about the same rate that we discover it, but a few decades later. Thus the rate of discovery predicts the rate of extraction. Worldwide, remember, the rate of discovery started declining decades ago. In other words, Hubbert's peak for oil discovery already occurred, decades ago. That gives an independent prediction of when Hubbert's peak for oil consumption will occur. It will occur, according to that method, within the next decade or so.

Not all geologists pay attention to this assessment. Many prefer to take the total amount known for sure to be in the ground and divide that by the rate at which it's getting used up. This is known in the industry as the R/P ratio—that is, the ratio of reserves to production. Depending on what data one uses, the R/P ratio is currently between forty and a hundred years. They conclude that if we continue to pump oil out of the ground and consume it at the same rate we are doing now, we will not have pumped the last drop for another forty to one hundred years.

Another point of disagreement concerns the total amount of oil that nature has produced on Earth. Over the period 1995–2000, the United States Geological Survey (USGS) made an exhaustive study of worldwide oil supplies. The resulting report concludes that, with 95 percent certainty, there was the equivalent of at least two trillion barrels when we started pumping. However, it also concludes with 50 percent probability that there were at least 2.7 trillion barrels—based on the expectation that, contrary to trends mentioned earlier, new discovery will continue at a brisk rate for at least thirty more years. The additional 0.7 trillion barrels to be unearthed would amount to discovering all over again all the oil that's now known to exist in the Middle East.

The fact is, the amount of known reserves is a very soft number. For one thing, it is usually a compilation of government or commercial figures from countries around the world, and those reported figures are at least sometimes slanted by political or economic considerations. Also, what we mean by "conventional" or "cheap" oil changes with time. As technology advances, the amount of reserves that can be economically tapped in known fields increases. The way the oil industry uses the term, the increase in recoverable oil counts as "discovery," and it accounts for much of the new discovery the USGS expects in the next thirty years. Finally, as oil starts to become scarce and the price per barrel goes up, the amount recoverable at that price will necessarily also increase. These are all tendencies that might help to push Hubbert's peak farther into the future than the most pessimistic predictions.

Nevertheless, all our experience with the consumption of natural resources suggests that the rate at which we use them up starts at zero, rises to a peak that will never be exceeded, and then declines back to zero as the supply becomes exhausted. There have been many instances of that behavior: coal mining in Pennsylvania, copper in northern Michigan, and many others, including oil in the lower forty-eight. That picture forms the fundamental basis of the views of Hubbert and his followers, but it is ignored by those who depend on the R/P ratio. Given that worldwide demand will continue to increase, as it has for well over a century, Hubbert's followers expect the crisis to occur when the peak is reached, rather than when the last drop is pumped. In other words, we will be in trouble when we've used up half the oil that existed, not all of it.

If you believe the Hubbert view—that the crisis comes when we reach the production peak rather than the last drop—but you accept the USGS estimate that there may have been an original amount of oil equivalent to 2.7 trillion barrels, then, compared with the earlier estimates, the crisis will be delayed by little more than a decade.* If Hubbert's followers are correct, we may be in for some difficult times in the near future. In an orderly, rational world, it might be possible for the gradually increasing gap between supply and demand for oil to be filled by some substitute. But anyone who remembers the oil crisis of 1973 knows that we don't live in such a world, especially when it comes to an irreversible shortage of oil. It's impossible to predict exactly what will happen, but we can all too easily envision a dying civilization,

---

*I have made this calculation using Hubbert techniques. Hubbert represented the rise and fall of oil discovery and extraction by a mathematical form known as the Logistic Curve (also known in business schools as the S-Shaped Curve). Others have used different bell-shaped curves known as Gaussian and Lorentzian Curves. They all give approximately the same results.

the landscape littered with the rusting hulks of useless SUVs. Worse, desperate attempts by one country or region to maintain its standard of living at the expense of others could lead to Oil War III. (Oil wars I and II are already history.) Knowledge of science is not useful in predicting whether or not such dire events will occur. Science is useful, however, in placing limits on what is possible.

To begin with, conventional oil is not the only oil. Once all the cheap oil is pumped, advanced methods can still squeeze a little more oil out of almost any field. These deposits are known as heavy oil: The more that is extracted, the heavier it gets. There are also deposits of what are known as oil sands and tar sands. Like the remains of depleted oil fields, these deposits are more difficult and expensive to extract; in essence, they are mined and their oil is extracted from the ore rather than just pumped out of the ground.

Then there is shale oil. As noted, conventional oil was created when source rock loaded with organic matter sank just deep enough in the earth for the organics to be cooked properly into oil. Oil shale is source rock that never sank deep enough to make oil. In Colorado, Wyoming, and Utah there is more shale oil than all the conventional oil in the world. However, shale oil in situ is not really oil at all; it was so named in order to attract investment. Instead it is kerogen, a waxy substance that can be made into oil if the rock containing it is mined, crushed, and heated.

Exploiting any of those resources will be more expensive, slower, and more environmentally damaging than pumping conventional oil. It will also require more energy input to get a given amount of energy out. Once the energy needed becomes equal to the energy produced, the game is lost. We are already using in our cars one fuel that may require more energy to produce than it provides: Ethanol made from corn is widely believed to be a net energy loser. As we progress down the fossil fuel list from light crude oil (the stuff we mostly use now) to heavy oil, oil sands, tar sands, and finally shale oil, the cost in energy progressively increases, as do other costs. Some experts believe that shale oil will always be a net energy loser.

Once past Hubbert's peak, as the gap between rising demand and falling supply grows, the rising price of oil may make those alternative fuels economically competitive, but even if they are net energy positive, it may not prove possible to get them into production fast enough to fill the growing gap. That's called the rate-of-conversion problem. Worse, the economic damage done by rapidly rising oil prices may undermine our ability to mount the huge industrial effort needed to get the new fuels into action.

Natural gas, which comes from overcooked source rock, is another alternative in the short term. Natural gas, mostly methane, is relatively easy to extract quickly, and transformation to a natural-gas economy could probably be accomplished more easily than is the case for other alternative fuels. Ordinary engines similar to the ones used in our cars can run on compressed natural gas. Alternatively, natural gas can be converted chemically into a liquid that could substitute for gasoline.* Even so, replacing the existing vehicles and gasoline distribution system, or building the industrial plant to convert methane to gasoline fast enough to make up for the missing oil, will be difficult. And even if this transformation is accomplished, success is only temporary. Hubbert's peak for natural gas is estimated to occur only a couple of decades after the one for oil.

---

*Liquid natural gas is a cryogenic (low-temperature) liquid that requires refrigeration and special handing. However natural gas can also be transformed chemically into other fuels that are liquid at normal temperatures.

There is also a possible fuel called methane hydrate, a solid that looks like ice but burns when ignited. Consisting of methane molecules trapped in a cage of water molecules, it forms when methane combines with water at temperatures close to the freezing point and under high pressure. Methane hydrate was discovered only a few decades ago, and so far there are a number of theories about where it might be found (under the Arctic permafrost, on the deep ocean floor, on the moons of Saturn), how much of it there is, and whether it might be mined (and used) successfully. Not much is known with certainty except that the stuff exists.

A huge amount of chemical potential energy is stored in the earth in the form of elemental carbon, or coal. As is true of the other fossil fuels, to extract the stored energy from coal, each atom of carbon must combine with oxygen to become a molecule of carbon dioxide, a greenhouse gas. But in addition to its inevitable CO_2 production, coal often comes with unpleasant impurities such as sulfur, mercury, and arsenic, none of which can be inexpensively extracted. Coal is a very dirty fuel.* Nevertheless, coal can be liquefied by combining it with hydrogen at high temperature and pressure—an expensive, energy-intensive process that Germany used out of desperation in World War II. If we take our chances on fouling the atmosphere and turn to coal as our primary fuel, we are told that there is enough of it in the ground to last for hundreds of years. That estimate, however, is like the R/P ratio for oil. It doesn't take into account the rising world population, the determination of the developing world to attain a high standard of living, and above all the Hubbert's peak effect, which is just as valid for coal as it is for oil. The simple fact is that if we turn to coal as a substitute for oil, the end of the age of fossil fuel, coal included, will probably come in this century.

Controlled nuclear fusion—energy obtained from fusing light nuclei into heavier ones—has long been seen as the ultimate energy source of the future. The technical problems that have prevented successful use of nuclear fusion up to now may someday be solved. Not in time to rescue us from the slide down the other side of Hubbert's peak, certainly, but perhaps someday. Then the fuel—at least initially—would be deuterium, a form of hydrogen found naturally in seawater, and lithium, a light element found in many common minerals.** There would be enough of both to last for a very long time. However, the conquest and practical use of nuclear fusion has proved to be very difficult. It has been said of both nuclear fusion and shale oil that they are the energy sources of the future, and always will be.

Nuclear fission, on the other hand, is a well-established technology. The fuel for this kind of reactor is the highly radioactive isotope uranium-235. The very word "nuclear" strikes fear into the hearts of many people—so much so that the utterly innocent imaging technique called nuclear magnetic resonance (NMR) by scientists had to be renamed magnetic resonance imaging (MRI) before the public could accept it for medical use. When the oil crisis occurs, the fear of nuclear energy is likely to recede, because of the compelling need for it. However, there will continue to be legistimate concerns about safety and nuclear waste

---

*The dangerous concentrations of mercury that are found in swordfish and tuna originate in coal-fired power plants.
**The nuclear reaction envisioned for fusion reactors is the fusion of deuterium and tritium, two isotopes of hydrogen. Tritium doesn't exist in nature, but the fusion reaction yields neutrons, which would be used to make the tritium in a lithium blanket. Thus the actual fuels are deuterium and lithium. See chapter 3 for further discussion.

disposal. Also, nucelar energy is suitable only for power plants or very large, heavy vehicles, such as ships and submarines. Don't look for nuclear cars or airplanes anytime soon.

What about the possibility that a huge new discovery of conventional oil will put off the problem for the foreseeable future? Better to believe in the tooth fairy. Oil geologists have gone to the ends of the earth searching for oil. There pobably isn't enough unexplored territory on this planet to contain a spectacular unknown oil field. The largest remaining accessible and unexplored area is the South China Sea; geologists consider it a promising (but not spectacularly so) region. It is unexplored because of conflicting ownership claims (by China, Taiwan, Vietnam, the Philippines, Malaysia, and Brunei) and murky international law governing mineral rights at sea. Other possible sites that come with big problems include central Siberia and the very deep oceans. Remember that in spite of intense worldwide effort, the rate of oil discovery started declining decades ago and has been in decline ever since. That is why the USGS assumption of thirty more years of rapid discovery seems questionable, even if it is really a prediction about future technology rather than future discovery.

But let us suppose for one euphoric moment that one more really big one is still out there waiting to be discovered. The largest oil field ever found is the Ghawar field in Saudi Arabia, whose eighty-seven billion barrels were discovered in 1948. If someone were to stumble onto another ninety-billion-barrel field tomorrow, Hubbert's peak would be delayed by a year or two, well within the uncertainty of the present estimates of when it will occur. It would hardly make any difference at all. That fact alone points up the sterility of the long-standing debate over drilling for oil in the Arctic National Wildlife Refuge in Alaska. If the ANWR is opened for drilling, its contribution to world oil supplies will be modest indeed. The best reason for not drilling there is not to protect the wildlife. It is to preserve the oil for future generations to use in petrochemicals, rather than burning it up in our cars.

Once Hubbert's peak is reached and oil supplies start to decline, how fast will the gap grow between supply and demand? That is a crucial question, and one that is almost impossible to answer with confidence. Here's rough attempt at guessing the answer. The upward trend at which the demand for oil has been growing amounts to an increase of a few percent per year. On the other side of the peak, we can guess that the available supply will decline at about the same rate, while the demand continues to grow at that rate. The gap, then, would increase at about, say, 5 percent per year. Therefore, ten years after the peak we would need a substitute for close to half the oil we use today—that is, a substitute for something like ten billion to fifteen billion barrels per year. Even in the absence of any major disruptions caused by the oil shortages after the peak, it is very difficult to see how an effective substitution can possibly be accomplished.

To be sure, the effects of the looming crisis could be greatly mitigated by taking steps to decrease the demand for oil. For example, with little sacrifice of convenience or comfort, we Americans could drive fuel-efficient hybrids rather than humongous gas guzzlers. There are countless other ways in which we could reduce our extravagant consumption of energy: redesigned cities, better insulated homes, improved public transporation, and so on. Such changes are beginning to be made, but there are powerful interests—like the oil companies and the automobile industry and its unions—opposing them.

Before we turn to prospects for the future, a little summing up is in order. The followers of King Hubbert may or may not be correct in their quantitative predictions of when the peak will occur. Regardless of that, they have taught us a very important lesson. The crisis will come not when we pump the last drop of oil but rather when the rate at which oil can be pumped out of ground starts to diminish. That means the crisis will come when we've used roughly half the oil that nature made for us. Any way you look at it, the problem is much closer than we previously imagined. Moreover, burning fossil fuels alters the atmosphere and could threaten the balmy, metastable state our planet is in. We have some very big problems to solve.

FUTURE SCENARIOS

So what does the future hold? We can easily sketch out a worst-case scenario and a best-case scenario.

Worst case: After Hubbert's peak, all efforts to produce, distribute, and consume alternative fuels fast enough to fill the gap between falling supplies and rising demand fail. Runaway inflation and worldwide depression leave many billions of people with no alternative but to burn coal in vast quantities for warmth, cooking, and primitive industry. The change in the greenhouse effect that results eventually tips Earth's climate into a new state hostile to life. End of story. In this instance, worst case really means worst case.

Best case: The worldwide disruptions that follow Hubbert's peak serve as a global wake-up call. A methane-based economy is successful in bridging the gap temporarily while nuclear power plants are built and the infrastructure for other alternative fuels is put in place. The world watches anxiously as each new Hubbert's peak estimate for uranium and oil shale makes front-page news.

No matter what else happens, this is the century in which we must learn to live without fossil fuels. Either we will be wise enough to do so before we have to, or we will be forced to do so when the stuff starts to run out. One way to accomplish that would be to return to life as it was lived in the eighteenth century, before we started to use much fossil fuel. That would require, among many other things, eliminating roughly 95 percent of the world's population. The other possibility is to devise a way of running a complex civilization approximating the one we have now which does not use fossil fuel. Do the necessary scientific and technical principles exist?

One of the more difficult problems will be finding a fuel for transportation. One possibility is that advanced electric batteries will make battery-powered electric vehicles practical. In the past decade, batteries packing many times as much energy in a given volume as the batteries commonly used in cars have been developed for use in mobile phones and portable computers. There is no reason why such advanced batteries can't become the basis of future means of transportation. Or the transportation fuel of the future might be hydrogen—not deuterium for thermonuclear fusion but ordinary hydrogen, to be burned as a fuel by old-fashioned combustion or used in hydrogen fuel cells, which produce electricity directly. Burning hydrogen or using it in fuel cells puts into the atmosphere nothing but water vapor.* Water

---

*However, hydrogen gas would also inevitably be leaked to the atmosphere. That would pose a threat to Earth's protective ozone layer. Other problems resulting from widespread use of hydrogen will inevitably arise.

vapor is a greenhouse gas, to be sure, but unlike carbon dioxide it cycles rapidly out of the atmosphere as rain or snow. Hydrogen is dangerous and difficult to handle and store, but so are gasoline and methane. Nature has not set aside a supply for us, but we can make it ourselves.

As the French engineer and thermodynamicist Sadi Carnot understood perfectly, you can't get something for nothing. Hydrogen is a high-potential-energy substance; that's precisely why it is valuable as a fuel. So is the working fluid of an electric battery. But thermodynamically speaking, hydrogen and batteries are not literally sources of energy. They are only means of storing and transporting it. That energy has to come from somewhere. Where will we get the energy, for example, to make hydrogen? Interestingly, one possible source is the potential energy stored in coal. There are existing processes that combine coal and steam to make hydrogen—and, inevitably, carbon dioxide. Hydrogen gas is produced from a slurry of water and coal using a calcium oxide-calcium carbonate intermediary reaction. The calcium carbonate is then converted back into calcium oxide (to be used over again) and carbon dioxide. In principle, the carbon dioxide could be separated and stored—"sequestered" is the current buzzword. Where could it be sequestered? That problem has not been solved yet (more about this in chapter 5). And in any case the coal will eventually run out, whereas we're trying to think long-term here.

The interior of the earth is heated by the decay of natural radioactive elements. In a sense, we live right on top of a vast nuclear reactor. Can't we use all that energy? We do, to some extent. It's called geothermal energy, and it's conveniently used for space heating in some places. Using it to generate power is more difficult. The temperature of Earth's interior rises with increasing depth, typically reaching the boiling point of water at a depth of about three miles. There are only a handful of places on Earth where a geothermal source rises to within drilling distance of the surface and thus can be used for power generation. Even in those places, using the heat to generate power often cools the source faster than its heat can be replenished. Geothermal energy will always be useful but probably never a major contributor. We should remember though that without geothermal energy we would never have had fossil fuel.

There is a cheap, plentiful supply of energy available for the taking—and, like geothermal energy, this one won't run out for billions of years. It's called sunlight. We now make very poor use of the sunlight that arrives at Earth. Farmers use it to grow food and fibers for textiles. A little bit is collected indirectly, in the form of hydroelectric and wind power. Here and there, solar cells provide energy for one use or another. But by and large, the solar energy that isn't reflected back into space just gets absorbed by the earth. We could learn to make better use of it along the way.

Sunlight is not very intense, as energy sources go. The flux of energy from the Sun amounts to 343 watts per square meter at the top of the atmosphere, averaged over Earth's entire surface and over an entire year. By comparison, the continuous per-capita consumption of electric power by Americans is 1,000 watts. Nevertheless, the solar power falling on the United States alone amounts to about ten thousand times as much electric power as even Americans consume. Both sunlight and nuclear energy can be used to make hydrogen or charge batteries, in a number of ways. There are chemicals and organisms that evolve hydrogen when sunlight is added. Sunlight makes electricity directly, in solar cells. Electricity can also be generated by using sunlight or nuclear energy as a source of heat to run a heat engine—such as a turbine—that can generate electricity. By means of electrolysis, electricity can make hydrogen from water. There is not much reason to doubt that hydrogen or advanced batteries can serve our transportation needs. At present, nuclear technology is far advanced compared to solar for all these purposes, but that could change.

So, technically, scientifically, the means may exist to build a civilization that has everything we think we need, without fossil fuels. There may be a future for us. The remaining question is, Can we get there? And if it is possible to live without burning fossil fuels, why wait until the fuels are all burned up? Why not get to work on it right now, before we do possible irreparable damage to the climate of our planet?